That Was Yvette

THAT WAS

YVETTE

The Biography of Yvette Guilbert,
The Great Diseuse

by Bettina Knapp and Myra Chipman

Holt, Rinehart and Winston

New York   Chicago

San Francisco

Copyright © 1964
by Bettina Knapp and Myra Chipman

Published simultaneously in Canada by Holt, Rinehart
and Winston of Canada, Limited.

Grateful acknowledgment is made to Basic Books
for permission to reprint two letters from
Sigmund Freud to Yvette Guilbert. These have
been reprinted from *Letters of Sigmund Freud*
selected and edited by Ernst L. Freud, copyright ©
1960 by Sigmund Freud Copyrights Ltd., London.

The translation of "Le roi a fait battre tambour"
is reprinted by permission of Ezra Pound.

Library of Congress Catalog Card Number: 64-14788

First Edition

July, 1965

Designer: Ernst Reichl
84990-0114
Printed in the United States of America

Acknowledgments

The authors wish to acknowledge with deep gratitude their indebtedness to all who have generously assisted in the research for this book or facilitated in any way its preparation.

Conspicuous among the many to whom we owe much are of course those devoted men and women of learning who staff reference libraries and museums, and who have made material available to us and shed light on our path in innumerable ways. Among the host of these benefactors have been Mr. John Neal Waddell, Columbia University Library; Mr. Robert H. Haynes, Widener Library, Harvard University; Miss Helen Willard, Shaw Theater Collection, Harvard University; Miss Margaret Hackett and staff of the Reference Department, Athenaeum Library, Boston; and Mlle. Marcelle Monval, Bibliothèque de l'Arsenal, Paris. We acknowledge with thanks also the many kindnesses extended to us by personnel of the New York Public Library; the Rare Book Department of the Boston Public Library; the Bibliothèque Nationale, Paris; Yale University Library; Chicago University Library; the Museum of Modern Art, New York; the British Museum, London; Theatermuseum, Munich.

In a biography, where much reliance must be placed on personal sources, the help of private individuals is of first importance, and in this area too the authors have been exceptionally fortunate. Not only recollections but unpublished letters, programs, documents, and photographs have been generously supplied by Mr. and Mrs. David Liebowitz, Dr. Eva Rosenfeld, Dr. Ernest Jones, Mr. Martin Freud, Dr. and Mrs. Vladimir Gurevich, Mrs. Theodore Josten, Mr. Hesketh Pearson, Mlle. Irene Aïtoff, M. André Cadou, Mme. Marcelle Broutin Bornay, Mme. Louis de Robert, Mlle. Gratiane de Gardilanne. Information regarding Madame Guilbert's broadcasting career in Marseilles was made available through the kindness of officials of Radiodiffusion-Télévision Française: M. Jacques Sallebert and Mme. Alice Lewitin, Director and Assistant Director, New York; and Mme. Odette Duchateau, Chef de Service aux Échanges Internationaux, Paris.

Dr. and Mme. Ado Avrane and Mlle. Denise Macagnò of Paris have lent invaluable aid in research and Miss Helen Perce and Mr. Hugh Edwards, The Art Institute of Chicago, counsel and assistance. For typing and transcribing, our thanks go to Elaine Graham Rosenfeld, and for suggestions and encouragement without stint to Prof. Alba Fazia Amoia, Mme. Elise Bani, Prof. and Mrs. Philip R. Sisson, Dr. Irving Fischer, and Dr. Morrison Levbarg.

BETTINA KNAPP and MYRA CHIPMAN

Introduction

A silhouette and a legend often are all that remain of a great *comédien.*
Frequently, only one or the other comes down to us. Molière leaves no
silhouette. Shakespeare leaves only a legend. Of many celebrated actors
it can be said that only a silhouette keeps them from oblivion. With
Yvette Guilbert everyone sees the tall, flexible, gawky, and flat-chested
girl, with a long neck and a nose in the air, as Steinlen drew her; or—to
capture her in her arresting essentials—a pair of long arms wearing black
gloves reaching up to her shoulders, caught, prophetically, by Toulouse-
Lautrec in the famous poster of the Divan Japonais, where the dancer
Jane Avril listens to the divette who is partially sketched in the background. One could, indeed, apply color to this phantom, add the henna
of the hair, the blood red of the large mouth, the chalky white of the
face, restore all the gesticulations of Toulouse-Lautrec's pitiless representations, and even try to track down the bas-relief in Dalou's statue
representing Song, lost amid the showy rooms in Paris' City Hall—but
posterity wants to remember only the tall and lanky girl, gloved in
black, whose fingers are crossed forever.

An even greater distance separates the legend and the ostensible truth,
for this legend itself is true if we consider the total and complex reality
of a living being who was overly simplified in the eyes of her contemporaries. Condemned to retain the image of what she had been during the period of her first triumphs, Yvette at sixty had perforce not
only to don the black gloves which she had come to hate, but also to
sing the trifling Xanrof songs with which she had achieved fame when
she was twenty-five years old. This is how she continues to live, within
the frame of an authenticated legend which is called history—this immortal interpreter of the realistic songs of *la belle époque,* which range
from unbridled humor to macabre horror. The lively and light couplets
of Fourneau who called himself Xanrof are incisively cut, seemingly to
bring out the clear diction of this virulent satirist, pieces which are to be
half sung, half spoken with the malice of discreet emphasis. The ironic

and bantering gaiety of Maurice Donnay, the corrosive power of Aristide Bruant, the *fin-de-siècle* perversity of Jean Lorrain, the pathetic bitterness of Jules Jouy: all these, thanks to Yvette, passed over the footlights and intoxicated an enthusiastic public. The Parisian audiences, difficult to conquer, still more difficult to hold, are very faithful in their own fashion, and were to prove it in her case.

Toward the year 1892 an equilibrium had to be established between the gross obscenities of the *caf'conc'* and the elegance of light poetry. The spirit of the Chat Noir singer, which was not loath to indulge in highly flavored Gallic humor but also knew how to turn a quatrain, offered a solution which Yvette immediately succeeded in adopting. The revival of such subject matter was developed along the path opened by realism, followed by naturalism and verism, but with a preference for the life of the common people of Paris in its least flattering aspects, coupled with an approach which permitted an alliance between drollery and cynicism, overbubbling gaiety and malice, irony and pity, indecency and detachment, humanity and terror.

How did this marvelous artist, who enchanted her contemporaries, succeed in fusing these elements? First, and above all perhaps is the mysterious role played by the human personality, certain aspects of which announce themselves at once in Yvette Guilbert. In the first place, she is a Parisian street urchin with all the defects and virtues of the kind (sometimes they amount to the same thing). She possesses an astonishing nerviness which nothing can deflect. "One must dare to demand," she says, and she tells very well how she did exactly that. Sometimes she goes too far, as she did when she took advantage of a banquet to ask Briand for the Legion of Honor. She displays a candor without bounds, is indifferent to sentiments of decorum or simple gratitude; her quarrel with Sarcey upon whose papers she overturns an ink well, is very funny; her recriminations against America are distressing. She has a keen mind, with an aptitude for seizing the main chance which propels her out of the miserable life in which she has been vegetating.

Chance plays a striking role in her career and she not only knows how to take advantage of it, but also how to give it a prod, sometimes to create it. Zidler one day encountered her in the street and suggested she become an equestrienne! It can certainly be said that he put her "foot in the stirrup." A conversation she overhears in a music store gives her the notion to propose herself for an engagement. At one time she feels the need of a certain type of song: in a bookstall on the quays she finds a Xanrof volume which answers her purpose.

Very poor, she is avid of everything. Can one reproach her for this? What she wishes above all, in the beginning, is to rise above her circumstances, taking her mother along with her. It is a real dime-novel situation. She will earn a lot of money. But her ambition soon transcends every other element. She wants to be an artist, a great artist. She envisions herself as a prophetess of art, and through some metempsychosis will convince herself of always having been just that: like Molière's Monsieur Jourdain who, in order to make certain of his noble rank, discovers that he was born a gentleman. The *diseuse,* in order to renew her repertoire as well as add dignity to it, which can only be achieved with the support and prestige of tradition, accumulates the largest collection of old French songs in the world. This self-taught woman plunges back in her studies as far as the Middle Ages, to the domain of Gaston Paris and Joseph Bédier. As a touching recompense, she will be admitted as a member of the Société des Anciens Textes. She will love to give song recitals combined with lectures (Hugues Le Roux at the Bodinière, in New York with Professor Becker of Bryn Mawr). The little girl who left school at such an early age develops a passion for culture. The *diseuse* of light songs now exhibits a longing for true poetry; she tries in her fashion to honor Baudelaire whom she may have seen to a large extent through the eyes of Rollinat and Richepin; she sincerely serves Villon, Verlaine, Laforgue, Jammes, and many others. While trying to embark upon a second career, sickness forces her to interrupt her activities and she finds herself so physically weakened that she is obliged to alter her manner of presentation and her material.

The final visible element of this personality, which was so Parisian, was her generosity. "I am not timid," she used to say. She could have added, "I am not mean." Forewarned since childhood against being the dupe of her heart, quick at repartee, informed in ways of protecting herself, not very sentimental (except in her memoirs when the past touches her), but open, humane, more generous than warm, possessing a wise and temperate pity, too energetic and hard-working herself to be truly indulgent of any weaknesses of will or inclination to vice, she was honest in all things. Completely indifferent to the flattery of gallantry, she might have even come to hate men because of the implacable grudge she bore against her father (what a song could be written about the latter's death scene!) had not Yvette's love for her mother so well filled her need for affection and had she not found the equivalent in the infinite devotion of her husband, Max Schiller. Her friendships, both masculine and feminine, give an impression of equilibrium and serenity. It was no small thing to have been praised by Sarcey, Adolphe Brisson, and Arthur Symons. It was glorious to have been admired by Bernard Shaw and Freud, loved by Duse, idolized by the most diverse audiences in the world. Her students were attached to her; she appreciated her collaborators. Aside from some difficulties with a great rival like Sarah Bernhardt or a few quarrels with critics and journalists, Yvette Guilbert managed well with mankind.

All this being said, the little girl once seemingly destined to become a seamstress could not have become the star of the French song without possessing a happy combination of intelligence and diligence of a sort that commands admiration. She was neither truly actress nor singer, yet she became the impeccable *diseuse* whose career, despite sickness, war, changes of fashion and taste, continued to flourish for half a century. She succeeded in transforming an unprepossessing physique into an instrument of *diction* by means of gesture and attitude. Her voice was pure, though not that of a great singer; an actor with words, she was capable of delineating and animating dozens of recognizable types, amusing or moving, by means of rhythmic patterns and the color of the tone. This double metamorphosis attests an innate sense, a talent which had only to be developed, that of an infallible art of mimicry, the origin of which I certainly believe manifested itself in her childish antics on Boulevard du Temple. Yvette—who owes to Maupassant her first name, which so well suits her patronymic—was already in seed form in the little Emma Laure Esther, whose exemplary life has been recounted by Bettina Knapp and Myra Chipman.

JEAN HYTIER COLUMBIA UNIVERSITY

*To David Liebowitz and Emily Gresser Liebowitz,
parents of Bettina Knapp, the authors affectionately
inscribe these pages.*

At the Ambassadeurs

That was Yvette. The blithe Ambassadeurs
Glitters, this Sunday of the Fête des Fleurs;
Here are the flowers, too, living flowers that blow
A night or two before the odours go;
And all the flowers of all the city ways
Are laughing, with Yvette, this day of days.
Laugh, with Yvette? But I must first forget,
Before I laugh, that I have heard Yvette.
For the flowers fade before her; see, the light
Dies out of that poor cheek, and leaves it white;
She sings of life, and mirth, and all that moves
Man's fancy in the carnival of loves;
And a chill shiver takes me as she sings
The pity of unpitied human things.

—Arthur Symons

Table of Contents

Yvette as a child

Yvette with her mother

At L'Horloge, summer of 1891

The new Yvette, 1902 (by Métivet)

The Sarcey feud, 1898 (by Willette)

Melba, Guilbert, and Bernhardt, 1894 (by Léandre)

Poster for *Les Ambassadeurs*

Toulouse-Lautrec caricature

Louis de Robert at twenty-four

Yvette and Max posing for illustration for *The Enigma*

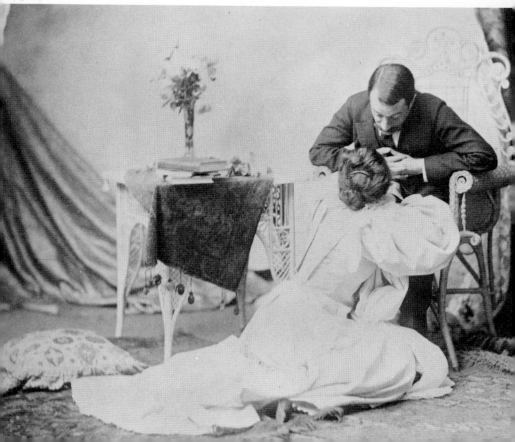

Yvette, 1901

Mon cher grand ami

Merci pour votre lettre! Non, je
ne crois pas que ce qui sort de moi
en scène soit "le surplus" supprimé
et employé, car si la vie m'a
fait connaître beaucoup de choses,
j'en ignore encore tellement!
Et pourtant je saurais les imaginer
sans les avoir "ressenties"
Je pourrais être la Tzarine, le
Tzar, Saint François d'Assise
Si un texte m'est donné
pour les exprimer, j'en éprouverai
le côté physique, par l'habitude
de transporter du cerveau à ma
chair, tout ce que j'ai à "faire voir"
à mon public —
C'est par les yeux, qu'on apprend
le plus de la vie des autres —
Mon œil à moi, est mon grand
révélateur! —

Letter from Yvette to Sigmund Freud, 1931

COMMISSARIAT GÉNÉRAL AUX QUESTIONS JUIVES

CERTIFICAT
4.453

DE NON-APPARTENANCE A LA RACE JUIVE

Sur le vu des pièces produites par l'intéressé, le Commissaire Général
aux Questions Juives constate que M⁻ GUILBERT Yvette Emma
Laure Esther née le 20 janvier 1865 à Paris (3ᵉ)
ne doit pas être regardé comme juif aux termes de la loi du 2 Juin 1941.
Paris, le 10 mars 1943

Nazi certificate attesting Yvette's
non-Jewish origin

Max Schiller

Hotel Nègre-Coste, Aix-en-Provence, where Yvette died, 1944

Part One

MAKING
THE MONKEY
blush

I

1865-1885

*Pour ma part je me promettais bien
de rire aux nez des galants quand il
en viendrait.*

—For my part, I made up my
mind to laugh in the face
of any suitor who might
come wooing me.

Chapter 1

In Paris, one January morning in 1885, a young lady barely turned twenty decided that because the day was fine she would take a walk along the Embankment. Her mind that morning was loaded with anxiety, as indeed it usually was, but as she strode along briskly beside the sun-spangled waters of the Seine, relishing the sense of invigoration that comes from exercise in clean crisp winter air, suddenly she found herself in an unexpected upsurge of good spirits.

She was an unusually tall and slender girl, and because she was, for the moment, filled with an ardor, a sense of well-being, that rightfully

17

belongs to twenty and that no amount of unhappiness can wholly stifle at that age, she was undoubtedly carrying herself exceptionally well. At any rate, she attracted the attention of a distinguished-looking gentleman of about sixty who happened to be walking behind her, and what ensued was one of those fateful incidents that life sometimes affords to spirited young ladies.

For a few minutes the gentleman followed her at a distance, studying her with what seemed a professionally appraising eye, and then, as if coming to a quick decision, he called to her: "Mademoiselle! Mademoiselle!"

Mademoiselle paid no heed, if anything merely stretched her long legs a little longer, and her admirer had to break into a run to catch up with her. The young lady, obviously not in the least interested in gentlemen, even distinguished-looking ones, who attempted to scrape acquaintance in the street, for some time turned a deaf ear to what this particular one was trying to say as he hurried along beside her.

"Mademoiselle, listen to me just a moment, please! I want to make you a business proposition. Don't be afraid of me! I won't hurt you. I only want to talk to you one minute. And please, please, don't walk so fast! Let me catch my breath!—Listen, my dear, I am Charles Zidler."

At this name the indifferent young person allowed her pace to slacken, and for the first time looked at the stranger carefully, though with a trace of skepticism.

"Charles Zidler, yes. Permit me," and he fumbled in his pocket and produced a card. "Mademoiselle is a working girl—am I correct? Let me assure you then, Mademoiselle, you do not need to remain one. You recognize me? You know that I manage the Hippodrome? Believe me when I tell you that with such a fine figure as yours you could become a magnificent circus rider!"

The young lady began to laugh.

"You do not think I know what I am talking about?"—indignantly. "Why, I could have you trained, Mademoiselle, and in two years' time you could be an *écuyère,* earning twenty thousand francs a year!"

At this the young lady stopped dead in her tracks, her eyes at last showing reluctant interest.

"I am serious, Mademoiselle. Twenty thousand francs. This could be for you the opportunity of a lifetime."

She became thoughtful. "But my mother might not consent."

"I will go to see her!"

"No, no! She would not like that."

"Well, then, you talk it over with her. Take your time, and when you have decided, come to see me," and Monsieur Zidler bowed a dignified farewell.

The young lady stood a moment as if dazed, watching the erect figure recede in the distance, then stared at the card in her hand. Who in Paris did not know the name of Zidler, of the Hippodrome?

In the 1880's Parisians were circus-mad, there being among the frivolities of the city no less than four permanent circuses; not housed under flimsy canvas tops, but in fine handsome buildings. Three were of wood, brick, or marble, but the fourth, the Hippodrome, giant of them all, which seated three thousand, was built of iron, the solidity of the edifice typifying the enduring place this brand of entertainment held in the affections of Parisians. Around the calendar, crowds flocked there for what were extravagantly billed as the most daring trapeze acts in all Europe, the cleverest clowning, the most accomplished horsemanship. The 80's, in fact, were the heyday of equestrianism.

Of the men who presided over these citadels of amusement none was so much a legend as Charles Zidler, partly because of his rags-to-riches history but chiefly because of his undoubted genius for pleasing the public. As a child of poverty, he had been apprenticed to a tanner when he was only ten; he was in his teens before he learned to read and write. How he became associated with Joseph Oller and his brother, circus entrepreneurs, nobody seemed to know. As the years went by, however, the boy who, as tanner's apprentice, had once wallowed in the stinking mud and tannin of the River Bièvre developed such a phenomenal flair for theatrical organization that he eventually became a partner in the numerous Oller enterprises.

Through years of exercising the iron hand over temperamental troupers Zidler had earned the reputation of being an ogre, though he could be gentle enough when he chose, and he always showed respect for any performer who worked honestly and conscientiously. He also had a reputation, in which he took excessive pride, for high ethical standards. "Oh, sure, Zidler is an old bear! He growls and shows his teeth when he has to. But," he would boast, "no one can say that he has ever broken his word." He was a star-maker, too, and his discriminating showman's eye was always alert for the new face, the new personality, that his infallible instinct would tell him was star material.

As most of this was general knowledge in Paris, it is to be presumed that even an unsophisticated young working girl would have been acquainted with the basic outline of his career, and certainly his importance, and hence it is not to be wondered at that this particular young lady on the Seine Embankment that winter morning of 1885 should have been struck with surprise at finding herself the recipient of an offer of employment from Charles Zidler. Recovering herself after a few moments of astonished contemplation of the card, she wheeled about abruptly and, apparently in some excitement, began retracing her steps.

Her new course lay in the general direction of the Marais, an ancient section of the city on the Right Bank, once pleasantly picturesque, now a teeming and melancholy slum. Taking short cuts that she apparently knew like a book, she half hurried, half ran, in and out of serpentine alleys where the sun, that lavished itself on Seine and boulevards, was never able wholly to penetrate; to dry the mold clinging to the cracked foundations of their rotting houses or sweeten the foul breath of their refuse heaps. When she arrived at a certain crumbling six-storied building, she plunged through its outer door into a dingy hallway almost as cold as the street itself. As she ran up the five flights of narrow, rope-banistered stairs leading to the apartment on the top floor, she passed half-open doors to other apartments, in which women, and children too, all wearing shawls or scarfs against the chill of their rooms, could be seen seated around tables, sewing or embroidering at top speed, or twisting bits of beadwork or feathers or ribbons into ornaments and gewgaws.

In the garret into which she burst a middle-aged woman, with a broad peasant face, was also sewing, but under a lamp, for although the room was up so high, it was semidark, having for a window only one of those small portholes known as *tabatières,* dear to eighteenth-century architects. It was almost bare of furniture; frigid from the drafts that penetrated the old, thin walls; and ill-smelling from the kerosene fumes of the lamp.

Rapidly the girl sketched the story of what had just happened. The other dropped her work to listen, her eyes shrewd with a countrywoman's caution, and at the end she made a vigorous gesture of exasperation.

"Emma Guilbert, you are a silly goose! Why do you suppose the pay for a circus rider is so high? Because the work is dangerous, of course! And what do you know about horses? Suppose you should break your leg—or worse, your neck? What's to become of us then?

Aren't things bad enough as they are? Indeed no! I forbid it. No circuses!" From the tone of the woman's voice it was obvious that there would be no appeal from this decision.

The girl could not deny that her mother was right. All too often one was hearing those days of another broken body picked up in the ring.

A few days later, when Emma Guilbert went to Zidler's office at the Hippodrome to report, regretfully, her answer, the great man greeted her with unexpected kindness. She had meant only to tell him briefly that her mother would not hear of her accepting his proposal. Instead, when he asked her to be seated and engaged her in conversation, the warm, paternal interest in his eyes put her at such ease that soon she found herself talking far more than she had intended. He was a comfortable sort of man to talk to, and from the questions he asked she could see that he seemed rather taken with her, that he really wanted to know all about her. Emma needed a confidant just at that time. It would be a relief to pour out to someone as sympathetic as Monsieur Zidler all that was pent up within her.

At the very beginning, she blurted out that if her life was difficult it was all because of her father.

Emma's maternal grandparents, Grandfather and Grandmother Lubrez, with their three young daughters, had moved to Normandy from Orchies, Departement du Nord, sometime in the late 1840's. The family had settled on a small farm near Saint-Lô, and there Emma's mother, Albine, and her two sisters had grown up in one of those ancient, steep-roofed Norman farmhouses.

Emma knew the place well, and loved it; she had lived there briefly as a child. She could never forget the great kitchen, with its strings of onions and dried herbs festooned from the rafters. Its walls were of dark clay, hung with polished brass saucepans, and in a corner stood one of those towering black Norman cupboards. And what a fireplace! Big enough for two men to stand in, where a huge oak log could smolder for days. She slept in an attic under the eaves, on a narrow cot that had once been her mother's, where there was a dormer window, open all summer, and swallows flew in and out as they wished. From that window in the morning she could look down into the barnyard and watch her grandfather scattering corn for his clucking hens; a long way in the distance, on a hillside, just visible over the treetops, the slate roof of a manor house glinted in the sun. Some mornings, when the dew was heavy, her grandmother would let her wade barefoot in the tall wet orchard grass.

Though Grandfather Lubrez was not a native Norman, he was as thrifty as one, and through the years, as he prospered, he set aside a sizable dowry for each of his daughters. Albine, who had been born in 1845, was only about eighteen when she met young Hippolyte Guilbert. His father was a farmer from the same region, of less consequence financially than Monsieur Lubrez, though the name Boisguilbert was an ancient one in Normandy.

Hippolyte was reddish-blond, tall, and muscular; and unlike most Norman peasants, who were traditionally an unpoetic, dour, and taciturn breed, he liked to talk; he could also sing. Never before had Albine listened to such a flow of ingratiating chatter, or known that songs could be so captivating. It was a headlong romance; within a month Hippolyte was asking for her hand.

Grandfather Lubrez did everything in his power to prevent the match. He recognized easily enough that this boy was not only impecunious; he was harebrained and unstable; it would be a shame to put a girl into such careless custody, not to mention a dowry built up through so many years of scrimping. But in the end he had to give in to Albine's tears.

The moment the wedding was over, Hippolyte took himself and his bride off to live in town. Feeling himself now a man of means, he told Albine that he had no intention of remaining a farmhand—he was no clodhopper; he had larger talents; he proposed to become a merchant. In a nice little shop in Saint-Lô, he said, they could double their investment in no time. To set up the shop he dipped into the dowry. He dipped again, after the shop failed, to dabble in real estate. One thing after another he tried, but nothing for long, and nothing succeeded. Finally he declared that the trouble was with Saint-Lô, incurably dull, provincial, stagnant. He would remove to Paris; Paris was the only place for an ambitious fellow.

In vain Grandfather and Grandmother Lubrez protested; like all peasants they distrusted that great city as a Jezebel, and they were saddened that Albine should be taken so far away from them, especially with a baby now near at hand. But Hippolyte was determined, and one morning in September, 1864, the young couple climbed aboard the little train from Cherbourg that leaped and swayed along its narrow roadbed, over the plains of Cotentin, straight into the heart of Paris.

Those were the days of the Second Empire, of Napoleon III and his lovely Empress Eugènie. Emma could remember the Emperor dimly, she said. From babyhood she had seen pictures of his handsome face, with its waxed mustachios, displayed in shop windows, and the bees and the crowned N's everywhere. And she had heard tales of the court balls at the Tuileries, with gilded carriages coming and going, and gentlemen in knee breeches, and lights blazing till dawn.

Many times her father had laughingly recalled the day he and Albine first saw Paris, and how bedazzled the two young bumpkins were. Though they had heard that the city was the beauty spot of Europe, more elegant and important now even than Rome, they were unprepared for its impressive opulence. As they gazed at the scene spread out before them, they could hardly believe their own eyes— the palaces, gardens, fountains; the historic Seine, and its bridges rich with sculpture; the famed boulevards, with their far vistas and perspectives, alive with spanking barouches; the sidewalk cafés, musical with the murmur of genteel voices and the clink of glasses.

Hippolyte was delighted over everything he saw and surer than ever now that he had made no mistake in forsaking a tight-fisted, tight-lipped peasant society for one of grace and graciousness in which he was convinced he could soon take his place. For Hippolyte had a plan: he intended to become an importer on a commission basis, *un commissionaire en marchandises,* of those Viennese knickknacks then so popular—candelabra, clocks, statuettes, morocco leather. Success and leisure would inevitably follow, and sophistication. Already he pictured himself a true *boulevardier.*

The section where he and Albine took their first lodgings, the Marais, center of the dressmaking and needle trades, was a far cry, however, from the Paris of the boulevards and the palaces. The house, 78 Rue du Temple, like all the others in that area, was dilapidated and malodorous; roaches scuttled openly and rats squealed in the walls. Yet Hippolyte was content. He had achieved his *pied-à-terre* in Paradise.

It was here, a few months later, January 20, 1865, that the baby was born—Emma Laure Esther—and for a while the young couple were happy and hopeful. As time went on, they moved about restlessly in the district, trying to better their conditions, once even achieving a flat with a miniscule balcony, which they gloated over as evidence of dawning prosperity. But it was not long before fond expectations began to fade. As importer in Paris, Hippolyte proved no more suc-

23

cessful than as shopkeeper in Saint-Lô. Twice the couple returned to Normandy, but not to stay; perhaps only because pulled by family ties or to show the grandparents the new baby.

Back in Paris, after the second sojourn in 1869, Hippolyte's continued incompetence eventually of course brought the financial affairs of the little family to a catastrophic conclusion—the bottom of the purse. The dowry was exhausted. Here was a situation to tear at the nerves, and when there was no longer even a loaf of bread in the cupboard, Albine had had no choice but to join the horde of needlewomen of the district. Then it was that the weepings and the quarrelings had begun, and Hippolyte's absences. Emma's earliest recollections were of those absences and the ugly silences when her father returned; the sulkiness that was even worse to bear than the hot words before he left. Sometimes he came back with money, but usually not; she learned that he had turned to gambling as a way of life. At first Hippolyte averted his eyes from the sight of his wife bent over her sewing, but before long he took it for granted. Eventually he demanded it.

"A wife should support herself and her child!" he flared at Albine one day when she reproached him. "Suppose you were a widow?"

In these domestic tensions Emma had been from the first her mother's child; she could not remember when she had not inwardly felt hostile toward her father.

By the time she was five there was little to choose between her and the other young street Arabs of her district whom she played with; she was as bold and saucy; spoke in the same gutter accent, learned the same dirty slang and smut. Like the rest, she learned too how to fight with her tongue; from the first a spate of invective was her ever-ready weapon. The main way in which she differed from the others was in a heritage she had received from her father: she sang as constantly and instinctively as any bird. Once the Guilberts had lived on Boulevard du Temple next to the Café Augeol, where working people of the neighborhood would gather over a beer and sing the songs then in vogue, especially those popularizd by the *café-concert* favorites Thérèsa, Judic, and Amiati; and there Hippolyte, with his passion for music, would often spend the evening with a couple of cronies, taking Emma along with him. The child would listen entranced and when she got home would reproduce every song. Once she had even been taken to see the great Thérèsa in person. From then on, nothing delighted her so much as to impersonate the diva by parading about in a long train formed by pinning a tablecloth to her belt, while the neighbors, listening to her incredibly accurate mimicry, would go into screams of laughter and afterward reward her with cakes. One of Amiati's songs, *La Fille d'Auberge*, she sang so incessantly that Albine often tried to bribe her into silence. "If you won't sing the Amiati song today, I will put twenty sous in your *tirelire*." It made no difference; the little show-off kept on singing it.

She could remember vividly the Franco-Prussian War. At first it affected the Guilberts very little; they merely joined the crowds cheering and shouting *"Vive l'Empereur!"* the day the ill-fated Napoleon III set off for the front, accompanied by the little Prince Imperial. She remembered when she first heard the *Marseillaise,* that red-hot incitement to revolution, so many years prohibited by law; it was after the debacle at Sedan, when Eugènie had fled the palace and the government had changed. The incendiary words were sweeping all over Belleville, the workingmen's district near which the Guilberts were then living, and Emma picked them up and sang them repeatedly, with gusto, to the embarrassment of her parents, who took no sides politically and wanted only to stay out of trouble.

She remembered the siege, and how often she was hungry, and how her mother hated the Germans for the scarcity of bread. But Albine's hatred was as nothing compared to the contempt expressed by the whole city the day the Prussian troops made their victory march down the entire length of the Champs Élysées. Emma was barely six, but she would never forget that day. All over Paris, black-bordered posters had ordered complete silence toward the Prussians: boycott them, ignore them, utter no single word. Shops and cafés were closed, statues draped in black. Thousands of onlookers lined the streets to witness the parade, but in a dead silence of mass hatred that was terrifying.

In the days of the Commune that followed, when the red flags were fluttering everywhere, her mother told her they were under siege again, this time from their own Adolphe Thiers, and nobody knew what the outcome would be, and so she absolutely *must* stop singing the *Marseillaise*. At first it was a very different kind of siege; there was enough to eat, the cafés were open, and crowds sauntered about unafraid, watching shells break occasionally in the distance. The troops from Versailles proceeded slowly and methodically, apparently in no hurry, advancing little by little outside the fortifications. When the suburb of Neuilly was evacuated, a mass of smoking ruins, the Guilberts joined the sight-seers who flocked out from Paris to gaze, and returned carrying armfuls of lilacs. Then the bombardment of the fortifications began.

Not long after, a delightful concert was held in the gardens of the Tuileries. It was a soft May day, and in the bright sunshine men and boys fished contentedly along the Seine. No one paid much attention to shells bursting in the Champs Élysées, and it was not until the end of the concert that it was discovered that for a whole hour the Versaillese had been inside the city gates.

From then on, Emma could no longer play outside. The seven days of the great fires began, the Communards putting the torch to petrol-soaked buildings as they retreated. Whole streets burned. Finally the battle narrowed down to the true center of resistance, some two or three districts on the fringe of Belleville, and for days the Guilberts were in the very eye of the hurricane, living from hand to mouth, keeping close within doors while bullets spat down their street.

Then suddenly all was over; the last fanatic barricade had fallen.

After the end of the war, as soon as public safety had been restored, Paris became mad with gaiety, as if society were trying to wipe out of mind as fast as possible the memory of crackling flames and streets running blood. The Opéra resumed, and there were balls and intimate supper parties. Those who could command carriages rode in them, to see and be seen; others promenaded, for the same reason. Clubs were crowded, and restaurants. The great salons opened their doors again. With so much going on, and wardrobes depleted by the war, almost over night a luxury market for women's clothes sprang into full operation.

At this point, Albine, who had tried her clever needle at one thing after another, now surprised everyone, herself included, by creating a new kind of hat—a concoction of horsehair base decorated with elaborate beadwork. Even more astonishing, the novelty caught on so rapidly that assistants had to be hired, and finally workshops opened, to supply the demand. To be able to devote herself completely to this unexpected piece of luck while it lasted and wring out of it every last sou of profit, Albine decided that Emma should be sent for a time to Grandfather and Grandmother Lubrez.

The time turned out to be longer than expected—two years, in fact, but a very happy two years; the only happy period Emma ever knew as a child. Under that ancient roof in Normandy no one quarreled, no one wept. When she went out to play, there was no horde of little child savages, with old, sharp eyes and fast, sharp talk, against whom she had to defend herself, tooth and claw; on Grandfather's farm all the open fields were hers.

Letters arrived from Albine occasionally, always about how hard she was working and how fast the business was growing; eighty women and girls—imagine!—now in her employ. She must get the business thoroughly established and she must save some money; then she would send for Emma.

One day the call came; Albine was ready for Emma to come back to her.

The little girl of eight whom the mother clasped hungrily to her bosom had shot up remarkably tall in her two years' absence, bony-thin and spindle-legged, and she was anything but pretty. When Hippolyte came toward her and she ducked her chin and wriggled uncomfortably away from him, he laughed and called her a little peasant and said it was high time she got away from the barnyard and learned a few manners.

The Guilberts were still living in the crowded workers' district which had been home to them from the first. Even in the intoxication of first affluence, Albine had resisted the temptation to move to a less proletarian neighborhood. First of all, she wanted to save money; but more especially she needed to be near her workshops, in which she spent nearly every waking moment.

Yet there were a few luxuries in evidence in the Guilbert apartment that Emma could not remember ever having seen before. Nice sheets on her bed, for example; pretty dresses for herself and a piano for her father; and Albine, perhaps trying to live up to her role as head of a business, was wearing a stylish false chignon, which somehow did not quite suit her broad flat face.

There was also a surprise in store; with the money that had been saved Emma was to be enrolled in a private school. How would she like that?

Hippolyte had prophesied that the little peasant would resist. As a young child she had been placed for a brief and wretched period in a kindergarten which she hated at the corner of Rue de Turenne and Rue de Saintonge. Here she had played incorrigibly in inkwells; proved herself a real *enfant terrible,* a thorn in the flesh for plump, pink little Madame Archimbault; and she had reformed only when she became enamoured of a new mistress, Mademoiselle Laboulaye. To Emma, this lady was nothing less than an enchantress, with her shiny-black corkscrew ringlets, and earrings of pink coral, and the tight dress of black velvet so long that it swept the floor. But the most fascinating thing about her was her black elbow-length gloves, which she never, never took off. Emma idolized her.

The school Albine had now selected was located in Saint-Mandé, just outside the fortifications, only a few kilometers from the Guilberts' section of Paris. In those days Saint-Mandé, a gay and pretty little *faubourg* wedged between the city wall and the Bois de Vincennes, contained several very genteel *pensionnats,* and one of them, the Pension Couard, 32 Chaussée de l'Etang, had been Albine's choice for Emma. It was not a small or insignificant school, for Mademoiselle Couard, the headmistress, kept a staff of five instructors. Of the hundred or more girls enrolled, some sixty were in a junior group of Emma's age, and there was a large garden attached to the *pension* where the children could play; no more would Emma have to depend for companionship on the little toughs of the Marais streets. The school was not inexpensive, either; in fact, Albine had taken a rather extravagant step. But there was the real advantage that Emma need not live at the school; she could be a day scholar, riding back and forth on a diminutive train of the Chemin de Fer de l'Est from the Gare de Vincennes, at the Place de la Bastille—very convenient—for a round-trip fare of less than two francs. When the little peasant learned that she could come home every night to her mother, she accepted the arrangement without protest.

For the next four years, then, Emma went to school. But she had an outside interest which she found more intriguing than books: her mother's workshops. In every spare hour and during her Thursday half-holidays she assisted in the shops, largely because she was fascinated by the uninhibited gossip she could listen to there. The talk horrified her—no intimacies were spared—but through it she felt she was finding out what life was really like. Inwardly the child bled with sympathy and indignation over the sordid tragedies the poor creatures retailed to each other. How she pitied the little *grisettes* and their inadvertent pregnancies, and the older women suffering from beatings, desertions, drunkenness. She could not help noting, moreover, that every one of these sufferers was the victim of a sweetheart or a husband or a father. Just like her mother, she thought, who slaved night and day for a man who contributed nothing more to the family welfare than occasional winnings from a gaming table. Worse, too; she knew now of her father's infidelities.

During these years Hippolyte apparently made sporadic efforts to remain on good terms with his daughter. As she grew older, he took her sometimes to the races, and he was fond of strumming accompaniments on the piano as she sang; he had the knack of playing by ear. At such times she loved him for his charm, his camaraderie, his talent as a musician, in spite of her general disapproval of his irresponsibility and his brutal treatment of her mother.

When Emma was twelve, disaster struck. Albine's business, which by now the Guilberts had come to assume was a lifetime insurance against want, suddenly began to slacken. The reason was simple: the fad for horsehair hats had run its course, and, try as she might, poor Albine could not devise another hit to take its place. Workers in the shop had to be discharged, the shop itself closed, and before long Emma stopped taking the morning train for Saint-Mandé. The few short years of prosperity had been nothing but illusion.

There was nothing for Albine to do but go back to the old struggle of trying to keep herself and twelve-year old Emma alive on whatever she could earn at home, this time assisted by Emma, who had threaded her first needle before she was five. But all her efforts were not enough; within a few months possessions had to be sold. The piano went, and the chairs and tables; even the linens and the pretty dresses. When there was nothing of value left, smaller, dirtier, colder quarters had to be accepted. The situation was particularly ironic because Paris in general was a cornucopia of prosperity. The Exhibition of 1878 was demonstrating to the world the French nation's recovery from the war. At the Trocadéro a huge balloon floated; Paris hotels overflowed with free-spending provincials; people danced in the streets in the summer nights, under the light of Venetian lanterns. Yet in the heart of all the optimism and easy money there remained the same old vacuum in which as always the very poor barely existed.

After a move into quarters more sordid than any the Guilberts had ever before endured, Hippolyte announced curtly one day that henceforth he would live elsewhere, and departed. Worthless as he had been as a husband and father, Albine was in agony over his desertion, and Emma, as she witnessesd her mother's suffering, vowed she would never forgive him.

From then on, the Guilberts were two, and side by side made an epic battle for survival. Work seemed to be more plentiful in the summers. Odd jobs, commissions for this and that, trickled in. One year it was bead flowers for funeral wreaths, again embroideries for ballroom slippers, or cravats or braces or umbrellas, once even nosebags for horses. But every winter, work would fall off, and then Albine would revert to making hats. By day the two would sew feverishly, and every night, from eight to midnight, laden with huge cardboard boxes, Albine wearing a pair of old boots that had belonged to Hippolyte, they would go out peddling their stock to small, dimly lit shops in the crooked back streets of Montmartre, Belleville, Clichy, Ménilmontant. They were humiliated by scant courtesy; brazenly cheated. Sometimes, in desperation, they rang bells of private houses in better districts, and here the humiliations were often keener. If they sold hats, they ate. They did not always sell.

Sometimes they trudged through rain and snow and sleet and came back with soaking feet, chilled to the bone in their thin garments, and the next morning in their icy rooms they would have to put their feet again into wet boots and pull on clothes still sodden. There were two smells, Emma learned, that belonged to beggars—their breath and their clothes—and from these she claimed she could always tell how long a derelict had starved. She had never been a strong girl. Now she became anemic from malnutrition and often fainted for no other reason than weakness.

On these nocturnal excursions it was inevitable that she should see terrible sights. Those were the hours when the most vicious inhabitants of Paris were abroad—the kind every great city spews up by night in its dark corners. Sots, thieves, *morphinomanes,* perverts, prostitutes, rapists, murderers—she came to know them all.

By the time she was sixteen, though painfully thin and still anemic, she was very tall, and one day it occurred to her to apply for a job as a model at Hentenarts', a fashionable dress shop in the Rue du Quatre Septembre. She was certainly no beauty—high cheekbones, wide thin lips, chin that jutted forward, a prominent fleshy nose with turned-up tip, and reddish-brown hair, dry, skimpy, and lusterless, drawn tightly back from her forehead—but because of her slender figure the proprietors agreed to hire her. They would give her her meals, provide her with a black silk dress to wear on duty, and pay in addition the solid sum of seventy-five francs a month. This was sheer manna from heaven.

Emma made a very successful model, learning quickly how to ply a buyer with drinks and run up sales with one hand, while warding off amatory advances with the other. But the Hentenarts were slave drivers. Employees were not allowed to sit down, this being before protective laws for women and children had been enacted, and from eight in the morning to nine at night their models paraded. The thick carpets of the showroom made Emma's feet burn, and her legs swelled to the point of torture. One hot July day, after she had modeled furs for two hours, she fainted in a New York buyer's lap, and would have been discharged if the kindhearted American had not threatened to take his custom elsewhere.

She lasted ten months with the stonyhearted Hentenarts and then fell ill of typhoid. Long weeks of slow convalescence followed and torments of anxiety.

During this dismal period, when she and her mother were existing mostly on bread and cheese, Emma found herself one morning in front of a rotisserie window, staring as if hypnotized at a handsome roast chicken, tantalizingly displayed on a bed of crisp cress. Finally the temptation became too strong, and without stopping to count the consequences, she flung into the shop and brazenly ordered the bird delivered to her mother. The chicken, when it arrived, was refused by Albine, who had no five francs to pay for it, but Emma, meeting the errand boy on the way back, plausibly talked the bird away from him, with a promise that she would drop into the shop the next day to pay the bill, and ran home with it in triumph.

"But," Albine protested, "we shan't have the five francs to pay for this in a month!"

"I don't care! The shopkeeper can wait! We're going to eat!"

It was a memorable orgy, but the price turned out to be higher than they expected. Every morning the errand boy was sent by the enraged shopkeeper to collect the money, and when he failed to get it, he would repair to the courtyard of the house and take revenge by shrieking for all to hear: "Crooks! That's what the Guilberts are! Chicken thieves!"

This daily rumpus went on until Emma and her mother were ashamed to go out, and their ears burned with embarrassment as they passed their neighbors on the stairs. At last someone, for the sake of peace, lent them the five francs.

When Emma had recovered enough strength, she got another job, this time as salesgirl in the dress department of the Magasins du Printemps. There the money was even better than at the Hentenarts', salary and commissions sometimes amounting to as much as one hundred and twenty-five francs a month. Life was more fun there, too;

she and the other girls would dance in the fitting rooms while the manager was out to lunch, and Emma would sing for them. But again the hours were killing—from seven to nine—and she often had not only to sell a dress but also to deliver it. Once more her health broke, and this time a longer period of recuperation was necessary.

One day Albine, who had heard not a word from her husband since his departure, received a letter from Villedieu-des-Poêles in Normandy. Madame Bochin, the wife of an inkeeper there, was writing to say that Monsieur Hippolyte Guilbert lay very ill in her house and begged that his wife and daughter would come to him, as he knew his end was near. He had been on his way from Paris to Saint-Lô but had taken sick en route and been unable to continue his journey. Though Emma rebelled strongly at going, in the end Albine's kind heart prevailed; the two borrowed money for the train fare and set forth.

It was August of 1882, and the day they arrived in Villedieu was one of Normandy's infrequent days of oppressive heat. Not a breath of air moved the leaves of the plane trees in the small central Place de la Republique, on which faced M. Bochin's square and austere *hôtellerie*. In front of the weather-worn, plastered façade of the little inn lay only the merest slice of shade. Inside the house, however, a shadowy hall reached back into cool interiors—oak-raftered rooms with whitewashed walls and waxed tile floors. A Sister from the local convent, Madame Bochin told Albine, was caring for the patient; the priest had been sent for to confess him; Monsieur Guilbert had been greatly anxious over whether his wife and daughter would come.

Albine went into the sick room while Emma waited in the hall, on a bench near the door, a bouquet of wilting fuchsias in her hands. After a while Albine came out, her eyes red. Hippolyte wanted to see Emma now.

Reluctantly the girl entered the room. Her father was lying in a great white-canopied bed, whose curtains that day had been twisted back to allow freer passage of air across his damp forehead. On the windowsill a wisp of a breeze played with a leaf of the Sister's breviary, but the Sister was not in the room.

The interview was extremely painful. Emma, not knowing what to say, laid the fuchsias on the bed beside her father, and Hippolyte in his weakness could only babble incoherently at first: "I repent—I repent—daughter—I repent." After a bit, however, he was able to speak with more composure. "Someday, Emma, soon perhaps, you will be marrying, and when you do, there is a favor I would like to ask. Will you remember me on your wedding day?"

Immediately the girl blazed in anger and incredibly cruel words leaped to her lips.

"I shall never marry!" she exploded. "Never! Why should I? I should be too miserable!"

For a long moment the dying man stared into his daughter's hate-filled eyes, then turned his face to the wall without a further word.

The funeral was typically Norman. There was no hearse in Villedieu, and Hippolyte's body was carried on a handcart by men of the town. The nuns and children of the convent formed an escort, dressed in white and chanting hymns and, to Emma's amusement, carrying lighted tapers in the bright sunshine. Down a winding road, between yellow wheatfields sprinkled with poppies and cornflowers, the procession, led by the curé, made its way. The cemetery was small and old and crowded, but somehow room had been found in a remote corner, and there the stranger was buried, under the traditional black cross of the Norman peasant.

That was about all there was to her story, Emma told Monsieur Zidler. Since then she and her mother had struggled on in much the same way. She had not dared to take another commercial job because of her health, so she had turned to sewing at home, like her mother. During Hentenart and Printemps days she had established connections with various women customers who liked to have their own "little dressmaker" for less important gowns. Most of these women she hated because of their meanness. One was a countess in the exclusive Parc Monceau district who used to fall into tantrums over every bill; another made her transfer labels of famous houses from other dresses into the ones Emma made; an American had skipped out, owing a large sum.

There was only one other person besides her mother to whom Emma was deeply attached. Relatives in Paris were few. She had an aunt and uncle. Her mother's sister Alice had married a Monsieur Jean Baptiste Broutin, and the couple lived in nearby Asnières. But they were not close to her heart. Her one dear friendship was with a young cousin, Adelina Gaillard, who had recently come to Paris from Sedan. Lina was a milliner, and the two girls often talked about how fine it would be if they had money enough to set up a little shop together; but these of course were only daydreams.

33

It was hard to believe that she would ever be able to find a solution to the problem of money. She thought of money night and day. That was why she had stopped so abruptly and listened so intently when Monsieur Zidler had pronounced the words "twenty thousand francs."

Marriage? Never. She knew too much about life from those poor women in the workshops, not to mention her own father. She hated men. Men had tried to entice her on the streets from the time she was eight, but she had known how to take care of herself; her mother had been very strict on such matters. Only once, and here Emma smiled a little at her adolescent absurdity, she had fallen in love. It was when she was not more than twelve, and the man, a Monsieur Puech, a middle-aged friend of her father's, had been entirely unaware of her infatuation until she had melodramatically offered herself to him; he had been very kind and tactful. The clerks and bookkeepers and buyers at Hentenarts' and Printemps who had tried to flirt with her she had always managed to put off with a joke—an off-color one, sometimes; how could a girl be prudish and hold a job? No, she wanted nothing of men.

She wanted merely to escape the tyranny of poverty. But how? She was twenty. What could she do?

II

1885 – 1899

Chapter 2

Monsieur Zidler had listened to Emma during her recital with absorbed interest and growing respect.

"My compliments, Mademoiselle," he said at the end, "on your intelligence and courage. Truly remarkable. And believe me, these are qualities that never go to waste. Someday a door will open for you; you will see. In the meantime, why not allow me to offer you a little pleasure? You like the theater? Well, then, let me send you passes. I get them from everywhere, you know. It will cheer you up to see a few plays. And keep in touch with me. When that door of yours opens, I should like to hear about it."

It was an inspiriting experience for a young nobody from the Marais to be treated with such cordiality by a man of Zidler's importance. Emma knew she was lacking in looks, ugly even, but she could not help knowing also that she had more wit than most of the simple working people she was surrounded by—morons, her father had called the mob—and with brains why should she not succeed at something? Mad as it might seem, she had her mind fixed on freeing herself from the murky precincts she had grown up in, and the everlasting sewing. Lately her mother's eyesight had begun to fail; she was afraid to think what would become of the two of them if her mother could no longer sew.

She was twenty, and of the two famous women with whose lives her own was to intertwine one was as yet completely unknown to her and the other barely heard of. Twenty, and with what a different attitude toward love than either of these, each of whom at her age had given birth to an illigitimate child. At her age, too, they had advanced far in their professions; were already known as rising young actresses. At that moment, what seemingly greater improbability could have been suggested than that the fortunes of this obscure young seamstress would ever be entangled with those of the Divine Sarah Bernhardt and the Great Eleanora Duse?

In her later years Emma gave varying accounts of what first put in her mind the idea of the stage as a profession. According to the best-known story, which appears in her memoirs, the kindhearted Zidler, man of his word, one day sent her tickets to a performance of Sarah Bernhardt in the Porte Saint-Martin Theatre, and Emma, who had never seen the Divine One, attended with a friend in high anticipation.

The two had hardly taken their places when a gentleman came in and sat down beside them on that odd invention of French theater architects, the *strapontin,* the backless seat that unfolds at the end of a row and on which the occupant perches uncomfortably in the aisle.

The curtain went up. . . . I was feverishly awaiting Bernhardt. At last a young woman came on the stage sumptuously clothed. It was Cleopatra! I listened, I gazed, I never missed a movement or lost a word; but when the act was over I was dismally disappointed. Mlle Masson was disappointed too. The man on the *strapontin* was so much amused by our criticisms that he informed us that Sarah Bernhardt had been taken ill in the theatre and that we had seen her understudy. He offered me his card: "Edmond Stoullig, dramatic critic." . . .

"Don't you admire the understudy?"

"No, monsieur."

"Why?"

"She speaks badly, and her sufferings don't seem real. So it seems to me," I added, half ashamed of being so positive.

He was so much interested the whole evening in what I said that he suddenly broke out: "Why don't you go on the stage, mademoiselle? You're clever, and you would be sure to succeed." And

36

he kept looking at me. And during the interval he kept repeating that I ought certainly to go on the stage.

"Here, I'll give you a line to an excellent teacher." And on his card he wrote "Landrol, 101 Rue Lafayette." "And I'll write him myself," he promised.

This anecdote finds corroboration in Brisson's "Portraits," in which Brisson relates the same story as told him by Stoullig. The name of the play, however, is obviously confused, as Bernhardt did not open in *Cléopâtre* until October 25, 1890, and by that time Emma was herself no longer an untutored working girl. Brisson recalls the play as *Théodora*. However, in the latter part of January, 1886, a Mademoiselle Barétry did appear as understudy in the Bernhardt play *Marion DeLorme,* and hence it is more probable that this is the play referred to.

Certain it is from his reviews later that Stoullig came to know Emma well, and that he became fond of her. It is also clear that about this time Monsieur Landrol, a prominent member of the company at the Gymnase, was accepting students of acting and possibly also of singing, and what more natural than that Stoullig, or perhaps Zidler, with his great admiration of his protegée, should send Emma to Landrol? Zidler may even have paid her tuition.

Landrol had a reputation for being severe. His methods were simple: he had no time to baby or cajole or cater to tender sensibilities. If a girl had talent, let her show it. If she could survive his rugged disciplines, he would eventually launch her by finding her a small part in some new piece that was being cast; from then on, she would be expected to fend for herself.

The vital question for Emma was: How long would such training take? No one could tell, of course. Should she risk it? Suppose she gave herself two years, during which she might still, she hoped, earn enough by sewing to keep herself at least at subsistence level; could she in this brief trial period prove the practicality of acting as a career?

Two years would be a long time with the belt a notch tighter, but the compulsion to try eventually became too strong to argue with. She felt it particularly after her first talk with Landrol and her first breath of the musty odor of backstage. Paris of the 80's teemed with theaters, some twenty or more in regular operation—fifty, according to Brander Matthews, if lesser ones in outlying districts were included —and among all these she may well have believed that there would be room for her in some small capacity. She was not seeking the stage as a *métier*, a dearly desired way of life, but very simply as a way of earning a living. Art was to her as yet a meaningless word; hunger was not. And after all, why not she, as well as anyone else? From babyhood she had been singing every tune on the street to entertain friends and neighbors.

Albine, who did not withhold her permission where there were no horses concerned, nevertheless built no castles; merely maintained her usual attitude of stolid Norman caution. Zidler, of course, applauded the move, joked about the hardships. "You may as well starve doing something amusing!" he laughed.

Emma found it not easy, however, to tell her cousin the news. Lina wept inconsolably, as if Emma had broken faith with her; the dream of the joint shop, it was clear, must be forever abandoned.

With the same thoroughness that she had given to her work as dressmaker, Emma began her study with Landrol, practicing diligently meticulous drills in diction, tone projection, phrasing, pace; struggling to achieve the gracefulness he demanded in stage business: how to enter, how to exit; how to stand, sit, rise, walk; how to faint; how to handle a train, or make one of those majestic sweeping crosses so popular with the stage directors of that day; memorizing the parts he assigned, rehearsing them, playing scenes with other students; learning to analyze roles, to build characterization.

Immediately she fell in love with the profession; it was as if a window had opened in her mind. To this seamstress, whose horizons had so lately been bounded by gores and hems and pinkings and rufflings, literature and art suddenly took on new meanings; libraries and museums became places of excitement. She began to read, indiscriminately—Balzac, Stendhal, Chateaubriand, Voltaire, Molière—and incessantly, as if she knew by instinct that she could never catch up on the years she had missed. She had always loved sculpture. Now she spent long hours in the Louvre, lost in wonder before the equilibrium of the Discobolus or the harmony of the Aphrodite of Melos.

It was sometime during this period of apprenticeship that Emma made her first important social contact, probably through Zidler, when she met Léon Sari, director of the Folies-Bergère. In this famed music hall, located at 32 Rue Richer—almost impudently where a monastery had once stood—the program even in those days was noted more for its nudity than its purity; for the lavish glitter of its revues;

for the fashionable demimondaines whose beauty, and occasionally talent, were on display behind its footlights. But the Folies had even more than its stage show to offer. Sari had created also the *promenoir,* that "mart of Venus," a circle inside the theater where spectators could stretch their legs between acts or have a drink at the bar, and where other elegant demimondaines were more immediately accessible than those behind the footlights.

Sari owned a country estate at Vaux, near Meulan, to which he was in the habit of inviting large weekend parties of theatrical friends. Here Papa Zidler was a regular guest, and Emma too was often invited. The estate lay beside the Seine, some thirty miles from Paris, in a beautiful stretch of unspoiled country. Beside the house was a garden; in front, a smooth expanse of greensward swept down to the river's edge. It was a wind-blown spot, with a far vista on sunny days; Emma fell in love with the place. Here, around a luncheon cloth spread on the grass, the clever ones exchanged backstage gossip, talked shop brilliantly, or in uninhibited mood set the air crackling with Gallic wisecracks. Just to listen to them was a stimulating experience for a young student.

One day at Vaux the subject of a stage name for Emma came up. A name, it was explained to her, was important: it should have a "ring" to it, and a "ring" the prosaic combination of "Emma Guilbert" clearly lacked. During the discussion that followed, a young man who happened to know Guy de Maupassant offered to ask that celebrity's opinion. Within a few days came a laconic reply. "Tell her to call herself Yvette," the great man counseled.

Yvette Guilbert. Completely satisfying, everyone agreed. Here was a name with a ring to it.

At the end of eight months Landrol wrote Stoullig that he considered Mademoiselle Guilbert the most intelligent pupil he had ever had. There is strong likelihood that the novice had made occasional amateur appearances during her training period, but her professional stage debut came when Landrol, or someone, procured for her the part of Madame de Nevers in *La Reine Margot,* from Dumas, which was to open in January, 1887, in the Bouffes-du-Nord. For this event the new Yvette needing funds to furbish up her wardrobe with, did not hesitate to apply to Papa Zidler, who responded with a lavish hundred francs.

Significant as this opening was for Yvette, it was characterized by an entire lack of notice by critics. Not a voice was lifted to announce the arrival of new star material. The performance seems to have been, indeed, a rather painful one. In a rented gown with headdress that wobbled, Yvette nervously strode back and forth across the stage so fast that her supposed attendants had to break into a trot to keep up with her. At one point she was all but paralyzed by sudden stage fright; at another laughed with the audience; and throughout forgot her cultivated accent and played duchess with guttersnipe overtones. But the simple-hearted public of the Bouffes-du-Nord, apparently kind to neophytes, found no fault, and she survived; in fact, she even appeared before the same public again as Baroness de Cérirères in *Princesse Georges.*

While she was still at the Bouffes-du-Nord, there came a piece of typical beginner's luck. Aciana, star of *Rigobert,* which had opened February 16 at the Théâtre Cluny in the Latin Quarter, fell ill, and Léon Marx, the manager, who had noted Yvette in *La Reine Margot* and *Princesse Georges,* asked her at short notice to step in Aciana's role. She played a month at the Cluny and pleased M. Marx so well that he offered to try to get her into a theater on the Boulevards.

The Boulevards! A magic name to Parisian pleasure seekers. There, in the dazzle of shops and cafés and theaters, was to be felt a certain bubbling up of good spirits, a special kind of *joie de vivre,* that existed nowhere else in the city. For the average theatergoer, the Grands Boulevards were the whole area from the Madeleine to the Bastille, but the real boulevard, *the* Boulevard, so-called, was the one that included the Boulevards de la Madeleine, des Capucines, and des Italiens as far the Opéra, particularly the section surrounding the Opéra. This was the territory of a special genre of Parisian, the *boulevardier,* that polished sophisticated being who twice a day sauntered through his domain—before dinner, during the "green hour," named for the color of the absinthe in so many glasses, and again after the play—and who would have expected the sky to fall if he missed a first night at the Variétés, the Vaudeville, the Gymnase, or the Ambigu.

But picking up an engagement in this hallowed area, as Yvette soon discovered, was not easy, and it must have been during those wearisome months when she was "at liberty" that she became acquainted with André Antoine's new Théâtre-Libre. In that much-talked-of dramatic laboratory the explosive chemicals of Ibsen, Tolstoi, and Zola were then being tested. Naturalism, having had its way with novels, was now attacking the stage, and under its blows the old authority was declining; the escapism of Augier, Dumas *fils,* and Sardou were giving way. A public that had only recently solaced itself with soothing syrups of romanticism was being replaced by one that fed hungrily on Zolaesque verisimilitude—uncompromising details, scrupulously observed, documented, and recorded.

To dodge the blows of the censor's ax on his shocking avant-garde plays, the director Antoine shrewdly restricted his audiences to subscribers and guests. The place was in Montmartre, the obscure little Passage de l'Élysée-des-Beaux-Arts, off the Place Pigalle, in a tiny hall where, said Jules Lemaître, "you could shake hands with the actors across the footlights and stretch your legs out into the prompter's box. The . . . audience was so close that illusion was an impossibility. We could feel ourselves akin to the spectators of the great days of the theatre, the fellows of Shakespeare and Molière." Yet in spite of these primitive conditions, nightly the miniature auditorium was crowded with intellectuals; here also Tout Paris flocked, that segment of Paris society which Brander Matthews described scornfully as "three hundred people who arrogate to themselves the title of all Paris . . . men of letters and of the world, artists, critics, ladies of good society and bad, bankers and do-nothings about town." Sitting night after night in the crowded, tiny Théâtre-Libre, watching the curtain go up on the new theatrical techniques being displayed there, listening avidly to challenging new social doctrines, Yvette soon became a disciple of the radical naturalistic movement.

Eventually, thanks to the exertions of Léon Marx, she was granted an interview with the noted Albert Brasseur, director of the Nouveautés who after listening to her audition, somewhat unenthusiastically engaged her. For bit parts only, however, Brasseur emphasized. The Nouveautés was a comedy theater, and frankly, he said, he lacked confidence in her for comedy roles; her expression was too melancholy.

Yvette, whose ego had instantly soared with the possession of a contract, was not greatly concerned over these reservations. The contract was the important thing, for with this scrap of paper she had achieved an objective that only a few months ago she would hardly have dared hope for: she was now a regular member of a real company at a first-class theater on the Boulevards! She was to open in *La Lycéene* on December 23, 1887, playing Anita; and at a princely salary—two hundred and fifty francs a month. At least it sounded princely until she began to realize that two hundred and fifty francs would hardly pay for her wardrobe.

One day some months later Brasseur fell into a directorial pet and started fuming again about her face.

"I have told you many times, Mademoiselle! Your face is sad enough to make one weep! You should go to the Odéon, the Gymnase. You'll never be any use to me!"

When Yvette flared back that her face couldn't be too sad because the Variétés had just made her an offer, Brasseur promptly retorted in undisguised relief, that in that case he would tear up his contract with her, and wished her luck. Parting remarks were not exactly polite on either side.

For long the Variétés, "where the Almanach de Gotha crowded the house," all gilt and sculptured decoration and jasper columns and thick carpets, had been considered the most truly Parisian of theatres; it has been described fully by Zola in *Nana:* its "garnet-coloured velvet seats"; . . . the ceiling "displaying figures of naked women and children floating among clouds"; the huge crystal gasolier "which blazed with prismatic hues . . . the light reflected on to the pit like a shower of gold . . ."

As steel to the magnet, young bloods arriving from London or Madrid would invariably gravitate to the Variétés, where the first half-dozen rows were traditionally reserved for males. In 1888, a little shabby perhaps with its years, heading toward its eventual nadir of squalor and odor of disinfectants, the house still exercised a fascination for Paris impuritans looking for a lively evening. Here the plays were, as Matthews reports, not long but always broad, and after the show patrons could step across to Tortoni's for a new refreshment, the *marquise*—pineapple ice floating in champagne.

Zidler had warned Yvette that she would never rise professionally as long as she was content to accept parts in curtain-raisers, and at the Variétés things did go better for her because the manager, Bertrand, at her badgering billed her now in the principal pieces, giving her roles in *Barbe Bleu* and *La Japonaise.* She was still getting only two hundred and fifty francs, but she tried to be patient about the money because she knew that even Réjane, already a great star, was making no more than a thousand francs.

Most advantageous of all for a newcomer to the profession was the superior company at the Variétés. Beside Réjane, there was the beloved Anna Damiens Israël, known everywhere as Judic, an actress of genuine comic power who first earned her fame in the *cafés-concerts* and the Folies-Bergère. And there were other celebrities—Dupuis; Louis Bouchenez, known as Baron; Christian; Lassouche. With deep absorption Landrol's most intelligent pupil studied these players at rehearsal and in performance, and they left an indelible mark on her style. They even taught her how to sing, she always claimed, because in later years when she had a new song to prepare she would instinctively devote herself first of all to acting it.

From her new associates she learned, too, some of the tricks and dodges of the acting trade. For example, how to recognize the people one has to keep on good terms with: this actress because her lover is an editor or dramatic critic; another because she is mistress of one of the shareholders of the theater; almost any author of a new play, who can so easily whittle down a part if he becomes annoyed or enlarge it a bit if judiciously flattered.

Not that she could see how any of this knowledge would ever really help her. Yvette, who habitually blurted out her mind with disconcerting candor, knew that she was not constituted for intrigue, and not being minded to barter sex for spotlight, she began to wonder how then she could ever rise to the top.

When she went to Zidler, as she always did with her thoughts, he smiled cynically.

"You have the virtue of courage, my dear, but in the theater one virtue has never been as handy as a couple of vices."

"But when shall I become a star?" she demanded.

He shook his head. "In Paris success for women is very slow—ten, maybe fifteen years."

And she had mentally allowed herself two!

These two years had indeed already elapsed when the Variétés closed for the summer of 1889 and she went off on a tour of the provinces with a company headed by Baron, with Jane May as leading woman. The piece was *Décoré,* by Meilhac and Halévy, in which Yvette played acceptably, but with no great distinction, her part of the Comtesse Carinti. She also appeared in the curtain-raiser *La Sarabande du Cardinal,* by the same authors.

Although the tour was uneventful, unexpectedly the summer marked a turning point in her life.

In the group was the personable and talented actor Baral, formerly of the Comédie Française and the Bouffes-Parisiens, and he and

Yvette, who both knew scores of songs, used to sing in the trains to amuse themselves and the others as the little troupe jounced along uncomfortably, from booking to booking, on the bare benches of third-class railway carriages. Baral was astounded at all the songs Yvette knew, and professed to be delighted by the style with which she delivered them.

"I can't understand, Yvette," he said again and again, "why, with your talent for singing, you don't clear out of the theater and make for the *café-concert*. Good heavens, it will take you ten years to earn as much in the theater as you could earn tomorrow in the *boui-bouis*. Granted, your voice is not musical enough for light opera, but it's still quite good enough for café singing. How much are you getting at the Variétés?"

"Two hundred and fifty francs."

"I'll bet you anything you want to name that you could begin at the Eldorado at six hundred."

"It's outrageous!" protested every other member of the company. "Advising a girl to leave the Boulevards!—especially a theater like the Variétés!—for those miserable, cheap *cafés-concerts!* Pay no attention to him, Yvette!"

But Yvette did pay attention. Somehow it had never occurred to her before that there might be money in the *cafés-concerts*.

Chapter 3

Marseilles, gateway from the Orient, is said to have been the first city in France to drink coffee. When the beverage was brought to Paris by the traveler Thévénot around 1650, the Turkish ambassador Soliman Aga quickly made it popular in society, but it remained for an Armenian named Pascal, in 1672, to open the first public room where the new brew could be generally sampled. When the bourgeoisie also pronounced in its favor, public establishments began to multiply, then gradually to turn themselves into places where people could eat as well as drink, and, in spite of Madame de Sévigné's pessimistic prediction that the coffee fad would never last, within a few years the café had become an accepted feature of Parisian life.

During the eighteenth century a related enterprise, referred to as the *café-chantant,* also came into being in Paris. The humble beginnings of what is now an enormously large and profitable segment of the amusement world took place in a little cellar restaurant called the Café des Aveugles, named after an orchestra of some half-dozen blind musicians who introduced the great novelty of playing jigs and tunes during the dinner hour; there was also a woman who sang with them at the top of her voice, and a ventriloquist. The new idea of combining frisky entertainment with food and drink so charmed diners and pleasure seekers alike that, from then on, more and more café managers might have been seen scurrying around to engage fiddlers and singers to enhance their own menus. By the middle of the nineteenth century the *café-chantant* had become an institution deeply entrenched in the customs and affections of the city, and after the phenomenal success, in 1848, of the Estaminet Lyrique, where a young tenor named Darcier filled the cash drawer month after month by bewitching the crowds with his silver tones, practically every café in Paris turned *café-chantant*. Later these "singing" cafés were often contemptuously referred to as "bellowing" ones (*cafés-beuglants*), many having little to offer but noise and cheap tunes.

In the 1860's, however, the whole genre took a new lease on life. It was then that one Emma Valadon, who came to be known only as Thérèsa—and always, affectionately, "the great Thérèsa"—leaped to stardom by her inimitable way of singing comic songs; became such a rage, in fact, that she was summoned by Napoleon III for a command performance in the Tuileries. Until the day of her final retirement, this great *artiste,* whom the child Emma Guilbert in tablecloth train had so delighted to mimic, continued to attract crowds wherever she sang, and it is she who is credited with having changed the status of the *café-chantant* to that of *café-concert,* to use the term common in the 80's.

The early *cafés-chantants* had been under tight police regulation. Staging and scenery, for example, would have been considered by the authorities as presupposing a play, and a play would simply not be licensed on the platform of a *café-chantant*. Even costumes were forbidden, and performers were thus restricted to conventional evening dress.

As the years passed, however, censorship relaxed in regard to the use of visual stage effects. Songs still had to be licensed, though even here a high degree of tolerance became the standard and by the 80's official curbs on unchaste commentary were largely nominal.

Though such compliance on the part of the censors naturally went far toward accounting for the popularity of the *café-concert,* there were other contributing elements, notably cheapness and convenience. Even the most inexpensive seat at a comedy, a drama, or the opera would cost the workingman fifty sous; if he wanted to be sure of seeing and hearing, five francs or more; and because he must hurry through his dinner, dress up a little, and arrive early to contend for a seat, what had been anticipated as pleasure might quickly deteriorate into irritation and fatigue. Worse, a degree of intellectual effort might be required to understand the piece. At the *café-concert,* on the other hand, a man could come and go as he wished during those boring hours between dinner and bed; drink and smoke and keep his hat on. Admission was cheap, or often free, though the customer naturally was expected to order refreshment at premium prices. To some cafés, those that catered to family groups, he could bring his wife and children, all dressed just as they were, munching chestnuts, chattering and relaxed.

By the 1880's, many varieties of the *caf'-conc'* had become available. Typical would be the regular concert hall, equipped only with a shallow platform, without scenery, at one end, and an orchestra of sorts. Sitting at the rear of the platform, "dressing the scene," would generally be found a half-circle of wonderful creatures known as *poseuses,* or *dames du bouquet,* brightly enameled as to complexion, fearfully and wonderfully coiffed, and wearing gowns that could hardly have been paid for out of the pittances the ladies legitimately earned by their presence there. Their presence, in fact, was all they contributed; they toiled not, neither did they sing, but served merely as decorative background for the real performance, having earned the designation of "bouquet ladies" by their traditional willingness to accept, with consequences, whatever flowers an admiring spectator might care to send up over the footlights.

There was also the subterranean type of *caf'-conc',* cellar dens where bodies were jam-packed and the air suffocating with stale breath and dense tobacco smoke; where only a dilapidated piano tinkled and flatted and performers often stood on packing cases in lieu of platforms, barely able to make themselves heard above the tumult and the shouting of customers and waiters alike. At the other extreme, a number of houses boasted real stages; were actually small theaters. Some were barbarously ornamented and tinseled and given over to nudes and naughtiness, but offered latticed boxes in which respectable matrons could mask their identity. A few, like the Châtelet and La

46

Scala, catered to a really well-mannered clientele; here programs would be less prurient. Pleasantest of all, of course, were the outdoor cafés in summer on the Champs-Élysées, where among trees and shrubbery, shut in by little more than vine-covered trellis walls, under chains of flickering yellow gas lamps that alternated tremulous glows and flickering shadows, an evening's entertainment shed much of its winter indoor stridency and achieved a witchery all its own.

To these cafés flocked a public ranging from the laborers of Belleville and the bureaucrats and businessmen of the Boulevard de Strasbourg to the bohemians of Montmartre and the Latin Quarter. Émile Blémont, writing in *L'Événement* in February, 1891, says that actually there were two *caf'-conc'* publics, totally distinct:

> On the one hand you will find the masses, a trifle heavy, a trifle slow, but simple-minded, sympathetic and generous. This public is composed of the loyal and steady workers in life, who come here for rest after their daily toil, and to get, without much trouble, a certain amount of cheap, but perfectly honest amusement. These people have an ideal of amusement which is as simple as their natures. . . .
>
> On the other hand, in these by no means unpicturesque places of amusement, . . . you will find another public which is, in some respects, more highly cultivated. They are the rakes, the eccentrics, the "déclassés" of literature or trade, forming the bohemia of the more well-to-do middle class, . . . This public is blasé, subtle, whimsical; prone to sudden exhibitions of feeling, and savage pleasantries; a public that has run through the whole gamut of emotions, and is always looking for some new sensation.
>
> These two publics side by side form a strange combination, a heterogeneous assembly where two entirely different classes sit close together but never intermingle.

Both publics, however, shared a common taste for laughter. The mob, in classic tradition, demanded the Rabelaisian belly laugh. They never tired of the drunk, with his farcically red nose, his cravat askew, his hat on crosswise, rattling on interminable details about everything he had drunk and vomited; or the antic, pantomiming the exigencies of a purge; or the keyhole witness, describing other bodily privacies with eyes, hips, broken words. Against this popular appetite for the obscene, Parisian censors were practically helpless. If lines were cut, performers substituted indecent mimicry.

More sophisticated listeners were capable of enjoying satire, but, sadly, performers were seldom capable of offering it. Taken as a whole, there was little evidence of social awareness in the *café-concert* either by men or women singers, other than occasional political partisanship, as for example during the height of popular enthusiasm over the would-be dictator Boulanger. Since with the mob natural gifts sufficed, most of the favorites had had little education, depending for success largely on spontaneity and pungent individuality. In general, the songs bawled out by the beefy middle-aged females or bleated out by the libertine little lambs had traditionally been composed in almost equal parts of smut, chauvinism, slapstick, and sugary sentimentality. Professionally speaking, these women performers were very small beer indeed, recruited for the most part from the bolder sort of milliners, or artists' models, or washed down from the higher reaches of the musical world—the opera or musical comedy—few Thérèsas or Judics or Amiatis having risen to stature in this all-but-impossible medium. Some had begun by learning songs by ear in a *caf'-conc'* "conservatory," such as the one directed by a Monsieur Duhem in Rue Sainte-Apolline. As Duhem was a composer and it was therefore to his financial advantage to have his works sung as often as possible, groups of girls, some thirty or forty at a time, would be drilled by a pianist and then sent out through the provinces, returning to Duhem for new repertory whenever the old one wore out. To supply the enormous and constant demand for new songs, a demand obviously far greater than a handful of composers could meet, a curious, almost monopolistic system had developed, which Theodore Child describes in the New York *Sun,* June 20, 1887:

> The observer who takes the trouble to examine the songs of the *café-concert* will find that the authors and musicians are few. Half a dozen names will recur constantly, and when we look into the matter we shall find that these names are those of managers, secretaries, or prominent *café-concert* artistes whose position puts into their hands means of coercion, and enables them to buy the words and music of a song for one, two, or three dollars or four dollars at the outside.
>
> But who are the real authors of the songs in question? Government employees, I have been informed, head the list, and this I can readily understand, for the government offices are the last and sure refuge of many mature poets and unsuccessful musicians, of whom

the foolish publish volumes of verse or of statistics, while the prudent produce dreadful couplets for the *café-concerts,* which are bought by purveyors, who in turn sell them to the managers and secretaries, who sign them and have them sung in public. These managers and secretaries are simple dealers in songs, believing only in success, avoiding all that is new and risky, and discouraging original effort. . . . it is perhaps time to risk something new. . . . the French *café-concert* is a sort of vast public bath of imbecility, ghastly comicality, and disguised priapism and scatology, the whole leavened by much good humor . . .

When young Mademoiselle Guilbert, prompted by Baral's fantastic prophecy of earning six hundred francs a month as a singer, began investigating the *café-concert,* she soon discovered that the Eldorado, Boulevard de Strasbourg, which Baral had mentioned, ranked easily, as one of the best of its kind; that it was indeed often referred to as the Comédie Française of song.

The celebrated critic Francisque Sarcey considered the Eldorado a real theater, and called it quite charming, with its stages, orchestra, three rows of boxes, and balconies. Including the café, it had cost nearly a million francs and excelled many legitimate theaters in appointments and comforts. It could accommodate fifteen hundred comfortably, each cushioned seat provided with side trays for glasses and plates. Here for two francs fifty centimes a patron could enjoy, with his pipe and his bottle of beer or wine, a whole evening of entertainment—acrobatics, clowning, singing; even a short theatrical piece.

The proprietress of the Eldorado, Madame Allemand, was in appearance a rather astonishing person. She wore habitually a grotesque hat, plumed like a hearse; diamonds were in her ears, turquoises on her fingers, gold chains about her neck, bracelets on her wrists, brooches on her aggressive breasts; and against her seamed old face, painted a pinkish mauve, purple lips and yellow teeth made a startling contrast. In spite of her eccentricities of dress, however, Madame was nobody's fool. She had already made one fortune managing a brewery in Marseilles and was now midstream in making another as *directrice* of entertainment at the Eldorado. It was Madame herself who auditioned performers, and it was she who listened with lackluster eye one morning in September, 1889, to an unknown young postulant

49

named Yvette Guilbert as she sang an air from the then-popular operetta *La Gamine de Paris.*

Fortunately for the young lady, two other listeners sitting in the rear of the theatre proved more appreciative of her talents than Madame. These were the Lyonnet twin brothers, popular singers of the day, who at the end of the audition spoke up forcefully in favor of Yvette, praising her diamond-cut diction, her modulations, her self-command. She had a glorious *élan,* they said; in time she could become something really extraordinary.

"This girl's good!" they exclaimed. "And she's different!"

So Madame halfheartedly allowed herself to be persuaded to a contract; the Lyonnets had picked winners for her before; she would take a chance. Yvette, emboldened at this breakthrough, pushed her luck a little further: it must be a three-year contract, she stipulated, with six hundred francs a month the first year, seven hundred the second, and eight hundred the third. Madame shrilled to high heaven over such avarice, but Yvette held her ground, and after a long session of fishwife haggling emerged, document in hand. Six hundred francs a month, just as Baral had predicted.

Floating on air, she hastened to seek release from her contract with Variétés.

"Well, well! So you have a voice, eh, Yvette?" Bertrand joked. "And a dozen or so smart new hit songs up your sleeve too, I suppose?"

This lighthearted reference to the problem of songs touched Yvette in a vulnerable spot. Everyone in show business knew that in the *caf'-conc'* the choice of material was crucial; songs were a singer's lifeline. In a city where literally thousands of ditties were being ground out every year for the hundreds of *cafés-concerts* going at full tilt, Yvette well realized that it would take an expert to sift the wheat from the chaff; she also realized that she was no such expert. Not only did she have no songs; at that moment she knew practically nothing about what the world of the *café-concert* would expect of her. Moreover, she had only two months before her opening date in November in which to find out. Where to begin?

She began by attending *cafés-concerts,* crowding her evenings with them one after another, studying the programs and making notes, and everywhere she went she was appalled by the low order of the entertainment presented, the poor caliber of the performers, and the stupidity of the audiences.

Nonetheless, she became convinced that the cabaret did offer a form of art, though to be sure one stated in very raw colors; rude and commonplace, but with a universal appeal, and, like its sister art of drama, a form of release and catharsis. What especially attracted her was that here was a theater without fixed rules, one in which the creative mind could enjoy a maximum of flexibility. As to the mediocre performers she listened to, Yvette, whose musical and dramatic background, slight as it was, probably surpassed theirs, sensed no formidable competition. Any singer of real intelligence, she believed, ought to be able to outstrip them quickly enough, and thus, viewed from the angle of self-interest, the medium offered real inducement.

But the audiences! Her heart sank when she compared these thick-headed, rowdy beer guzzlers with the suave crowds at the Variétés. Landrol's most intelligent pupil was shrewd enough to admit that she could hardly expect to change uneducated tastes, and Madame Allemand's parting words, "Be sure your songs are funny, young lady!" kept ringing in her ears. Yet she could not endure the thought of dishing up such nauseating balderdash as she had listened to everywhere. The *Sun* correspondent, therefore, was not long alone in his opinion that "it is perhaps time to risk something new" in *café-concert* entertainment. Mademoiselle Guilbert, surveying the scene through her keen young eyes, came immediately and independently to the same conclusion. Something new was indeed needed: something meaningful. Furthermore, ambition was burgeoning fast within her; eventually she would be satisfied, she knew, with nothing less than star billing, and stars are not born on assembly lines. Clearly the problem was to find unhackneyed material.

One day, armed with her precious Eldorado contract so that she could get songs free, she turned in at Benoit's, the music publishers, to see what she could unearth. While she was riffling through a heap of trite music laid before her, she overheard a conversation going on nearby between Benoit and another man, who, it developed, was Verdellet, director of the Casino in Lyons.

"Do you happen to know a singer I can pick up at this season?" Verdellet was saying. "I need a semi-star for a ten-day engagement—not too expensive—from one of the good *concerts*— but not an agent in town can seem to lay hands on one. Any suggestions?"

"Sorry, I'm afraid I haven't," said Benoit.

Immediately it flashed into Yvette's mind that there seemed something almost providential in this unexpected bit of intelligence, and, following a strong impulse, she rose and walked coolly over to Verdellet.

"Pardon, Monsieur, you need a singer? May I suggest myself? I have been playing at the Variétés and am now engaged to open at the Eldorado in November. Until then I would be available," and she pulled out of her pocket the contract on which Madame Allemand's signature was hardly more than dry.

Verdellet glanced at the document, noted the salary of six hundred francs, and became interested. Just about what he wanted—a semistar. The girl seemed pretty serious, thin, and humorless, but her poise and self-confidence impressed him, and besides—the Eldorado.

"What style do you sing, Mademoiselle? Humorous or sentimental?"

"Humorous, Monsieur."

"I regret to say I don't know your work, Mademoiselle, but the Variétés and Eldorado are good houses. Would you accept four hundred francs and expenses for ten days, with star billing of course?"

Mademoiselle, had he known, would have signed for nothing, merely for the sake of an out-of-town tryout before the all-important début at the Eldorado.

For Lyons she quickly decided on four rollicking songs which had recently been made the vogue in Paris by Demay, a popular comedienne, but which she felt sure would be new in the provinces, and began practicing them assiduously.

Lyons was the antithesis of Paris—a grimy industrial town, clouded with mists from its rivers and smoke from its chimneys. Yvette felt ill at ease in it from the moment she arrived, and the more so when she encountered on every billboard gaudy posters featuring the arrival at the Casino of Yvette Guilbert, artiste from the Paris Variétés. Verdellet had kept his word; she was being given star billing. Her heart aquake, she was thankful she had been astute enough to prepare those four sure-fire songs.

At the theater that night, waiting her turn in the wings, she found herself trembling from stage fright. On the stage was a barrel-bellied peroxide blonde singer, perspiring freely and red as a lobster from her exertions. The lady's ample bosom heaved and her eyes fairly popped out of her head as she yelled her indecencies above a hurdy-gurdy sort of accompaniment. The house was filled with students from the university, who sang the choruses lustily with her, cheered and stamped their feet, and clapped her back again and again. A hit performance.

She was followed by the diminutive comedian Wély, a *café-concert* favorite from Paris, who, like Yvette, after the Casino engagement was slated to open at the Eldorado. Wély sang about a pretty lady undressing in a bathing machine as described by a Peeping Tom, but every now and then interrupted his indelicate musings with bursts of Tyrolese yodeling. The enthusiasm out front left no doubt that Wély also was a hit. The young men went into ecstasies. More stampings and encores. The show was really rolling.

Now it was Yvette's turn. The star emerged, tall and poker-dignified in a chaste pearl-embroidered frock, with puffed sleeves and high neckline, that she had worn in her last play at the Variétés. In her terror her face had gone paste-white and her lips were quivering. She heard a kind of gasp go up as she walked down to the footlights. To an audience where lusts were in full cry, this pallid, emaciated creature must have seemed as unreal as an apparition, sexless as a figurine. There was a moment of stunned silence, and then abruptly laughter broke out—the wrong kind—followed by boos, hoots, quips. The jeering cascaded down upon her from all sides.

"Where'd they find that string bean?"—"God, what a skinny!"— "Flat as a pancake!"—"It's a freak!"

"Where's her bosom?" a voice trumpeted over the hubbub.

"She left it in her trunk!" another voice yelled back, and at this witticism the house rocked. Over the bedlam, Yvette tried to begin her first song, but in vain. Some of the young gentlemen, tickled with the image of the star's curves left in her trunk, started to repeat the insulting exchange, chanting it to the tune of a popular song: "*Où sont les tétons? Où sont les tétons?*"—"*Ils sont dans la malle! Ils sont dans la malle!*", while all the time the gibes and catcalls continued. As the uproar mounted, Yvette had no choice but to walk off, her songs unsung, and the stage manager quickly rang down the curtain.

Almost in a faint, hardly able to see for the black, swimming mist before her eyes, Yvette stumbled to her dressing room. She was cold as ice, and her heart seemed almost to have stopped beating. As she sat there, stunned, motionless, Verdellet knocked at her door. He was understandably disturbed.

"My dear girl, you're not supposed to walk on stage as if you were entering a drawing room! You've got to liven up a bit. Don't be so stiff; throw yourself around more. Notice how the others do it, and

53

imitate them. Try it that way tomorrow night. Perhaps things will go better."

Things went no better. The press meantime had ridiculed her, and her next appearance on stage was the signal for the audience to break out again into open mockery. For five nights the Lyons public steadfastly, almost sadistically, refused to listen to her, and then Verdellet gave up.

"Take my advice, Mademoiselle," he said, not unkindly, as he paid her off, "you are simply not the type for the *café-concert*. Your physique, your looks, your gait—everything is wrong. It makes people depressed just to look at you. The *café-concert* wants the jolly kind. Believe me, Mademoiselle, you should go back to acting."

Yvette, who had been crying for the whole five days and worrying over what would happen to her contract with the Eldorado if Madame Allemand found out about the Lyons fiasco, as she might well do from Wély, took refuge in an old tactic of her father's—bluster.

"Monsieur," she snapped, "the fact is that your *café-concert* is out of date and hopelessly stupid! Your songs have no salt, no pepper, no rhyme, no reason. You have paid me forty francs a day. That is at the rate of twelve hundred francs a month, isn't it? Now listen to me, Monsieur. Before a year has gone by, you will be offering me twelve hundred francs a night! Do you hear?"—her voice rising—"A night!"

But despite all her defensive vehemence, when Yvette set off for Paris next morning, her heart was heavy, and it was heavier still when she arrived home and discovered that her pocket had been picked on the train of the four hundred francs Verdellet had given her. It was a penniless, sobbing, distraught girl that Albine folded into her sympathetic arms that night—all cockiness gone—overwhelmed by an unutterable dread of the future, particularly of bracelet-jangling Madame Allemand.

Chapter 4

The date of the Eldorado opening drew near. Yvette, though now frightened nearly out of her wits, continued doggedly to practice her songs. One day Albine, who had been listening to her for several days, could keep silence no longer.

"My poor child, I really believe Monsieur Verdellet was right. You

54

should go back to the stage. Those café singers have something you lack. Believe me, dear girl, you are on the wrong road."

After that, it took a good deal of will power to keep on.

The evening arrived. She had been placed on the program at ten o'clock, the choice spot. The hall was full, but when she came on stage, she was received by a polite but frigid silence. She began her first number, her voice rising delicate and clear, building up a series of bright blocks of sound to a shiny climax. When she had finished, stillness dropped again like a curtain. The audience did not seem actually hostile, merely stonily unresponsive. She gave her second number; the same implacable silence. At the end, burning with humiliation, she withdrew without a single handclap. The indifference of the crowd was almost palpable. Back stage, a hulking comedienne was sniggering over Yvette's figure. "Scrawny as an Englishwoman, and she thinks she can do *café-concert!*"

For two whole weeks, in an extremity of misery, Yvette endured the same indifference from her audiences, and then Madame Allemand shifted her to eight o'clock. This was putting her back again to curtain-raiser status. Henceforth she would open the performance—a significant change, for nobody ever arived at eight and she would be singing to empty benches:—"wiping the boards."

One night some friends from the Variétés came to hear her, bringing with them the critic Bisson. Later in her dressing room Bisson remonstrated with her.

"You should go back to the stage, Yvette. Look here, you are an intelligent girl—you want to be a star. You have heard Judic sing at the Variétés. Can't you recognize the difference between her and you? Can't you see that you can never be like Judic?"

"That's not the point," Yvette argued stubbornly. "What you are saying is that there is only one style of singing! These café singers are all dull and tiresome, simply because they are imitating each other. Judic has one style—Thérèsa another. I intend to develop one of my own. What's wrong with that?"

"Only that you may not last long enough!" M. Bisson warned.

He was nearer right than he realized. It was shortly thereafter that Madame Allemand issued an ultimatum: either leave, or play in the one-act sketches which rounded off the programs; salary cut from six hundred to two hundred francs a month. But no more singing!

"As a singer you are ridiculous, Mademoiselle—I put it to you plainly! You freeze the public!"

At this, Yvette froze Madame. With icy calm she chose to leave rather than accept demotion, and for an exit speech had recourse again, as with Verdellet, to lofty braggadocio.

"Before next season, Madame, you will be offering me six hundred francs, not per month but per night!"

At this unexpected burst of fantasy, Madame, caught off guard, nearly choked in convulsions of derisive laughter.

Secretly, Yvette was crushed to earth. Twice sacked in two months! Perhaps her critics were right. Was she after all on the wrong road, as even her mother had agreed? More tears, sleepless nights, frantic self-analysis. In the end she decided she would make one more try— one only.

The Eden Concert, Boulevard Sebastopol, was an establishment of far different stripe from the Eldorado. It was one of those family cafés, where sketches and songs breathed a simple, fresh-air whole-someness, with never a word, not even a *double-entendre,* to bring a blush to the cheek of the most circumspect. In the beginning the Eden had been a very modest club, specializing in short plays and brief, routine revues. But in December, 1889, at the beginning of the World's Fair of that year, it began operating on a larger scale. Revues took on color, excitement, originality. Novelties were added, as for example, the Friday programs of ancient *chansons* of old France, which beguiled the interest of such poets as François Coppée and Sully Prud'homme and the critical attention of Sarcey. These pro-grams fascinated Yvette, who had not known before how deep were the roots of song in her country.

At this time the Eden also was presided over by a woman, Madame Castellano Saint-Ange, reputed to be a kindly soul, who had made her money in butter in the Halles before she turned to concert man-agement. It happened that she was just then in deep mourning for a daughter about Yvette's age, and so when Yvette presented herself for employment, Madame Saint-Ange, under the sway of sentiment, hired her almost on the spot. Salary, again six hundred francs; con-tract, two years.

Here, Yvette felt, was the long-needed turn in her luck. Here there would be no problem of either being funny or getting fired; not even of what songs to sing. Madame's musical director was charming old Eugène Baillet, a talented poet-singer, and it was he who chose suitable fare for the family public that streamed nightly into the

Eden. With her financial future thus temporarily assured by the contract Madame Saint-Ange had given her, Yvette made immediate plans to use her spare time to develop a repertoire of her own, something for the future, along lines that had dimly begun to take shape in her thoughts. The repertoire she envisioned was of Balzacian range—and its main concern should be *la verité*.

For Yvette was beginning to entertain a revolutionary idea. During the last two years in which she had been acquainting herself with the new concepts invading the novel and the theater, the principles of realism had struck deep root in her mind, and she had been dismayed to recognize in the *café-concert* the same stereotypes of mawkishness and artificiality against which writers generally were in revolt. Popular song clearly was not keeping pace with the times; she winced at its monstrous crudities. It cried out for new vein, a new approach. The lifelikeness that had already been introduced into fiction and drama should be possible in song. At a couple of unusual cabarets in Montmartre—Le Mirliton and Le Chat Noir—couplets of the kind she wanted had in fact been heard, but those resorts were not for the masses. She coveted songs of the same *esprit* for the lowly *caf'-conc'*.

By this time she had accepted the premise that to become a *café-concert* success one must make the public laugh. Very well; she was no stranger to dirty jokes. But there are many kinds of laughter. She thought also in terms of laughter on the edge of pity, of laughter that tore the heart, of laughter that was afraid to laugh. The songs she wanted would have to be in the modern idiom; songs she could make her own, could stamp with her own individuality.

Obviously she needed exceptional lyrics. Everything hinged on ideas, words, situations. She searched and searched.

One day at a bookstall on the Seine Embankment she picked up a small volume called *Les Chansons sans gêne*, by someone named Xanrof. It fascinated her so much that, standing there on the quay, she read the little book all through. Incredibly, these were the lyrics she had been looking for. How amusing, how young they were, sparkling with a raillery typical of the Latin Quarter. Here was Paris through the eyes of a student. The tunes too were good. She had never heard of Xanrof, but never mind. No one was being featured in these songs; these were what she wanted. She bought the little book for eight sous and hurried home.

While she was in Lyons, she had herself composed a few verses which she now asked the composer Byrec to set to music. She called

57

the song *La Pocharde,* and added it to her Xanrof collection. These numbers would be the nucleus of that new element that she would some day try out, when opportunity presented itself.

The taunts of the boorish Lyonnais had caused Yvette to become concerned about her silhouette. It was her lack of *la belle poitrine,* the feminine attribute which the Frenchman of that day looked on with most favor, that had caused the students of Lyons to riot. As H. G. Ibels reported: "The bosom is one of the favorite topics for fun at the *café-concert,* an inexhaustible subject for pleasantries and interest. Everybody gabbles about bosoms—the real ones, the false ones, the firm and young ones, the straying ones, the low ones ... people respect nothing ..." Even Bernhardt was ribbed unmercifully; it was claimed that she was so thin that she had been known to hide behind her riding whip; one favorite fable was that one day an empty carriage drove up to her theater and Bernhardt got out. But Sarah was at the top of the ladder; she could afford such waggery. Yvette, to achieve a few curves, even if slight ones, now adopted the fashionable tight corset, drawing in her waistline to an elfin nineteen inches, which by contrast, she persuaded herself, created at least a suggestion of swelling bust and hips. Physicians everywhere were expostulating with women, pleading with them to give up the dangerous fad of tight lacing, pointing out the evils that were bound to follow, but Yvette, determined on at least some modicum of feminine allure, paid no heed.

As to her plain face, which was quite as much a problem as her figure, she decided to make a virtue of her natural pallor; emphasize it by rice powder to masklike whiteness. The dull hair should be hennaed to an eye-catching Titian. The mouth she would keep wide and thin; lacquer it a geranium red to enhance her teeth, which were white and beautiful—almost her only good feature. For eyeshadow, to enlarge and irradiate the expressive eyes, she would use a brown smoke produced by holding a porcelain bowl above a lighted candle. Her neck was phenomenally long and slender, and she had a comedy trick of stretching it until it seemed even longer. At the Eden the other players joked about it and called it the "neck that unrolled." But even the comic neck and the ugly nose and jutting chin which she could do nothing about would eventually become assets too, for the caricaturists would add them to the red hair, the white-mask face, the smoky eyes, the red slash of a mouth, and from the ensemble etch her likeness on the memories of millions.

By now she had learned the importance to an actress of uniqueness, and in costume she had resolved not to conform to any existing image in the public mind. In an era when women's dresses were loaded with distracting fripperies, she settled on a model of unadorned simplicity, so classically simple that she was able to sew the gowns herself, tying around the wasp waistline sashes made merely of wide satin ribbons. For audacity she concentrated on a V-neckline that plunged to the middle both front and back. Not a jewel; not an accessory. The end result was the boldness of a cunningly contrived portrait, with emphasis on the subject herself, looking distinguished and well-bred despite the daring of her decolleté. The final touch of individuality she achieved by a pair of long black gloves that reached almost to the shoulder.

In later years Yvette used to claim that she selected black for the gloves on the basis of economy, but Yvette was capable of being disingenuous, and in view of the effectiveness of black with light-colored dresses she might well have selected it at any cost. Or was she perhaps unconsciously imitating the incomparable Mademoiselle Laboulaye, whose long black gloves had so entranced her, years ago, in Madame Archimbault's kindergarten classes?

At any rate, it was the gloves that became her trademark.

With June came the closing of the Eden. Yvette had been only a moderate success, but at least the curtain had not been rung down on her. Critics for the most part had ignored her, one of them referring to her merely as "a lanky girl, as thin as a thread." But she could stick at least two feathers in her cap. She had been invited to sing at a mammoth benefit performance at the Trocadéro, where some of the biggest stars in France were to appear, and an agent had booked a month of her free time in Liège for double what she had been getting at the Eden.

What probably delighted Yvette most about the Trocadéro benefit was that the novelist Pierre Loti was to be a guest of honor. In 1890 Lieutenant Julien Viaud of the French Navy, whose pen name was Pierre Loti, was at the height of his career. As a sailor, he had painstakingly kept a careful diary of his promiscuities, including his probings into harems, and drawing on this record had written a series of exotic romances that were nothing if not frank. In these he detailed his affairs with his Tahitian Rarahu, his Circassian Aziyadé, his Japanese Mme. Chrysanthème, heroines who may well have been, as

Professor Harry Levin suggests, "actually heroes in private life." Women adored him for his libertine pen; men scorned him for his effeminate habit of wearing make-up and high heels. For long Yvette had been one of his avid readers; now she was to have the opportunity to sing before him.

The evening went exceptionally well. She presented an unpublished song by a young man whom a friend of hers had recently met at a Latin Quarter party held in a café near the Sorbonne. It was one of those larkish cellar gatherings that Left Bank students loved—lusty jokes and much horseplay. During the evening a young law student, Léon Fourneau, had sung some amusing solos of his own composing, and through her friend Yvette had learned that the singer Fourneau was none other than the author Xanrof whose *Chansons sans gêne* she had so recently acquired.

Fourneau was a strange fellow, with curious talents and even more curious habits; a contradiction even in appearance, looking more like a cleric than a bohemian in the dark suit and Roman collar which he invariably affected. Forced by his family into a profession for which he had no taste, he had sought compensation in an avocation more to his liking. At night, after shutting his law books with a sigh, he would repair to some cozy café in the Latin Quarter or in Montmartre where he would pre-empt a table in a corner, order his bottle of wine, lay out sheets of paper, and, aloof from humanity but observant of it, compose his verses; later he would set them to music. When Fourneau had first proposed to publish his slim volume, his professors at the university had sternly disapproved. As a future member of the bar, he must maintain a degree of dignity; publish either anonymously or under a pseudonym, they ruled. Fourneau in Latin was Fornax, which did not quite please the young poet as a nom de plume, so by anagram Fornax had been turned into Xanrof. The songs he sang at the party were delicate in nuances, risqué, irreverent, satirical, and it was one of these that Yvette chose for her appearance at the Trocadéro.

It was easy to give Xanrof's characters a three-dimensional quality, and that night she adopted a technique of half singing and half speaking that served her well. Despite the wretched acoustics of the great hall, her diction was so perfect that her words fell crystal clear on the ears of her auditors, resisting the distortions and reverberations that troubled more experienced singers than herself. But she looked in vain for a good word from the critics. Only the great names on the program were singled out.

The twelve-hundred-franc fee Yvette would get from her month's engagement in Liège was flattering, but more important was the fact that this would be her first experience outside her own country. In a foreign city, far from Paris skeptics, she would dare to try out the Xanrof songs, which, she felt instinctively, constituted a sort of minor *comédie humaine,* descanting as they did on the whims, gaucheries, and vices of modern Parisians. In gently caustic tone the songs covered a wide range of subjects, from the debauches of student life to the habits of the petty bourgeoisie. Though the prevailing attitude was that of irony, now and then through the lines sounded strains of sweetness or pure drollery. Best of all, the verses were new, unhackneyed; this was not the old Paris singing of itself in stale accents; this was Paris through the eyes of a sharp young sophisticate. Incidents were presented in terms of the contemporary realism she demanded; recognizable little vignettes of Paris life, done in firm, virile strokes.

On the evening of the Liège premiere the Pavillon de Flore was full, the audience friendly. Yvette was wearing white that night, with a black sash in which she had tucked a deep pink rose, and of course the black gloves; in her manner there was for the first time a touch of self-assurance.

For her opening number she had chosen Xanrof's *Le Fiacre.* This farce-whimsey describes a Paris cabdriver, jolting along over the cobbles behind his old nag and listening appreciatively to the goings-on between a pair of lovers inside the cab.—"Léon, do be careful of your glasses!"—As he jogs along, he shouts every now and then the sort of things a cabdriver would shout to his horse:

> *Un fiacre allait trottinant*
> *Cahin, caha,*
> *Hu' dia! Hop la!*
> *Un fiacre allait trottinant,*
> *Jaune, avec un cocher blanc.*

An elderly man in the street observes the approaching carriage and recognizes the beautiful lady within in the arms of her lover. It is his wife, and the lover is young and handsome! Angrily he rushes toward the cab, slips—*diable!*—and falls in the mud. The lady in turn recognizes her husband—confusion! alarm!—what to do? Well—cynically—what can one do? Since all is now discovered, what need to flee? And the lovers fall to embracing once more—ah, the cruelty of youth!—while the cab rolls on—*allait trottinant.*

Yvette once said of the text of a song: "It is just a few threads on which one builds an airy structure." Often her listeners who had been profoundly affected by one of her performances would say to her afterward: "What is it you do to a song? When I read the words of what you sing, there seems so little meaning to them." So it was with *Le Fiacre.* Actually the song had first been done briefly by Felicia Mallet, but no one remembered Mallet after hearing Yvette in it once. With her, the whole thing shone with the iridescence of creative imagination; not a hearer doubted the verity of the situation, the immediacy of the dilemma. The words were innocent, the manner she adopted demure, but the suggestion she conveyed was of the most abandoned behavior. Her listeners reddened and roared.

Feeling for the first time a stimulating sense of rapport with her audience, she launched into her second song, *L'Hôtel du Numéro 3,* in which the humor was more broad-gauge. This is a story about student boarders in a rooming house near the Sorbonne, a flea-ridden establishment in the days when modern conveniences were luxuries of the rich and a poor student must get along on three francs a day; where everything was held in common, share and share alike—combs, towels, and the not-too-pretty chambermaid.

> *J'habite près de l'École de médecine,*
> *Au premier, tout comme un bourgeois;*
> *Une demeure magnifique, divine*
> *À L'Hôtel du No. 3. . . .*
>
> *La bonne n'est pas une très belle fille*
> *Mais nous n'tenons pas au minois,*
> *On lui fait la cour en famille*
> *À L'Hôtel du No. 3.*

The laughs during this were so hearty that for good measure she added another off-color student song, *La Complainte des 4 z'étudiants,* again accentuating a demure, almost saintly air, singing suggestive lines without a hint of sensuality and playing naïveté to the hilt. The more detached she appeared, to the point of seeming almost unaware of the character of the story she was telling, the more the house doubled up in laughter. The contradiction between the outward seeming of the young singer, so virginal in her white satin and fresh rose, and the bawdy character of the song was not lost on the earthy Flemings.

That night she presented also her own song, *La Pocharde,* the story of a young girl who has had too much champagne at her sister's wedding breakfast and is talking a great deal of nonsense. She knows she is tipsy, doesn't care, and wants to stay that way. Here is the familiar "drunk" motif, but with a difference, with a concealed trigger. This is not the well-known lush, a butt for ridicule, but a lovely young lady; she may be funny, awkward, silly, but she is not degraded; she must be portrayed not as a stereotype but as an individual. One laughs at her, but there is a shiver underlying the laugh, a shiver that comes from the indefinable conviction of having just witnessed an innocent girl take the first luckless step that is fated in time to lead her to the tragedy of chronic drunkenness; to utter ruin.

> *Je viens d'la noce à ma soeur Annette,*
> *Et, comm' le champagne y pleuvait,*
> *Je n'vous l'cach' pas, je suis pompette*
> *Car j'ai pincé mon p'tit plumet, . . .*

The words are banal; again it was the vividness of the characterization that counted, a vividness deriving in part from the singer's economy of style in physical interpretation. Gestures being largely suppressed, the few that were used became starkly emphatic. But it was mainly through the nuances of voice and the expressiveness of the facial mask, with its magnetic eyes, that implications were conveyed. Yvette sang with the brilliance and spontaneity of a bird, seeming never to care whether she was on or slightly off key, in a voice that could be melodious and lilting, or coarse and harsh.

She gave many encores that opening night in Liège before she had satisfied the appetites of the good burghers, and at the end found herself taking curtain call after curtain call, on each making a slow, very low, appreciative, but formal bow. After the Liège engagement she sang also at the Alcazar, a small music hall in Brussels, before she returned to Paris, and here she duplicated her triumphs at the Pavillon de Flore.

During that summer of 1890, young Mademoiselle Guilbert, balancing in the scales the kudos in Belgium against the hisses in Lyons, saw that the one now easily outweighed the other. Yet even as she nightly took her many encores and made her low, grave bows, she could never forget Molière wandering in the provinces and yearning for Paris, that sweet city without whose approval no other applause, however loud or prolonged, could ever fill his actor's cup to the brim.

While in Liège, she had met again the dramatist Ludovic Halévy, librettist of *Barbe Bleu,* in which she had played Héloise, one of Bluebeard's wives, in October, 1888, at the Variétés. Describing the meeting, Halévy later wrote:

> . . . You came to me. You recalled to me that you had played a small, a very small, part in a revival of Offenbach's *Blue Beard* at the Variétés. I did not remember. You were a little sad, a little discouraged. . . . Paris . . . Paris . . . It was Paris that you wanted. And how to conquer Paris?

Chapter 5

Brilliant *fin de siècle* days—a moot point when they began. Possibly the whole decade of the 90's might justifiably be included; it might even be argued that in Paris the period was inaugurated by the Exposition of 1889, which took Science as its keynote and publicized itself by rearing the mighty Eiffel Tower as the newest wonder of the world. This engineering marvel was not accomplished without opposition from many Parisians, who feared it would prove an artistic monstrosity. In the end, however, the "great jet of steel" captured everyone by the very audacity of its skyward thrust, its immense intricacy, and a certain unaccountable airy grace that somehow stirred the beholder. Even Edmond de Goncourt, a most vocal opponent, after he had ascended it by one of its crawling elevators and dined in the sky, was impressed:

> The lift in motion feels something like a ship getting under way. From the top you can see, farther than you could ever have thought, the extent, the magnificence, the Babylonian immensity of Paris. Under the setting sun the angles of masonry catch up color, and the sweeping lines of the horizon closing down upon the slope of Montmartre make the town look, as the light slowly fades, like a vast illuminated ruin.

64

It was inevitable that insistence upon Science as the new and illimitable frontier of the human mind should launch an era in which men would be forced to relinquish forever many old concepts. Obviously an end to something had been reached, and though the man in the street might not be able to say precisely what, for want of a more exact term he could safely call it the end of a century. This handy title, however, as every thoughtful person recognized, carried implications far beyond the passing of an arbitrary date in the Gregorian calendar. In the light that Science was throwing on an imperfect world, it meant not only a dislocation from the old but more especially a fumbling toward the new; an exciting interplay of nostalgia and bewilderment; of intellectual sobriety and intoxication; of caution and unbridled curiosity. With shackles of the past dropping, and new freedoms inviting both mind and senses, the 90's became understandably over-exhilarated; the Nineties became Gay. Dull days were clearly over, moralizing no longer fashionable, and *fin de siècle,* by interpretation, quickly came to signify ultramodernity—a letting go.

When Yvette returned to Paris, one fact loomed large in her mind in connection with the Belgium trip: that she had first tasted success because she had had for the first time a modern repertoire She was indignant, therefore, when she found Madame Saint-Ange strangely unimpressed by foreign press notices, however complimentary, and cool to the new songs which Yvette begged her to listen to.

"That stuff is not for the Eden," Madame ruled. "The only one our customers might possibly put up with is your *La Pocharde.* Try that if you like. The Xanrof ones—bah!"

Coming on the heels of those ovations in Brussels and Liège, Madame Saint-Ange's obduracy seemed unreasonable to a degree. In fact, it rankled deeply.

So, when *La Pocharde* broke all records by running for a month, to warm applause from audiences even if not noticed by critics, she felt triumphant enough to demand a raise. Naturally Madame Saint-Ange resisted any such inroads on her purse, adding as insult to injury: "I must say, my girl, your head has certainly been turned!"

At this, Yvette permitted her smoldering resentment to burst into a flame of rage. She would quit, she vowed. Madame Duparc was earning a hundred francs a night, she only twenty; she had as much talent as Duparc; she had proved it. She was being exploited. She would quit. It was another of her arrogant, vainglorious tirades, which nevertheless failed to produce any effect on blasé Madame Saint-Ange, who had probably listened to many such in her time and who could hardly have been expected to recognize in this one all its mingled motivations of egotism and self-will, and more especially the compulsion for quick success because of an all-too-vivid memory of hunger. At the threat to leave, Madame merely shrugged and reminded Yvette that for a breach of contract she would be legally liable to damages of ten thousand francs.

"Very well!" the girl screamed, in complete abandonment of common sense. "I'll pay your ten thousand francs!" And she stormed out. The fact that she had no idea how she could ever raise such sum seemed at the moment irrelevant.

Yvette had always shown a tendency toward bombast and quick, unbridled anger, unconsciously imitated from a weak father. In fact, the record of her early days in the theater provides several instances, which she herself never hesitated to relate and always with apparent self-approval, yet which illustrate character traits that at times must have been trying to her associates. In her very first engagement at the Bouffes-du-Nord she had made fun of an old actor during a performance because she was displeased with what she considered his surliness to a girl who was having difficulty with her lines. When she was reproved by the manager for sauciness and reminded that as a rank beginner she had behaved badly, her reply was: "Beginner or not, I helped the girl who had lost her voice. As for the old man, I don't care a hang!" At the Eldorado her impertinence to the director during rehearsals had cost her fines on more than one occasion.

Albine, always prudent and circumspect, heard the news of the broken contract with dismay. That Yvette should make herself liable for such a catastrophic sum—not to mention throwing overboard an excellent salary—seemed sheer madness. How could they now pay the rent for the new apartment in the Rue Saint-Lazare, with its pretty chintzes, its books and piano? She must have wondered if her daughter, like her husband, had been born lacking a certain balance wheel.

A significant difference existed between the two, however. Whereas Hippolyte's conceit had been based on nothing more substantial than self-love and delusions, the daughter's rashness was to some degree justified by self-knowledge. Yvette had seen for some time that at the Eden she would be forever fettered in the choice of repertoire, a restriction that promised to be more and more irritating after the proofs she had enjoyed in Belgium of the rightness of her own selections. Moreover, Boulevard Sebastopol was not The Boulevard; one could not conquer Paris by vegetating there. If the time had come when the Eden could no longer serve her purposes, by all means it should be summarily cast aside. Instinctively, then, she may have forced the issue with Madame Saint-Ange in subconscious defiance, with a readiness to accept consequences; she may have taken a calculated risk. At any rate, whether by impulse or half-formed design, when she found the fat irrevocably in the fire and fled, as usual, to Zidler for comfort, she looked for him this time, not at the old Hippodrome, but at his new venture, the Moulin Rouge in Montmartre.

Fin de siècle Montmartre—what a milieu the words conjure up; a milieu now become legendary. This little hill, once a grassy spot where windmills lazily flapped their sails, by the seventeenth century had become a village of evil reputation outside the city walls, where police were hard put to it to prevent crimes of violence. By the nineteenth century the hill had been folded within the city walls and half tamed into a historic little jumble of streets and tangled roofs and gables, its ancient stone and plaster walls of maddeningly subtle tints of blue-gray, with a few old weather-blackened mills still on its summit; a hill that since the 1880's had drawn to itself so many artists and poets to immortalize it that before the century was over it had come to belong not to Paris but the world. By then its every ferment and fad down through the years had been made known: its traditional urge toward the untrammeled life, its cherished prerogatives of eccentricity, its excesses and bacchanales. Unhappily, aspects of the old sinister life persisted too, in an underworld of doss houses and *maisons closes,* of establishments where a pipe of opium was a peccadillo compared to the unspeakable practices and where picturesque squalor gave way unashamedly to depravity.

Not until *fin de siècle* years, however, did Montmartre come to be regarded as synonymous with a certain type of night life that sprang up during this period, one in which cafés, cabarets, dance halls, and brothels figured heavily. Cafés of the district ranged from fly-blown, crowded little holes like the Lapin Agile, where beer slopped over on marble-topped tables, and creepy, off-color, "atmospheric" retreats for perverts, like Le Hanneton and La Souris, to a few really smart and expensive hostelries like the Café de la Place and L'Abbaye de Thélème. *Cafés-concerts* were mainly of a variation known as the *cabaret artistique,* a kind peculiar to bohemia and used as clublike meeting places by artists, musicians, and men of letters.

67

The most noted of these, the Chat Noir in the Rue Laval, was claimed by some to be the most original, the most authentically French cabaret of its kind ever known in Paris. Immediately it had struck a new note. The group that gathered there under its pioneering proprietor, Rodolphe Salis, had already made a name for wit. To the sophisticated professional entertainment offered by Salis were nightly added other features contributed spontaneously and gratis by the artist-patrons. Polished, daring, amusing, every act could be depended on to stir up comment. The talented habitués even published a weekly journal filled with ribbing nonsense; they instituted Friday "literary evenings," where they debated literature fiercely, recited poetry of their own making, and gave concerts and shadow-plays. Tall stained-glass windows suggested a *vieux Paris* atmosphere; rooms were massive, smoke-darkened, medieval; waiters wore the costume of the august French Academy, and Salis, playfully obsequious, addressed his clients as "Your lordship," "Your ladyship." But the place was more than a stage set, a fashionable night spot, a bedlam of drunken gaiety, a witch's cauldron of dissolute doings, a literary club, a studio for artists. Its brilliant avant-garde entertainment was a microcosm of the life of the times, breathing a spirit which gave its name to the era—*l'esprit du Chat Noir;* a look at life that was, as one of its literary members, Maurice Donnay said, eclectic: by turn "joking, ironic, tender, naturalistic, realistic, idealistic, cynical, lyric, *fumiste,* religious, mystic, Christian, pagan, anarchistic, chauvinistic, republican, reactionary"—anything and everything except boring.

Chic and original as the Chat Noir and other *cabarets artistiques* were, however, it was the dance halls that won the widest notoriety for Montmartre. For years at the old Elysée-Montmartre, for example, ever since the introduction of the lascivious *quadrille naturaliste,* a harassed gentleman named Courtelat du Roché had been waging an uneven battle to preserve enough decency on the dance floor to keep the proprietors out of jail. The *quadrille,* or *chahut,* which made its appearance in the 80's as an outgrowth of the can-can, carried only two fundamental prescriptions for the girl dancers—*le port d'armes,* performed by standing on one foot and holding the other up high over the head, and *le grand écart,* or split, a sinking to the floor with legs spread right and left in an absolutely straight line. Beyond these, the dancers followed their own fancies, which included a great deal of high kicking by the girls, since kicking was then the rage everywhere, and turning of cartwheels, both of which afforded

68

viewers the excitation of endless billows of lace frills and the flashing gleam of black silk legs. For such acrobatics, drawers were supposed to be *de rigueur;* but as poor M. du Roché discovered, this was a custom more honored in the breach than the breeches by the hoydens of the Elysée, who paid no heed to the gentle harangues of their Père Pudeur—Papa Modesty—as they scornfully called him, and went nonchalantly on their provocative way.

In 1890, chief competitor among all the dance halls was the flamboyant Moulin Rouge, opened by Zidler the year before to raid the pocketbooks of the thousands flocking to the Exposition. Its location had been chosen against the earnest advice of all the experts, who insisted that the nucleus of night life in Montmartre had always been, and must always remain, the Boulevard Rochechouart. But canny Zidler, for the sake of a lighter overhead, had dared to build five hundred yards west of the goldfields, confident that enough rocketry in his advertising and spice in his shows would alter the nocturnal habits of Montmartre pleasure seekers. The artist Willette, commissioned to create an eye-catching exterior, set up on the roof of the building a screamingly red windmill, with an illuminated, slowly revolving wheel, that could be seen by all Paris and is still remembered as the showy symbol of those riotous years. Debonair Jules Chéret, later known as The Poster King, was just then beginning to make the walls of Paris sing with his brilliant palette, his pretty, red-haired model "Chérette" smiling on the passers-by in a multiplicity of aspects, and with the posters Jules designed, Zidler plastered the hoardings far and wide.

The place caught on from the beginning, partly because of Zidler's magic name and partly because there was nothing else quite like it in Paris. Not exclusively a variety theater, nor a public ballroom, nor a beer hall with music, it managed to combine something of all these, and more, beneath its ample roof. But with minor differences. Its list of *consommations* ran all the way from Schiedam schnapps to champagne and from *limonade gazeuse* to Madeira. There were variety stages, but performers were only perfunctorily looked at; the big show was played on its immense dance floor.

The building itself was one-story, squatting in the midst of five-story apartment houses, with its back to the Cemetery of Montmartre and its front facing the Place Blanche. At the entrance, reminder of the tradition of roistering that had always clung about the very name of Montmartre, a large stained-glass window told the story of olden times, when the original mills were the center of village life, and peasants who came to sell their grain remained to be gulled by peddlers, jugglers, and winesellers set up in booths around the green.

Adjoining the Mill, but hidden from the street, was a large garden where Zidler had thrown in extra attractions. Here were fountains, flowery nooks, a band, dancing girls; a tiny concert stage, used for songs and vaudeville when weather permitted, and a ring where bare-bosomy ladies trotted donkeyback. Here was the prodigious elephant, standing two stories high, with a little red-lighted balcony on each of his sides, brought over from the Palace of Fairies in the late Exposition. Spiral stairs inside his legs led up to a roomy belly, where patrons looking for supersalacious entertainment could repair to enjoy a *danse du ventre* wriggled by impudent young things in Arab dress.

The interior of the Mill, done in hard wood and decorated with flags of all nations, was one great dance floor surrounded on all four sides by galleries equipped with tables for refreshments. Here charmers of the *promenoir* could sip their cherry brandy and watch the antics of the dancers or, as the spirit moved them, exhibit their gowns and smiles and shed their perfumes by joining in the never-ending walk-around, leered at by roués of all nations. Tall mirrors doubled the scene in size and animation; a mixture of gas jets, shaded pink and white, and electric bulbs, tulip-shaped and colored cream and blush-rose, lighted it with a soft brilliance.

At one side of the great hall was the small winter concert stage. By eight-thirty, when the stage show began, perhaps a couple of hundred patrons would have arrived. These few, who wanted their money's worth, would come early, order their bock or coffee or liqueurs, and sit listening to the whole bill—from the lady in the pink tights, caterwauling of her misadventures, to the learned-dog and trained-seal acts—variety turns that are the same yesterday, to-day, and tomorrow, from Tokyo to Timbuctoo. But again with a variation: the last number was always a performance of the *quadrille naturaliste* by four headliners, as a prelude to its performance on the dance floor by a whole flock of participants. Montmartre managers saw no point in keeping the high kickers on stage, so that, as Zidler said, a man would need a telescope. No, indeed; put the kickers where an audience could crowd around.

For his dance floor Zidler assembled in female talent the biggest attractions of the day. La Goulue (The Glutton), dainty Jane Avril

70

(The Mélinite), Grille d'Egout (Sewer-Grating, because her teeth were so widely spaced), Rayon d'Or (Golden Ray, because of her red hair), Nini Patte en l'Air, Sauterelle, Trompe-la-Mort, Vole-au-Vent, Étoile Filante—all the fanciful names were there, lured away from rival establishments by Zidler's higher salaries. They were a wild crew, too, these *quadrillistes;* it took the iron hand of a Zidler to keep them in line.

By the middle of the evening the number of spectators would have increased to perhaps two thousand, and the overcrowded, overheated, overperfumed hall would be ringing with laughter and conversation. To announce the dance-floor performance, promptly at ten-thirty a roll of drums would thunder forth from the circus-sized orchestra, the *quadrillistes* would run in and take their places, and from then to twelve-thirty, to the loudest music ever blared out in Paris, the big show was on.

Sterling Heilig, a journalist of the day, described it as a "tarantula-stung" performance:

In substance it is a transformation of the peaceful quadrille of the parlor, as if it had been suddenly awakened, stung by a tarantula. In place of the slow and decorous walk-about, with its discreet alternations and gentle oppositions of heads and arms and whirls of prudent limbs, they have substituted fantastic bounds and goat-like leapings, where starched and lace-bedizened petticoats act to frame in and to artistically balance black silk stockings held firm by monstrous satin garters. And the foot goes up! Five times, ten times, twenty times it darts so high above the head that you would think it was a little bird.

It was this spectacle that brought the crowds in night after night, the gorgeous melée of movement, light, and color appealing violently to every primitive instinct. Performers on the dance floor grasped their partners with intimacy—even couples of the same sex were allowed here—and leaped and bounded, "goat-like," until the whole hall seemed to seethe with emanations of animal energy.

Queen of these licentious revels, because of her daring and vitality as a *quadrilliste,* was undoubtedly Louise Weber, once a laundress, now known only as La Goulue, The Glutton, because of her greed; a woman endlessly stuffing herself with victuals and strong drink. She was a shrewd, coarse virago, pretty in a hussy sort of way, with a certain grand air about her, wearing always bangs to her eyebrows, kiss curls over her temples, and a Psyche knot twisted tightly on top of her head. Morally she was completely abandoned, indiscriminate in her affairs, which reputedly included both men and women; an habituée of Madame Palmyre's notorious haunt for Lesbians, La Souris. Like her betters in the theater, she too craved to stand out from the crowd, and where Sarah had her lions and Réjane her team of white mules, La Goulue affected a pet goat that accompanied her on her strolls and often to rehearsals.

Her partner, Valentine Desossé, The Boneless One, grotesque as a gargoyle, was quite as imaginative a dancer as she. Tall, cadaverous, lugubrious in expression, wearing always a greasy, battered stove-pipe hat, frock coat, and skin-tight trousers, he looked like nothing so much as a caricature of an undertaker. But the undertaker had double-jointed rubber legs and when he danced, he flung them about with such suppleness that they earned for him his nickname.

In the quadrille, with The Boneless One as partner, La Goulue was a whirlwind. At the finish of her act, with one hand holding a slim black leg high over her head, she would spin around and around interminably, spreading out her yards of black lace into a mammoth umbrella, end by knocking off her partner's hat with one last smart kick, and then sink into her split. Her professional hallmark of individuality in costume, somewhat more raffish than Yvette's black gloves, was the scarlet heart on the seat of her black panties, which she revealed to her audiences by facing away from their applause and bowing disrespectfully, with a flip of her skirts over her head.

"So now why shouldn't I sing in your cabaret?" Yvette demanded of Zidler, after she had confessed her precipitate flight from the Eden's security and stagnation. "Montmartre would understand me and my songs."

"You may," Zidler replied, "though, as you realize, my cabaret is only an hors d'oeuvre to the dance hall. However, I'll put you on from eight thirty to nine, and if you can get another engagement elsewhere for later in the evening, I'll have no objection to your taking it. Only your songs mustn't be too subtle."

"I'll come," said Yvette. "And I have a new song that is not at all subtle."

It was largely the tradespeople of the neighborhood who filtered in to the Mill between eight and nine, the smart set never showing up before nine-thirty at least, and it was this early group whose carnal appetites Yvette was supposed to whet. Her new song, entitled *Miss Valérie*, burlesqued an English nurse, ready to "turn her hand to anything" for her old gentleman patients. Wearing a long, tightly buttoned, high-collared mackintosh, hair slicked back severely under a prim bonnet and the inevitable English umbrella tucked under her arm, she was a perfect replica of the prudish Englishwoman of that day who never failed to tickle the funnybone of the French; and nightly the Montmartrois went into screams of laughter as Yvette, imitating an English accent, described Nurse Valérie's cold complaisance to the advances of silly old dodderers. It was a libertine song, chosen for the libertine atmosphere of the Mill, and with it, and others of the same ilk, Yvette soon began to build up a little following. When word got around that young Mademoiselle Guilbert, in spite of her virginal airs and recherché appearance, was an accomplished teaser, more patrons began arriving early to add an extra fillip to their evening, and before long crowds had perceptibly thickened in the Mill from eight to nine.

One night the critic René Maizeroy happened to look in on the cabaret, and the following morning an article devoted to the unique new singer at the Moulin Rouge appeared in the journal *Gil Blas*. When Zidler saw the review, he came rushing into Yvette's dressing room, brandishing the paper "like a flag of victory." He knew well enough the importance of a first Parisian "rave."

Here one is likely to pause a moment in mild surprise to wonder at a man of Zidler's stature becoming excited over a press notice concerning one of his second-string entertainers; even speculate as to just what degree of intimacy between the veteran impresario and the young actress such excitement might suggest. Zidler, virile, attractive in his rough way, had for years secretly kept a mistress, a young woman of thirty-odd, though presumably this fact might not have guaranteed his total disinterest in an adventure with Yvette. Yvette always maintained that Zidler was purely paternal in his attitude, which may well be the truth. To be sure, he addressed her affectionately, in the familiar second person singular; but the familiar, affectionate form of address to a young woman is no rarity in the theater, especially from an older man. It is abundantly clear that he showed her many favors—sending her theater tickets, lending her money, exercising his influence in her behalf, counseling and consoling her—and there is evidence that people winked about them. But rumors of an affair between the two Yvette always labeled as stupid and baseless. Not that complete credence need be placed on these denials, which would be understandable; moreover, Yvette was by nature secretive about her relationships with men and in all instances carefully camouflaged them.

Perhaps the main argument in support of the quasi-paternal role which Yvette claims for Zidler lies in Yvette herself—her absorption in self and career, her mother-centered emotional life, her settled conviction that men were to be avoided as lovers, and her tendency to place any older man whom she liked in the position of father. An ideal father would naturally provide. Père Zidler, as she always called him, performed this function. Best of all, a father was safe. To a career-obsessed woman, men exist only as servants to one overweening desire, and Yvette may have sensed the needless folly of becoming entangled in a liaison with a man who, without her running any risks, was already serving her interests in every way she demanded. It would have been natural enough, on the other hand, that there should exist a tie between the two—both slum-born, upwardly mobile socially, dedicated to unremitting work, instinctive money-makers; both possessed of a certain fundamental effrontery. Zidler, mature and surfeited with attainments, could hardly have failed to recognize in Yvette the traits of one destined for a rise in life parallel to his own and to be attracted thereby.

With Yvette, Père Zidler was to prove only the first of a line of "fathers," some of whom she dubbed "godfather." The critic Stoullig later was proud to proclaim himself one of these. "Go to hear my little god-daughter!" he urged in Le National. "She is worth the trouble!" To Yvette the paternal relationship apparently filled a long-felt need, signifying as it did approval, affection—but not too much!—and acceptance of a benign responsibility on the part of the supposed parent.

Chapter 6

One night shortly after the Gil Blas review, Jehan Sarrazin, host of the Divan Japonais, a cabaret artistique at 75 Rue des Martyrs, almost within a stone's throw of the Moulin Rouge, dropped in at the Mill to take a look at the new attraction, the girl with the innocent mien and the earthy message, and before he left he had offered her an engagement at his own place at a later hour every evening. As something of this sort had been specifically foreseen and approved by Zidler, Yvette accepted. The new arrangement would mean an exact doubling of salary. She would now be earning forty francs a night, a munificent twelve hundred a month.

The Divan Japonais, as small and intimate as the Moulin Rouge was huge and self-assertive, as specialized in its clientele as the other was heterogeneous, offered the perfect setting for Yvette's talent. Probably not more than a couple of hundred could squeeze into it, but those few considered themselves the intellectual elite of Montmartre. Interior decoration was naïvely incongruous; exotic Japanese murals and the Japanese costumes of waiters and musicians—anything Japanese was high fashion at the time—combined unblushingly with Louis Philippe chairs; not to mention the manager's businesslike wife, glasses on nose, presiding over the cash drawer and also strictly non-Oriental.

The manager himself, Jehan Sarrazin, had been an olive merchant in the provinces until, fired with the belief that he was a poet, he had abandoned the ways of trade and set off to Paris in search of literary rewards. What must have been his pained astonishment when editors and publishers consistently declined to buy a word he wrote! The age-old problem of genius thwarted, Jehan, however, found his own way of solving. With little packets made up of a dozen olives wrapped in a sheet of his poems, he wandered in and out of the cafés of Montmartre, offering his wares to the customers and thereby achieving the minor fame of becoming known as *le poète aux olives*.

Now that he had acquired a café of his own, he still kept up his quaint custom, but it was not for the olives or the poems that the intelligentsia foregathered here. Jehan was an excellent judge of entertainment, and it was his ideal to include in his cabaret the liveliest examples of avant-garde wit in Paris. "*Le Théâtre Français de la chanson*," the Divan was often called.

For the choicer spirits among his patrons Jehan provided a sanctum in the basement where a more sophisticated brand of fun might be offered until a later hour than that afforded the general public upstairs. Here could be found at their favorite tables, night after night, the artists Willette, Léandre, Bac, Steinlen, Forain, Capiello; and the sculptor Lalou. Of writers there would be Auriol and Henri Dumont and Alphonse Allais, and the *chansonniers* Xanrof and Mac-

Nab; the journalists Maizeroy of *Gil Blas,* Catulle Mendès of *l'Echo de Paris;* the editors Perivier of *Le Figaro* and Meyer of *Le Gaulois.* The critics Bisson and Bauer often came and, feared by all, the fierce Sarcey.

If it is true, as has been claimed, that Jehan Sarrazin lived "in a cold sweat of terror at the prospect of having his cabaret raided," part of his apprehension unquestionably stemmed from the contributions of Mademoiselle Guilbert. Yvette, who now had the complete freedom of choice in subject matter she had long been demanding, took full advantage of it. Standing on the tiny stage, whose lights gleaming through the dense billows of smoke in the room lent it a kind of shimmering, dreamlike quality, she nightly sang her *grossièretés,* in true naturalist tradition never hesitating at the crudest language. Some of her lyrics, it is true, were biting or sardonic rather than gross; a few even glowed with pity or chastised with wit, but always it was a degraded or morbid side of life they were preoccupied with. These were songs with a glitter all their own, though undeniably a darkened glitter.

The censors, prosaic men more concerned with morals than with art, often failed to see eye to eye with her on the literary merit of her choices, finding—and correctly, it must be granted—some of them purely pornographic. To the harried inspectors of popular literature the fact that obscenities were presented by a singer with a complete lack of coarse gesticulations, with indeed an air of almost classic detachment, made little difference. There is no question that during the previous decade in France the products of the school of naturalism had inspired another whole school, that of thinly disguised pornography, which the civil servants appointed to protect the public morals of Paris were admittedly ill-equipped to combat. One would need the wisdom of a Solomon, they complained. Where did art leave off and nastiness begin, anyway? Why did the much-touted "slice of life" always have to concern itself with gutter levels? How could a conscientious inspector prevent the dry rot of corruption from spreading through the body politic and at the same time avoid being stigmatized as an ignoramus or a blighting reactionary?

One day Yvette was peremptorily called in to the censor's office in regard to her new song *Les Vierges.* This was touching her in a tender spot, for *Les Vierges,* a bitterly ironic attack on feminine virtue, was currently a favorite number at the Divan Japonais; some nights she had to repeat it as many as three times. The title itself was scandalous, the censors averred. And then the language—the vilest *double-entendres!* The whole text reeked with indecent allusions. And no "slice of life" excuse possible for this particular enormity either.

Personally Yvette and the censors, Bernheim, Desfossés, and Desforges, were on excellent terms, and apparently she and the office boy as well. For a five-franc tip that young man often allowed her to help herself to the official stamp, with which she was able to visa many of her songs that might otherwise have had rough passage with Messrs. B, D, and D, as being—to use her own euphemism—*"un peu décolletées."* Another ruse she employed was to provide the censors with specially expurgated versions of her verses; perhaps no one would check. In one of her *"décolletées,"* called innocently enough *Celles qu'on respecte* ("Women One Respects"), Yvette sang in cool tones, with her air of what Arthur Symons later called "depraved virginity," of the ways whereby dissolute women of fashion deceived their husbands, a little trifle from which Don Juan himself might have picked up pointers. Regarding another, *Le petit Cochon,* even the daring young lady of Montmartre sought advice before she introduced it. Catulle Mendès, on whom she tried it out, feared that audiences would be offended by the theme—the everyday *ménage-à-trois* of Paris—but Alfred Capus shrugged: "Nonsense! Adultery is a well-established custom!" Both judgments went astray. Though the song was intended as a satire, particularly of the "pig" who shakes the hand of the man whom he has just cuckolded, the underlying meaning got lost. The public saw only the picture—*"Le petit cochon, avec sa queue en tire-bouchon"*—and roared.

It was at the Divan Japonais that Yvette first came under the notice of a man who was undoubtedly one of the strangest figures in Paris at that time, the Count Henri de Toulouse-Lautrec Monfa. Persons meeting the count for the first time, unprepared, often failed to keep their features under control and exhibited involuntarily a sort of instinctive horror. For the most gifted Parisian painter of the 90's, who was capturing in one brilliant sketch after another the living essence of the night life of Montmartre, was a dwarf, a freakish gnome, with a peculiarly ugly and repulsive face. It was only on further acquaintance that the strange creature would be discovered to be also an aristocrat of ancient lineage, polished in manners and witty in conversation. Lautrec had solved his problem of deformity as best he could by forgetting the life of horse and hounds to which he had been born and losing himself in Paris, especially that Paris where genius was

77

welcomed and abnormality met with total tolerance—Montmartre. His debauches became, in time, legendary in the district. In the amusement places he was accepted without question; in them he found his companionship; in their light, glitter, animation, and color, the source of much of his artistic inspiration. Seated every night in one of his favorite resorts, always at the same table in order to have the same angle of vision, Lautrec sketched satirically one after another of the personalities who caught his fancy, sometimes in foreground, sometimes in background, pitiless toward all in his definitions of character and his almost clinical exposure of social decadence. The little artist's eyes were not slow in noting the coolly ironic newcomer Guilbert; that she was someone not to be overlooked his intuition instantly recognized. The poster that he made for the Divan Japonais in 1892 presents the dancer Jane Avril listening with an air of profound attention to a truncated Yvette who is shown on stage in the background, headless but entirely recognizable, her hands in the long black gloves loosely clasped before her.

Contemporaneously with the Divan Japonais and not far from it, another cabaret was operating, Le Mirliton, at 84 Boulevard Rochechouart. Here songs in a rich baritone were being poured forth in the night air, the singer being that modern François Villon, the handsome and hard-hitting Aristide Bruant. Today, in various Lautrec posters, Bruant still stands before us, virile and swashbuckling as life, picturesque in his broad-brimmed black felt hat, with a black cape and red scarf slipping back over his shoulders.

Like Yvette, he too had known slum years, and it was of the poor and depraved that he sang. Among his friends of the underworld he searched out the raw material that went into his ballads, for which he wrote music as well as words. At first his songs had been light in tone, and with them he amused *café-concert* audiences. Later their tone changed. They became stark with indignation, angry songs bearing the stench of the slums, told in slum argots, in the cant of thieves and hoodlums, ugly songs, describing incidents in the shadowed lines of beggars, gravediggers, dopesters—"their savageries, brutal affections, drunken gaieties, obscene delights." His *À Saint-Ouen,* for example, throws a searchlight on the sad wretches—tuberculars, syphilitics, alcoholics—who spend their days picking in refuse pails for rags to sell, inhaling the malodors of putrefaction to the point of nausea. Those appalling ragpickers! Yvette too had seen them as a child and would never be able to forget them. At ten years of age, how frightened she had been in passing by the Rue Quincampoix, a little dark, lugubrious street where rats as big as cats ran from one heap of ordure to another, while ragpickers disputed the trash from the kitchens. These people curse the day they were born. A woman gives birth in the street.

> *Un jour qui faisait pas beau*
> *Pas ben loin du bord de l'eau*
> *Près d'la Seine,*
> *Là où qu'pouss' des moissons*
> *De culs d'bouteilles et d'tessons,*
> *Dans la Plaine,*
> *Ma mer' m'a fait dans un coin*
> *À Saint-Ouen.*

In *Dans la Rue,* Bruant describes young girls who earn a living by prostitution, and young boys with a similar bent who eventually lose their masculinity. From his songs audiences winced to learn the desperate sordidness of Paris flophouses and brothels, and the sleeping cribs under bridges and in open lots.

When he acquired his own *cabaret artistique,* Le Mirliton, he continued singing these songs, though, ironically, his real success stemmed not so much from them as from an unexpected incident. Losing his temper one night, he began flinging insults at a guest and was astonished when the patron laughed hugely, taking the incident as a prepared joke. The next night the man returned, with friends, all apparently expecting the same rough treatment. They got it, of course, Bruant being an astute showman, and from then on, epithets and contumely were standard practice at Le Mirliton: "Shut up, you bastards! Over here, ladies! Next to that fat blob. That's all right! There are only five of you on that bench. Hell! Squeeze in over there at the end. And you, you chump, sit down over there with your two whores."

Yvette and Bruant had met earlier at Léon Sari's, and they had become the best of friends. "I adored Bruant," Yvette always declared. "He loved the down-and-outs as Francis of Assisi loved the lepers, in all pity." Inevitably she was attracted to his songs by virtue of their uncompromising naturalism, their passion for filth and abnormality, and very soon was singing them herself at the Divan,

79

thereby bringing him—another irony—more fame than his own performances of them had brought.

As Yvette's popularity increased at the Divan Japonais, so did the length of her program, and soon the hour from ten to eleven became known as Yvette's hour. The room where she sang was so low-ceilinged that there was barely space on stage for a performer to stand, and in this restricted area intense heat from the gas footlights rose in suffocating waves. On that broiling platform, her dress almost singed by the flare of the too-close lights, Yvette underwent every night sixty minutes of physical martyrdom, but she also tasted the joy of professional triumphs.

The connoisseurs of the Divan held that a large part of her total fascination lay in her unusual methods of delivery. With her, every song became a miniature drama in which, knowing full well that she did not possess a first-class singing voice, she more and more called on the techniques of acting. Music was always an integral part of her performance, and she never entirely lost the thread of melody; but to secure an effect, she never hesitated to sing off key, or to break into something resembling a half-spoken recitative, or even to fully speak occasional words and phrases. Yet the result was distinctly never recitation to music; it was instead something unique, inimitably her own, a blend of two modes of expression, and because of it she was sometimes referred to as a *diseuse*.

Meantime the Moulin Rouge appearances were, of course, continuing; Yvette had therefore two publics and two salaries. Yet in spite of all her new satisfactions, whenever she spilled over to Zidler in what was for her a new sense of euphoria, he repeatedly warned her not to lose her sense of values.

"Remember this," he kept telling her, "no one makes a real reputation before just a handful of artists or in a fad like my Mill. Success in Montmartre! There's no such thing! For real success you've got to get back down there in Paris itself."

For once, however, Yvette found it hard to believe Père Zidler, and that fall of 1890 felt herself falling under the enchantment of optimism. "I had done with poverty forever!" she exulted, and for the first time since her miserable childhood she began to believe in the possibility of happiness for herself.

It was fun, those mellow September nights, when a crowd of young fellows used to walk beside her open carriage all the way home to Rue Saint-Lazare, through the half-empty streets, under a star-sprinkled sky. They did not pay her the time-honored compliment of taking the horses from the shafts and pulling her carriage themselves, as their grandfathers had done for Jenny Lind, but they well served her vanity. By now she had come to enjoy masculine adulation *en masse* —that emotional warmth reaching up to her across the footlights. Here was a form of love to which she could respond with coquettish pretenses of warmth in return; it gave her a pleasing sensation, like the glow of wine in the stomach that makes it easy to smile across the uplifted glass. She liked this kind of homage; nothing was demanded of her in return except more songs, and these she would always be ready to offer. When she reached her own door, it was pleasant to listen to the deep-voiced farewells fading away in the night: *"Bon soir, Yvette!"*—*"À demain, Yvette!"*—*"Bravo, Yvette!"* She felt a distinct affection toward these lads; it was safe to love a crowd.

That fall of 1890 Auguste Musleck and his wife Sidonie, proprietors of the Concert Parisien, found themselves in a serious financial predicament.

Auguste, reputed to have followed any number of occupations— stableboy, swimming teacher, wood gilder, saloonkeeper of the more dubious type, and who knows what else—had recently decided to take a fling at purveying *café-concert* entertainment instead of rotgut liquors, and to that end had purchased the well-known Concert Parisien, Faubourg Saint-Denis. This was one of the oldest *cafés-concerts* in the city; along with the Eldorado, the Gaîté, the Folies-Bèrgere, the Ambassadeurs, and the Pavillon de l'Horloge, it dated back to Second Empire days. At the time he bought it, it had been having hard sledding financially and, unfortunately, under his management fared no better, possibly because Auguste could not bring himself to trust his agent's choice of talent and insisted on making his own. As a last resort, to win back the public, as he hoped, the befuddled man had appealed to *"la grande Thérèsa"* to come for a two-weeks' engagement. But although receipts did go up during her stay, the remedy had come too late. Bankruptcy loomed, and Auguste and Sidonie had decided to give up as a mirage their expectation of becoming concert managers and to throw no more good money after bad.

It was Zidler who relayed to Yvette the gossip that the Parisien was about to close its doors. A pity, too, because the house was in an excellent location—two steps from Boulevard Rochechouart—and exceptionally well appointed. Mirrors, carpets, and chairs were fresh and new; boxes richly upholstered in velvet; even electricity had been installed. A place, in short, to attract the carriage trade.

As Zidler talked, Yvette suddenly experienced a thunderclap of an idea. She was now beginning to be known in the Paris press; she had saved a little money. Why not try to star herself at the Concert Parisien? She could hardly wait to interview the Muslecks.

She found Monsieur a grossly fat man, with a flaming-red face, weak eyes forever streaming water, and a heavy mustache which he continually sucked. His natural expression was that of a rather quaint rascal, except when he was preparing some deceit or other, when he would assume an expression so exaggeratedly open-eyed and honest that even a child should have been instinctively on guard. Madame was a fluffy, simpering blonde, trying to act the lady.

"I have a thousand francs," Yvette told the strange pair bluntly, "which I will give you for advertising. With this you can cover Paris with posters. You know my name? You know my reputation at the Moulin Rouge and the Divan Japonais?"

To her surprise and disgust, Musleck hedged: he had never heard of her, he said. The thousand francs apparently spoke loud in his ear, however, for he did agree to look into her record and it was left that she should come back to him the next day but one for his decision.

How Zidler and Sarrazin laughed at the grotesqueness of the creature when they told Yvette about Auguste's visits of inquiry to them.

"I swear he gilded a pair of handcuffs to make that watch chain he drapes across his belly!" Zidler roared.

But both Zidler and Sarrazin must have convinced Auguste that the adventurous young lady who was prepared to invest in his moribund business was in truth well on the road to becoming "somebody," for when she returned he treated her warmly. Yes, he would accept the thousand francs and in return would put up twenty thousand "butterflies" all over Paris, done by some fine artist, and with a caption that he had himself devised: *Yvette Guilbert, La Diseuse Fin de Siècle, le 5 Octobre, au Concert Parisien.*

It was in this odd way then, and from the lips of this most unlikely person, that Yvette first heard the slogan which was to be forever after associated with her name, quoted around the world, and in the end would make of her a symbol of those confused, decadent, rebellious *fin de siècle* years.

A contract was duly drawn up, its term three years in length, stipulating a salary of a hundred francs a night the first season, two hundred the second, and three hundred the third, with the customary ten-thousand-franc forfeit against whichever party might break the bond. It is to be assumed that both signatories accepted the forfeit clause with tongue in cheek: Musleck because if he really went bankrupt, no one would be able to collect from him anyway; Yvette because of her previous experience with Madame Saint-Ange. When she had told Zidler about leaving the Eden under forfeit, that realist had merely shrugged and advised her not to worry: the law would never sanction a fine amounting to more than a quarter of a month's salary.

On her first day in her new quarters, as Yvette arranged her cosmetics on the dressing table, her eye was caught by something shining on the floor. She picked it up; it was a hairpin, dropped apparently by the last occupant, *la grande Thérèsa*. Yvette, remembering the precocious gamine who had once mimicked Thérèsa, switching behind her the make-believe train of tablecloth, looked at the little object in her hand very tenderly for a long minute or two, then put it carefully away in her purse for a talisman.

On opening night the Muslecks were highly apprehensive. By this time they had caught on to the fact that their new singer refused to wear jewelry or to gesticulate, they had listened with sinking hearts to rehearsals of what seemed to them queer and unfunny songs, and they could not help wondering if they had not been handsomely taken in after all. As for Yvette, she was even more apprehensive. The house was packed; in the audience it was comforting to recognize many old friends from the Moulin Rouge and the Divan, but there too, for the first time, she saw the sphinx-faced first-string critics. To meet the definitive test of a true Boulevard opening, she had prepared a couple of new songs with calculated shocks. She hoped they were not too risky.

The clowns and acrobats did their turns; singers Armand and Clovis chimed their couplets and disappeared; the applause died away; it was time for the new attraction. When next the lights dimmed and the curtain rose, a hush fell over the house. Standing there so strikingly tall, the Titian red of her hair flaming around the chalky pallor of her face, Yvette was the embodiment of Sinet's arresting poster of her. A moment's silence, and then, to the accompaniment of a piano's crashing chords, rose a full-throated, electrifying cry:

> *Peuple de Navarre et de France,*
> *Des Batignoll's et du Jura,*
> *Oyez une triste romance.*
> *Oï! aï! ma mère, oï! aï! papa!*
> *C'est l'horrible mésaventure*
> *Q'eut, il y a quelque temps qu'ca s'passa,*
> *Un professeur d'littérature.*
> *Oï! aï! ma mère, oï! aï! papa!*

As the song progressed, the audience, caught up in suspense, recognized the beginnings of the familiar and well-loved story of Héloïse and Abélard. Familiar, yet tonight strange, for eventually it dawned on the hearers that this was not after all the heartbreaking medieval tragedy. This was a new version by Xanrof, of unexpected coloring, loaded with indecencies, and ending with a ribald treatment of the theme of mutilation. The song laid the ax of ridicule to traditional sympathy for the two doomed lovers, inverted every accepted value in the tale, and left nothing remaining but the lechery of a priest, to whom a punishment hilariously suited to the crime had been meted out. The tragic idea was thoroughly travestied, and the audience, after they had caught their breaths, found themselves shrieking in hysterical laughter where they had formerly wept and suffered.

After other more conventional songs—the gay and naughty *Le Petit Rigolo, Le Papillon qui passe, Les Femmes, La Pocharde*— came the second "shock," the frightful, bloody *Ma Tête*. This was Secrétan's song of the guillotine that playwright Victorien Sardou had particularly urged her not to attempt. "A guillotine on stage!" he had shuddered. "Atrocious! People will throw things at you!"

The hero-villain-victim of *Ma Tête* is an apache murderer, condemned to public death by the descending blade. The scene is a spot outside the prison walls at La Place de la Roquette, and the words are the man's thoughts, his interior dialogue. Through the bravado verses the apache reveals his relationship to a prostitute who, according to custom, gave a large part of her earnings for "protection." By this arrangement the "protector" was in return committed unreservedly to her defense, his knife or revolver always at her need. Now this man has killed; has been condemned. Roused at dawn of his last day, he washes and puts on the garments of the condemned; is conducted by guards out of the prison toward the place of execution. It is his end. But the journey is sufficiently slow-paced for his fevered imagination to envisage fully the spectacle of his severed head rolling from his body into the basket. He almost swaggers a little at the thought of the respectful crowd doffing headgear to salute the hero who by his death will pay all debts.

> Et puis voilà, j'suis condamné,
> Parce qu'il est prouvé qu' j'assassiné
> Il faut qu' j'attende pale, vanné
> Le moment suprême de la guillotine,
> Et puis un beau jour on m'dira
> C'est pour ce matin! Faites votr' toilette!
> J'sortirai, la foul' salu'ra
>   Ma tête!

In this song the singer made use of suggestive bits of costume—a red scarf around her neck and a hooligan's black cap. Describing the act and its effects on audiences, Harold Simpson later wrote:

. . . she depicts the recklessness, the strange strain of vanity, and the devil-may-care humour which go to make the character of this type of wasted humanity, born and brought up in an atmosphere of criminal viciousness. For the moment it is not Yvette Guilbert who stands there, singing of this curious creature, but the creature himself . . . Vicious he may be, and wholly bad; but we cannot resist a sneaking sympathy for him, as he goes on his way to his predestined end. . . . He deserved his end, of course, but only because Fate made him what he was. This is the feeling that Yvette Guilbert imparts . . . the play of her facial expression, and, above all, of her eyes, as the story gradually draws towards its tragic climax, are things that dwell indelibly in the memory. And then the breathless silence which accompanies the words:
"J'sortirai, la foul' salu'ra—"
the pause during which she removes the black cap from her head and holds it out at arm's length; the dull thud with which the cap falls to the ground; . . .

Weights had been sewn into the cap, and more than anything else it was this thud on the floor that gave the last, almost unbearable turn of the screw to the taut, agonized nerves of the audience. At that sound they could hear, they could see, the blade slicing through flesh and feel the impact of the pitiful bloody head in the basket. And then the final despairing cry—more a gasp than a cry—"Ma tête!"

At the end, as Yvette crumpled into her low bows and listened to the bravos and applause rocking the theater, she must have known beyond doubt that she had won her morning's accolade from the sphinxes.

Chapter 7

L'avez-vous entendue?

Have you heard her? This was the question that now swept across Paris. Overnight a new name was being pronounced—Yvette Guilbert.

Ten—fifteen—years to succeed in Paris, Zidler had said, but for once the wizard had been proved wrong. Yvette had made it in five. As for salary, she found it exhilarating to calculate that in two years she would be earning almost as much as the great Coquelin the elder of the Comédie Française; in three years she would surpass him.

Critics smiled a little patronizingly over the newcomer's assumption of the term *fin de siècle* as belonging exclusively to her and her particular brand of song, but the general public seemed to understand perfectly and to cede it to her. To them it meant the novelty she brought: modernity itself: the songs half spoken; the shivers—*les frissons*—that half delighted; the laughs that half curdled; the obscenities that more than half shocked. Though paunchy Auguste Musleck could not for the life of him understand what all the gloved applause was about—to him and his Sidonie such songs were all but meaningless and their delivery clearly substandard—he understood well enough his box-office receipts. Also his eyes bulged a little when the Russian Grand Duke Alexis engaged four boxes one night, and still more when the Duke and his *entourage* stormed Yvette's dressing room after her turn.

The tight little self-contained world of the Paris *café-concert* understood, too, where managers followed the rises and dips in personal fortunes of each entertainer as closely as brokers follow fluctuations of the stock market. Of these none were more sensitive to Yvette's explosive success than Eldorado's Madame Allemand, of the waving plumes and jangling bracelets, and her son-in-law, Monsieur Marchand, new director of the Folies-Bergère and manager of La Scala, another of the important *cafés-concerts* of the city. After some weeks of watching Tout Paris stampede into the Concert Parisien while La Scala stood half empty, M. Marchand decided to attempt the classic maneuver of capturing the attraction away from his competitor and dispatched Madame Allemand, as go-between, to offer the new star four hundred francs a night to appear at La Scala. As to the ten-thousand-franc forfeit, Madame was to beg Yvette not to concern herself about that.

Four hundred francs nightly at La Scala as compared to one hundred at the Parisien—could such an offer be less than irresistible? Yet, to Madame's consternation, the new star asked time to consider.

More significant than the packed houses of the Concert Parisien and the nightly applause that was now hers, these overtures of Madame Allemand carried meaning to Yvette. Clearly there had been a shift in positions. Now it was she who was in the driver's seat, and immediately the shrewdness inherited from generations of bargaining peasant ancestors came into play, reinforced by an instinct for strategy all her own.

"Monsieur Musleck," she said the next day, going as usual straight to the point, "look at the crowds I am drawing here. You must admit that you are making a great deal more money from my name than either of us expected. So it is only fair that we should draw up a new contract. I must have more salary."

Musleck, who naturally had no intention of relinquishing a sou of his heaven-sent solvency, tried to laugh off such nonsense; when pressed, began to bluster.

"More salary, my eye! Why, you don't even know how to make gestures like the other singers! I give you a hundred francs a day and you stand with your hands on your stomach like a stuffed eel!" Yvette's temper signals began to fly, but he paid no heed and bumbled along: "And what a costume! You look absolutely poverty-stricken in those plain dresses of yours, without a scrap of trimming. Not even a jewel! Besides, you know as well as I do that songs are supposed to be sung, and your singing, I must say, is pretty poor—half of it is spoken!"

Yvette's low threshold of tolerance had long since been reached, and she now began to strike back. The quarrel ended when she burst into tears and announced: "Very well, then! I'm through with you! And Madame Allemand will pay your forfeit!"

The unexpected mention of the formidable Allemand was a knife-thrust, she could see, but Musleck pretended not to believe her.

"All right, all right, let her pay it!" he bluffed.

That night Albine counseled patience. "Give him a little time. When he finds out you are speaking the truth, he'll probably offer four hundred himself."

"He'll bully me, too, on my choice of songs."

"Have the new contract framed so that he can't."

Musleck of course came around eventually; he had little choice, indeed, unless he wanted to kill the goose that was laying his golden eggs. So, saving face as best he could, he assumed an air of benevolence, patted his little girl on the shoulder, and told Yvette to forget that cock-and-bull story about Madame Allemand and La Scala. Maybe he would give her a raise after all. How much did she want?

Yvette, who had had time to consult Zidler, now gave the knife an extra twist.

"Five hundred francs, Monsieur." Musleck's red face flamed even redder, and he started an angry protest. "But of course, Monsieur! La Scala will give me four hundred. Here, read this letter if you don't believe me." And she flashed before his eyes a written offer from Madame Allemand.

The revised contract to which Musleck had to knuckle gave her five hundred francs a night the first year, six hundred the second, and seven hundred the third, with a forfeit of a hundred thousand; full liberty in choice of songs; and—a final twist of the blade—permission to appear elsewhere, if opportunity provided, after her turn at the Parisien was over. Musleck agreed to these ridiculous terms, he confided later to one of the Ollers, because he meant to make his fortune out of La Guilbert while she was in demand. Naturally, after a season or two she would lose her value, and then he'd find some way of getting rid of her. It didn't stand to reason that a girl with her queer program could last very long.

At one stroke, therefore, the new legal instrument had raised Yvette's immediate earnings some twelve thousand francs a month, and further provided the star with an enormous added potential. In a few brief weeks her market value had pyramided to a spectacular degree. Moreover, if anything further was needed to heighten her prestige, it was the flock of imitators that now quickly sprang up around the town. Pseudo-Yvettes blossomed right and left.

It must have been about this time that Yvette met one of the most vicious and dreaded reviewers of Paris. This was Jean Lorrain, poet, novelist, playwright, and critic, writing reviews under the pen name of Restif de la Bretonne, an eighteenth-century author known for his publicly scandalous life. Lorrain, a Norman whose real name was Paul Duval, was then a man of thirty-five, notorious for his use of make-up, his face always rouged and powdered more heavily than any actress's, his eyes shadowed a turquoise blue, his hair dyed red. But even more talked of than his make-up were the cameos that loaded his fingers. It was said that he counted on his rings to do as much for his renown as his writings.

Unfortunately, he also had habits of a more serious nature than his make-up or his rings or his extravagant cravats or his reputation for using ether. The Paris *marlous,* or bullies, appealed strongly to Lorrain, and on night prowls he frequented their haunts under the bridges, went to their dance halls, hung around their cafés, redolent of fried fish and absinthe, and wrote nakedly about his experiences. He was embarrassingly candid, parading freely the details of his life as sodomist.

The strange creature was also a profound student of literature, intelligent and artistic. But in his writings there was a cruel streak. His poems of biting irony mocked the sordid creatures he associated with; his malevolence made them his puppets; he took pleasure in provoking laughter at the besottedness of the wretched, preferring to shame and damn rather than to arouse sympathy, like Bruant. Lorrain had devoted a number of columns in *L'Echo* to Yvette, writing always with an edge of sarcasm, dubbing her work "divinely perverse." Yet despite his amiable contempt, such was his influence that these reviews had perhaps done as much toward establishing her reputation as others more directly laudatory.

She is the very latest thing in up-to-date Paris; we shall have the Christmas hawkers selling toy models of her soon on the Boulevards. Her fame has spread from the Cafe Concert to the street already. "Yvette! Yvette!" Her name is in everyone's mouth. . . .

And it seems but yesterday that she was obscure and unknown, save to a few night-revellers, stranded in an idle moment at Montmartre, this Montmartre which has made her what she is, cadaverous and intensely modern, with a sort of bitter and deadly modernity . . .

Has she talent, you may ask? Sometimes, yes. Beauty? No! She is not exactly beautiful, nor exactly the reverse . . .

She is long, oh, so long! and thin, so thin! . . . Long, too long, thin arms, clad in long black gloves . . . with a bodice that always seems about to slip off her shoulders . . . There is something about her, in fact, that is disturbing, peculiar and very individual . . .

Her enunciation is clean-cut and precise; words and sentences emerge from her carmined lips with a wonderful clearness, as though cut out with scissors. She has no voice, but very quaint intonations . . .

With individuals of Jean's effeminate type, Yvette was always able to make friends easily, perhaps because this was another class of men from whom she feared no emotional involvement. Indifferent to their moral standards, she could freely enjoy their undoubted abilities to amuse. With Jean, however, there were practical reasons for cultivating friendship. Besides being a critic, Jean was a writer of off-beat, erotic songs, some witty, some merely unhallowed, which he aspired to have launched, and the song problem being what it was, Yvette, on her part, was alert to any source of usable material.

After his first meeting with Yvette, he sent her *La Peur d'aimer:*

J'ai peur d'aimer, mais je voudrais
Pourtant connaître ce que c'est . . .
Comme un fruit dans la bouche
Qui fondrait jusqu'au fond
Du coeur, un vrai bon bon
Qui sucre ce qu'il touche . . .

J'ai peur d'aimer et cependant
Quand un beau gars a l'oeil ardent
Torse plein, taille mince
Me frôle, au fond d'mon emoi
Je sens un rien qui me pince
Et prise d'un petit froid
Vrai demoiselle de province
J'pâlis et je reste coi.

Why Yvette rejected these lines on the grounds of pornography, having already accepted many no less indecent, is not immediately clear. When Lorrain, offended, accused her of being provincial, she suggested that he write a satire in a pseudo-classical style, involving, if he wished, a definite vice. She would be willing to sing about "dubious and unhealthy people who draw chills from all." The outcome of this suggestion was *Fleur de Berge,* which the author prophesied, and accurately, would become one of her most celebrated numbers. "If this one suits you," he wrote, "we will compose many others, O future mother of my children. I kneel at your feet." Keeping his part of the promise, for many years, from whatever place Jean traveled to or visited, he would send her poems as he wrote them, and through these years a strange kind of friendship grew up between the two. It was a friendship marred by frequent conflicts and tangled mis-understandings, which finally ended in a public quarrel and a com-plete break.

Lorrain's malice, Yvette discovered, could even be turned against her. One of his poems, *Decadente,* she refused to sing, because in it he did not hesitate to ridicule her "silhouette" and to attack her character. Sometimes, when he was angry, he ridiculed her in his column. Remembering his vitriolic pen, Yvette was unquestionably wise in keeping guardedly in his good books. She recognized that he was dangerous. As she once said, "I knew the ogre could be useful to me if meantime he didn't decide to eat me."

There was, however, another writer very unlike Jean Lorrain, whom she had first met at the Divan Japonais and who had followed her to the Concert Parisien. This was Louis de Robert, of *L'Echo,* a slight, goodlooking young fellow, barely twenty, with his spurs still to win, who nevertheless carried himself with something of an air of distinction despite his lack of years and achievements. This young man was frankly a lover, and what to do with a lover Yvette could not imagine. Moreover, at the moment she did not greatly care, being much too occupied with riding the glittering crest of her wave.

Like Yvette, De Robert was a native Parisian, but between their origins existed an enormous gulf. Where a little girl of peasant stock had grown up on the streets of a slum, a little boy, sprung from a family of gentility, had been carefully reared and educated. In tem-perament, too, in every approach to life, it would be hard to find two personalities more dissimilar. It is likely Yvette had never before encountered anyone of Louis' fine-grained nature—sensitive, intro-spective, aristocratic. Where she was aggressive or boastful, he was reticent; where she was frankly a child of the people, he spoke in other accents.

With a suitor of such modest manners Yvette must have been deceived into assuming that here was someone easily put off; instead she soon found that there was no divesting herself of his attachment. If one can judge by reading between the lines of his later writings, she treated him cavalierly, even rudely; yet after every cruel incident he would come back, hurt but unyielding. He was five years her junior; she treated him condescendingly; he gave not an inch. She laughed openly at his "puppy love"; the puppy merely set his teeth and hung on. In the end, she must have decided that this stripling would after all prove no real threat to her cherished inaccessibility, that with him she could still keep the upper hand. Because of his years and his slight stature, there was a certain balance of physical power on her side; and, increasingly, of course, there was that other balance of power—the fame now spreading, which she was already beginning to accept as her due. Little by little, then, she appears to have accepted Louis as an intimate, perhaps irked at first by his ardor, but in spite of herself drawn to him. She must be given credit for having early recognized his promise of genuine achievement. He was already ad-dressing himself toward becoming a novelist; the artist in his nature spoke to her, and this was a voice she could not ignore.

The earliest description we have of Louis de Robert is from the pen of his close friend Paul Faure, who years later described their first meeting in July, 1897, and though Louis was then a few years older than at the time of his first acquaintance with Yvette, his appearance could not have been greatly changed. Faure, who was that summer a guest of Pierre Loti at Bidassoa, went to the station to meet Louis, coming down from Paris also as a guest; rapidly he sketches the figure of the faultlessly groomed young man, valises in hand, who jumped lightly from the train, wearing his *barbiche noir* and *cravate lavallière;* recalls the lively, myopic eyes behind the glasses and the quick, crackling quality of his speech.

Faure, who during a long lifetime came to know Louis probably more intimately than did any other human being, presents his nature as one that through the years developed many facets, his personality as one that bristled with extremes. Seeming tender, dreamy, melancholy, lacking in energy, he proved himself endowed with strong will and great courage. Gay, teasing, full of fantasy, he was also proud and deeply loving. As he first came into Yvette's life, however, he was predominantly a boy in the agonies of hopeless love, laying his heart sentimentally at the feet of a hardheaded young woman who since adolescence had been telling herself that she wanted nothing to do with *l'amour.*

The relationship that grew up between the two is not easy to understand; from the first it was carefully camouflaged by Yvette. Nevertheless, equivocal as it eventually proved, it was probably the only redeeming masculine interest in those emotionally arid years of Yvette's young womanhood, when natural sex drives were being most unnaturally strangled at birth; when the personal perversity of a constant turning away from love was accompanied by the artistic "perversity" Jean Lorrain and other critics had already noted—that preoccupation with the morbid and macabre mingled with the lewd and the scatologic. It was a relationship in which—again reading between the lines—Louis became as regular a visitor in Yvette's dressing room at the theater as in her apartment; acted as escort whenever an escort was needed; was known everywhere as her closest intimate; and if the affections he offered were at first frequently trampled on, that after all is a situation not uncommon between an indifferent young woman and a persistent wooer.

The Parisian public, about this time, was being about equally diverted by a sensational new political philosophy known as anarchism and certain very lively goings on at the Théâtre Porte Saint-Martin. The Divine Sarah's affairs were as usual at a boiling point. For a quarter of a century the greatest actress in the world had been playing out openly, for all to see, her succession of liaisons. "*J'ai eté une des plus grandes amoureuses du mon temps,*" she once murmured modestly; perhaps she might as truly have said, "*de tout temps.*" As Joanne Richardson explains the phenomenon:

Sarah, the natural daughter of a Second Empire cocotte, was to inherit the morals of a cocotte and of the Second Empire. Was she ever truly in love? It may well be doubted. She was young, she was ardent, she was to know the traditional temptations of her profession, and being an unwanted child, she wanted love all the more. But she was in love with love, not with her lovers; she enjoyed the physical pleasure, not the subtle, all-pervading understanding, the spiritual affection.

Be this as it may, Paris had smiled indulgently through the years at her long series of amatory escapades, and when finally Sarah, madly infatuated, married the handsome actor Damala, ten years her junior —even eloping to England to bring off the affair—her public thrilled over the drama of it all. When the marriage soured over his infidelities, and Sarah fled for consolation into the arms of the burly, bearded poet Jean Richepin, the change in her private life was no secret. When she and Damala reunited, sentimentalists' eyes misted. Then suddenly Damala was dead; Sarah cruelly widowed at forty-five. But now, only one year later—*Quand même!*—here was the dear idol, appearing in Sardou's *Cléopâtre* and, in the opinion of the critics, carrying everything before her more magnificently than ever.

Among those enthralled by Sarah's latest performance was that newer star whom Sarah had not yet deigned to notice, undoubtedly because of the acknowledged difference in caste between the world of the legitimate theater and that of the *café-concert*. Yvette, as much under the spell of the incomparable one as anyone else, while she witnessed the play did not, however, lay aside her critical faculties.

In my youthful eyes, she represented the romantic splendour of the "actress" and the skilled seductiveness of the courtesan of the olden time. When I watched her play Cleopatra, it was as though (so it seemed to me) she brought back to life the dead centuries and all the glories of bygone Byzantium. . . . All the same, I must admit that, although she surprised me at first and later on amused me and always astonished me, yet by her art she was never capable of carrying me off my feet. My heart refused to be taken in by the tricks of her voice or of her jerky enunciation, which sometimes made her words rattle and click like castanets, but which sacrificed truth for the sake of elaboration.

The mischievous Xanrof, however, looked on the same play through less reverent lenses. This was the era, it must be remembered, when, as Yvette herself had so bitterly discovered in Lyons, no part of the female anatomy was sacred to funmakers and even Sarah, who was as flat-chested as Yvette, had long been a source of foolery by cartoonists. Hence, when in *Cléopâtre* the tragic queen commits suicide by placing an asp in her bosom, the gesture proved suggestive to Xanrof's impudent sense of humor. The result was a song, practically *lèse-majesté*, which the young student wrote and Yvette sang ("created," in terms of contemporary reviewers) at the Parisien under the title of *Le Petit Serpent de Sarah*.

> *C'était un pauv' petit serpent*
> *Qu'avait rien à s'mett sous la dent.*
> *On l'amène à Monsieur Sardou*
> *Qui, pour les animaux, est doux.*
> *Il m'engagera, pensa-t-il,*
> *Lui qu'a déjá fait l'crocodil'.*

He was a poor little serpent, Yvette mourned in hoarse graveyard tones, who had not a morsel of food to sink his teeth into. Somebody took him to M. Sardou, known to be tender to animals, and the very next morning Sardou took him to Sarah (whose heart, croons the song maliciously, is not of wood, but of gold, like her voice). Now when *le petit serpent* sees Sarah, so thin, so supple, he cries out: "I recognize her! She's my mamma!" And Sarah, in turn, makes the same mistake; she thinks *le petit serpent* is indeed her offspring, tries to give it her breast but, alas, can find none to give. She tries and tries, but all in vain. So what will become of the poor serpent? Why, he will die, of course, one of these nights, on the desert of Sarah's bosom, the poor little serpent who has nothing—but nothing!—to sink his teeth into.

The saucy little jingle took the city by storm, even capturing the redoubtable Sarcey. Writing of Yvette, December 24, 1890, he said:

> *. . . sa voix est juste; sa diction d'une netteté rare. Elle a beaucoup de vivacité et de grace. Elle est quelqu'un. Elle nous a chanté Le petit Serpent de Xanrof. C'était à mourir de rire.*

Truly enough, everyone was dying of laughter, including the dramatist Sardou; everyone, that is, except Sarah, who had at last taken notice.

Chapter 8

In the rear of the Parisien was a little corner reserved for friends which soon became a kind of informal club for a small circle of admirers who had first known Yvette at the Divan and who now followed her here, dropping in almost every night for her turn. It was a circle made up largely of those who did posters of her, wrote articles about her, and made songs for her.

During the late 80's, according to Adolph Brisson, writing in *Les Annales* of October, 1890, as if to meet the need complained of earlier by Theodore Child, a legion of young *poètes-chansonniers* sprang up in Paris and won quick renown. Three whom Brisson mentions, all wits from the Chat Noir, became regular contributors to Yvette's programs: MacNab, who died in the flower of youth but who produced little gems of the ironic and macabre type; Xanrof, whom Brisson describes as filled with warmth and liveliness, "darting arrows at police, government, established institutions"; and Jules Jouy. To these would be added, as time went on, Victor Meusy, Émile Bessière, Eugène Le Mercier, Pierre Trimouillat, Paul Delmet, Maurice Rollinat, Jacques Redelsperger, and a multitude of others. Although Yvette still scoured libraries—she was rapidly becoming a connoisseur of usable lyrics—she was also immeasurably assisted by this new poet host, eager to have her as *créatrice* of their compositions.

Jules Jouy had much to offer her somber tastes. He was an unprepossessing creature, with jumpy features, an eternal cigarette drooping from the corner of an unsmiling mouth, and eyes that looked in opposite directions, but his approach to life was made to order for Yvette. He had known actual hunger and the horror of having no bed, and his naturalism, like Bruant's, uncovered the sore spots of Paris. He described the prostitutes imprisoned at Saint-Lazare; wove brutal dramas about the shiftless poor, constantly on the move, refugees from civilization, adhering to their own codes or to none at all.

Another who contributed to her repertoire was Maurice Donnay, that facile, ingenious playwright-prince of light comedies, an indulgent observer of life and morals. Yvette and Donnay had become acquainted in Moulin Rouge days, when he used to drop in often to listen to *Miss Valérie,* which he found uproariously funny. Like Xanrof, he had studied for another profession but had found his way instead into literature. At the time he and Yvette met, he was as young as she, and lighthearted, and the two found themselves instantly *simpático*. Yvette always said she "adored" him, but there was no hint of romance, and to this statement Donnay in his memoirs, *Des Souvenirs,* agrees. He had, she says, "a smiling eye sparkling with mischief, . . . one was never near him without hearing some witticism. . . . How delightful he was! When he writes to me, he signs himself 'the friend of your childhood,' or 'yours for life.' And he kisses me when we meet and says: 'I jump on your neck like a blessed holy medal.' "

Perhaps the most celebrated of Donnay's chansons, one which he himself originally recited in the cabarets of Montmartre, but which reached the general public through Yvette, was the hymn to sexual depravity entitled *Eros Vanné:*

> *Je ne suis le Dieu qui jette*
> *Les amants aux bords des fossés*
> *Et dont la rapide sagette*
> *Couche des couples enlacés,*
> *Le Dieu qui sème, qui féconde*
> *Et qui garde vigilamment*
> *La vielle Loi qui donne au monde*
> *L'éternel rajeunissement. . . .*
> *Elles ne sont point prolifiques*
> *Mes unions, évidemment;*
> *J'assiste aux amours saphiques*
> *Des femmes qui n'ont point d'amants.*
> *Je suis le Dieu des Morphinées*
> *En quête de frissons nouveaux,*
> *Je suis le Dieu des Raffinées*
> *Dont je détraque les cerveaux.*

When the song was published, it was under a cover designed by Toulouse-Lautrec. Although Lautrec's sexual excesses were well known, they did not include perversions, as could almost be guessed by the unsympathetic illustration here provided, which conveys no great relish for the subject matter. The design depicts two Lesbians, "mannish, hard-featured women," says Gerstle Mack, who are drinking at a bar, "while an unhappy naked little Eros, crippled and deformed, stands disconsolately beside them; . . ."

One night when Donnay brought her some other verses, Yvette made up a little tune for them on the spot, and so was born *Adolphe, ou le jeune homme triste.* This song, along with *Les Vieux Messieurs,* another of Donnay's, both also published with cover drawings by Lautrec, seemed never to lose their popularity; for many years Yvette used them.

In the early 90's the smart, pretentious Nouveau Cirque on the Rue Saint-Honoré, founded in 1886 by Joseph Oller, stood high on the list of society musts in Paris. To the Nouveau Cirque, audiences came in evening dress; first nights were of first importance. Boxes were filled with men from the exclusive clubs—the Jockey, the Pommes de Terre, l'Épatant; impeccable Paris dandies, who spoke in their own crisp idiom. Even the manager, Monsieur Donval, husband of the great Thérèsa, behaved with such correctness that his aristocratic patrons sometimes treated him as an equal and shook hands with him. It was in the Nouveau Cirque that the clowns Footit and Chocolat, the latter a dancing, singing Negro immortalized by Lautrec, romped through an act that became as celebrated as, later, the Fratellinis'.

Though it was therefore considered flattering to be invited to play the Nouveau Cirque, Yvette, when approached by M. Donval, at first demurred on the grounds that a large arena would not offer the best background for her intimate style. The Cirque, however, was in such high vogue that she eventually agreed, making her debut there January 16, 1891, and playing on a small stage specially set up in the center where she could appear to advantage. After her act every night, clubmen would mob her dressing room to be presented, with Donval rubbing his hands and boasting: "I have known the two glories of song—Thérèsa and Guilbert."

Another complimentary type of engagement soon began to be offered also. This was the benefit performance, so frequently mentioned in the Paris press of this period. To such performances, usually given for the relief of some member of the theatrical profession ill or out of luck, performers freely contributed their services. To be invited to appear at these affairs implied status as a drawing card, and from now on Yvette was seldom omitted from them. There is no record that she ever refused to serve; as one who remembered only too well her own dark days, she was always quick with sympathy.

Under date of January 24, *Le Gaulois* reports an imitation, performed *"le plus drôlement du monde,"* by Mademoiselle Pieroy of *"la divette Mademoiselle Yvette Guilbert.*" The incident is significant on two counts. Yvette is now of sufficient public interest to warrant a satire. She is also an acknowledged "divette"; in only a matter of time she will be a "diva."

Still Zidler was not satisfied to let his protégée rest on her oars.

"Paris is not enough! France is not enough! A career worth the name has to be international. Give yourself a couple of years here, and then you must be off!—travel! Look at Bernhardt—thirteen months on tour and she comes back with eight hundred thousand francs clear profit. And this month she's starting all over again. You'll do the same—you'll tour Europe and America, too. Mark my words!"

The most important event of the winter was a new kind of publicity, on a higher level than any Yvette had thus far known, which introduced her to a better public.

At 18 Rue Saint-Lazare, very near the apartment in which she was now living, a unique enterprise had recently been founded. In a hall originally used as a picture gallery, a certain Charles Bodinier, who for many years had been associated with the Comédie Française as play-reader, had opened an experimental student theater which he named the Théâtre d'Application. At the far end of the gallery he had constructed a small stage and in the rest of the available space had installed theater seats, even a balcony and a few boxes, to hold a tiny audience of hardly more than two hundred. As a director, Bodinier proved to be a man of taste and originality, and in consequence his dramatic productions were well patronized in spite of his limited facilities.

But this was not all. In Brussels at that time semischolarly lectures, delivered as matinees, were proving immensely popular, and Bodinier conceived the idea of instituting a similar series in Paris. Success was immediate, his Wednesday afternoons at the minuscule Théâtre d'Application, offering such distinguished names as Lemaître, Brunetière, Barrès, Donnay, proving of even greater drawing power than the Théâtre Français Tuesdays. As the front of the hall was still used as a gallery for pictures and sculptures, artists and the art-loving public were among his subscribers, as well as professors and actors, poets and journalists. Even satiated socialites climbed his long flight of stairs in large numbers. All in all, a distinguished clientele had been built up for this self-consciously exclusive little venture, in which, with the suave M. Bodinier acting as host, the subscribers could meet and mingle for a couple of hours in an afternoon as if they were in a drawing room.

Tastes of the group were liberal. Aristide Bruant had been brought in from the outer boulevards for the benefit of those who would have hesitated to submit to his rough tongue at Le Mirliton, and now, when newspapers were sounding the tocsin over the new Mademoiselle Guilbert, the inventive director devised a series of lectures on the history of French song, with Yvette singing some of the works discussed. The lecturer he had in mind—to serve, as it were, as framework for the real attraction, the divette herself—was Hugues Le Roux, journalist, African explorer, and speaker of exceptional eloquence.

In characteristic fashion, Yvette gives varying accounts of how she and Le Roux originally met. In her memoirs she states that he was first introduced to her by M. Bodinier; in another story he "discovered" her in Printemps days. Le Roux himself wrote that the first time he heard her sing was at the Trocadéro engagement. There, he said, Yvette, accustomed to singing *en plein air* and above the general confusion of a *caf'-conc'*, was as much at ease in the great auditorium as a swallow in a church. "*Elle avait la merveilleuse diction qui vous envoie les mots comme un coup d'aile, . . .*" Soon he had joined the long line of "daddies," styling himself her "*père noble,*" taking her on sight-seeing expeditions into doss houses, escorting her to the Chat Noir, letting himself be known as one of her most extravagant admirers.

Now, when Paris was completely hers and along every street bloomed the posters from which, in her ball gown, she smiled at her adorers, decorated by the legend "*Guilbert . . . fin de siècle*" in great black letters, Le Roux became struck one day by certain implications he thought he discerned in her "silhouette." Did it hint, he wondered, a decline of the Rubens ideal of womanly beauty and the arrival of an entirely new concept, one which would be a "strange mixture of femininity and slenderness, of perversity and candor"?

Writing in *Le Temps* of February, 1891, Le Roux was perhaps the first journalist to attempt to present a psychological analysis of the new favorite; in his own words, "a definition of the nature of Mademoiselle Guilbert." This he does by describing a scene in the studio of Edouard Lormier, the sculptor, when Yvette posed for the first time for a clay model of the bust which the artist was to make of her. Le Roux for days had been searching vainly for an answer to the riddle of what Yvette truly was, and now the thought occurred to him that only through the penetration of an artist's creative imagination would that answer ever be found. He watched intently, therefore, while Lormier started modeling.

"Sculptors," he writes, "have so strong a classical education that, placed before a face to portray, they seek behind that mortal head the divine prototype of which it is a reflection." A few minutes only sufficed for Lormier to bring into being the vague outlines of a face that could be none other than *"la chaste image de Diane."* To Le Roux this revelation seemed entirely believable. ". . . was not Diana the 'ingénue' of Olympus, the maid who fled in terror from her suitors, patroness of all young girls who want to be delivered from all undesirable Actaeons?" But as the sculptor kept on working, Le Roux gave a sudden cry. Diana had disappeared. The artist, after his dream of the general type, was now seeking the personality of his subject, and in the second incarnation under his hands Yvette emerged, completely alive and vivid, as a laughing figure of a young fauness. At this Le Roux jumped up and delightedly shook him by the hand.

"My dear Lormier, . . . you have just brought light into the darkness where I was lost. Without speaking a word . . . you have defined for me that sweet and indefinable state of soul we call ingenuousness.

"Yes, that is it, that is exactly it. In general essence it is the purity, the intact virginity of Diana; in its individual form it is the laugh of the young fauness who knows that she is made to love, who wishes to be loved. And between these two extremes, which are the confines of ingenuousness, lies an exquisite province, a charming Eden, a paradise to lose, around which men revolve, charmed, attracted, ravished; the kingdom of Yvette. Sing, Yvette, sing to seduce us, whatever you wish . . . it does not matter. . . ."

A strictly romantic appraisal, in which, nevertheless, lies a hint of prophecy in the image of fatuous males forever revolving, "charmed, attracted, ravished"—which is to say, perpetually teased but never gratified; always seduced by the fauness but never entering her kingdom.

The first appearance of Le Roux and Yvette at the Théâtre d'Application was set for February 5, 1891, and immediately the district gendarmerie found themselves confronted with a traffic problem. On the days of Yvette's matinees the Rue Saint-Lazare became so choked with carriages that the distracted police ordered vehicles routed to side streets, and it took all Yvette's charm to persuade the Prefect to rescind the edict, allowing the carriages to approach the theater single file, deposit their owners, and later, after the performance, to pick them up in the same way. Eventually there were two, and later three, matinees a week, but still the stream of carriages never failed.

Such mad success of a *café-concert* star within the récherché precincts of the Théâtre d'Application—that sanctum of art, almost the Conservatoire itself—had stunned reporters. Nonetheless, Émile Blémont took the "pretty savage" seriously enough to try to explain the phenomenon of her triumph with cultured audiences. At the Concert Parisien, he said, Yvette operated on the frontier of the Paris that works and the Paris that amuses itself and undertook to respond simultaneously to the artistic postulations of both. She could conquer gross souls by the vulgarity of the morsels she tossed out and at the same time charm delicate ones by the perfection of her enunciation. When she began to sing, she reminded one of a schoolgirl when prizes were about to be given out; when she delivered her appalling crudities, it was with almost an astonished air that she should find herself saying such words. Her exaggeratedly décolleté gown delighted the lower classes, who seldom wore anything but work clothes, and her spicy rhymes revived tastes dulled by insipidity. She offered an equal attraction to subscribers to *La Revue des Deux Mondes* and the Théâtre Libre and to regular readers of the *Petit Journal*. In short, therefore, Blémont affirmed that if Guilbert was succeeding at the classic Théâtre d'Application, it was precisely because she had a classic talent.

For each of their joint appearances Le Roux and Yvette at first received a hundred and fifty francs apiece, but it was not long before they were striking for a fee exactly doubled, and getting it. That clause in Yvette's contract with Musleck which allowed her freedom for outside engagements was beginning to pay off. She was now performing at both the Parisien and the Nouveau Cirque in the evenings, as well as at the Théâtre d'Application for matinees. Her strength seemed inexhaustible.

It was Yvette who invented the name of "*La Bodinière*" for the unique little theatre, a name that caught everyone's fancy. Even the press adopted it.

One day at La Bodinière the urbane Count Guy de Kerveguen and his sister made themselves known to Yvette. The Count, a Guilbert devotee, wished to offer a bit of advice and also hoped to open other doors. He proposed to introduce the new star as entertainer into the drawing rooms of Paris, where, he claimed, no *café-concert* actress had ever set foot. His sister would suggest to her friends that Yvette be invited to sing at evening parties; he himself, as a member of four of the leading clubs of Paris, would also recommend her.

"But Mademoiselle," he concluded, "be sure to ask a big fee. At least five hundred francs."

Even Yvette gasped at this. "No one would ever give such a sum!"

"You can ask a thousand francs, Mademoiselle, if you play your cards right. And now I come to my advice: when you've made enough money and can afford it, take your talents back to the theater. You are too great for the *café-concert*."

Sardou was another who told Yvette that winter that she was properly not so much a chanteuse as a comedienne; she reminded him sometimes, he said, of Desolée and of Déjazet.

"Why do you never play in comedy?" he demanded one day.

"I'm waiting to make my name first in song."

"Ah, but then it will be too late!" he cried. "Paris will have you ticketed, and you will have to sing to the end of your days!"

Sardou knew his Paris well.

Ever since those classical concerts on Friday evenings at the Eden, Yvette's interest in the ancient songs of France had been keen. Now, under the guidance of Le Roux, her knowledge of the subject grew rapidly and she began, almost as a hobby, to collect a repertoire of the old *chansons*. It was inspiration as well as challenge, once or twice a week, before discriminating hearers, to relinquish the *fin-de-siècle* mood and try to recapture the medieval tone and temper; each period fed the other; she felt herself growing as an artist.

Other offers began to pour in; the divette needed seven-league boots: more benefits, more *soirées;* a ballet at the Folies-Bergère with Yvette wearing on her gown *le petit serpent de Sarah.* The first of many bits of gay doggerel:

> *Vingt-trois ans, la taille bien prise,*
> *Nez au vent, le front découvert;*
> *Un bon rire qui plaît et grise:*
> *C'est Yvette Guilbert.*

May brought a flying tour of the provinces where, in Lyons, at the very Casino from which—so long ago it now seemed—she had been shipped back to Paris in disgrace, she now paid off her score by fulfilling the bravado prophecy she had made that night of rage and humiliation. Or almost fulfilling: she had sworn she would return for twelve hundred francs; actually she accepted eleven hundred.

Back in Paris in June, there occurred what the press characterized as an event of "gigantic proportions."

The Champs-Élysées, like many thoroughfares, had always had its "right side" and its "wrong side." On its right side, where the pavements were thronged day and night, stood two of the city's most crowded *cafés-concerts,* the Alcazar and the Ambassadeurs; on the wrong side, where almost nobody passed, the little Horloge.

Every *caf'-conc'* in Paris had its quaint history, but certainly none was more unusual than that of the Horloge. This fine old establishment was at that time being operated by the rich Stein family from Vienna, who had rented its pavilion for the sake of a cherished little daughter of delicate health who was required to live as much as possible in the open air. In the garden there was a small stage for summer entertainment, which the Steins, under terms of their lease, were obliged to continue. The Steins were so wealthy that they were not concerned with making money, but chose their attractions purely to amuse the young invalid, who would lie on her balcony every night from eight to nine to be amused. For her clowns performed antics and an orchestra played favorite tunes. A few patrons with children would wander in from the street, but hardly enough to be called a real audience.

One day Yvette was astonished to receive a visit from the Steins, who begged to know if she would sing at the Horloge; their daughter had requested it. Nice songs only, of course, and not late, so that the child could go to sleep early. They hoped still to keep the quiet, almost private, tone of the place, and since they were situated on the wrong side of the street, they believed that crowds would continue to pass them by. Something about the circumstances intrigued Yvette; the Steins were cultivated and charming; she accepted.

When the papers announced that Guilbert would sing at the Horloge during the summer months for the next two years, Zidler protested vigorously what he considered a hideous error in judgment.

"It's no better than a graveyard for you!" he spluttered to Yvette.

"Why, it's the wrong side of the Champs-Élysées! Not a soul will cross that street, and you're agreeing to be buried alive there for two years!"

But Yvette persisted. She opened early in June, and what followed became theatrical history. The little garden that night overflowed; chairs and glasses had to be hastily borrowed, while the child from her balcony watched the new hubbub in incredulous delight. All summer the crowds crossed over, until Zidler, happy to be proved wrong, had to concede that it was "a miracle." Every week Yvette, with her seemingly endless resources of energy, added five new songs to her repertoire. Receipts were so heavy that after only a few days M. Stein voluntarily doubled her fee. On August 14, the night of her last performance for the season, a surge of carriages crammed the streets from the Rue Royale down to the Étoile, wheel to wheel, coming to a stop before the little Horloge, with its lights gleaming like jewels among the leafy trees. Said *Le Gaulois: "Dieu me pardonne, c'est un première et non pas une dernière."* Front rows were heavily Tout Paris, including that most formidable of social arbiters, the Prince de Sagan. *"Paris est fou de sa divette,"* the reporter gushed.

The triumphal summer was marred by one untoward incident. In July the Minister of Finance, wishing to give a party with entertainment to the members of his Budget Commission, invited a number of prominent actors and singers, including Yvette and the Coquelins, to entertain his guests. As reported by Sergines in *Les Annales*—for the incident caused considerable gossip—the Coquelins created consternation by refusing to appear if a divette from the *café-concert* preceded them on the program. Such an institution as the *café-concert*, Coquelin *cadet* pontificated, was "in absolute opposition to the general law of Art." Art consists of indication, of permissive divination, and not of delineation. He did not deny Mademoiselle Guilbert's perfect diction, but he absolutely disagreed that from an artistic point of view hers was a superior *genre*. "Art must be elegant and correct; art is something distinguished, not something vulgar, within everybody's grasp."

It must have come as something of a surprise to everyone when Mademoiselle Guilbert, never a shrinking violet regarding her prerogatives, agreed that the Coquelins were entirely correct. And she was quite sincere. The *café-concert* was indeed vulgar, both socially and artistically. She recognized that as an art form it could not compare with legitimate theater, especially of the standards of the

Comédie Française. Nonetheless, the sting of the Coquelins' public insult went deep and lingered. That there would inevitably be similar incidents in her future she could not avoid facing. To compensate, she would have to keep her mind firmly fixed on the other side of the ledger—the side that compared her bank balance with that of the Coquelins.

By the time Mademoiselle Guilbert reopened at the Concert Parisien in the fall of 1891, she had acquired an English-speaking press as well as a French. During the summer an American reporter had interviewed her:

> Even Paris has a new toy. It is a woman, and the whole gay capital is at her feet.
>
> On the boulevards, in the clubs, in the cafés, everywhere, it is one constant query:—Have you heard Guilbert?
>
> One sees her pictures right and left, on wall and window. The papers never tire of singing her praise. The boys in the streets whistle her favorite airs. The shopkeepers use her name to attract attention to their goods. There is the Yvette Guilbert hat and toothpaste. . . .
>
> A year ago Yvette Guilbert was practically unknown. She is one of those rare geniuses that take us by surprise. . . . At the time I write she is indisputably the most talked of and, by all odds, the most popular woman in Paris.
>
> . . . hundreds are turned away nightly from the Horloge. This is not the customary "thousands turned away" of the imaginative but well-meaning advance agent, but a genuine indisputable fact witnessed by all who have had to crush through a perspiring mob to get even a distant glimpse of the new feature. No such triumph as this has been known since the palmiest days of Thérèsa. . . .
>
> Is it surprising that the new singer is the talk of Paris, or that the theatres, concerts, and even private special gatherings fight as to who shall have her? She sings nearly as much in private drawing rooms, noble and plebeian, as she does on the stage, and nearly trebles her income by so doing. . . .
>
> She also received a royal summons to sing at Marlborough House before the Prince of Wales. Yvette wired back to London saying she would not go for less than 10,000 f. To this somewhat extravagant demand no answer was vouchsafed, . . .

But the "divette" is independent of princes. She sings in two halls a night, and makes full $60,000 a year. She is rapidly accumulating money, yet lives simply and quietly in a small apartment in the Rue St. Lazare.

It was there that I made her acquaintance some few weeks back. . . . In answer to my query, I was ushered into the "salon" by an obsequious valet, . . .

It was a pretty little room, all hung in red cretonne. It was plainly the interior of an artiste. The colors were in harmony, the draperies and furniture in good taste and the general arrangement of bric-a-brac, books and pictures and plants suggested the hand of an artistic eye. The room was low and looked on to the busy Rue St. Lazare. The principal thing which struck the eye was a handsome piano, bearing evidence of hard work and littered with music and all kinds and manner of songs. Over the piano was a painting of the "divette" by Gervex. To the right on a stand, I admired a handsome bust of her by Van Straeten, . . .

Later in 1891 Yvette's Spartan way of life somewhat softened. In November *Le Gaulois* reported her removal to a spacious airy apartment at 2 Rue de Portalis. Here walls covered with white satin spelled new opulence. On the piano rested a shiny new guitar, for Yvette was learning to strum some of her own accompaniments.

For the Parisien's Christmas season Surtac and Halévy concocted an elaborate revue, *Páris à la Blague,* summing up amusing events of the past year. It was the usual flesh show, against a background representing the façade of the Concert Parisien, with a climax of bicyclists—cycling had recently become the maddest of fads—riding round and round to the rhythms of brass and the rolling of drums. Yvette's number was another caustic impersonation of Bernhardt. Sarah had set sail on her second international odyssey that spring, and to *Le Petit Serpent* Yvette now added a scene in the stateroom of a steamship about to leave Le Havre for the United States. In this burlesque Sarah rages against the captain for refusing permission to bring her menagerie of pet dogs and panthers aboard, then sings some shoddy and outworn ballads in her well-known *voix d'or*. It was a stinging piece of ridicule, Yvette mocking Sarah's languid poses and melting glances, and her way of larding her words with those long-held, quavering "golden tones." When the applause quieted, the *compère* would call out: "You ought now, Madame Sarah, to imitate

Yvette Guilbert." "That's easy," Yvette would say in the person of Bernhardt, and then launch into the *tour de force* of a double impersonation: imitating Bernhardt imitating Guilbert.

Critics during this period kept a close watch on the newcomer and her techniques. E. Armand wrote in the *Revue d'Art Dramatique:*

> Her prominent cheeks hollow under the eyes into great shadows that give her, according to Jean Lorrain, "the allurement of a young and smiling death's head." She possesses a mixture of ingenuousness and perverse grace which, in spite of everything, is seductive and draws to herself the sympathy of a blasé *boulevardier* public. . . . She produces a profound impression.

Sarcey, however, seeing her on December 20, 1891, after a lapse of some months, allowed himself a few captious remarks. *"Elle n'est pas en progres,"* he complained, and, though Parisians in general were enraptured, he deplored as unhappy her choice of songs. "She was more simple and frank in former days," the old man sighed.

Actually Yvette was still frank, especially about the money she was earning, seeming never to tire of telling reporters the size of her fees. To André Galdemar she boasted of having made in that year 210,000 francs. The great Coquelin himself was reputed to have earned only 69,000.

"But I am not proud," she proclaimed. "I live modestly, telling myself this can't last. People say Yvette is a miser, as tight as four sous. What do I care? I don't like jewels and gewgaws. What good are they? They don't make me pretty, do they? Besides it's to my ugliness that I owe my position. If I had been pretty, perhaps I would not have worked. I have very simple tastes, and I see myself already retired to the country, walking in my garden in the bright sunshine. Ah, the sun! When the sun shines, I feel as if I could climb the Eiffel Tower on a rope!"

Chapter 9

Just before midnight of March 5, 1892, close-packed lines of shiny carriages, reminiscent of those that for so many months had been surging up to the doors of the Concert Parisien, La Bodinière, and the Horloge, could be seen stopping to discharge their occupants under the brilliantly lighted marquee of the Théâtre des Nouveautés where, in tiny flaming jets of gas, the name of Yvette Guilbert was spelled forth. The piece was Léon Xanrof's new revue, *Paris Nouveautés.*

This comparatively new method of name-publicizing by lights was not overlooked by *Le Gaulois:* "Finally she enters. Who? Yvette Guilbert, *parbleu,* whose name flames in letters of fire [*lettres de feu*] at the door of the theater."

L'Illustration, in spoofing vein, elaborated:

... Yvette Guilbert is the only one who has the right, according to her contract, to have her name in gas lamps [*lettres de feu sur les motifs de gaz allumés*] in Paris near the café-concert where she sings. O ultramodern revelation! What is the humble headline of the actor compared to the light of the diva! It is merely the declaration of the presence of a renowned artist in a play. But ... the right to have one's name in lights is to ... enter into the luminous Pantheon of the firmament. Here it is, here it is, the *Brevet supérieur,* ... *la lettre de feu.*

In the revised agreement which Yvette had jockeyed Musleck into signing, she had specified freedom to accept outside engagements concurrently with the term of her contract at the Parisien, a privilege which she had already exercised at the Nouveau Cirque and La Bodinière. The new engagement in the Xanrof revue had been made possible, like that in the Cirque, by a simple matter of scheduling. After concluding her turn at the Parisien at eleven, Yvette could jump into a carriage and be driven to the Nouveautés in time to appear on that stage at midnight. Proper enough, one might think, and why Musleck should now suddenly charge upon his star like a maddened bull, filing suit for breach of contract and demanding a forfeit of a hundred thousand francs, is something of a mystery.

Perhaps the journalistic tralala over *les lettres de feu* angered him. Or possibly *les lettres* themselves; perhaps he interpreted them to mean that his chief drawing card was being lured away.

Such was not the case, of course. During January and February of 1892 Yvette had continued faithfully, week after week, creating one new song after another at his pretty *bonbonnière,* responding generously every night to the wildly applauding audiences by giving encore after encore: "The brilliant artiste, called back over and over again sings up to ten songs. The curtain goes up and down and up and down again, until the gracious Yvette disappears in a hurricane of bravos."

Or he may have been actuated mainly by greed. Certainly he could not have found it pleasing to watch the rivers of gold which, as he may have reasoned, should have been flowing into the till of the Parisien being diverted into that of the Nouveautés. The Bodinière matinees were different; they attracted a group that would never have come to the Parisien anyway. But the Nouveautés catered to much the same public as the Parisien; the whole situation must have been intensely irritating. Still, for a while there seemed to be nothing he could do about it, until Yvette made what proved to be a misstep. When she began singing at Sunday matinees at the Nouveautés as well as at evening performances, Musleck promptly served upon her his *papier timbre*.

Étienne Desgranges, in his column "*Chronique Parisienne,*" March 20, 1892, stated concisely the gist of the quarrel:

> "But I have the right," says Mlle Yvette, "to sing at the Nouveautés in a matinee, since I have finished my stint the night before at the Concert Parisien."
>
> "Not at all," answers Musleck. "Sunday at five in the afternoon, Yvette Guilbert's work has not as yet started, and she belongs to me until ten at night."

In the several weeks' interim before the suit came to trial, a war of nerves ensued between the two antagonists that seems to have somewhat damaged the dignity of the divette. During these hostilities, according to Yvette, the bumbling and ineffectual Musleck suddenly became downright dangerous. Even thirty-five years later, her autobiography presents a highly colored version of the affair. Musleck, it is claimed, threatened to "do her in," and she was obliged to seek police protection every night between her dressing room and the stage. The picture of a homicidal Musleck does not entirely square with the one previously drawn of a loutish publican whose worst faults were corpulence, ever-streaming eyes, and cupidity. But Yvette is more often emotional in her judgments than logical, and in seeking police escort perhaps she was merely overwrought.

The press played up the controversy *ad nauseam,* and in the end at least one journalist could not refrain from expressing a boredom that was perhaps shared by others:

> Yvette Guilbert is talented, . . . and I am always among the first to applaud her. But I would prefer not knowing how much she earns . . . nor what she counts on earning later. Knowing all this ruins the pleasure I derive from hearing her sing. I am no longer under the spell of her artistry when I have to say to myself in listening to one of her songs: "This now costs such-and-such a number of louis." M. Musleck interests me perhaps more, for he is merely a businessman trying to get himself out of a bad situation.

M. Musleck did not wholly succeed in the endeavor, nor, in point of fact, deserve to, for Yvette had been a bonanza for him from the start. He failed to collect the damages he was suing for, and the rupture in relations between the two eventually led to the end of their association.

Late in May, after the season's closing of the Parisien, when Yvette reopened for the summer at the little outdoor pavilion of the Horloge, the box office there was so besieged that a second one had to be provided and reservations accepted by telephone; all this in the face of trump counterattractions being offered by two big competitors on the opposite side of the Champs-Élysées—Paulus at the Alcazar and Bruant at the Ambassadeurs.

It would have been impossible to find three more popular names with which to woo the Parisian pleasure seeker those warm June nights than Guilbert, Paulus, and Bruant, yet the critic Gaston Jollivet, surveying them in *Le Gaulois,* flattened the spirits of all impartially; all had deteriorated. Yvette Guilbert has always made her audiences laugh; less this year, however, than last. Paulus does not make anyone laugh any more, and as for Bruant, he never drew a laugh."

In particular, Jollivet complained that the Guilbertian repertoire no longer scintillated, that the songs were trite; and, as if this were not enough, Sarcey, writing for *Le Temps,* dipped his pen in gall to agree. Sarcey, furthermore, charged that Yvette's delivery had changed, had become mannered. She was always seeking effects, he said, dragging out words, overemphasizing them, with the result that some of her old chefs-d'oeuvres, *Le Fiacre,* for example, had become intolerably dull.

Reading these waspish comments, Yvette felt the first chill of fear strike to her heart. Climbing to the top had been difficult, but staying there might prove more so. Some critics, to be sure, had been kind. But pudgy little old Sarcey was potentate of them all. No authority was comparable to his; it was his opinion that mattered.

Late summer brought the fulfillment of a wish long cherished, though more as dream than hope—a meeting with Pierre Loti. The season at the Horloge completed, Yvette had played four days in Brussels in August and then gone on tour through France, closing in Biarritz. Loti, as Lieutenant Viaud of the French Navy, was at that time commanding the *Javelot,* a little gunboat stationed at the mouth of the Bidassoa, close to his summer home at Hendaye, which looked across to Spain. Here Louis de Robert had been his summer guest, and it was Louis who arranged the meeting and came to Biarritz to fetch Yvette.

Loti, who had been elected the previous year member of the French Academy in spite of savage opposition from some quarters, was now more talked about than ever, and more than ever Yvette had been yearning to know him. One of the facets of his strange character was an excessive personal vanity: "I would give the whole world," he once mourned, "for the good looks which I lack!" Yvette, however, found no fault with his appearance the day she first met him. The well-groomed officer who greeted her aboard his trig little naval cutter looked extremely attractive, she thought, in his dress uniform of blue jacket with brass buttons and his white trousers:

His thin face tanned by the wind and the sun was lighted by wonderful eyes, eyes as of translucent enamel, with flashes of fire, eyes that one could never forget, . . . Did he use atropine to distend his pupils, like the Arab and Egyptian women? I don't know, but certainly Loti's eyes held one and fascinated all those who knew him . . . he was elegant and distinguished-looking, very simple, affable, but without familiarity, and his voice was as gentle as a woman's. At this first interview he said: "You are very young, mademoiselle. It is magnificent at your age to have such a success."

"A passing success, monsieur, fashion, excitement, perhaps. . . . It is not success, but talent that one must have so as to last. Have I really talent, that is what I don't know! . . ."

Pierre Loti never forgot that, and reminded me of it on many occasions. He kept his promise and came to see me in Paris several times. One day he . . . begged me to sing him some old popular songs; his enthusiasm delighted me.

"There! that's the true spirit of the race, and what a richness there is in it! . . . You will come to it, Yvette, you will come to that beautiful poetry which is universally human, and you will gather fresh laurels more noble and lasting when you make yourself its minstrel!"

Still under the Musleck contract, Yvette returned in the fall of 1892 to the Parisien, she and Auguste apparently having agreed to patch up their differences in favor of the box office. *Le Gaulois* chronicled the brilliant reopening on September 10; later quoted Sarcey, who, invoking the mightiest name behind the footlights, now referred to Yvette as the Sarah Bernhardt of the *café-concert,* and found her repertoire improved if not her technique; described the crowded houses that continued through the autumn. On October 15 she was praised for an eighteenth-century *chanson, La Mouselette*—Le Roux's tuition was bearing fruit.

Yvette remembers it as being also in 1892 when she was first invited to appear at the Chat Noir—a gesture of thanks, as she modestly puts it, for having been the first to bring to the Boulevards the chatnoiresques verses of the group's most celebrated *chansonniers:* Donnay, Jouy, Rollinat, Xanrof, Bruant, Richepin. Her reception that night was so warm that she was pronounced *"de la maison"*; in fact, she remained so, for many subsequent appearances.

On December 15, in a new revue at the Parisien, *Cligne en haut, cligne en bas,* she launched what was to become one of her most celebrated numbers, the *Fleur de Berge* of Jean Lorrain.

Fleur de Berge is a love song full of a girl's memories of sensual moments, with a passionate wailing for the " 'skin' of the male" which the girl "had in the blood."

> *Y m'app'lait sa gosse, sa petite môme,*
> *Dans l'jour, en bateau . . .*
> *J'étais foll' de lui, et d'sa peau;*
> *Y m'caressait, fallait voir comme.*
> *C'était un gas, c'était un homme!*

113

L'soir au Lion d'Or, par des temps d'neige,
Au coin d'un bon feu
Y m'faisait des tas de sortilèges
Pour m'monter un peu

Caressant comme un chat qui miaule.
D'suite y riochait
M'disant: "Viens-tu voir à la piaule
C'que d'vient ton brochet. . . ."

In the end, the passionate yearnings give way to the girl's reproaches against Fate for letting her die of consumption: *L'Ciel est canaille, y faut mourir quand on est heureuse.* "Heaven's always pulling dirty tricks—making you die just when you're happy." In this song Yvette avoided the easy and obvious—the tough, husky voice of a street-walker—and sang instead in tones virgin pure, as if the girl had been sweetened and spiritualized by the experience of love; thus idealized, the words became, says Yvette, "Botticellian."

"*Tout est superbe*," raved *Le Gaulois* of *Cligne en haut.* "*Yvette Guilbert a remporté un succès triomphal . . . On l'a rappellé bissée, trissée. Le public était insatiable.*" At the end of such ovations, when she had literally sung herself out with encores, would come the regret-ful, almost whispered, words, "*Je n'en puis plus,*"—"I am exhausted" —the deep slumping bow, and, finally, the reluctant release by her hearers.

Yvette, fortunately for an inquiring posterity, was a favorite subject for the press interview, then a journalistic innovation. One day a reporter asked her the banal question that sooner or later is asked of all stars: How does one achieve fame? Is there a formula for success? Yvette, choosing to write her reply for publication, made a frolicsome but half-ironic answer, one that was ever after quoted against her as evidence of a dominant concern for money:

Monsieur,
You ask for my formula on how to become a star. *Mon Dieu,* it is very simple.
First, I asked a louis per performance; they gave it to me.

Then   4 louis . . . they gave it to me.

  " 10 "   . . .   "   "   " " "

  " 20 "   . . .   "   "   " " "

  " 25 "   . . .   "   "   " " "

  " 35 "   . . .   "   "   " " "

. . . You see that I am revealing my entire system, and that it is not a bit complicated People think it is very difficult. Here is the proof to the contrary! But one must dare to ask; I am not timid. . . .

A thousand compliments, dear monsieur.

Yvette Guilbert

In spite of accusations of avarice leveled against her, however, it was always admitted that Yvette had "a good heart"; that she was always ready to contribute her services in behalf of those in distress. On one occasion this instinct of generosity functioned even in the face of bitter personal attack, and, by the strangest of fates, from a source she would least have expected.

The great Thérèsa, retiring because of age, had publicly disapproved the new favorite's repertoire; the songs, she said, lacked taste; in fact, they were scandalous; Yvette owed her acclaim less to talent than to her assumption of that absurd term *fin de siècle;* her popularity could not last, and the young woman had better make her financial hay while she could. Obviously Thérèsa knew nothing of how, years ago, she had been admired and impersonated by a brazen little gamine in Rue du Temple, or of how, not many months since, a stray hairpin of hers had been picked up in the dressing room of the Concert Parisien by that same gamine and cherished as a talisman. But in February, 1893, shortly after Thérèsa's strictures had appeared in the newspapers, the young star, when asked to perform at a farewell benefit at the Gaîté in honor of the old star, readily agreed. The wheel of fortune had come full turn.

At Number 2 Rue de Portalis that winter of 1892–93 the piano and the guitar were seldom silent. Not only was the divette singing nightly at the Parisien and continuing her matinees at La Bodinière, she was also accepting invitations to the saturation point to entertain in the houses of the wealthy. Count de Kerveguen and his sister had done their work well. The Princesse de Sagan had been the first to engage her, then the Marquis de Massa, the Duc de Modène, and the Marquise de Saint-Paul; after these, innumerable doors had opened, especially of those hostesses who were following the fad of the hour, "the five o'clock," and who now began to book Yvette weeks in advance for their *soirées*. Interestingly, too, it was not only Yvette's most innocent numbers that were called for at the most select five o'clocks. At these affairs, where her fame made the divette the center of attention, men flocked about her first through curiosity, then were often surprised to find themselves lingering, fascinated by her wit.

Under such constant pressure a new repertoire had to be always in process of preparation. Practice could never end. Toil, says the proverb, is the sire of fame, and Yvette, with her inherited Norman capacity for dogged, driving, systematic effort, was beginning to develop a hard-and-fast philosophy toward work.

To young De Robert, who found himself being repeatedly put off from seeing his inamorata because she was too busy, such a philosophy was irritatingly unfeminine. There was little he could do, however, except to snatch every moment she would allow: waiting in her dressing room, driving her home, calling at her apartment, accompanying her to the five o'clocks. His own journalistic work was prospering well enough—this was the year he left *L'Echo* for *Le Journal* —but he was impatient for the time when he would turn to writing the books he dreamed of. Also he chafed at finding himself held in thrall by his fruitless passion for a self-absorbed young woman, a passion that seemed to grow more absurd in proportion as its object became more unattainable. Yvette was being more and more sought after, feted. Her clothes were copied; in social circles black gloves had replaced white. Midinettes sang her airs in the streets. Her lightest word was picked up by the swarm of reporters that always followed her. It was a frustrating situation for a suitor. True, he remained her closest friend and their names were constantly linked together. But it was not enough; he strenuously insisted on being more than a friend, much more.

One day in March, 1893, Yvette received an invitation to sing for the septuagenarian composer Gounod at his home. She was flattered, but also apprehensive, for Gounod was reputed to have a crabbed tongue. A story was going the rounds that when a lady who lately rose to sing one of his songs had quavered to him: "Oh, Maestro, how frightened I am!" the old man had muttered sourly: "*Et moi aussi.*"

But the day Yvette rang the bell at his house on the elegant Place Malesherbes, looking appropriately elegant herself in a skirt of black and pink stripes and bodice of black trimmed with heavy ecru lace, she was received with such courtesy by Gounod and his entire family that she felt immediately at ease. To pay her respects gracefully, she had chosen for her first song one in which Gounod had written the musical setting for a poem by Sully Prud'homme. It is a measure of her esteem for the great man that when the last note had died away, she looked, and felt, abashed.

"Never," she confessed to him meekly, "have I regretted more my lack of musical training."

To which Gounod gravely answered:

"Never take any singing lessons. Your professor will kill your power of expression by giving you a 'pretty voice,' which means a flat voice. And then you will be one of the thousands. You will be like Judic, whose voice is pretty, charming and nothing else.... You yourself have created your own style, so preserve it."

Her heart lifted by this praise, Yvette poured out more and more songs, one after another, for almost two hours, while the Gounod family sat entranced. Finally Gounod asked for *La Coupe du roi de Thule,* from his opera *Faust.* Frightened, for this was a song she knew only by ear, she nevertheless complied with the request, Gounod following her on the piano.

". . . you have sung it admirably [he said at the end] . . . particularly I liked that intentional vagueness in the diction, for that is just the way it should be sung, as a woman would actually sing while she was doing work about the house—but that is just what my opera singers don't understand. . . ."

Then—a still greater compliment—Gounod, accompanied by one of his daughters, sang for Yvette.

A New York newspaper of February 10, 1893, had referred to Mademoiselle Yvette Guilbert as "the young woman whose success in Parisian concert halls has been so great that Russia is longing for her at Sarah Bernhardt prices," and speculated on the possibility of her being captured for the forthcoming Chicago World's Fair of 1893 "if a slight difficulty, a matter of one hundred thousand francs or twenty thousand dollars, is gotten over." On being interviewed regarding her choice between the two foreign countries, Yvette had merely shrugged. If the United States would give more for a glimpse of her than Russia, she would be happy to make the trip. However, as she tried out her English on the reporter and spoke of her intention of someday singing in English as well as French, she was perhaps not so indifferent to the results of the *pourparlers* then under way as she was pleased to pretend.

For America was the Land of the Dollar, and Yvette "dared to ask." According to every contemporary testimony, she was taking her good fortune with fingers crossed. And understandably so. Witness was not wanting to the volatility of the Parisian public; Yvette had sung at too many benefits to doubt that fact; and she had herself already felt the critics' stab when her repertoire had faltered ever so slightly. To reap the harvest then where the stand of grain was thickest; to seize the day, since there well might be no morrow—these were her frank objectives. Reporters, who never tired of asking her about her earnings, found her still willing to talk freely, if perhaps not always accurately. Whether the variations to be found in the astronomic sums quoted in the press of those days stem from a divette's mood of the moment or a reporter's carelessness it would be impossible now to establish. As time went on, Yvette would learn to exploit more and more deliberately the topic of her fabulous earnings; she may even have believed that it was something people demanded to hear about, part of her legend, on which it would not be good policy to be silent.

Meantime, it was generally considered most unusual that she continued to live so quietly in the Rue de Portalis, and especially that she still refused to wear jewels. The only new feature in her way of life had been her purchase the previous year of a country home. Léon Sari had fallen on evil days, and when his estate in Vaux, where she had so frequently been a guest in her student days and for which she had always felt a strong attraction, came on the market, she had promptly bought it. It was an ugly enough house, with an agglomeration of bastard-chalet gables, confusing roof lines and ungainly chimneys; in bad repair, too; she had to make extensive improvements. She also added new stables, and their red-tile roofs brightened up the green of the fields. Here, enclosed in white fences, she could keep the two superb black horses presented to her by a gentleman in whose house she sang one evening. She liked the Seine rolling nearby, and the fruit garden that adjoined the house, where grapes hung on the arbors and peaches loaded the trees in August; and she enjoyed her new role of chatelaine and the novelty of being photographed with a gentle brindle cow, though she did not go as far as another queen and play milkmaid. Her dear Maurice Donnay owned an estate, "La Prieure," within four kilometers. Zola was even nearer; from her upstairs windows could be seen "Medan," with its several houses, each named after one of his books; and Zola himself often pedaled by, looking, she thought, more like a seedy lawyer than a celebrated writer. The spot was sightly and open, and it gratified a slum child's passion for the sun. Symbolically, too, it must have meant the sun to one who barely six years before had been a self-conscious nobody on the lawn and today was the self-possessed proprietor.

From a practical standpoint "La Rive," as she called it, was ideal. Here Albine could be installed each summer, and from here Yvette could easily travel back and forth by train to Paris and her engagements. Although during the period of Yvette's rapid rise to wealth Albine was seldom seen or mentioned by the press in connection with her limelighted daughter, her domestic influence had remained constant. Love for her mother continued to be Yvette's dominant motivation.

There were so many years that I suffered at the sight of my widowed mother, always working, always watching out for me, always fatigued, and especially always weeping over our two lives, that at the age of twenty . . . I could see nothing in the world more indispensable, more pressing, than to lighten her efforts, and twenty francs a day represented to me the end of her struggles and the beginning of her rest. So when I earned them for the first time, . . . what joy! . . . I was and I still am what the *boulevardiers* . . . call a mamma's girl. Yes, indeed. . . . Filial love is an ideal, like any other.

One wonders whether Louis de Robert was ever aware of the obsessive nature of this filial love; of its possible rivalry to his own suit. Perhaps not, since he himself in later years was to wear a leash of the same silver cord.

To indulge Albine's Norman passion for fine needlework, Yvette, now that she was rich, began spending large sums of money on embroidered lingerie for her mother. Some thirty thousand francs, she claimed; or even allowing for exaggeration, still probably an extravagant amount. It makes an interesting vignette—the picture of an aging peasant woman, whose hands could no longer hold a needle or whose eyes see to use one, bending in delight over her tardy hoard of finery; fingering with a connoisseur's enjoyment the pieces that she must have known she would probably never live long enough to wear; perhaps even wondering which old neighbors in the Marais may have worked the exquisite designs.

Chapter 10

On January 23, 1893, a relatively unknown Italian tragedienne—unknown, at least, to the theater publics of Paris and London, which were what counted—opened, with almost no preliminary fanfare, in the Fifth Avenue Theater in New York. The play, audaciously, was *La Dame aux Camélias,* in which the newcomer was to all intents throwing down the gauntlet to Sarah. Eleonora Duse had been seen earlier in a tour of South America and, more recently, in a few European capitals, in each of which she had received an enthusiastic press. Critical comparisons of her Italianate concept of the role of Marguerite Gauthier and Bernhardt's Gallic one had brought the challenger off usually the winner. Personal qualities, too, had demanded respect—a deep sincerity and humility, a certain sad dignity, and an utter lack of showiness.

Not that the name of Duse was free from gossip. Far from it. There were plenty of open references to the illegitimate infant that had died. It was also public knowledge that her marriage with sober, middle-aged Tebaldo Checchi had broken up over her affair with Flavio Andò, director and leading man of her company. That the Andò fire had subsequently cooled was not so well known, since for pecuniary reasons it was considered wiser for the stage lovers to continue in the public mind as prototypes of the real. There was also that matter of her relationship of long standing with composer-librettist Boito. And other liaisons were hinted at.

Duse's American debut took place during a brilliant period of New York theatrical history, in a city accustomed to diversified stage fare. Through the entire nineteenth century, from the time of the famous Park Theater down, New York audiences had known no dearth of excellent entertainment. Scores of distinguished transatlantic singers and players had trooped across their boards, including many of Duse's own compatriots—Mario, Salvini, Ristori. Those were the palmy days of great managers, great companies, great stars, if not always great plays, and all in the grand tradition. In the New York scene Duse's producers, the brothers Carl and Theodor Rosenfeld, whom Odell refers to as "manager-adventurers," were alert, ambitious, rising young men of the theater, recently come over from Berlin, who had sensed the increasing importance of the new Italian personality and through their connections with the Continental agent Tänczner had signed her and her company for an American tour.

The tour, unfortunately, began as something of a nightmare for the star. To provide herself with a little time for rest before the New York opening, Duse had elected to sail alone, in advance of her troupe. It was a harrowing trip, in vilest winter weather, and when she walked down the gangplank in New York, looking ill, dowdy, and untheatric, the Rosenfelds, waiting for her on the pier, failed to recognize her and she was obliged to drive unattended to her hotel, almost overcome with desolation. But these were only the first of many jarring experiences. She hated the tumult of New York. She was frustrated by the language barrier. Worst of all, she was constantly being infuriated by what she considered the intrusion of the press upon her privacy and she was sickened by their vulgarity. In vain her managers reminded her that Sarah had dripped treacle to New York newsmen; that in America even royalty would run risks in not answering silly questions good-naturedly. Too late she found the warning true; on opening night her snubs were reflected in rows of empty seats.

As producers, the Rosenfelds well knew the hairline of emotional tolerance that must not be crossed with any prima donna, and it can be imagined with what anxiety they noted the worsening state of mind of their Duse. Here was an artist of hypersensitivity, already disturbed to the danger point by the hardships of her journey and the uncongeniality of her surroundings, and now humiliated by a lame opening. In spite of critical approval, the New York public was anything but won. Also the managers must have feared for the hazards of the road tour that lay ahead—Chicago, in turmoil with its Exposition; Boston, capable of being chillier than New York, both in temperature and social climate. Even under normal circumstances, Duse was known to be mercurial, her artistry varying from performance to performance. Now, unless this resentful, discouraged, homesick woman could be somehow reassured, the situation might easily deteriorate into downright failure.

Luckily, somewhere in their fevered deliberations, Carl and Theodor Rosenfeld had the inspiration of where to turn for help: brother-in-law Max.

Max Schiller and his sister Rose, wife of Theodor, both born in Jassy, Roumania, were the two youngest children of Aaron and Bertha Schiller-Wechsler. For generations the ancestral roots of the Schiller-Wechsler family had gone deep into Eastern European culture and tradition. Max and Rose's maternal grandfather had been chief banker of the Regent of that part of Roumania called Walachia, famous for horsebreeding, and at the beginning of the nineteenth century, when Roumanian Jews enjoyed considerable liberties, was reputed to have been very prosperous, even a landowner; a man who built his own synagogue and behaved in a grandseigneurial manner. After 1866, however, when the Roumanian government took away citizenship from Jews, and persecution and confiscations ensued, the history of Aaron and Bertha and their six children became one of reduced circumstances and uneasy living. After three years in Czernowitz, then under Austrian rule, they removed to Berlin. Of his fortune Aaron had still remaining only some three hundred thousand marks, and most of this he lost, little by little, on the stock exchange, the family all the time struggling to retain, in spite of creeping penury, what shreds they could of former elegant ways of life.

Max, a dreamy, sensitive youth, had always wanted to become a violinist, but his father boxed his ears and ordered him instead to enter a course in chemistry. This led him in due time to a doctor's degree, after which he obtained a position in a Berlin biochemical factory and, as the months went by, apparently became so well oriented as a scientist that his father must have believed him thoroughly cured of all that early nonsense about music.

But the staid career of the rising young biochemist suffered an interruption one day in 1892 when he received a letter from his brother-in-law Theodor Rosenfeld in faraway America. Max's sister Rose, newly pregnant, was acutely unhappy in a strange land; could Max come to New York for a few months to keep her spirits up until the confinement should be well over? As to temporary employment he need not worry. The Rosenfeld brothers had many enterprises afoot. Only the year before, cherishing dreams of reviving a German theater for the benefit of New York's fast-growing German population, they had re-opened the old Thalia, where German plays had first appeared in 1879. That very year they were also producing at the famous Union Square Theater, and—their trump card—they would shortly introduce the Italian newcomer Duse at the Fifth Avenue. Nor were these prospects all; there were others. With the plentiful grist going through their mill, certainly Max could find occupation.

It was an appeal not to be refused, and scientist Max Schiller (the Wechsler had by that time been dropped) set out as soon as he could on this unforeseen excursion to the New World, as it was then called.

Max, just turned thirty-two, was handsome and amiable, cultured and intelligent, and women found him irresistible. To endearing qualities of perception and tact the final touch of charm was added by his beautifully polished Continental manners. While he apparently made no effort to interest women, they turned to him like flowers to the sun, seeming to recognize instinctively in his warm personality a tenderness and understanding to meet their deepest needs. If in him they also vaguely suspected a fundamental weakness under all the attractive overlay, they seemed not to mind; young Dr. Schiller was the very image of any fastidious woman's dream.

In the present emergency with the emotionally disturbed Duse, the Rosenfelds must then have blessed the happy fate that had only so recently put this paragon on their staff. Here would be the ideal person to represent their management and at the same time stand as buffer between Duse's sensitivity and American crassness. Moreover, Max was a linguist. He could converse with Duse in French and so supply her yearning for sympathetic human contact. Someone would have to travel with the company on those rigorous road engagements, and who better fitted than he?

No account exists of the meeting of Max and Eleonora. Records indicate, however, an improvement in La Duse's spirits and an extension of the tour into April.

Years, many years, afterward, a record of another kind was made, first in the memory, and later still in the letters, of the child Eva, born to Rose and Theodor that eventful year of 1892. Sitting in the Grand Hotel in Paris one night in the 1940's, Dr. Eva Rosenfeld, then a famous London psychologist, listened to a very old man, looking backward long after Duse's death and just before his own, as he described the love affair and eventual liaison that grew up between himself and the lonely Eleonora in the weeks and months that followed their meeting. To a passionate woman of the theater, homesick for Europe and hungry for congenial companionship, it may well have seemed that the handsome young Roumanian-German who so urbanely anticipated her every need was the only civilized creature in the whole raw and detestable American landscape.

In Paris, Guilbert and Bernhardt and Duse soon thereafter began to move closer in their orbits, closer to the day of inevitable general comparison with each other; all three so diverse in character, yet all to become in the public mind so nearly equal in magnitude and so closely associated. That Sarah's days of unqualified praise were drawing to a close had already been suggested in London in 1892; Duse's subtle charm meantime had just begun to extend beyond Italy, and Guilbert's fame to spill over the boundaries of France.

In March, 1893, Sarah had dropped in on Paris only long enough to buy the Théâtre de la Renaissance and be off again, this time to South America, on the last lap of her second world tour, one that ended in September in Lisbon.

"Have you heard about the fortune Bernhardt brought back!" everyone was gossiping. "Three and a half million francs!"

That same month of March, when it was announced in the Paris papers one day that Guilbert was not to renew her contract with the Parisien, Madame Allemand lost no time in calling at 2 Rue de Portalis. Perhaps now the divette would lend an ear to the son-in-law at La Scala. Five hundred francs a night she offered.

"Six hundred," replied Yvette.

"But, my child, you are on the wane," sniffed Madame.

"Then you should not be offering five hundred. When you sent me away from the Eldorado and I was earning six hundred francs a month, I said I would come back to you only if you gave me six hundred francs a night. And six hundred it shall be."

Yvette had wreaked her vengeance on the Casino at Lyons; now she was obdurate in fulfilling also her mad prophecy with La Allemand. In the end the agitated plumes and the noisy bracelets could only admit defeat. It was still a bargain well worth making for Allemand and Marchand, for the Eldorado had already captured the popular star Judic, and with Yvette snared for La Scala there would be little else for these canny impresarios to do but sit at receipt of custom. As a street ditty put it:

Judic regne à l'Eldorado,
À La Scala triomphe Yvette
(Do, ré, mi, fa, sol, la, si, do.)
Judic regne à l'Eldorado
Sur ces deux divas, ridendo,
Taillons une simple bavette.
Judic regne à l'Eldorado,
À La Scala triomphe Yvette.

The contract that was signed in March, 1893, to begin the following September 29, was for a period of three years, four months a year in two periods of two months each, to permit the diva Yvette time for foreign travel—Zidler's advice of long standing—and the right to appear for two months elsewhere in Paris in the summer.

In accepting the La Scala offer Yvette had not lost in prestige. La Scala, 13 Boulevard de Strasbourg, almost opposite the Eldorado, was, like the Eldorado, a real theater, with the conventional interior design of orchestra seats, boxes, and galleries. In both houses elaborate revues were presented, "splendidly mounted," says Gaston Jollivet, "and with magnificent choruses. In fact, there is little to choose between these establishments and others labeled theaters, except that here patrons are permitted to smoke and keep on their hats." Because of its excellent bills, La Scala attracted a public of better than average means.

The beloved Steins of the Horloge had sold their pavilion the previous year to M. and Mme. Debasta, a couple whom Yvette found crude and distasteful. Madame was, like La Goulue, an ex-washerwoman. Monsieur was "dark, handsome, becurled, with waxed moustache, and flashing black eyes, a real Don Juan lady killer." With his jewels and his hair oil and his bright yellow gloves. Yvette found him so obnoxious that her heart "curdled" inside her whenever he came near. When, in the summer of 1892, Debasta had offered voluntarily to renew her contract at a thumping raise—one thousand francs a night—Yvette became suspicious. Such generosity could hardly spring from good will; there must be reasons not appearing on the surface. But when she played for time before signing, as she had with Madame Allemand, Debasta angrily refused. Sign now or never, he snapped.

"Never, then," said Yvette coolly.

The next day, while she was lunching at the Ambassadeurs across the street, Pierre Ducarre, the manager, came to her table and made an offer of fifty thousand francs for his *caf'-conc'* for the next season. Debasta's real motives thus came to light. Don Juan had somehow learned of Ducarre's intentions and had hoped to forestall his rival by an unheard-of sixty thousand and a quick signature on the line. In spite of the difference in salary, Zidler, who had never approved the Horloge, strongly advised his ward to sign with Ducarre; Ducarre, he said, was a thoroughly decent sort.

Then [Yvette relates] there happened to me something unique in the annals of the theatre: Debasta on hearing of this business realized my dislike of him, and not being able to prevent my escape (as I was going to his rival for less money) actually offered me the same sum of 50,000 francs to come to the Champs-Élysées and do nothing at all, not sing a note! He was ready to buy my silence.

Les Ambassadeurs, at which Yvette made her formal debut June 2, 1893, was large and animated, and the ultimate in chic. In May, the audiences were notoriously noisy; singers had to be engaged for their lungs, dancers for their abandon.

Elise Faure [writes Yvette] yelled above the orchestra and overcame as best she could the yells, the catcalls, the banging of saucers, the clinking of spoons, the choruses bellowed by the audience, and when Violette, the dancer, came on the rowdier sports used to call out: "Take off your drawers!" "Higher!" "Let's see!"

And Paulus! One night he was so furious that he called out: "If you *must* sing, then for God's sake keep in time with me."

But with the opening of the real season in June, the atmosphere immediately changed. When the racing season brought the world of fashion to Paris, audiences became cosmopolitan and observed ordinary decorum—barring perhaps the night of the Grand Prix.

The garden was particularly agreeable. Says Mack, "One would think oneself in a great park, a guest at some royal fete." The restaurant was on a raised terrace at the rear, overlooking the open-air rows of seats, with a roofed stage at the far end. On stormy nights a huge tarpaulin was stretched over the orchestra, but though this served to keep spectators dry, it also functioned as a drum on which

126

heavy rain could sometimes drown out the voices of the entertainers.

Yvette opened at Les Ambassadeurs with a grisly piece called *La Danse Macabre des Foetus*, a tidbit of horror with which its author MacNab had once chilled hearers at the Chat Noir. The preoccupation of poets with the macabre was not new—one thinks, for example, of George Moore's "Ode to a Dead Body" in the 1870's—but to the audiences of the Champs Élysées MacNab's verses were nothing short of revolting.

> At the mere sound of the title, at the very first words [Yvette writes], the women would sit up in horror and the men stiff and pained. Horrible memories of carbolic, of midwives, of hopes and disappointments, would rise to their minds and could be read in every face. . . .
>
> Unforgettable those nightmarish pictures, this fresco of imps so ludicrously soaking in spirits of wine! How can one help laughing at what we are before we begin to weep over what we shall some day become? Oh, these fruits of love! grotesque figures, evoked under the great trees of the Champs Élysées that dappled my face with green as though it was lit up by the chemist's colored flagons. It was uncanny.

Far more palatable than the "fresco of imps" the patrons at Les Ambassadeurs found Donnay's fresco of *Les Vieux Messieurs*, an unsparing description of aging rogues who cannot give up their perennial pursuit of very young girls:

> *Plus laids que de prêtres boudhistes,*
> *Ils s'en vont suivant les modistes*
> *Avec les airs astucieux*
> *Les vieux Messieurs.*
> *Cachochymes et rachitiques*
> *Ils s'en vont le long des boutiques,*
> *Lorgnant les trottins vicieux*
> *Les vieux Messieurs.*

They even loathingly approved Jules Jouy's savage *La Pierreuse*. Typical of Yvette's "song with the shiver," this was another tale of beheading in which, as in *Ma Tête*, Yvette dared again to bring the guillotine on stage. But from a different standpoint. In *Ma Tête* the hearer is identified with the victim of the guillotine; in *La Pierreuse* with an observer.

A *pierreuse* is a garrotter's decoy. The song describes one of these harpies prowling about the fortifications of Paris at night, entrapping a belated passer-by in conversation, then summoning her accomplice by the weird cry *Pi-ouit!* The apache-murderer is caught and sentenced to death, and the song describes his execution as witnessed by his sweetheart, La Pierreuse, as she callously mingles with the crowd at La Roquette. Her eyes follow her lover as he appears at the prison door, accompanied by the priest trying to console him. But he has no spirit; he collapses and has to be carried to his bloody end.

> J' l'aperçois la-bas ... sous la porte ...
> Le curé lui parle sans témoins ...
> Sur la bascule, il faut qu'on l'porte
> Un camarade l'appelle de loin ...
>   Pi-ouit!
> Y n'y a a pas l'temps de l'dire deux fois
> On l'couche sur la chose en bois!
> Tirlipiton! Hue donc! Aie donc!
> L'bourreau tire le cordon;
> La tête, le tronc
> Tombent, dans l'panier de son;
> C'que, ca s'fait vite!
>   Pi-ouit!

Bernard Shaw, some years later reviewing a performance of this song, wrote:

> ... the subsequent operations are described in a perfect war dance of a refrain ... the last verse describes ... the guillotining of the robber; and so hideously exquisite is the singing of this verse that you can see the woman in the crowd at La Roquette; you hear the half-choked repetition of the familiar signal with which she salutes the wretch as he is hurried out; you positively see his head flying off; above all, you feel with a shudder how the creature's impulses of terror and grief are overcome by the bestial excitement of seeing the great State show of killing a man in the most sensational way. Just as people would not flog children if they could realize the true effect of the ceremony on the child's pet playmates, to whom it is supposed to be a wholesome warning, so the French Govern-

ment would certainly abolish public executions . . . if they would go and hear Mlle. Guilbert sing "La Pierreuse."

It may have been as early as Divan Japonais days when the English essayist and critic Arthur Symons first lost his heart to Yvette, and throughout her career he remained her faithful rhapsodist. As early as 1892 he was writing in the *St. James's Gazette:*

Now to me Yvette Guilbert was exquisite from the first moment. "Exquisite!" I said under my breath, as I first saw her come upon the stage. She sang *Sainte Galette,* and as I listened . . . I felt a cold shiver run down my back, that *frisson* which no dramatic art, save that of Sarah Bernhardt, had ever given me. I had heard about her, but it was not quite this that I was expecting, so poignant, so human, that I could scarcely endure the pity of it. . . . It must be said too that she can do pure comedy—that she can be merely, deliciously gay. There is one of her songs in which she laughs, chuckles, and trills a rapid flurry of broken words and phrases, with the sudden, spontaneous, irresponsible mirth of a bird. But where she is most herself is in a manner of tragic comedy which has never been seen on the music-hall stage from the beginning. It is the profoundly sad and essentially serious comedy which one sees in Forain's marvellous designs—those rapid outlines which, with a turn of a pencil, give you the whole existence of those base sections of society which our art in England is mainly forced to ignore. People call the art of Forain immoral, they call Yvette Guilbert's songs immoral. That is merely the conventional misuse of a conventional word. . . . She brings before you the real life drama of the streets, of the pot-house; she shows you the seamy side of life behind the scenes; she calls things by their right names. But there is not a touch of sensuality about her, she is neither contaminated nor contaminating by what she sings; she is simply a great, impersonal dramatic artist, who sings realism as others write it.

In . . . *Sainte Galette,* she represents a denizen of the Quartier Bréda praying in her room, at nightfall, to "Our Lady of Cash"— the great omnipotent "Sainte Galette.". . . And as Yvette Guilbert sings, in her quiet, thrilling voice, which becomes harsher, for effect, in the lower notes, which becomes a moan, in that recurrent cry of "Sainte Galette," it is the note of sheer tragedy that she strikes. She literally shook me; she made me shiver; she brought tears to my eyes. . . .

The difference between Yvette Guilbert and every other singer on the variety stage is the difference between Sarah Bernhardt and every other actress. . . . The word "creation" has come to have a casual enough meaning in regard to any new performance on the stage, but in this case it is an epithet of simple justice. This new, subtle tourmentée way of singing the miseries of the poor and the vices of the miserable is absolutely a creation; it brings at once a new order of subject and a novel manner of presentment into the comic repertoire, and it lifts the entertainment of the music-hall into a really high region of art.

Next season at La Scala, Yvette introduced Jean Lorrain's sensational *La Morphinée;* the theme abnormality, the story that of a morphine addict who brushes both love and death. This perverse poem contains heartbreaking and terrible moments, suggesting hidden elements in a human spirit longing to escape from fantasy and hallucination. Its rush of passionately rebellious words sweeps the audience along on a dark tide of horrified sympathy.

> *J'peux plus dormir; dès qu'il fait noir*
> *J'vois grouiller un tas d'choses dans l'sombre*
> *Des chauves-souris, des grands yeux d'ombre*
> *Puis des rats comme dans l'Assommoir.*
>
> *Alors j'prends l'flacon qui console*
> *Vite une piqûre et ça m'remet*
> *C'est d'puis c'matin ma troisième fiole*
> *J'm'en déshabitu'rai jamais.*
>
> *Si j'vis comme une hallucinée*
> *C'est d'puis qu'un homme m'a plantée là*
> *Ca m'a chaviré l'coeur . . . voilà*
> *D'autres boivent, moi, je m'suis morphinée.*
>
> *La morphin'! Mais c'est un peu d'rêve,*
> *Un peu d'oubli! L'oubli, c'est tout.*

Paris was stunned by the song. Edmond de Goncourt praised it; Burne-Jones longed to paint the singer; the Duke of Serbia paid his homage by kissing the singer's hand. Of it Symons wrote:

La Morphinée is sheer tragedy: . . . it tells all the horrors of a life enslaved by morphine . . . the rise of the voice, into a dull, yet intense monotony, at the words "*je suis hallucinée*," is one of the most thrilling effects that even Yvette has ever obtained. The whole thing—sordid, horrible, crazed, as it is—is, as a piece of acting, incomparably expressive, and it is always restrained within the severest artistic limits.

Yvette herself apparently did not at first fully realize what psychological depths she was probing in her songs that made vice seem immediate and understandable. To every casual hearer she seemed to be suggesting that it is an element lurking close to the surface in each human personality, secretly cherished; that in given circumstances any man or woman may become as abandoned as any one of her most immoral examples; that dark forces exist, inextricably tangled in the webs of the soul, prepared to attack at any moment the serene cosmos of spirit and reduce it to chaos. Beware, beware of yourselves, she seemed to be saying. What profound chords of guilt these songs of abnormality must have been striking were evidenced by the intensity of her audience response; it was a fearsome thought—the instability of one's own will to escape evil. That she herself could participate and yet seem to stand aloof, both observer and observed, seemed to critics not the least extraordinary feature of these evocations of horror.

The autumn of '93 was mad with work, including in October a double-starred bill at the Folies-Bergère featuring both Judic and Guilbert. In November the bill was triple-starred by the addition of the sensational American dancer, Loie Fuller, clad only in scarf and flames. In December, under terms of her contract with La Scala, Yvette was free for a short tour.

It was the dead of winter in the Roumanian city of Bucharest. The new red, white, and gold Théâtre des Variétés which Yvette was supposed to inaugurate was not quite ready, and she was obliged to appear instead in the Grand Pavilion, a former Exposition building, lighted for the emergency only by hundreds of candles. At the end of the concert, the candles were distributed to the audience, and a crowd of men, in high, gleaming boots and tall astrakhan caps, escorted her carriage through the snowy streets all the way back to her hotel, with much good-natured shouting and singing, the lighted tapers tossing all about her in the night.

It was when she reached Vienna that Yvette first heard the name of Eleanora Duse. Everywhere she looked along the elegant promenade of the Ring, she was startled to see huge posters reading: *Au Ronacher, Théâtre des Variétés, à 10 heures, Yvette Guilbert, la Duse de la Chanson*. Still unsophisticated enough to mistake a Viennese banker's flamboyantly uniformed and plumed concierge for a royal personage, Yvette was equally limited in her knowledge of theatrical figures outside Paris, and immediately her ego was outraged. Who, the darling of the Paris boulevards demanded, blazing into the office of the theater, was this Duse? Why should the celebrated name of Guilbert be associated with that name?

When she reached Brussels she discovered why. She attended the theater where Duse was playing the lady of the camellias and within five minutes was spellbound: "I was . . . hypnotized by this strange woman who suffered, bled, died for love. Coming out of the theatre, I sat till two in the morning writing an article for the *Indépendance Belge*. My article was accepted, and Duse never forgot it."

With her always exquisite courtesy, Duse sent Yvette a note of thanks for the tribute, and it was this incident that laid the foundation for the deep friendship that sprang up between the two women.

Years later, in referring to her outburst in Vienna, how freely Yvette admitted her *niaiserie*: ". . . *et j'étais bête, et j'étais idiote, et j'étais ignare, et j'étais ridicule . . . Mais j'étais comme ça*"; how humbly she acknowledged that in point of fact the shoe was on the other foot: ". . . *que l'honneur était pour moi très grand qu'on voulut bien rapprocher mon nom de celui de cette unique créature.*"

Chapter 11

The years 1893 and 1894 were ones of great inspiration for the crippled artist-gnome who had adopted every milieu of the amusement world of *fin-de-siècle* Paris as his own—dance hall, cabaret, race track, circus, *maison close,* theater, opera—and from each was cynically delineating on his easel an astonishing range of astonishing models.

Frankly interested in what he called phenomena, this dissolute historian of low life, whose "scrutiny of music hall and haunts of vice compared to Baudelaire's," could hardly have escaped being intrigued by the racy appearance and personality of La Guilbert. Though Lautrec had known her in a general way since Moulin Rouge days—had even sketched her incidentally as in the Jane Avril poster—suddenly he became, as it were, intoxicated by her, preferring her, according to his friend Gustave Coquiot, to all other models. From show to show he followed his new idol, and from song to song. But when he submitted to her in July, 1894, a sketch of a poster he proposed making of her—the one now preserved in the Musée Albi, "which shows her full face, the neck *brandi,* the mouth teasing, the eyebrows in circumflex accent, the hands widespread, one little finger lifted, detailing a couplet that one guesses is obscene"—Yvette was annoyed. "Don't make me so frightfully ugly," she wrote pettishly, returning the sketch.

Lautrec accordingly put aside the poster, but not the subject. His pursuit of her did not slacken. He drew her in the wings; entering or leaving stage; bowing; singing; full face and profile; each sketch capturing and holding some vivid moment, flashing it out in delicate but sure strokes.

One can only speculate as to why such an obsessive interest in Yvette should have seized Lautrec at this time. Claude Roger-Marx believes that this man, burdened with deformity, was more receptive to the exceptional than the normal, to inharmony than harmony. It is clear that he was fascinated by the sordid and the cruel; that it was often among the artificial or the vulgar or the impure that he sought his truth. In this cult of ugliness Yvette's philosophy was demonstrably pacing his own; as much of his painting dealt with "horrible creatures, the larvae of vice and poverty," so also did many of Yvette's songs. In spite of the fact, therefore, that her extreme height and slenderness offered the widest possible contrast to Lautrec's cruelly stunted physique, Roger-Marx suggests that the artist, as he listened to her satirical character probings, may have experienced the eerie sensation that he was gazing into a mirror; that in this extraordinary woman he was face to face with nothing less than a *café-concert* Lautrec.

As to style, Roger-Marx observes:

Between his style and Yvette's the parallelism is constant. Sweetness and ferocity, triviality and refinement, phlegm and *outrance* have equal part in their designs, for Yvette designs herself each night, and it is precisely the *jeu* that plays from the crown of her red head to the tips of the gloves, the leaps of humor modeling a face whose proportions change constantly, which incite that other mime —the painter—to suggest and fix this mobility and dynamism.

Yvette was not flattered by Lautrec's preoccupation with her as model; in fact, she continued to be revolted by his representations of her and incensed that of all his stage models she should be the only one singled out for actual caricature. Poster artist Chéret, Bac, Sinet were men she could understand; to them she would entrust the work of showering the walls of Paris with prettifications of her face and figure. With originality, a wealth of fantasy, and sureness of touch she had caricatured herself through her standardized stage "silhouette," emphasizing her excessive height, flat chest, clown's pallor, wide red mouth, and black gloves, but she could not readily enjoy the same techniques of exaggeration when employed against her by a painter. Nor was she ever able to understand that she and Lautrec—to whom incidentally she at first attached little importance—were following their research into "character and epic deformation" with almost the same methods, animated by the very same comic demon.

Yvette first met Lautrec the day Donnay brought him to her home for luncheon, when his unexpectedly hideous aspect, she says, so shocked her footman and her mother that social amenities temporarily suffered.

A dark enormous head, the face high-complexioned and very black of beard; oily, greasy skin; a nose large enough for two; and a mouth—a mouth like a cut from ear to ear, looking almost like an open wound! The flesh of the lips thick and violet-pink, flattened and indecent-looking! I am struck dumb, and then my eyes plunge into those of Lautrec. Oh, how beautiful they are, large, wide, full of warmth, surprisingly bright and full of light!

As I continue to look into his eyes, Lautrec, aware of my gaze, snatches off his glasses. He knows his one redeeming feature and offers it to me wholeheartedly.

Then follows a description of the bizarre luncheon scene, where Yvette's anxiety as to how she should seat this dwarf at an ordinary dinner table was solved by his prompt, agile leap onto his chair. Although his chin was only a few inches above the cloth, he was able to plunge the food, she says, into "that gash of a mouth. . . . When the fish came with the *rémoulade* sauce there was a sound of splashing."

One of Lautrec's characteristics, as everyone knew, was his habit of taking up residence, from time to time, for long periods in various brothels. One day he explained to Yvette his reasons for seeking out such depraved environments; he wanted, he said, to witness the breaking down of the barriers of reserve, to probe the feelings of the inmates.

He often declared: "Everywhere and always there is beauty, even in ugliness; it is thrilling to discover it where no one else has yet noticed it." On other occasions, cynical and pained, he would say that Don Juans were just "beasts of love with women and lovers merely demented animals."

"Oh, yes, love, love!" Lautrec would say. "You can sing it in every key, Yvette, but my dear, hold your nose . . . love, my poor Yvette, love *doesn't exist*." And he rapped out each syllable.

". . . And you should see the faces they make! Look here! Here are some loves and some lovers; just look at 'em!" And he opened a little album where the sellers and buyers of love were crucified, stigmatized without mercy, crudely, horribly, deliberately deformed by him, while he delighted in their bestiality. . . . It was as if they avenged him for his physical deformities while he chuckled: "Eh, what mugs they've got, these Romeos and Juliets!"

On another occasion, when Yvette was looking at some of his drawings of herself which she considered distortions as savage as those of the brothels, she could not control her irritation.

"Really, Lautrec," she exploded, "you are the genius of deformity!" To this typically Guilbertian lack of tact, Lautrec made a frigidly formal bow and replied with cutting courtesy: "*Mais naturellement!*" It irked Yvette that Lautrec had never presented her with any of his sketches of her, as so many other artists had done, and one day when he was at her house she asked him outright for a drawing of herself; she had a whim for having one made into a tile for a tea-table top. Lautrec responded by still another caricature, which he offered to her to autograph, and at sight of which her temper flared again. "Little monster!! You have made a horror of me!!" she inscribed heartlessly on the drawing. However, when she eventually received a completed plaque bearing the design, epithet and all, she accepted it, testament as it was to her scorpion tongue.

The climax of the touchy situation between artist and divette came in 1894 with the publication, without her permission, of Lautrec's *L'Album: Yvette Guilbert,* with text by Gustave Geffroy, a collection so uniformly unflattering that both Albine and Jean Lorrain urged Yvette to sue the artist for defamation. Fortunately, discerning critical comment appeared in the press in time to prevent her from committing such a colossal blunder. When in *La Justice* of September Georges Clemenceau wrote in high praise of the artistry of the lithographs, her anger abated to a point where she was even willing to autograph copies.

It was a rugged relationship, the Lautrec-Guilbert one; no softness, only a relentless give and take; half friendship, half enmity.

In 1894 an obscure French army officer, a Captain Alfred Dreyfus, was court-martialed for espionage. Dreyfus, a Jew, protested his innocence, and charges of anti-Semitism, leveled against the army, began to resound through the country. Incredible bitterness sprang up between Dreyfusards and anti-Dreyfusards. "For one who did not live through the poignant days of 1894 and 1895," reminisces man-about-town André de Fouquières, "it is difficult to imagine the climate of the Affair—the polemics, the duels, the lawsuits, the ruptures of friendship engendered by the accusation and condemnation of Captain Dreyfus. Was he a puppet in the hands of powerful personages?" After the trial was over and the Captain had been removed to Devils Island to begin serving his sentence, the fiery controversy died down a little, but, unhappily for the army, the embers continued to smolder and refused to die completely.

Louis de Robert became embroiled on behalf of Dreyfus, but there is no record that the prodigious Affair made any impact on Yvette, the reason being perhaps that the year 1894 was proving an *annus mirabilis* in her personal life. The overtures that had been made to her earlier for a command performance at Marlborough House had not materialized because, as gossip had it, she had overreached herself in the matter of the fee. But the time had now come when, with her star invincibly in the ascendant, she actually would sing for Albert Edward, and at an even higher figure.

One night while she was playing at La Scala, a telephone message was relayed to her dressing room from the Bristol Hotel in Cannes.

Could she come in two days' time to sing at a private party? She might name her own fee. Yvette's relayed answer was routine: she regretted that it would be impossible to interrupt her booking at La Scala. Immediately another call came through, this time to the manager, M. Marchand, who made the same reply, only more sharply. Nevertheless, the cheeky caller from Cannes insisted on a personal word with Mademoiselle Guilbert herself.

When Yvette, thoroughly annoyed, was finally brought to the manager's phone, she demanded of the Bristol: "Who on earth is the ignoramus who can't understand that when I am actually playing in Paris I can't possibly leave Paris?"

"Mrs. Ogden Goelet, an American," was the reply.

"I don't know her!" snapped Yvette.

The Bristol Hotel speaker launched into panegyrics on Mrs. Goelet's wealth and social status. The occasion was to be a dinner party, and the point was reiterated that money was no object.

Marchand, fidgeting nearby and half-hearing the monologue pouring over the wires, finally whispered: "Call this fellow's bluff! Quote him a fee that will shut him up!"

"How much?" Yvette whispered back.

"Fifteen thousand francs!"

Promptly lending herself to the joke, Yvette interrupted the flood of persuasion. "But Monsieur, I cannot stir from Paris for less than fifteen thousand francs!"

"Agreed!" said Cannes delightedly. "Fifteen thousand!" And while divette and manager stared at each other thunderstruck, through the telephone receiver poured further voluble explanation that the Prince of Wales would be guest of honor at the dinner party, and it was he who had expressed a particular desire to hear Mademoiselle Guilbert.

On the appointed night in the Goelet drawing room in Cannes, after being strictly cautioned by her hostess to submit only her "least risqué" songs, Yvette was presented to the Prince.

Very respectfully I bowed and took the hand he held out. He stopped a moment to look at me closely, then said, *"Quelle distinction, mademoiselle. Cela vaut une célébrité,"*. . .

At last my turn came to sing. I rose and went to the piano; the Prince of Wales followed me and took a chair near me. He continued to smile at me in a friendly fashion during my first "select" songs; then . . . speaking low so that no one else could hear: "Dear Mlle Guilbert, why don't you let me hear your songs of Montmartre? I have read so many articles about your way of interpreting the spirit of the Chat Noir."

"Your Highness, I am somewhat puzzled by what you say, for Mrs. Goelet has asked me on your account to sing songs *pour jeunes filles*." The Prince laughed so heartily that there was a sudden silence among the guests; he took advantage of it to say that he would ask to be allowed to suggest the songs he would like to hear. Everyone heartily agreed, and the Prince, leaning on the piano, asked for the most delightfully Parisian items of my *répertoire*.

When the evening was over, the Prince, with his characteristic affability, said to Yvette, "You must tell me, Mademoiselle, if there is ever anything I can do for you."

"I am soon coming to London," the young lady who dared to ask replied unhesitatingly. "Will Your Highness give me your patronage?"

The timing for the Cannes incident, which took place March 14, could not have been more propitious, for on April 29 Yvette was to leave for London and a ten-day engagement. In London it was the era of the slightly rowdy but fundamentally innocuous music-hall miscellany—little Letty Lind, who almost whispered rather than sang; comedian Dan Leno; improviser Marie Lloyd and mimic Cissy Loftus; Vesta Tilley, of the male impersonations; Little Tich the clown, of the big boots and indignant eye; Katie Lawrence, with her "Daisy, Daisy, give me your answer, do"; May Yohe, in her polka dots, who had married the Hope diamond; costersinger Albert Chevalier, and all the others—the entire bill of fare a welter of trivialities and platitudes in which as yet not one voice had spoken in terms of life itself, or serious commentary thereon. It was a question, therefore, even though La Guilbert's fame had long since crossed the Channel, to what extent middle-class British *pudeur* could accept the Guilbertian spade-is-a-spade brand of repertoire and the vocabulary that stopped at nothing.

Yvette, registered at the Savoy, promptly fell under the spell of British solid mahogany and solid comfort and took the whole British scene to her heart. The *London Daily Graphic* reports Mademoiselle's wide-eyed comments: her astonishment at finding London audiences so sophisticated—everyone in evening dress and women more decolletée than in Paris; the theaters so well constructed, tasteful, handsome in *mise-en-scène,* and so clean; shops overflowing with beautiful goods unknown in Paris; agreeable people, many of whom spoke French and made the stranger welcome.

To launch publicity, Yvette held a kind of preview of her program for curious but slightly embarrassed members of the fourth estate, in which she offered samples from her repertoire. As to her opening at the Empire May 9, Yvette details her impressions:

> What a fine music-hall it was! . . . and what an orchestra . . . sixty well-trained musicians! What taste, what luxury in the ballet. . . . What artistic dignity in the choice of programmes, what quiet elegance in production! But then the three men responsible for the management were gentlemen who in Paris might have belonged to the Jockey Club. . . . George Edwardes, the manager, man about town, lived like a lord, elegant in speech and manners; Hitchins, distinguished, clever, well-born, looked after the establishment with the manners of an aristocrat; Tennant, the least gentlemanly, something of a roisterer, saw to the Promenade to make sure that the girls should be beautiful, smart, and—decent in behavior.
>
> On the night of my first appearance George Edwardes insisted on giving me his arm to lead me on to the stage when I took my curtain call. It made a sensation. . . . I had a glorious bouquet, which he made me carry as I went on with him, the flowers falling in long streamers to my feet. We had a tremendous ovation, and George Edwardes, still keeping me on his arm, addressed the audience for a full five minutes. I understood nothing of his speech, but four times I heard "This adorable Yvette Guilbert"—that was all I could catch.

In spite of Yvette's claim to an "ovation," her general reception might have been characterized nevertheless as a trifle cool. Undeniably she was caviar, even to hearers who understood French, and not all did. Some critics objected to her use of drawling recitative; complained of monotony; found her songs deficient in melody—nothing for the pit and gallery to whistle.

George Bernard Shaw, however, the first to recognize that a new planet had just swum into the ken of the English vaudeville public, brushed these objections aside in the *World* of May 16, 1894:

Another great artist has come. . . . It amuses her to tell interviewers that she cannot sing and has no gestures; but I need not say that there would be very little fun for her in that if she were not one of the best singers and pantomimists in Europe. She divided her programme [at the Savoy Hotel] in three parts: Ironic songs, Dramatic songs, and—but perhaps I had better use the French heading here, and say "Chansons Légères." For though Mlle. Guilbert sings the hymns of a very ancient faith, profusely endowed and sincerely upheld among us, we deny it a name and an establishment. Its "Chansons Ironiques" are delivered by her with a fine intensity of mordant expression that would not be possible without profound conviction beneath it; and if there is anything that I am certain of after hearing her sing "Les Vierges," it is the perfect integrity of her self-respect in an attitude towards life which is distinctly not that of a British matron. . . . I was not in the least shocked or disgusted, though my unlimited cognition of an artist's right to take any side of life whatever as subject-matter for artistic treatment makes me most indignantly resentful of any attempt to abuse my tolerance by coarse jesting. . . .

Technically Mlle. Guilbert is a highly accomplished artist. She makes all her effects in the simplest way and with perfect judgment. Like the ancient Greeks, not to mention the modern music-hall artists, she relies on the middle and low registers of her voice, they being the best suited for perfectly well-controlled declaration; but her cantabile is charming, thanks to a fine ear and a delicate rhythmic faculty.

During this visit and later ones—for she would return to London many times—Yvette was to make many interesting social contacts; she would be engaged to sing in salons as exclusive as those of the five o'clocks in Paris. In London she would again see Henri de Rochefort, exiled firebrand of the Second Empire and later Communard; he would entertain her in his well-appointed house and present her with a pair of Louis XIV candlesticks, offering many sour animadversions on the general dismalness of living with a race of people who, so he averred, were totally lacking in humor. "Glory to Yvette Guilbert," he once wrote, "who made the English laugh." In London her fame would become so great that Bliss and Sands would publish in 1898, an English edition of the Lautrec lithographs, with text by Arthur Byl. In London a spirited brunette would one day affectionately accost her in a lobby, arms outstretched: "At last we meet! Do you know that you have given me my best lessons in diction? Let me kiss you!" and thus would begin a lifelong friendship with beautiful Emma Calvé.

Meantime, Prince Albert Edward, always mindful of his obligations in gallantry, had not forgotten to speak a word in her behalf. At royal request, Sir Arthur Sullivan gave a dinner at which she sang for, so she claimed, an unprecedented twenty thousand francs and at which she was seated between the Prince and the Austrian ambassador. During the after-dinner entertainment, Edward and the Duke of Connaught delighted the company by breaking out into an impromptu whistling duet.

Years earlier, Bernhardt had been at pains to create the impression of intimacy with the Prince, writing once to her stage manager: "I've just come back from the Prince of Wales. It is twenty past one. I can't rehearse any more at this hour. The Prince has kept me since eleven. . . ." Yvette, on the contrary, had there been any intimacy between her and the Prince, would have been at as great pains to draw a red herring across the trail. Actually there is no real evidence that she ever enjoyed from Edward anything more than the huge princely good will, although it is true that tongues did wag, especially in later years, when the two met summer after summer in Marienbad. But when did tongues not wag about Edward?

June, 1894, brought a return to the Ambassadeurs, where in spite of a rainy month every seat in the garden continued to be filled. In July, Yvette held a charity fête at "La Rive," the first of many such kermesses, to benefit the old and infirm of Vaux. It was a day of frolic, with a sense of freedom and jollity among the guests and much boating on the Seine and everywhere reporters snapping pictures, including one of Yvette saucily sticking out her tongue at the photographer.

In October came the reopening of La Scala, which during the summer had been transformed from a typical smoky music hall to "*une salle coquette*," airy, well ventilated, tasteful, sumptuous, and it was in this pristine setting that Yvette launched what was to prove one of her most hideous and terrifying chefs d'oeuvres, Jules Jouy's *La Soûlarde*.

The song itself *Figaro* called a drama of misery, bloodcurdling as a tale from Poe, dolorous as an etching by Goya. "We were all chills down the back, we were moved to our very entrails. This is no longer art of the *café-concert,* this is art absolute." Sarcey also felt a physical effect: a nightmare pressing on the chest, an anguish in the throat.

The story is about a drunken old woman, lurching, half mad, along the street, surrounded by a jeering crowd, pelted by cabbages and rubbish. Every three lines, like the lugubrious striking of a clock, came the repeated refrain *"La Soûlarde!"*, which the singer diversified with infinite delicacy and even a strange audacity, on the last syllable of the word breaking with the piano and leaning on the sound in a way to suggest the sadistic screams and taunts of the pursuing gamins. The audience, Sarcey said, was chilled to the marrow. As to Yvette's delivery, his sharp eyes noted a few changes. "The face, formerly immobile, has taken on expression . . . the arms that hung inert . . . show life; she is the same, but not the same; even her diction is transformed; she has become more dramatic."

Reviewing *La Soûlarde* on the occasion of Yvette's second visit to London, Stanley Makower wrote in the *Yellow Book:*

> . . . when Yvette Guilbert is telling you about the drunken woman, though you shudder, it is not with disgust—for the thing is transfigured by her into something different. . . . When she steps outside the characters of the scene, crying out against the profanity of ridicule and raising a plea for the woman to pass unmolested, she conveys in her voice a suggestion of that universal humanity which binds the world together. The subtlety of this is indescribable. . . . It is just this poetry of vision which robs these songs of all their horror, for it is in the beautifying of the terrible that lies the supremacy of her art.

It was evidently sometime during this year of good fortune that Yvette had taken the important step of acquiring her own town house in Paris. In fact, she had one built. It stood near the Parc Monceau, on the Avenue des Villiers but fronting also on Boulevard Berthier, close to the old fortifications—a house with two addresses: 79 Avenue des Villiers and 23 bis Boulevard Berthier.

Her German architect Schoelkorpf, writes De Fouquières, "had had the courage not to take his inspiration from either Gothic or Renaissance, like those in the immediate vicinity. He elected to 'go modern.'" Not only did Yvette "go modern" in her architecture, she also probably scandalized her more conservative neighbors by a detail rampant with self-advertisement. Over the porte-cochere, supporting a balcony on the story above, a large, ugly, smiling head of Yvette, sculptured by Rouillère, thrust out on its long neck from the façade like the figurehead on the prow of a vessel.

Within, a large drawing room, with pink satin walls and marble floors, furnished in the period of Louis Philippe, overflowed, in true *fin-de-siècle* clutter, with bibelots, statuettes, drawings, antique curios. Beyond, on the other side of folding doors, was the divette's library of music collections, now of formidable size, where her grand piano stood, always heavily littered with songs. In the dining room, decorated in the style of the late Middle Ages, stood a long refectory table and massive carved mahogany sideboard. The house throughout was filled with artists' representations of her—drawings, oils, posters, busts —by Steinlen, Granié, Léandre, Bac, the German Carl von Stetten, Willette, Chéret, Capiello. "The Gallery of Yvettes," her friends called it.

The house itself, according to De Fouquières, was subsequently torn down in the march of modern living to make way for apartments, and what became of the sculptured figurehead was never known.

As early as the fall of 1894 Yvette was in residence at the house of two addresses, from which she writes to Lautrec in a—for her— unusually tactful, or chastened, vein, evidently soon after reading in September Clemenceau's praise of the Geffroy-Lautrec album:

Cher ami
    Thank you for your lovely drawings for the book by Geoffroy [sic]. I am delighted! delighted! and you have all my gratitude believe me. Are you in Paris? If so, come to my new house, 79 avenue de Villiers, for lunch next week.
        Kind regards and again thanks.
                              Yvette

Chapter 12

To cap the events of Yvette's *annus mirabilis* came the publication of Louis de Robert's first novel, *Un Tendre,* a book in which the divette moves through the pages clearly recognizable as heroine. It is also a book which, like Pierre Loti's romances, purports to relate, under the thinnest possible guise of fiction, details of a bona fide love affair: in the case of *Un Tendre,* an affair between the author and Yvette. It is a history of a young man's first love, and the sentimentalist referred to in the title is of course none other than De Robert himself. In calling himself *"un tendre,"* the author was perhaps not far wrong; at least, one of his friends, the artist Forain, many years later, after a certain famous abdication, made an interesting comparison: *"De Robert, c'est un tendre. Windsor aussi. Je pourrais lui prêter ma devise: Je ne crains que mon coeur."*

That the book created a sensation goes without saying. Not that the knowledge of indiscretions on the part of a popular star would be likely to come as a surprise to a Parisian public, who might indeed have been less surprised at a liaison than at the lack of one. Nor probably would most people have found it hard to believe that the attractive young De Robert had been this star's secret choice all along, for the two had been seen together a great deal. It was merely that the fierce light that beat constantly upon Yvette made everything pertaining to her of intense concern.

The fictional device of spicy revelations prudently veiled was no literary novelty, the *roman à clef* dating back, in fact, to the seventeenth century, to a series of interminably long novels which made this type of literature fashionable. Madame de Sevigné was one who loved the parlor game of trying to guess identities of shepherds, nymphs, and Roman soldiers. The nineteenth century, too, had had its examples of these appeals to curiosity and eroticism, and Loti's books especially could not have been lacking in influence on young De Robert. Only a few years later the kiss-and-tell school of writing would reach its zenith—or nadir—of sensationalism with D'Annunzio's *Il fuoco,* in which would be disclosed the Italian playwright's most intimate relationships with Eleanora Duse.

As to *Un Tendre,* the book itself is a fascinating puzzle. A few details are clearly fictional; some parts are unmistakably factual, and others open to speculation. The story goes something like this:

Clairin, a young artist (Louis de Robert), is visited in his studio by Jeanne Saulnier, a popular singer (Yvette), who wants to meet him because of a painting he has just exhibited that is attracting a great deal of attention. The subject is a red-haired peasant woman, a perfect likeness of Jeanne, whom the artist, oddly enough, has never seen. Clairin is described as "a young, delicate-looking man with light hair and a fresh complexion. A slight moustache covered his upper lip; his smile disclosed fine, white teeth." He is not much a man of the world, this Clairin, almost a hermit, indeed. But he is happy in his solitude and has no other desire than to work.

Jeanne is "tall and slender and looked pretty in her spring gown. . . . contrasted with her red hair her face seemed quite white." Clairin is captivated by her. His artist's eye notices the hair is dyed; sees the face as roguish and serious at the same time; marks the mobility of features; vividness of gestures. He is enchanted by her conversation, capricious and full of the unexpected. She tells him about herself.

Other women were all jealous and detested her, just as if it were her fault if she had been lucky, if she loved her work, if she were less stupid than the others. The theater had tempted her and she had ventured to try it . . . she had succeeded. She worked hard enough to try to please, rehearsing, experimenting. There were nights when she could not sleep after studying, when her head was feverish, and the next day what headaches! But it was so delightful to learn new songs and to sing them, to have a public of one's own, to recite to it as one would speak to friends in a drawing room.

Clairin becomes caught up in her orbit; attends evening parties where Jeanne sings, where the "rosy color of his youthful and girl-like face contrasted oddly with his fashionably cut dress suit." At the soirées, she talks animatedly to the men who surround her, so tall that her shock of red hair flames above their heads. At one of these affairs Clairin meets Rosel, described as an amateur playwright, "a man in the forties, very fat, jovial faced and with a heavy moustache. . . . Both seemed very intimate and addressed each other in the familiar second person singular." Paris had coupled the names of Rosel and Jeanne.

But no one knew their true relations. Jeanne was a strange woman and nothing amused her so much as to give the outside world a false opinion concerning herself. She passed her time in deceiving everybody in this regard and very few had ever been able to read her or could say what her true character really was. Others, her friends, seeing her so frank, so free in her manners, so mannish, believed her to be without desire, and declared she had a cold temperament. Both were mistaken. Jeanne was simply a sensible woman who had been able to restrain her feelings and lead a virtuous life by sheer force of will. Having started from nothing, she had courageously climbed her way up the ladder, and her patience and tenacity had won for her a brilliant position in the artistic world. Seeing her lanky body, her droll eyes, now laughing, now sad, it was difficult to believe that that little red-haired head contained so much lucidity and intelligence. Her personality presented something abnormal, a disconcerting phenomenon of cerebral refinement and feminine force.

Eventually Jeanne sits to Clairin for a portrait, arriving in the studio "like a gust of wind, filling it with her chatter, the frou-frou of her skirts, and her hearty, spontaneous laughter." During the sittings Clairin learns still more about her. "She herself was a little sovereign, having her courtiers, her newspapers, her public. She had her enemies also; she could not avoid that. One can accomplish nothing without elbowing others, and it is the fittest who survives." After she leaves, a persistent odor of heliotrope lingers in the studio.

When Clairin questions her about Rosel, she protests.

Was he like all the others? Did he, too, believe in those stupid stories? No, indeed. Rosel was nothing to her. . . . She lived very quietly, having no time to think of such things. . . . That surprised him, doubtless, yet it was true. No man and no intrigues. She was in too much need of her brain and her independence. Besides, she lived as she did in order to retain her own self-respect. . . .

And by snatches she told him her life. First she had been a model in a dressmaking establishment, and later . . . she went on the stage as a super. She made up her mind that one day she would become a great public favorite. This idea became fixed in her head, and all her wishes were always realized. But the beginning was hard . . . and then she endured all kinds of misery in the provinces from vulgar audiences, who greeted her appearance with hisses and derision. . . .

Ah, how well she remembered those early days, those days of utter blackness and despair. In spite of all, she had kept up her courage, she had worked hard, sat up all night, rehearsing twenty times the same words, the same part, studying, seeking a natural attitude, a gesture, a smile, an intonation. At last she seemed to be at the end of her troubles, having found an engagement at a Paris music hall at twenty francs a night. Twenty francs a day was sufficient for her and her mother to live on, and it gave her so much encouragement to think that she was able to defray all their daily expenses that she took an obstinate pride in devoting herself solely to hard work and in leading a quiet and virtuous life, in wresting success from Fortune by sheer force of will.

That is why she was earning today what she wanted. She had half a million invested in good securities, a fine piece of property in the country where her mother lived, and "thirty thousand francs' worth of lingerie." As she furnished the figures there came over her face the serious and thoughtful expression of the thrifty and economical housekeeper. . . .

He made inquiries and learned that Jeanne lived very quietly and that if some malicious gossips winked when speaking of Rosel, every one acknowledged that she was never seen in disreputable places. If she had a liaison she was very prudent, for no one was cognizant of it.

As to Rosel:

"How absurd you are, to keep mentioning him. Rosel is my clown, my jester, if you must know. I am paid twenty-five louis every evening to amuse the public; he amuses me for nothing. Rosel likes to be seen with me. It is his vanity. He would miss it if his friends, when they met him, did not say: 'Well, how is Saulnier?' "

And now, having started on this subject, she made fun of Rosel. He was so fat and homely. When he was eating, his eyes became moist and wept all down his cheeks as if they were melting. Could a woman be in love with such a man? This essentially feminine observation convinced Clairin.

Clairin is by now hopelessly in love, and very unhappy because of Jeanne's indifference. In her dressing room, lined with mirrors, he watches her make up: "She was again using the powder puff, which ran over her neck like a little white mouse." He declares his passion, protesting that he loves her more deeply than anyone else. "They all say that," she replies, pinning on her flowers. When he pleads to be her only friend, she says that that would be too monotonous, gives him his hat and sends him away. "When you are more reasonable, you may come and see me again." Constantly she urges on him the necessity of working hard in his career. He tells her of his ambition to achieve fame, to be someday her one friend.

Their relationship ripens into intimacy, and he becomes a frequent visitor in her apartment.

All its furnishings, entirely characteristic of the owner, were unconventional and artistic. Strangely fashioned bric-a-brac, rare pieces of porcelain and china, oddly fashioned stools and chairs, pieces of sculpture, including several busts of herself, books, canvases framed and unframed, were all heaped together in picturesque confusion.

Here Clairin met the bohemians, who formed the little court that Jeanne dragged after her, like a procession, on first nights. . . . Their wit, like their costumes, had the cut of a good house. They were all exactly alike, and they addressed each other familiarly.

Clairin is embarrassed by their free language and manners, blushing "to the roots of his hair." They make so much fun of him that finally he comes only when Jeanne is alone. She has a great passion for flowers, and her apartment is always filled with them. "Flowers everywhere—white lilacs, white roses, white pinks."

The tantalizing situation continues. One day he kisses her, and she becomes angry. He writes a contrite letter and she comes to his studio "with a smile that meant she was sure of herself and her power." Next day she again chills his heart "with an indifferent and bored air."

Finally her attitude becomes "indulgent, more affectionate." She no longer hurries his departure or bursts into her mocking laughter. "Bashful Clairin, with his virgin heart and chaste soul, was not a lover in the usual meaning of the term," and he tells her that he has never loved before. She, however, confesses that she has had *une grande passion,* for a man who waited five years for her and whom she made to endure all misery because she did not want to show her love. One day she surrendered, "forgetting that this man was not free." The liaison lasted two years, in a "small isolated pavilion at the end of a solitary court" in Auteuil, "where they could live quietly, far from the world, far from their friends." "I was the happiest woman in Paris," she declares. "I really lived." Then came a note from the man: "My wife knows all. . . . Let us say farewell." She had not even the right to weep. "Women such as I must laugh; . . . I sang in the evening . . . not a sign of distress in my voice or my eyes." When all was over, she went to Auteuil, destroyed mementos, sobbed madly.

"Now I know what the great passions of men are worth. . . . I shall never have faith in anything."

One evening Jeanne admits to a sisterly love for Clairin. They plan to meet next day at five in the Bois, on the Acacias. As Clairin waits, Rosel comes by, upbraids him with paying Jeanne too much attention. "Everyone's talking." Jeanne fails to keep the appointment, and Clairin spends the night walking the streets, crazed with suffering. The next day he decides to leave Paris, but as he is packing, Jeanne arrives at his studio. "You came to try your power over me . . . to laugh at me, to mock the courage I displayed in wishing to go. You are a cruel woman. . . . I am being consumed because you do not love me." After this outburst she weakens and he kisses her. "Suppose I were to tell you that I love you too?" Jeanne says as she goes out.

Sunday in her apartment there is more lovemaking, and he whispers a few words in her ear "with a manner and in a tone as if asking for something which he scarcely hoped would be given to him. . . . 'Never,' she replied emphatically. 'Yes, I do love you, only you must have patience.'"

And so the cat-and-mouse game goes on, Clairin maddened by her indifference, real or feigned; jealous, but always restraining himself lest he make himself unbearable and thus lose her entirely. "He was so humble that it pleased her vanity."

One day as they are driving, they pass a man whom Jeanne speaks to, in an embarrassed manner. Clairin demands to know if this is the man she loved; she denies it. The man, Forge, soon calls on Clairin at his studio on the pretext of wanting to buy a painting. When Clairin confronts Jeanne with Forge's card and declares that he does not believe her denial, she betrays herself, protesting, however, that Forge no longer means anything to her.

One night Rosel, Clairin, and Jeanne go to the Moulin Rouge after the theater. Here Jeanne is, of course, recognized; girls stop dancing and come boldly up to stare with admiring curiosity at the "celebrated star who made so much money, and whose pictures were pasted everywhere on the walls of Paris." While Rosel is dancing with a girl, Jeanne and Clairin run out together. "It was another Jeanne, a simple, girlish Jeanne, that had come to life in this scene of her childhood." As they pass a wineshop she used to know, on the impulse of the moment they go inside. In a small, dirty back room, where they take a table, they see an old man bent over his absinthe. He does not recognize Jeanne, but she knows him, and after he goes out she tells Clairin the story of her schoolgirl infatuation for Puech, her father's friend.

"That old man was Puech?"

"How odd life is."

From now on the two see each other constantly; they walk in the Bois, he calls for her at the theater. One night in the carriage Jeanne touches Clairin's forehead "with warm, exquisite little kisses." But on an afternoon in her carriage, when Clairin thinks she is about to yield, she chances to see Forge again, changes suddenly and drives home.

One day Clairin receives an invitation to go to Meulan to Jeanne's summer home. They go down by train, accompanied by her cousin, a young boy; Rosel, clearly jealous, is also a member of the party. The house exterior at Meulan suggests a Swiss chalet; carefully laid out grounds stretch down to the banks of the Seine. There they meet her mother, a "stout elderly woman, simply dressed," and a man in a white suit. He is her uncle, a widower, who looks after the property. There are terraces, with vines and grapes; a lawn with daisies; stables and horses—all Jeanne's, including an island in the Seine.

After luncheon Jeanne and Clairin go down to the boathouse, take a boat and row over to the island. Here, so intimates the author, comes at last Jeanne's capitulation.

But back in Paris, quarrels break out. Clairin sees Jeanne and Forge walking together and charges her with resuming the old relationship. She admits it. "You are my wife, you have not the right to go back to him." Infuriatingly she starts putting him off again, asking him to be reasonable, to be her friend, to be strong and work. Clairin serves notice on Forge that if his attentions to Jeanne do not cease, he will be faced with the choice between a public scandal and a duel.

Convinced that the affair is continuing, however, in spite of his warning, Clairin, encountering his rival one night in the lobby at the Variétés, threatens to cane him then and there. To quiet him Forge agrees to a duel; next morning the two men, armed with pistols and accompanied by their seconds, meet near Chaton. Both fire and both miss.

From here on the story suddenly changes tone and moves quietly and undramatically to the end. Clairin, it is true, goes alone one day on a sentimental journey to the island, but when he next meets Jeanne a few months later, she finds him, to her surprise, very calm, wholly absorbed again in his art. They greet each other casually, though agreeing to remain good friends. The change in Clairin's attitude, is, moreover, sincere. The young man feels as if Forge's bullet had not missed him but killed him, and that a kind of resurrection now awaits him—one of return to work and achievement.

Though departures from strict fact abound in minor details of this work, the general basis of truth is too clear to be denied: the suggestion of Yvette's peasant origin—though one would hardly expect such class-consciousness on the part of an enamoured young suitor; Yvette's appearance and personality, including the dyed hair and the ebullient temperament; the outline of her theatrical career; the salons at which she sang; her superior intelligence and philosophy of hard work; her queening it with public and press; her enemies; her wealth, even to the thirty-thousand-francs' worth of lingerie; her ostensibly virginal life, which she was always at pains to stress; her bohemian coterie, with their uninhibited speech; her apartment crowded with busts and pictures of herself; her country estate, complete with Swiss chalet and stout, elderly mother; her love of flowers—all these points tally so perfectly with known facts that the reader may well be tempted to accept as authentic the account *in toto*.

On second thoughts, however, certain elements seem questionable. For example, the duel; though affairs of honor were not infrequent, De Robert seems hardly the type to call out a man. If the duel is assumed, however, to be poetic license, it can be accepted as good craftsmanship; a device to shock the unaccepted lover back to his senses and his true career, art.

It is even harder to believe that a public personality, followed as closely by reporters as Yvette was at that time, could have kept an affair hidden for two years, in Auteuil or anywhere else. To preserve such secrecy over so long a period would have required a benevolent conspiracy of silence on the part of every journalist in Paris. In later years reporters were not slow in speculating about possible romantic interests of the divette, but at this stage of her life such observations are lacking. Yet even granting complete delicacy on the part of numberless persons in the secret, a larger question looms. The Forge affair is represented as *un grand amour;* mere lust is not suggested. But Yvette's capacity for *un grand amour* is another matter. Yvette, we know, was self-assertive, and to accept a situation that would have required her to submerge her ego—to take on anonymity for the sake of a married lover—seems a violation of her nature. A willingness to surrender self for another has appeared nowhere else in her life. Perhaps then the whole Forge story should be considered as poetic license also, another complication introduced to heighten reader interest; or, perhaps even more likely, a fabrication of Yvette's, tossed off impromptu one day to De Robert to account for her coldness to him.

But assuming that such an affair had existed, the identity of the man remains a conundrum. While there probably can be no complete discounting the possibility of Père Zidler in some kind of amatory relationship in earlier days, the Forge incident seems not to relate to him. Forge is the most shadowy character in the book, and the few details about him describe a rather different person from Zidler. The supposed Forge is a paterfamilias; as to appearance, he is referred to merely as "athletic."

Regarding the identity of Rosel, however, more definite clues exist. Were it not for one detail, the figure of Hugues Le Roux might leap to mind. Le Roux had certainly been seen in public with Yvette a great deal, and his extravagant admiration of her was well known. But there is another candidate. Rosel, says De Robert, is "very fat, jovial faced and with a heavy moustache." And Jeanne, making fun of Rosel, says that when he is eating "his eyes became moist and wept all down his cheeks as if they were melting." It seems significant that these details correspond closely to the description Yvette herself gives in her autobiography of a man she carefully characterizes first as a lout and then as an enemy—none other than the litigious Auguste Musleck, husband of Sidonie and manager of the Concert Parisien. Granted that there might easily have been in Yvette's actual acquaintance a number of fat men with mustaches, the detail of the streaming, melting eyes—which De Robert particularly remarked and which thirty years later Yvette still remembered to note in her memoirs—is passing strange. That De Robert may have metamorphosed a lowly concert manager into a playwright would be merely another instance of literary manipulation; that Yvette excoriates him years later in her own book may perhaps be taken as further substantiation of De Robert's claim of the care she invariably took to camouflage personal relationships.

A touch of historicity appears in the incident of old Puech, where even the real name is used. Here Yvette's schoolgirl crush on her father's middle-aged friend has been enlarged to appear as a real affair, no doubt for heightened literary effect. Whether the author ever actually saw an old man bent over his absinthe or merely heard about him through Yvette is immaterial. Puech is identifiable, Yvette being reported elsewhere as telling the same story.

Centrally, however, the main interest in the book lies with none of the three supposed previous lovers—Forge, Rosel, or Puech—but with Clairin and Jeanne. Was there a bona fide affair between De Robert and Yvette? Certainly there existed a close emotional tie. And arguing from Yvette's predilection for the red-herring technique, one notes that in her autobiography, where she boasts of her wide acquaintance with men of letters who admired her, she makes only the barest mention of Louis de Robert. So little is said, in fact, that one is tempted to believe that De Robert may have been hitting the nail precisely on the head when, knowing her as well as he did, he wrote that as to her private life it amused Yvette to deceive everyone; that few had ever been able to say what her true character was.

Accepting then, as it seems one must, the central truth of a siege laid by De Robert to Yvette's heart, one can find little to doubt in the details by which his campaign is presented in the novel—the visits to her dressing room, her apartment, her country house; the walks and carriage rides; the many letters and telegrams. Equally believable are the coquetry and the teasing. There remains only the question of Yvette's final surrender, a question that contemporary readers apparently found simple enough to answer: no denials issued from the divette. That is, at the time of the French edition. Later, when the American edition appeared—but that is another story.

Though *Un Tendre* stands below the level of first-rate writing, at the time of its publication the book made its claim on the interest of critics as the first full-length serious work of a young man already favorably known by his shorter tales. In *Siècle* a reviewer speaks of its "exquisite freshness and extreme delicacy of sensibility." As to the suffering of the young Clairin, the theme which fills the book, he writes: "The analysis of this first passion, so sincere and ardent, is done in delightful fashion; charming in sentiment; there are details so tenderly described, so profoundly true, that they bring tears to the eyes"; after which the reviewer ends with a discreet reference to the identity of Jeanne Saulnier, recognizable as "one of our most celebrated divettes, whose posters have popularized to the limit a slim silhouette and golden hair."

Chapter 13

In the 1890's in New York, a German immigrant named Oscar Hammerstein—future *entrepreneur* of Melba, Tetrazzini, Calvé, Garden, Cavalieri—was beginning to cut a wide swath as theatrical manager. The New York of that decade was an appropriate place in which to display his particular talents for size and splendor, for the city, in its own *fin-de-siècle* spirit, was exhibiting the most pronounced extravagances of its history. If the American Eighties had been Elegant, the Nineties were *Ne plus ultra*. Broadway gleamed in marble, luxury hotels were rising, palaces and châteaux spawned for blocks along Fifth Avenue. The gilded age had never been more affluent, nor entertainment more plentiful and diverse. Besides the legitimate theater, there were operas and ballets, and in musical shows Lillian Russell, all peaches and cream and dripping with diamonds, was perennially ready to throb and bloom and enchant the gallery gods; nor was there any lack of "concert saloons," variants of the London music hall and the Paris *café-concert*.

Hammerstein had built his first theater in 1889, and from then on had indulged himself in ambitious dramatic and musical attractions. Although he constantly walked a financial tightrope, and although his personal relations with his stars were not always harmonious, he had earned the reputation of paying his performers liberally and promptly. After his Harlem Opera House in 1889 and his Columbus Theater in 1890, he had followed with his oversized Manhattan Opera House. Here, in a structure too big for anything but opera and where for some months his ventures proved unrewarding, he finally found himself forced to take emergency measures for revenue.

In 1893 the variety show was prospering mightily in New York. Messrs. Koster and Bial, in an establishment not unlike the typical *café-concert* of Paris, were turning crowds away nightly for lack of room, and out of their huge but homeless public and Hammerstein's huge but empty Manhattan Opera House was born the idea of coalition. The Opera House, with alternate rows of seats removed and tables installed, became Koster and Bial's Music Hall, and, with bar and lounge added, a kind of Folies-Bergère was created.

Within two years, however, this seemingly ideal arrangement was wrecked by a violent disagreement between Hammerstein and the other two men, which ended in Hammerstein resigning from the corporation with the melodramatic threat to build a music hall of his own that would put his erstwhile partners permanently out of business.

The new three-million-dollar Olympia which he built on Broadway between Forty-fourth and Forty-fifth streets was claimed to be the biggest music hall in the world. The enterprise included three other related projects—a concert hall, a theater, and a roof garden—with ample supplements of bar, Oriental café, billiard room, smoking room, lounges, and promenades; all for fifty cents admission. But being initially most concerned with his vast Olympia, Hammerstein immediately began, through overseas agents, to lay plans for importation on a grand scale of internationally known headliners, offering fees no European could resist. High on his list of desirables, of course, was Guilbert.

In Paris meantime, in the fall of 1894, a rash of rumors had broken out to the effect that the divette was being solicited also for other foreign engagements: to Berlin for a month, at seventy-five thousand francs; to Russia for two months. Consulted as to the truth of these rumors, Yvette had replied flatly: "To Russia, yes! To Germany, never!" The childhood memory of that hated Prussian victory march down the Champs-Élysées had apparently not faded from her mind. Also it should be remembered that in 1894 the recently formed Dual Alliance between France and Russia was immensely popular. France, facing the very real threat of the Triple Alliance of Germany, Austria-Hungary, and Italy, had warmly embraced the great northern bear. Indeed, everything in the fashionable world was, to adopt the title of one of Jean Lorrain's books, *Très russes,* and Yvette would not have been insensible of the distinction a visit to St. Petersburg would confer. Nothing definite, however, materialized immediately from any of these overtures; what did materialize was a return engagement to London and the Empire Theater in December, followed in January, 1895, by a trip to Italy.

The London engagement is memorable because, in anticipation of it, Toulouse-Lautrec created his one and only flattering representation of Yvette, a commission for *Le Rire,* in which the singer stands leaning forward, hands under chin, frankly sentimentalized. For this the artist asked his subject to pose in her new song, the English "Linger Longer, Loo," which she was about to try out on London audiences, while he sketched her brilliantly with a few telling strokes. "Linger Longer, Loo" had been popularized in London by Cissy Loftus; as

Yvette sang it, it was a delicious burlesque both of the banality of the piece and the mannerisms of Loftus. Loftus, on her part, had already joined the growing number of Guilbert imitators.

The English went wild over the take-off; now took the foreigner unreservedly to their bosom; thought her "an ugly charmer," accepting her perhaps on the basis of Bacon's dictum that there is no exquisite beauty without some strangeness in the proportion. They approved too of Béranger's *La Grand'mère*, classical verses that had been sung by three generations of French and that Yvette made as compelling as any modern vignette. Wearing a white cap, Yvette, as a tottering grandmother, sang in an affably cracked voice an old woman's reminiscences of her early indiscretions, each confession in the series less veiled than the preceding one. Clement Scott, of the *Illustrated London News*, comparing her techniques with those of other forms of art, maintained that Yvette was "an impressionist of the finest touch."

Of the Italian venture, regrettably, nothing so happy can be related. It was an era of such unfriendly Italo-French relations that French performers rarely ventured before Italian audiences. In Rome, Judic had been booed off the stage and the management had refused payment, Italian theater managers of the day being notoriously indifferent to contracts. In Naples, where Yvette was booked, anti-French feelings were so strong that her agent, a M. Gainnet, decided it would be prudent to accompany his star, not only to demand her salary each night before the ghost walked but to watch over her safety. Yvette may have found it picturesque to be escorted to and from her hotel by a *carabiniere* sitting beside her coachman, but she could hardly have been pleased with her first-night public, turbulent and hostile; so ill-behaved that Francesco Crispi, then Italian premier, who was in her audience, sent flowers backstage and apologized for his countrymen. To offset such disappointments, however, she reveled in her first glimpses of the beauties of Naples and the wonders of Pompeii. "Ah, my career! How much happiness I owe you! A poor girl, without the money that you brought me, how could I have seen so many marvels, how could I have traveled? That was my true success, my glorious recompense: to travel! to travel!"

Not long after the return from Italy, arrangements for an American trip under the Hammerstein auspices were completed. The New York *Sun* of March 24, 1895, reporting that competition for Guilbert between agents of Koster and Bial versus those of Hammerstein had been stiff beyond precedent, prognosticated gloomily: "The success of the singer here is a matter of very serious doubt. . . . It is a pretty well established fact that actors who do not speak English rarely make money in New York."

The amount of the fee finally agreed upon was widely publicized: $4,000 a week; $16,000 for a month's engagement. When it is remembered that money values in the 90's should be multiplied perhaps by four to arrive at their present equivalent, it can be seen why the total, some $64,000 today, was considered newsworthy, and why, from that date on, metropolitan papers and sophisticated magazines joined in one of the most extravagant advance publicity campaigns yet given to a visiting artist.

When the news was announced in Paris, the divette received a sacerdotal benediction from the high priest of criticism, Sarcey himself: "I would not turn her back from this; she is ripe for export."

After the signing of the American contract, as if in reaction to such a boiling-up of phenomenal doings, the spring of 1895 settled down to a purely predictable routine. Nightly the star continued to fill La Scala; the Bodinière matinees continued, as did the special galas here and there; constantly Yvette lent her name to benefits, one of which, as fortune whimsically decreed, was for the Lyonnet brothers, who on that momentous morning of her first audition for the *café-concert* stage had argued so stoutly with Madame Allemand in her behalf. Then it was summer again, with Albine installed in the country and Yvette taking the train down from Paris as often as she could; again the precious weeks at "La Rive," with their bright days and fragrant evenings; and always faintly in the distance the voice of the river she loved so well. Summer, and again the Ambassadeurs, where in the witching soft night air there was never an empty seat in the great gaslighted garden. One evening, according to *Le Gaulois,* two hundred persons stood to hear her.

It must have been sometime in November of this year that Yvette received, through her good friend the critic Henri Bauer, an invitation almost tantamount to another command performance before royalty: Would she sing for Bernhardt? Bernhardt wanted to hear the new favorite, but, as Bauer tactfully explained, would find it difficult to go to a *café-concert.* Yvette, who like everyone else in Paris, had heard about the house on Boulevard Péirère where in the salon the famous satin-lined coffin shared prominence with a cage of lions, accepted out of curiosity, only to find, however, when she arrived that the scene was somewhat less Gothic than reported; the lion cage, for example, was empty, though the smell remained.

Bernhardt was her most gracious self that night, full of compliments on the singer's impeccable articulation. To Yvette, as she was leaving, she said, "I don't think you've been to America yet, Mademoiselle Guilbert?"

"I am going there in three weeks, Madame."

"Delightful! I shall arrive a few days after you, so do come and see me."

With this she put into Yvette's hands a box in which lay one of her own fans, with a card enclosed: "Mademoiselle, please accept this fan in grateful remembrance of your visit to me, and believe me affectionately and admiringly yours, Sarah Bernhardt."

Although the Olympia technically opened on November 25, 1895, with R. A. Barnet's *Excelsior,* to a mob curiosity-wild over the gigantic entertainment complex, it was Yvette Guilbert who, on December 16, led off the series of foreign artists that had been recruited. It was on Yvette and her power to attract a public large enough for his financial needs that Hammerstein was gambling.

In Paris, before she set out for New York, American correspondents had been for some time securing advance interviews, in some of which the divette's remarks were, to say the least, fanciful. One of the most amazing of these was that granted to a dazzled representative of the New York *World* in the drawing room of her house on Boulevard Berthier shortly before her sailing. She swept into the room clad in ruby velvet trimmed with sable, assumed a captivating pose, and started pouring into the gentleman's ear what in the light of known facts today can be considered only as saucy nonsense. Stars are not notably accurate in reporting on themselves: what better example than Bernhardt? One recalls Dumas' cruel quip about Sarah's mendacity: *"Elle est si menteuse qu'elle est peut-être grasse!"* The story which Yvette retailed that day went something like this:

Her father had been a stockbroker, who had speculated and lost; her mother a straw-hat manufacturer. She herself had had the very best education, especially in music, and until the age of sixteen had lived in a pension. At twenty she had met, through her father, the love of her life. (Shades of Puech again!)

For six years I was perfectly happy. I knew nothing, I cared for nothing, except this one true affection, and then one day I awakened to the painful sensation that I had been deceived. I did not become reckless as most people do under a hard sorrow; I did not throw myself away in dissipation, drink or anything of that sort, but I pulled myself together and determined to go on the stage. Meanwhile as a result of my sorrow I became anemic. My father died, and my mother and I were left alone, having lost all we had by the death of my father.

Then I went to the Concert Parisien, making my debut five years ago . . . having written and composed all my songs. In fact, every song which I have sung has been suggested or composed by me, and in my own style. . . .

Now a significant new note:

My ambition now, as I am rich, is to marry. I don't say that all those reports about Mr. Hirsch, of England, and myself are untrue; I am thinking seriously of taking the step, and I am very fond of him. He is a man of brains, and I prefer men of that type to a man who only provides money for bills.

And so on and on, until in a farewell burst of charm: "*Et voilà, ça c'est tout. Au revoir. Venez déjeuner avec moi avant mon départ.*"

Whether the legend of *le grand amour* was originally launched by *Un Tendre,* or conceived by Yvette in a desire to show herself as interesting romantically as Bernhardt and Duse, who can say? But having been now officially adopted by Yvette, it persisted in a number of forms. Sometimes the beloved was a gay deceiver, sometimes he met an untimely death.

Henceforth, Yvette's stories, if reported accurately by the press, will be found to include a variety of fictions based on who knows what unverifiable germs of fact. Sometimes her father was a rich commission merchant. Sometimes she was "convent bred"—a nod to fashion —and had left the stage because she refused to "go to the bad." Her mother had had an embroidery shop in the Rue Helder; or sometimes it was a school of embroidery. Yvette had posed as model in artists' studios. Aurelian Scholl, managing editor of *L'Echo,* once tried her as a reporter, but she had been obliged to leave because the men reporters were jealous. Again, it was Hugues Le Roux who, after discovering her in Le Printemps, had later introduced her to other Paris journalists.

In practically all interviews, though figures fluctuate widely, references occur to the large fees. American commentators made elaborate comparison of Yvette's earnings with those of Lottie Collins, Adelina Patti, Nordica, Jean de Reszke, Emma Eames. Hilary Bell, writing for the New York *Press* shortly before her arrival, startled his readers by the following estimate:

> Yvette is paid for eight days, computing the day at twelve hours of continual work, more than the President of the United States receives for his four years in office. Her income a minute is about $75, ... larger than that of the Astors, Vanderbilts or the Emperor of Russia.

Mainly, however, it is the recurring new element in the interviews of this time that captures attention—the astonishing about-face in relation to love and marriage. At thirty Yvette had seemingly freed herself to a degree from the former father-domination of her thoughts, and on the eve of her departure for America was frankly in search of a mate. The unidentified Mr. Hirsch will live for posterity only as a momentary candidate for that honor, and from now on, the diva will be answering glibly the stereotyped query of reporters regarding her concept of the ideal husband.

In one of these off-the-cuff definitions she asserted:

> I like brainy men, literary men—men with ideas. . . . The cerebral quality is what enchants me . . . I hate fools. I hate Johnnies. Ah! *Quelles bêtes.* They talk, and talk, and give birth to no single idea. They disgust me.

In another more considered statement she seems to have been thinking in terms of being doted upon. Her husband, she affirmed, must "love me as a child, whose every caprice is catered to—like a sweetheart, like a sister." He must be "a person who will be competent to place a profound value on a dollar." Unquestionably an appetite for matrimony had been tardily aroused. Still, she must be "catered to." Nowhere does she indicate willingness to relinquish her cherished sense of supremacy.

On December 8, the day of her long-heralded arrival in New York, the metropolitan press pulled out all its stops. In contrast to Duse, Yvette never let slip an opportunity to confide in reporters, and at her press conference that evening she told a group of eager listeners that shortly before she left Paris fourteen hundred students had attended a benefit of hers, that they had taken her horses out of the shafts and dragged her carriage themselves, and that it had required three hundred gendarmes to keep order (it is true that on November 21 she had given a benefit for students at the Eldorado); and that next winter she was to play a three-weeks' engagement in St. Petersburg for 100,000 francs.

Perhaps she rattled on a little too loquaciously, for here and there the judicious grieved:

There is something pathetic in Guilbert's statement that she must make money while the sunshine of her popularity lasts; in her apprehension that the public may soon tire of her; in her frank argument that she is not in this business for her health. . . . May we not feel reasonable and anxious concern over this gifted and hitherto original performer when she shows her gowns to reporters, and relates with pride that her carriage was drawn by foolish students of the Quartier Latin, and rejoices over her engagements to sing before royalty?

Unfortunately, the old, characteristic tactlessness also came to the fore. No, she did not think she would like America, it was too far from home. She would never come again. No, she would not sing any American songs, they were too stupid.

To her manager she was downright rude. That morning, as she debarked, she had found Hammerstein waiting for her at the foot of the gangplank and from the first seems to have taken an intense dislike to him. "Greasy, dark, Oriental," he appeared to her, and his manner overfamiliar. In the carriage en route to the Savoy, when he invited her to supper, she snubbed him unmercifully. Later, when, as she says, "puffing up like a peacock and trying to take my hand," he asked whether his name was known in Paris, she replied that it was.

"What do they say?"
"That you're a fool." And with that I buried my hands in my muff. He was much offended.

Such lack of finesse from a star in dealing with her impresario, however much a vulgarian he may have been, is a little hard to understand. As time went on and trouble began to brew between them, Yvette, blind as usual to her own shortcomings, castigated Hammerstein for his enmity toward her, which she could not understand.

A few days later, Bernhardt arrived, and Yvette's publicity took a surprising turn.

"What is your opinion of Yvette Guilbert as an artist, Madame?" was one of the first questions put to Sarah by the press.

"Yvette Guilbert? *Connais pas!*" the Divine One replied promptly.

Connais pas! Bombshell! Bernhardt didn't know Guilbert! The startled reporters went scurrying pell-mell to Yvette. Would she care to reply to this astonishing statement?

Outraged by what she considered professional perfidy, Yvette emphatically would and did reply, not forgetting to exhibit the fan that Sarah had so lately presented to her and its accompanying note, with pungent commentary that provided first-rate copy. Yvette did not forgive the incident and for a long time thereafter waged a nasty sort of verbal warfare against Sarah.

As she had done in London, Yvette in New York sang privately at her hotel before a group of newsmen prior to her opening, so that the anticipated indecencies of her repertoire might be fully exploited in advance to sensation-loving New Yorkers. Speculators had bought out the Olympia for opening night, and seats were selling for as much as fifteen dollars. Said one writer: ". . . the scenes that took place at her debut at the Olympia amounted almost to frenzy." The music hall's "ascending tiers of boxes . . . were all filled. The parterre was crowded with all New York, in the lobbies surged the hoipolloi." Openly impatient for the divette's appearance, the crowd drowned with conversation the grabbag of luckless performers who preceded her on the bill. One after another the bright phantoms took their places and then vanished: Mademoiselle Fransetty, Charles Lifflon, Les Anders, My Fancy, the Avolos, Flo Banks, Signor Gennaro, Charles Urdoho —names long since forgotten.

In her dressing room, wearing a diaphanous white gown embroidered in pale yellow, with yellow ribbons tied around her tiny waist, waiting her turn at 9:20, Yvette was almost stiff with stage fright. Then: "Loose curtains fell. They were pushed aside almost immediately and the $16,000 Yvette faced the feverish audience."

By the end of the next forty minutes she had led her new public through a strangely violent world of haunted and macabre figures: *Les Ingénues*, about "presumably innocent girls who are not"; *La Soûlarde*, the drunken; *Ma Grandmère*, with her senile revelations; *Ça fait toujours plaisir*, from the operetta *La Femme à Narcisse*, a young man's erotic dream; *À la Villette*, sharply etched portrait of a pimp; *La Pierreuse*, criminal woman of the streets. Then, at ten o'clock, abruptly the enchantress called off the spell; with her mocking burlesque in English, "Linger Longer, Loo," brought her listeners smartly back to the sidewalks of New York.

Backstage, the perpetrator of the three-million-dollar gamble, who had been almost as nervous as the singer herself, listened to the applause rocking his mammoth auditorium, and relaxed behind a big cigar.

Not a critic could deny that, in spite of the fact that few of her audience were bilingual, La Guilbert had scored heavily, but even those who admired her artistry could not always applaud her choice of songs. "She is fully the genius which Paris took her to be," said the *Sun* next morning, "but she applies her great talent to the prostitution of dramatic art and the degradation of the theatrical business." Others looked down their noses at her talent: called her work "utterly non-extraordinary"; regarded some of her songs as not immoral but "simply imbecile," "stupid, maudlin."

The *Times* entered the dispute in general on the side of the affirmative:

Several of these ballads are distinctly, almost terribly, moral. . . . What the diseuse says is not, "These things exist and are amusing," but "These things exist and are frightful." The distinction is enormous; it is that between morality and immorality.

The *World* hailed her as "the most gigantic histrionic satirist of the day"; linked her with Bernhardt:

Such diction as Guilbert's you cannot hear even at the Théâtre Français. For does not Sarah the Great "grasseyer" her r's even in Racine? Yvette, I do declare, is the greatest mistress of the art of diction upon the French stage . . .

And also with Duse:

[During the last ten years] two artists have overthrown all the schools, the traditions, and the methods that had gone before. Duse has created a new tragic style, and Yvette Guilbert—well, will it be possible to listen to the smirking, prancing, painted, short-skirted dolls after hearing her? I doubt it.

Meltzer, also in the *World,* dared utter a prophecy that Yvette's impact might even change the whole course of American drama:

The fiction of American prudishness has been killed, the word "shocking" has been eliminated from the dictionary. No more can it be used with reference to American sensitiveness in matters of morals. No more need managers use the pruning-knife. No more need French plays be adapted. . . . Yvette has sung her songs verbatim et literatim, with their Rabelaisian wit and their Zolaesque naturalism, and they have been applauded and encored. . . . And this in a community where managers exist who transform Camilles into jilted maidens, moral peccadilloes into statutory crimes, and liaisons into flirtations; who disguise and pervert the excesses of human passion by the use of the transparent veil of hypocrisy.

But of sober critiques the masses of any nationality very sensibly seldom take heed. The man in the street next day was satisfied to sing or whistle:

Yvette, divette! Yvette, chérie!
'Twas au Concert Parisien
In gay Paree, you captured me
And I'm your dévoué since then.
Could I but tell you—ah, diable!
You know *que vous êtes adorable.*

In spite of all the acclaim, however, there was an ugly side to the New York engagement, for Yvette was not long in encountering the same social discrimination as in Paris. Melba, currently playing at the Metropolitan Opera House, refused to lunch with her.

"With that *chanteuse?* At the most, she might have been invited to come for dessert, for a fee, to sing one of her couplets."

When the remark was repeated to her, Yvette showed her claws. "I quite understand," she purred demurely. "I am of humble birth, but Madame Melba of course belongs to the royal family of France." As it was an open secret that Melba was mistress of the Duc d'Orleans, this *riposte feline* drew blood and Melba slashed back.

Various singers then in New York, including Melba, Plancon, Nordica, and Guilbert, had agreed to contribute their services to a benefit for the French Hospital, to be held at the Metropolitan. Now, Melba, when she heard that she and Guilbert were being billed on the same program, made such a shocking row that Maurice Grau, who was running the show, besought Guilbert to have the generosity to withdraw. She refused.

"My dear fellow, you have engaged me for a concert at 3000 francs and you have told me my appearance would be a good thing for me, because certain people would come to hear me who would not care to go to a music hall. I shall sing then. I shall give my 3000 francs to any needy compatriots in New York, but I intend to sing."

And Yvette did sing. It was Mesdames Melba, Plancon, and Nordica who withdrew. Yvette sang, in spite of the fact that patrons who took their opera reverently were "astounded at what they called Guilbert's effrontery in venturing within the sacred precincts of the temple of music"; and one man was overheard to say on leaving that it seemed to him almost "like playing skittles in church."

These were triumphs of a sort, but not of the happy kind. Nor could Yvette have been pleased when certain fashionable patronesses refused to attend a matinee of hers at Sherry's ballroom arranged by one M. Le Cocq de Lautreppe—a kind of Bodinière affair, with De Lautreppe playing the part of Le Roux—and a second matinee was actually canceled because of society's frowns.

Shortly after the close of the Olympia engagement, in the New York *World* of January 16, 1896, appeared the following announcement: "Ted D. Marks today assumes the management of Guilbert's short American tour," a notice suggesting that relations between Hammerstein and his star had perhaps lapsed into such hopeless disrepair that a change of impresario had become imperative. "Teddy," usually referred to by newspapers as a "well-known theatrical manager," was a debonair gentleman noted for dressing to the hilt, always seen wearing a glossy top hat, frock coat, and huge carnation *boutonnière,* and it was under the aegis of this Beau Brummell that Yvette set forth.

The first important booking was Boston, which in those days laid great claim to cultural pre-eminence and considered its own aristocratic appraisals of the arts more discerning than vulgar New York's. Boston critics had already reviewed Yvette adversely both in Paris and at the Olympia, and T. Jefferson Coolidge, who had heard Yvette in Paris "at Count d'O———'s," had found her "a canaille of the worst description." A fashionable crowd, nevertheless, including gilded youth from Harvard and radiant buds from Back Bay who knew French better than their chaperones, streamed into the old Music Hall the night of January 17, 1896, to level their opera glasses and judge for themselves.

Next day in the more choosy Boston papers the divette's work was dubbed "sewer sketches"; her talents said to be used in "apotheosizing the useless; in gilding refined tin"; she was accused of enjoying an imposing reputation "without having deserved it." But some papers carried raves, and there was again the comparison of stature which was now becoming inevitable—Bernhardt, Duse, Guilbert.

Returning to New York at the end of the tour (Boston, Brooklyn, Washington, Philadelphia, Chicago), Yvette took time before dashing aboard the *St. Louis,* Paris-bound, to tell a *World* reporter that there was absolutely no basis for the rumor that she was engaged to be married to the sartorially resplendent Mr. Marks.

Chapter 14

Back in Paris, a correspondent of *Figaro,* calling one morning in February, 1896, at the house with two addresses, found Mademoiselle Guilbert kneeling on the floor in the middle of a roomful of half-unpacked boxes, absorbed in an Edison phonograph she had brought back from New York. The record she was playing was one Calvé had made for her, and it contained a personal message filled with lavish praise and affection. The reporter listened to it admiringly.

Yes, her trip had been eminently satisfying. *"Superbe, mon voyage—adorable, les Americains!"* Had he heard the Negro song she learned over there—"I Want You, Mah Honey"? *Exquise!* Negro songs with banjo accompaniment were all the rage in America. In New York she had already tried out another song in English, "Her

166

Golden Hair Was Hanging Down Her Back." *Succès fou!* In fact, her next concern would be to perfect herself in speaking English. "Then you will go back?" *"Parbleu!"* Her two months must have been profitable? Oh, something between 170,000 and 190,000 francs. " 'Nice, isn't it?' artlessly." She glided gracefully over "the impression she had produced in critical Boston"; Bernhardt and Melba "lay heavy on her heart." But it was good to be home! In her dear Paris.

On February 17, loaded with fresh laurels, the divette was back at La Scala, again packing the house, again listening to the frenetic bravos, again meeting the incessant demand for more and more songs. In April, Marchand attempted a lengthening of her engagement, but her return to the Empire in London prevented. By June 2, it was time to recommence at the Ambassadeurs, where, says *Le Gaulois,* she was again engaged for sixty summer appearances at a fee of 50,000 francs. "Let us add, however, that Yvette has just signed with a New York director for the coming winter for the same number of appearances, for which she will receive 400,000 francs."

Autumn brought to Parisians two intriguing novelties—a visit of state from Their Imperial Russian Majesties, Tsar Nicholas II and the Tsarina, over whom the city went quite mad, and the appearance of their *caf'-conc'* idol in a new role, that of writer.

To a book entitled *Femmes de Théâtre* by Ferdinand Bac, a collection of drawings of "elegant and perverse, but not frankly debauched" women, accompanied by *double-entendre* captions, Yvette had contributed the preface. In America the book was something "which the father of a family might keep in the office safe under lock and key lest the office boy find it," but in latitudinarian Paris, the work swept quickly through three editions. The preface, however, was a puzzle. In this lighthearted context, why should Yvette have spent so much heavy sarcasm on the lack of talents and morals of actresses in general, with a strongly implied suggestion that she herself did not belong to these ranks? Such sentiments, taken at face value, would suggest a holier-than-thou attitude. Was she serious or joking?

Because of the long and tender friendship between herself and Donnay, Yvette had always hoped that the playwright would one day tailor for her a starring vehicle. But by temperament Donnay was fearful, and he could not overcome his dread of a fiasco. For a woman of Yvette's reputation, suppose what he wrote missed fire, as he put it?

"Tu comprends, avec toi . . . c'est très difficile . . . dans ce que tu fais, tu n'as que des succès, si avec moi tu fais un four, hein, qu'est-ce qu'on dira? On dira: comment! Donnay avait Yvette Guilbert et voila ce qu'il en a tiré!"

Again and again ideas had been discussed, sometimes even beginnings made, but always the end result had been the same: Yvette would wait in vain for the promised comedy.

Then one day in the fall of 1896, into her fertile brain leaped what she considered a genuine inspiration. A volume of erotic poems, *Astarte,* and a novel, *Aphrodite,* had recently made Pierre Louÿs the current favorite of the Parisian reading public. In the novel Yvette believed she discerned choice material for a musical comedy, with thoughts of course of herself in the leading role, but the fame of the author gave her pause. Pierre Louÿs might not regard with favor a proposal from a *caf'-conc'* singer to star in his chef-d'oeuvre.

She took her idea first to Donnay and then to Saint-Saëns. At the prospect of having Louÿs as collaborator, Donnay forgot his timidity, and as for the composer, he had often told Yvette that the day she found a text that pleased her he would provide the musical setting. With these two unimpeachable names in her support, therefore, Yvette dared to approach M. Louÿs and to her delight found him immediately and ardently interested. He believed a combination of Donnay, Saint-Saëns, and Guilbert would be one that any box office would welcome; *nihil obstat.* In high enthusiasm deliberations began.

Unfortunately they were short lived. At the very outset M. Louÿs took the unusually modest position that it would be inappropriate for his name to appear as co-author of the musical; he would be entirely content to have the new work fathered by Donnay and Saint-Saëns. But Donnay violently disagreed. What?—assume sole responsibility for the adaptation of such a formidable success as *Aphrodite? Jamais!* Saint-Saëns sided with Donnay; he too considered the novel far too important for the author not to be associated with the librettist. In a sudden tangle of Gallic excitability the playwright refused to proceed and the author refused to give way, while Yvette frantically tried to persuade Saint-Saëns and Donnay that the joint value of their two names would outweigh even that of Louÿs. Not one of the principals would yield an inch. The whole beautiful dream evaporated.

The outcome of the affair, however, did not mar Louÿs' extravagantly high regard for Yvette, whom he considered a satirist of first rank. "Satire, you know," he said to her one day, "is eternal.... Homer is dead, but Juvenal is still alive; Aristophanes created Molière, who owes him his eternity. Donnay, Saint-Saëns, Pierre Louÿs will add nothing to what you are. Don't regret what escapes you, Mademoiselle. Time will prove your riches."

Early in December of that year, when Yvette came down the gangplank in New York a second time, it was to fall, figuratively, into the waiting arms of Teddy Marks and Albert Bial. This time she would be appearing under Koster and Bial in their Thirty-fourth Street house, reputedly for $6000 a week, and Teddy seems to have been retained in some promotional capacity.

Animated and chattering volubly in better English than before, she told reporters proudly that she was arriving with three new American songs: "I Want You, Mah Honey," "I Want to See the Old Home," and "My Pearl Is a Bowery Girl." To give verisimilitude to the last, she declared her intention of spending some time on the Bowery, studying its mores and vowels at first hand. As things turned out, her investigations seem to have been confined to a brief visit to Chinatown, where her cicerone was the colorful Chuck Connors, an authentic Bowery inhabitant known widely as "the mayor of Chinatown," and where she created something of a sensation on Doyers Street, stepping out of a satin-lined and perfumed brougham in her silks and velvets.

A few days later, Alan Dale of the *Journal,* calling at the Savoy to interview Yvette on her scathing attack in Bac on her professional colleagues, found her practicing at the piano with the faithful Teddy turning the music. The preface? Oh, that, Yvette airily declared, had been designed to trim down the pretensions of certain actresses whose memoirs had been appearing in *Figaro.* When Sardou produces a play, the divette explained, he always asks for four or five artists; the rest may be actresses; the difference is supposed to be obvious. She deplored the fact that in the public mind, however, both were lumped together as actresses, those endowed with the divine spark and those with merely pretty faces. "It's enough to make one die laughing. . . . Such wearisome protestations of virginity of soul! They asked me to write. What could I do? I am an *artiste.* I am not an actress, so I took up my pen and I whipped them all with the weapon of satire." The true "artist," said Yvette, she who has the innate gift of tragedy, or comedy, or song, or of imitation, has nothing in common with "these jades, these gigolettes," "silly janitors' daughters who take to the stage because it gives them an opportunity to lead jolly lives profitably. ... They have no more talent than a cat. They want to enlarge their clientele—you understand what I mean by clientele, *n'est-ce pas?*"

Mr. Dale ventured to suggest, gently, that even "artists" possibly were not all unsullied.

"Ah," she gurgles with a shrug, "that is their business. ... What artists do does not concern the public. ..."

I see a yearning look in the eyes of Teddy [Dale goes on], to whom gossip affianced Yvette some time ago. And I cannot resist the petty temptation ... of asking her whether she is to blossom forth as Yvette Guilbert-Marks.

And how she laughs. ... "I am always being affianced," she says. "When I was in Vienna, I was the fiancée of the Duke of Bulgaria. When I was in Roumania, they betrothed me to the German Consul. It amuses me."

According to the *World,* however, the name of Teddy Marks, all protestations to the contrary, had been linked with Guilbert's, even in Europe.

Teddy Marks has been highly indignant at current statements to the effect that Yvette Guilbert did not go into "society" while in our sweet and courteous city. As Teddy Marks is not to become Mr. Yvette Guilbert—although a Berlin contemporary announces his engagement to the concert-hall star—his assertions may be looked upon as merely managerial.

The cold shoulders she had encountered on her previous New York visit may have affected Yvette more deeply than she would have cared to admit, if one can believe the following, from the same account:

She is charming to meet, but charming with a sort of haughty self-esteem. She is so fearful of being snubbed that she is on her guard all the time. When I met her, I wanted her to tell me something about her humble origin. Artists who have risen from the ranks are generally very proud of narrating stories of their obscure days when a loaf of bread was a luxury and a dish of soup a joy forever. I said to Yvette, "I believe you were born in the Rue du

Temple, Paris?" I expected a vivacious affirmative and a string of anecdotal paragraphs. Not so. Yvette looked a trifle uncomfortable, eyed me rather glassily, remarked indifferently, "Mais, oui," and dropped the subject.

As on the previous visit, when Bernhardt snorted her scornful *"Connais pas!"*, Yvette's luck for opportune publicity operated once more. It was just before the Koster and Bial opening on December 14 that the evangelist Dwight D. Moody, speaking at a Cooper Union meeting, immoderately attacked her repertoire, especially singling out for condemnation the song *La Glu,* by Jean Richepin. "I don't think Sodom ever produced anything like that!" pronounced Mr. Moody, after he had read to his scandalized listeners a translation of the song.

La Glu, based on a Breton legend, with musical setting by Gounod, was considered in Paris one of the most terrible dramas in Yvette's repertoire of terror. As translated by Arthur Symons, it reads:

> There was once a lad—alack for his lot,
> And he loved one who loved him not.
> She said to him, "Go bring to my feet
> Thy mother's heart for my dog's meat.
> Get thee home; slay her, nor wait!"
> He took the heart and he ran with it straight,
> As he ran he fell to the ground.
> And in the clay the heart rolled round.
> The heart spoke, and he heard it say—
> He heard the heart say in his ear,
> "Hast hurt thyself, my dear, oh my dear?"

A refrain, *Et lonlon laire, et lonlon la*—essential to the French version—occurs six times in the song, each time summing up the basic situation. In the first, sad and tender, it limns the love of the boy and his dejection at being rebuffed. Next it underscores the hideous cruelty of the girl when she orders him to kill his mother. When the boy rushes off to do her bidding, the refrain screams the ferocity of the deed. When he trips and falls, it breathes his fear of being caught; his panic and exhaustion. In the fifth verse, it stops the boy's breath in supreme horror. At the end it suggests an echo of the dead mother's voice, plaintive, full of anxiety; faint, as if coming from beyond this world.

Following the Reverend Mr. Moody's tirade, the *World* promptly took photographs of Yvette, illustrating her poses and gestures in *La Glu,* and within a few days an energetic New York press had fanned a negligible flame into a raging controversy. District Attorney W. M. K. Olcott hoped to prevent the singing of such brutal songs in public; the Reverend Charles H. Parkhurst found the singer's tastes "morbid, coarse"; Commander Ballington Booth called the piece "inhuman, demoralizing"; the W.C.T.U. petitioned a convention of Methodist ministers to sweep clean; to protest Yvette's entire repertoire countrywide.

Useless for defenders of the song to deny any connection with the Fifth Commandment; or to point out that though the fable reveals the heartlessness of coquetry and the slavery of infatuation, beyond all else its crowning idea is the undying tenderness of a mother's love.

How the charming Max Schiller happened to come into Yvette's life that winter of 1896 is not entirely clear. Yvette says that he was introduced to her by the journalist Arthur Hornblow, after Hornblow had dragged him to one of her performances.

The Rosenfeld family, however, preserve a different tradition. According to Dr. Eva Rosenfeld, Max was asked by a dramatic critic to deputize for him at one of Yvette's performances and at first refused, on the grounds that he could not abide variety shows. Nevertheless, he was reluctantly persuaded to go. Next morning when Yvette read her reviews, she was so impressed by Max's comment that she asked the paper to send her the man who had written it. If Hornblow was the critic for whom Max had substituted, a partial meshing of these two accounts may be possible.

The meeting of Max and Yvette must have been a case of love at first sight, in spite of all seeming obstacles. To ask how this German-hating Frenchwoman came to love a man so alien to her—a Jew from an Eastern country, educated in Berlin, with strong German ties—would be to pose a thoroughly illogical question, the blind bowboy's butt shaft having been always so notably erratic. Dr. Rosenfeld, theorizing on the attraction between the two, wrote:

> ... it is obvious that in all centuries they [the European Jews] had a proficiency for studying the needs of man. Max Schiller ... was one of those gifted men in whose life tending and protecting was a vocation. It would be wrong to call him a German, and it would be

equally wrong to call him an Eastern Jew. I would liken him most of all to a Medieval Knight ... who once he chose a master whom he could serve would surrender his life to this service unconditionally.

One who "had a proficiency for studying the needs of man"; with whom "tending and protecting was a vocation"; who would "surrender his life to this service unconditionally"—a man with these characteristics would certainly not have been often encountered in the rough-and-tumble of Yvette's experience, and it is likely that only such a man could have come to terms with her artist's egocentricity.

Yvette, at that particular period, must have been ripe for being tended and protected. Underlying all her fame lay the memory of the bitter poverty behind her and the nagging fear of what might lie ahead if her luck should run out; the prospect of a never-ending struggle in a profession where no holds are barred, no quarter given; the humiliation of being looked down on in certain circles, in spite of her money, her power, her indisputable genius. In Max she met for the first time a mature tenderness that wrapped itself around her, warmed her, cushioned her. Here was no "fool," no "Johnnie," fatuously fluttering around a stage door; no opportunist. Subconsciously, she must have been from the first demanding of a mate complete self-abnegation. Here, miraculously, it was being offered. Furthermore, if, as she had often said, it was cerebral quality that enchanted her, certainly Max was highly intelligent, and his cultural background far exceeded her own. Did she want to be loved "as a child, whose every caprice is catered to"? To Max, her every caprice was law. If she required "A person who will be competent to place a profound value on a dollar," Max would try, earnestly.

Almost at once the two became lovers. Max had rooms upstairs in the house of his brother-in-law, Theodor Rosenfeld, at Seventy-second Street, corner of Fifth Avenue, and it was here that the liaison was carried on, and with such secrecy—and luck—that, almost incredibly, no word ever reached the public of the many nights Yvette spent there. The Rosenfeld family were well aware of the relationship, but they too had succumbed to Yvette's charm and did not condemn it.

After her four weeks under Koster and Bial, Yvette again was off on the road, this time in a wider swing than before—Montreal, Toronto, Buffalo, Detroit, Chicago, St. Louis, Louisville, Memphis, New Orleans. To her, this tour would be a voyage of exploration of a truly new world, concerning which she was by now intensely curious. In Montreal, she was intrigued to find Norman French being spoken; seats for her concert sold at opera prices; babies were named for her; she discovered in a shop a deck of playing cards illustrated by contemporary celebrities that carried her own face on the ace of clubs. Toronto, then in its pioneer stage, she pronounced a "horror of a town" and marveled that in it could be found so many cultured women, richly dressed. She was told that the populace could neither speak nor understand French and that her hearers had come only to gape at her, as they previously gaped at Bernhardt. In Buffalo, on her birthday, January 20, she was thrilled by the majesty of Niagara; here her audience was commonplace. In Detroit she encountered for the first time the fearful mystery of the bed which folds down from an *armoire* and which she mightily distrusted, suspecting it might treacherously leap back of itself some night and swallow her alive.

At every hotel along the way would be waiting for her a long, adoring letter from her lover. In Chicago Max joined her, and here an announcement was made which created a considerable ripple of astonishment in theatrical circles:

> Yvette Guilbert ... has just signed a contract to appear under the management of Dr. Schiller of New York. ...
>
> "It may interest the public to know [she said] that I shall return to this country again, but not as a singer. While I have some contracts yet to fulfill abroad, I shall organize a company in the meantime, and will prepare for my appearance on the legitimate stage, as you call it here. ... Dr. Schiller suggested such a plan when in New York. ... My first part will be 'La Dame aux Camélias,' I intend then to produce some fresh adaptations of Italian plays, and an adaptation of a very dramatic Russian play."

The project never materialized, but even the consideration of such a radical change of direction suggests that her new manager may have been trying to point her to higher ground. On the other hand, the idea may have sprung chiefly from social causes, from a resentment of the galling necessity of always being forced to sit below the salt in the presence of "real" actors and singers. Or there may have been practical considerations. In New York the divette's initial appeal had been to curiosity, and curiosity is soon appeased. If Yvette wished to return to

America and its dollars—as what player did not?—to return as actress might well be the better strategy.

A degree of skepticism as well as astonishment was also voiced by critics. Yvette on her own terms in the realm of the *café-concert* was incomparable; but as contender with Bernhardt and Duse on their terms, even Guilbert might be overplaying her hand.

Yvette Guilbert is one of the brainiest and most magnetic women before the public today. But Yvette as Camille, and Camille in English! . . . Can a woman whose strange genius has something sardonic, satanic, demoniac in it ever act emotional roles and be convincing?

No one of course could have guessed that the scheme had been conceived and fashioned under the enchantment of new love.

All in good order the American continent unrolled before her fascinated gaze. In the Palmer Hotel in Chicago Yvette condemned the famous floor paved with silver dollars: "To walk on a fortune, when so many are perishing with hunger, in this America so cruel to the poor—it makes the heart bitter." In Chicago she was told that the only thing Americans really bowed to was success. She had succeeded, against great odds; her success was the basis of American interest in her, not her art; for Americans she was an inspiration to go and do likewise. In St. Louis someone snipped a piece from her sash as a souvenir. In Louisville and Memphis she was horrified at the filth and the primitive conditions. Loie Fuller, whom she encountered en route, gave her an opal and counseled her to go to Mexico. No, she was bound for Louisiana. The deep South captivated her, especially the Negroes in their picturesque dress. One night in New Orleans so many exotic flowers were loaded upon her after a concert that she could not bear their perfume and shared them with her Creole servitor Felix.

Then it was time to go home. She had experienced at first hand the great upsurge of raw energy that was North America of the 90's; had run the gamut of a continent from its live Indians in Montreal to cigar-store Indians in New Orleans; she had walked its wooden sidewalks, feasted on its beefsteak and quail, talked with its hotel-keepers, coachmen, slaves; shuddered at its ugliness, its cultural un-couthness; and had everywhere been quick in criticism of what she did not like.

175

A short period of time elapsed in New York between Yvette's return after the road tour and her departure for Europe, and it must have been during this period that one of the most bizarre literary collaborations on record was consummated—between Yvette, Louis de Robert, and Max Schiller. An American version of *Un Tendre,* to be entitled *The Enigma,* was then under way for the Judge Publishing Company, 110 Fifth Avenue, and for it Yvette had agreed to write a preface. In France, readers had not been shocked by the implications of De Robert's text; but in the United States, as Victorian in moral standards as Britain itself, the attitude of the public would presumably be less tolerant. Not only had Yvette been recently pilloried by the *La Glu* incident; in spite of all the popular adulation, some of her notices had been condemnatory, as witness Boston; and she had been under a cloud socially in New York as well. It must then have been in hope of wooing American public opinion to a belief in her respectability that in the preface which she wrote for *The Enigma* she certified that all statements made in the book about herself were true, with one exception—that concerning the favors which the author implied to have been granted to himself. This claim she dismissed as poetic license.

At this point reason falters. Not only has personal dignity been thrown to the winds, but what has become of judgment? Why trouble to deny Clairin and admit Forge? It was a witless thing to do, and the press was not slow to suggest the profit motive. The American version, moreover, was to be illustrated by photographs, taken by Pach in New York, in which Yvette herself would pose. Had the public realized the relationship then existing between her and the gentleman who doubled for De Robert in these photographs, the jabs of criticism might well have given way to snickers of amusement. For the gentleman-double, who in fact resembled Louis rather closely, was none other than the infatuated Dr. Max Schiller!

A few weeks after her return to France, the engagement of Mademoiselle Yvette Guilbert to Dr. Max Schiller was announced in the American press, and Dr. Schiller began a series of trips to Paris. The date originally set for the wedding had been May 15, but at the last moment the official who was to have performed the ceremony ruled that legal requirements had not been fully complied with. Under French law, one of the parties to a marriage contract must have resided at least six months in the *arrondissement* in which the banns were published. Dr. Schiller had made the mistake of posting banns in the *arrondissement* in which he was living temporarily. But the mistake could be corrected. The banns would now be posted in the district in which Yvette had lived for several years.

In Paris, meantime, it had been observed by several reporters that since her betrothal the chief votary of the song-with-a-shudder, apparently now viewing life *tout en rose,* was including more themes of gaiety in her programs than formerly. To illustrate, *Le Gaulois* prayed its readers not to miss her latest bit of ribaldry, *L'Aveugle et le paralytique.* This beguiling ditty concerns two street beggars, a blind man and a paralytic, who are represented as being invited by a charitable cocotte to her rooms. The invitation poses a problem, but after careful pondering the two decide to accept, for, as the blind man says:

> *Tu regard'ras pour moi,*
> *Je marcherai pour toi . . .*

That spring the whimsical Fates decided to indulge themselves in a pretty caprice. They would loop and tie together three golden threads they happened to be spinning at the moment into one great glittering ornamental knot. And thus it happened that on June 14, 1897, the three greatest names in the European theater shared honors in Paris on the same bill. The occasion was a benefit held in Bernhardt's beautiful Théâtre de la Renaissance to raise money for the erection of a statue of Alexandre Dumas, a prestige event where everyone who counted in Parisian society, politics, literature, and art foregathered. That night Bernhardt and Duse starred in scenes from repertoire, and Guilbert appeared in a sort of monologue, one of the *Lettres de Femmes* by Marcel Prévost. The affair took place during the period of Duse's first engagement in Paris; the fateful liaison with D'Annunzio had only recently begun.

But though the world was unquestionably brighter now for Yvette than ever before in her life, there remained one deep shadow: Madame Guilbert's stern opposition to her daughter's approaching marriage. The fact that Max Schiller was a Jew would have automatically disqualified him at any time in the eyes of the strictly Catholic Albine, but now her hostility found encouragement in the recent flaring up again of the Dreyfus Affair. The exoneration of Captain Dreyfus did not come until 1906, and meantime France, still split angrily into two violently opposing camps, was riddled with anti-Semitism; even the

177

validity of marriage between Catholic and Jew was coming under question.

But in romance as in every other aspect of her life the inflexible will of Yvette prevailed. Naturally the ceremony would have to be a civil one; but this would not trouble Yvette, who was a freethinker and not a churchgoer.

At ten o'clock on the evening of June 22, 1897, a reporter inquired of an usher at the Ambassadeurs whether Madame Schiller would sing that night.

"We have no Madame Schiller on the program," was the reply.

"Madame Yvette Guilbert, I mean."

"Ah, Guilbert! But why should she not sing? She sings every night at ten thirty."

"Because she was married this afternoon to Monsieur Schiller, a young American chemist."

"Guilbert married!" gasped the youth. "We knew nothing about it!" And off he sped to whisper the news to his fellow ushers. By ten thirty, the whisper had run all through the audience: "*Mademoiselle Yvette s'est mariée aujourd'hui!*"

Would she appear?

She appeared; at her usual time, clad in white, and singing her usual quota of songs. So far as could be seen, there was no departure from her nightly schedule—save one detail. The long black gloves were missing.

After her turn was over, the same reporter lost no time in seeking an interview. He found the bride in high spirits and, as always, ready to talk. The wedding had been kept a dead secret except for a choice few invited guests: Monsieur Boulard, an American journalist, and Monsieur George, an architect, friends of the bridegroom; Jacques Redelsperger, one of Yvette's songwriters; Ferdinand Bac; the beloved cousin, Lina Gaillard; and a friend, Viscount Linière. The ceremony had been performed by Deputy-Mayor Tamburini, of the Seventeenth Arondissement. She had worn a pearl-gray suit with white lace blouse; a gray hat with black aigrette. Afterward the wedding dinner, intimate as the wedding itself, had been held in her house. The menu? Mussels *marinières,* served in their colorful shells; leek and potato soup; roast pheasant, rice, and vegetables; tossed salad and assorted cheeses; crèpes suzettes. Champagne, of course, and everyone very gay. The reporter, a model of tact, forbore to remark on the absence from the party of both Louis de Robert and the mother of the bride.

He need not have worried over either. Even stubborn Albine was to give way, or at least halfway, to her son-in-law's irresistible charm for women. And within a few months, at the home of a mutual friend, Tristan Bernard, distinguished wit, sportsman, author, and editor of *La Revue Blanche,* Yvette and Max would be found lunching cozily with Louis.

Chapter 15

It would be delightfully romantic to be able to relate that Louis de Robert's heart had been broken and his career wrecked by Yvette's marriage to Max Schiller. In all candor it must be admitted, however, that facts urge other conclusions. As to career, following the publication of *Un Tendre,* a spate of other books poured out from Louis' pen between the years 1894 and 1899: *Fragiles, Papa, L'Envers d'une courtisane, L'Anneau et la première femme, Lettres d'un Enfant, La Reprise, Ninette.* Even erotically, according to Faure, Louis seems not to have been seriously affected. In 1898 the two young bloods had passing affairs with a couple of Basque girls. Regarding Yvette, in an undated letter sometime prior to 1900, he is found writing to Faure:

Last night Yvette back. There is at La Scala a very pretty girl whom I would much like to know. I am going to prowl behind scenes a few nights to make her acquaintance. What shoulders, what a bosom, what a waist. And the haunches and thighs firm and supple. . . . It is ten of twelve. I slept badly. I am going to lunch at Yvette's house.

No, the heart appears not permanently damaged. On the contrary it would seem that the young man is outgrowing his self-styled role of sentimentalist and is making the most of his experience in theatrical dressing rooms. Whatever had existed between him and Yvette seems now, in the best tradition of Gallic sophistication, to have been realistically put aside; what is being substituted, as events were to prove, is a comfortable *entente cordiale* with both Max and Yvette.

"Yvette Guilbert is going to Germany," noted Jules Renard in his *Journal inedit* in November, 1897. "She is being paid almost 40,000 francs for ten engagements."

Here is an abrupt *volte-face* on the part of a young lady who had so recently sworn, "Germany, never!" Yvette accounts for it by saying that she had not believed that her songs, with their *"esprit chatnoir-esque,"* would be understood by the stolid Teutons and that in response to inquiries she had therefore jestingly quoted a figure so absurdly high that she thought it would never be accepted. More likely perhaps that her anti-Prussian attitude had been softened and her appreciation of German culture enlarged by her German-bred husband. Or that her eyes had been opened by the Rosenfeld brothers-in-law to the importance of Berlin as a theatrical center. Carl and Theodor were themselves back in Berlin now, their New York career at an end, and were operating an enterprise called the Passage Theater —a variety theater and two cabarets—at 22 Unter den Linden.

At any rate, the step proved to have been well taken professionally, the *Lokal Anzeiger* testifying to the thunders of applause with which Yvette was received in the Apollo Theatre, a music hall, in December of 1897. On this occasion she had agreed to give as usual a preview performance to some two hundred members of the press for publicity purposes, but just before beginning the preview she suddenly suffered one of her seizures of acute stage fright. The fear of a thorough critical drubbing all but paralyzed her. Suppose these men proved teasing, mischievous—what might they not do to tarnish her reputation? Later, during the reception that followed, she was astonished to find that the Berlin Sarceys not only spoke excellent French but were thoroughly documented on her world of the *caf'-conc'*, and in their subsequent reviews, to her further surprise, she found a greater appreciation of herself as an artist than in Paris. "In Paris they lauded my songs; in Germany my art of singing them. In Paris I was Yvette of a new repertoire; in Germany the exponent of a new art. My talent as interpreter always took precedence."

To the rich professional satisfactions of the Berlin appearances were added the pleasure of the personal debut with Max's family, who were in a flurry of mingled awe and pride over the new daughter-in-law. It was during this visit of 1897 that Eva Rosenfeld, then a child of five, first saw her uncle's famous wife:

My first . . . conscious memory of Yvette is a little concert she gave to . . . my grandparents, who lived in a suburb of Berlin. . . . Already her fame was worldwide, . . . and this great artist came to the home of her humble parents-in-law where all their grandchildren had assembled and sang to us the chansons which had conquered the world... I have never forgotten my enthralment, from that moment I belonged to her, heart and soul.

Hardly had the divette reopened at La Scala in the fall of 1898 than she came under unexpected censure from Sarcey. In the past this critic had delighted in her subtleties, her originality; now suddenly he claimed retrogression of a serious nature:

What an unbearable manner she has formed! She drags on the last syllables of the verses with a sort of prolonged moan which, by dint of endless repetition, finally irritates the nerves painfully. She makes pauses; you think she is holding the word back merely to send it out more strongly; not at all; she purposely lets the end of the phrase drop or utters it in speech so rapid that it is impossible to understand anything. In the perpetual jugglery there is an enervating affectation. She carries affectation into everything.

The unhappy result of this onslaught was an open feud between critic and star, played out in the press, that dumbfounded the public and shed little luster on the name of either participant. Parisians found themselves at a crossroads. It was unthinkable to question a verdict of Sarcey's. It was equally unthinkable to discredit Guilbert's genius; as Sarcey sarcastically complained, every day newspapers burned incense at her altar.

The first brickbat Yvette hurled in retaliation was a public statement that Sarcey had written not objectively but maliciously because he had been obliged to buy a ticket for her performance. In reply, Sarcey advised her that instead of wasting time writing letters to the press she would do better "to act upon the advice of a critic who may be right, even though he paid for his seat." Yvette then charged that Sarcey's real motive had been disgruntlement because, for her forthcoming tour of Russia, she had turned down an offer from his friend Gunsbourg in favor of a higher bid, and she ended with a verbal jab below the belt—a fleer at the critic's obesity. It was time, she said, for artists to speak out:

Artists fear Sarcey, though they have no high opinion of him.
... When I think that the admirable Duse was prevented from coming to Paris because of a savage criticism from the Sarcey Belly

[*le Ventre Sarcey*] after Sarcey had seen her in Vienna. . . . It's enough to make one groan.

Gunsbourg, when informed of her statements, wrote *Figaro* denying that he had ever offered Mademoiselle Guilbert a contract; in fact, that he had ever written her. Yvette quoted communications received from Gunsbourg's agents and displayed to reporters a dossier filled with correspondence. Rumor had it that she even called on Sarcey, brushed aside the servant who tried to keep her out, and forced her way into his study to denounce him:

> "You are an insolent cad who makes cowardly attacks upon a woman."
> ". . . as a woman, Mlle. Guilbert is nothing to me. What I say of her public character cannot affect her innocent private reputation."
> The sarcasm was too much for Yvette. She jumped up in a white rage.
> "I regret," said M. Sarcey, waving his hand toward the pile of paper on his desk, "that pile of white sheets must be covered before noon, and if we have no more to say to each other—"
> The raging divette seized the brass inkstand and in a flash overturned it on the sheets.
> "They were to be dirtied. They are dirtied," she said, striking a pose.

M. Sarcey bowed, and rang for the servant to show her out.
And so the stories made their rounds, losing nothing, one may be sure, in the telling, until the Affaire Guilbert-Sarcey rivaled in popular concern the Affaire Dreyfus. Unquestionably, the incident left its mark on Yvette. She never forgave Sarcey, never ceased hating him.

It was inevitable that St. Petersburg as well as Berlin should finally demand Guilbert in person on its stages; she had already been seen there in a number of imitations. The interest was reciprocal: Yvette was quite as eager to see as to be seen. Actually, however, she saw little in St. Petersburg that snowy December of 1898 that pleased her. It was a disagreeable trip that she and Max had made, on a train filled with verminous rabble, and with a corpse aboard. The Nemetti theater in which she was billed was shabby and cramped; there was a strike of the company the night of her debut, and from nine to eleven, to save the situation for her manager, she held forth alone, without benefit of assisting talent or stage effects, and with a curtailed repertoire, all Xanrof and Donnay songs having been prohibited by the censor. Attendance continued poor until she received nobility's nod of approval, appearing first before the Grand Duke Paul and later at a fête given by the Grand Duchess Constantin. Throughout her stay in Russia she was filled with pity over the misery of the poor and openly voiced her disapproval of what she called the superstitious piety of the wretched masses; the roubles wasted on votive lights should have been spent on food. Moscow was better. There she was struck by the semioriental aspect of the city, the dazzle of gilded and painted domes, and the ornate awesomeness of palaces and cathedrals.

Other new countries, too, were added to her itinerary. In March, 1899, Yvette returned to La Scala from a triumphal progress that had carried her to Denmark, Sweden, Portugal, Spain. In Copenhagen, students swarmed on stage to crown her with a white toque symbolically ornamented with laurel. Yvette privately considered Madrid a failure because King Alphonse laughed so stupidly in all the wrong places; but in Lisbon, when she made her final exit from the theater at the end of her engagement, young Latins gallantly threw their great black capes on the ground to form a carpet of honor for her to walk on.

In June, 1899, it was announced that, in anticipation of her next winter's trip, the divette had just signed a contract for fifty appearances in Berlin, Vienna, and Budapest for 150,000 francs. Meantime she would play in the operetta *Zut pour Yvette!,* current attraction at the Ambassadeurs.

Why should she ever have worried over a change in fortune? *Zut pour Sarcey!*

On October 4, 1899, *Le Gaulois* reported that Guilbert had opened brilliantly the night before at the Folies-Bergère, in a new program calculated to attract crowds for weeks to come. It was something of a shock to the Parisian public, therefore, to read ten days later in the same journal that the star would be obliged to cancel all appearances, both in Paris and abroad. Her doctors had ordered an absolute rest of several months.

A secret that Yvette had been courageously concealing from the public thus came out in the open. For several years she had been plagued by recurrent knifelike pains around the waist. "Hardly had I overcome the difficulty of earning my living," she writes, "before

Death came creeping toward me; ... teasing and torturing me ... with his claws in my entrails, taking me by the waist (that slim and supple waist of which I was so proud!)." As time went on, the seizures had become more frequent and acute. Often an attack would come during a performance; then she would cry out, sob, vomit, become so weak that she could barely walk. Make-up, streaming off in floods of perspiration, would have to be renewed again and again. Yet at the cry of the callboy, "Mademoiselle Guilbert on stage," her indomitable will would produce a physical transformation. From some secret spiritual resource she would find strength to rise above her agony, and as she stood before the public singing without a trace of effort her *Cahin caha* or her *Et lonlon laire et lonlon la,* no listener could have guessed the physical torment she was surmounting. It was a situation known only to a few intimates; one not to be acknowledged openly. In the accelerated tempo of a star's life, everything is predicated on boundless health—contracts no less than crowded houses. To the attacks of pain stoicism had for a long time seemed the only answer. Now even stoicism no longer served.

Soon the papers were headlining new developments: Guilbert must undergo surgery to correct a kidney complaint caused by excessively tight lacing. Readers were reminded of the famed svelte, nineteen-inch waistline.

For years the subject had been agitated—to lace or not to lace—and medical advice poured out on women to avoid excess of vanity. But though physicians' tirades were generally discounted, some difference of opinion had lately arisen even among women themselves. Among actresses, Mrs. Leslie Carter had abjured corsets, as had Elsie de Wolfe, and the increase of interest in athletics, especially cycling, had led many other women to leave them off. Now the word that Yvette Guilbert must submit to the loss of a kidney aroused to new heights the ardor of anti-corseteers the fashionable world around. Her name, predicted the New York *Journal* solemnly, was destined "to go down through the ages as a warning most dreadful to all tight-lacers!"

In 1899 the removal of a kidney was an operation attended with great hazard, and when, on the night of her last performance, Yvette caught sight of her surgeon, Dr. Albaran, in the audience, for a moment she could hardly proceed. So he knew it was his last chance to see her!

But Yvette did not die, though for weeks she hovered on the brink of death. "I prayed," she wrote later, "and decided that I would live."

In the end, life did come back to her, though very, very slowly; hope and self-confidence even more slowly. One night at her dressing table she noticed two fine silvery strands in her hair. Yvette was thirty-four. It was her fearsome first glimpse of the specter of age; she plucked them out and put them away carefully. "I shall look at them daily," she said. "They will remind me that I have strength to live and the will to compel fortune still to smile on me."

Eventually, when she was strong enough, far-reaching decisions had to be taken: one of Europe's most talked-about careers had dramatically crashed. Max had earlier told reporters that his wife would retire to private life at some indeterminate time. Had that time now arrived?

It was the eve of the Paris Exposition of 1900. Again the city would be crowded for months to come with amusement seekers from home and abroad; it would be hard for them to imagine a Guilbertless Paris. As for Yvette, to withdraw now from the *café-concert* would be a disastrous loss of opportunity to extend her fame to every civilized corner of the globe. The Exposition was to include a Théâtre de la Chanson, in which every poet and *chansonnier* whom Paris counted as witty or original would be heard and in which Yvette was already scheduled to appear. In addition, hundreds of thousands of new admirers would be flocking to La Scala and Les Ambassadeurs. Earnings would be spiraling ever upward.

But—

What of those other considerations the divette had long been wrestling with in secret? From the beginning she had been warned away from the *café-concert*. She remembered in particular one magic evening at the home of Charpentier, the publisher, when she had sung for a selected group of *littérateurs*.

That evening how life smiled on me . . . when after two hours of singing I was feverishly happy as each guest came up to me with words of praise . . . and all with the same advice to leave the *"Boui-Bouis"* (the halls).

In nostalgic mood she now turned over the pages of a morocco-bound album of laudatory letters, many from guests of that evening, which she treasured above the whole body of her press critiques: letters from Zola, Edmond de Goncourt, Alphonse Daudet, Paul

185

Hervieu, Marcel Prévost, Pierre Loti, Octave Mirbeau, Henri Lavedan, Jean Richepin, Catulle Mendès, Robert de Montesquiou, François Coppée, Jules Massenet, Jules Lemaître, André Theuriet, Ludovic Halévy, Jules Clarétie, Paul Bourget, and many others. How often she found in them the same thought reiterated—that her artistry was being lamentably wasted. Hervieu called her a great tragedienne; Daudet wished he were young and strong enough to write a lyrical drama for her; Mirbeau demanded for her a modern Shakespeare.

It had remained for kind Count de Kerveguen to put into words the situation that she already knew she must one day come to grips with:

"You see, my dear," he said to me, "your great good fortune is your talent, but your misfortune is the place where you have to display it.

"... the mass, the crowd, is drawn to you by your songs; the daring, naughty words, that is what attracts them ... if you were to change your *repertoire* they would drop you immediately.

"... When you are rich you can build yourself some kind of place where people can come and hear you in the things that you really enjoy doing, and you will always find a select audience who will be drawn by your talent; but for the present don't deceive yourself; the public only comes to enjoy your *repertoire* ... your artistic quality is unnoticed. If you want only genuine admiration for your talent itself then you must leave the *café-concert,* but remember you must give up the idea of making money."

There it was, baldly stated—The Dilemma. It had not seemed a serious one at first, to a money-hungry young woman who cared not a whit what dirty words she put into her mouth.

But in the ten crowded years from 1889 to 1899 much had happened. She had matured intellectually as well as artistically. To her intellectual interests she owed acquaintance with some of the most brilliant artists and men of letters of France. She had married a man of taste. Particularly, she had discovered for herself the riches of song as an art. Inspired first by the Friday classical concerts at the Eden, she had enjoyed later, at the Bodinière, months of study in the old French *chanson* under the tutelage of Le Roux. In fact, concurrently with her public career as "queen of improprieties," she had for some years been indulging a passion for research on the subject. As early as 1894, she had been reported as daily frequenting the Bibliothèque Nationale and other libraries, poring over old song collections.

"To get out of my environment, to create a new *repertoire,*" she writes, "that was my dream," and she had chafed that, as Kerveguen had so well said, it could be only a dream.

The Dilemma had not been made any easier by the *declassée* status she had been forced to accept as an entertainer on the lowest level of the theatrical profession. How much longer should a woman of her stature be expected to endure the slights of the Coquelins and the Melbas? Respectability beckoned seductively—a respectability equivalent to that offered by the Comédie Française and the Metropolitan. To achieve it, she had only to leave behind forever the smoke-filled *caf'-conc',* and its overflowing coffers, for the chaste atmosphere of the concert hall or the serious art of the legitimate theatre.

Now, too, the fears that had always haunted her of the inevitability of a declining vogue seemed to be materializing. She worried over whether Sarcey had damaged her and, after the floodtide of Exposition tourists ebbed out of Paris, whether he would renew his attacks. London had been unkind. As recently as May, one English critic had declared that the "old pictorial power, the old ironic salt, are gone from her songs. . . . Once she belonged to French Naturalism. Now she belongs only to the music halls." These were tiny cracks in the foundations; were they serious? Was the "old ironic salt" part and parcel of her old struggle against odds? Was her very good fortune—her new domestic happiness and her affluence—undermining her as an artist? Art admits no relaxation. Did she need new goals?

Dare she, at thirty-four, hope for success in pursuing new goals?

H. G. Ibels once said that the answer to her immense success in the *café-concert* was to be found solely in her unique intelligence and unremitting toil. As to the first, Yvette had been intelligent enough to reject stereotyped material and to address herself directly to her immense corps of *poétes-chansonniers,* knowing with a sure instinct the kind of songs to demand from them that would make her name and theirs. As to her capacity for work, Ibels said that to fully comprehend the energy she poured into her preparation one would have to see and hear her study a song for weeks, word by word, couplet by couplet, seeking its strongest emphases, filling its silences with eloquent mimicry, daring even to convey its most subtle impressions by sheer rigidity; in a word, achieving what every true artist strives for—maximum of effect with minimum of effort.

Arthur Symons had already recorded another quality not to be overlooked: will power. "Other women are just as clever as I am," she had once said to him, "but if I make up my mind that I will do a thing, I always do it. I try, and try, and try, until I succeed."

But beyond the endowment of intelligence and the trojan virtues of industry and will power, Yvette knew that she was also an innovator. Not wholly in manner, where she was not the first or only stylist in the technique of "depraved virginity." On the stage, assumed modesty had been the forte of Eve La Vallière; in dance, the success of dreamy, remote Jane Avril derived in part from what Symons called "the last refinement . . . of perversity"—perverted sanctity; "absinthe in the guise of milk." But in the *café-concert* Yvette had brought the technique to new heights; in the song pornographic she had made herself the muse of deadpan; she had brought about new directions through her introduction of naturalism into the medium of the *caf'-conc'*.

Would the qualities that brought her to such heights in her twenties still serve for her thirties? Was the time for a change propitious?

In the deliberations that took place over these questions during the long weeks and months of Yvette's convalescence, it can hardly be doubted on which side the fastidious Max stood. Money need not now be of first consideration; ergo, the Dilemma no longer existed. By all means, with her great talent, her new treasures of research, her widespread reputation—*Vanity Fair* had recently claimed that Yvette Guilbert was "one of the first half-dozen women most prominent in contemporary newspaper discussion"—she could and should change course. Dramatists had often suggested starring her in their new plays; there was always possible a return to the abandoned project of forming her own company; or there was the prestige of the concert hall, with classical repertoire and elite audiences. She remembered what Mirbeau had once said to her: "You must know that you have genius, or you are not worthy to have it."

Long ago, in Concert Parisien days, Émile Blémont had said of La Guilbert that though her mien would make an angel swoon, the words she uttered would make a monkey blush.

Let her be done now, once and for all, Max urged, with making the monkey blush.

Part Two

MAKING
THE ANGELS
SWOON

I

1899 – 1922

Un artiste est un prêtre,
un serviteur divin.

—An artist is a priest,
a divine servant.

Chapter 1

"*J'appartiens à Maxime*," read the inscription on the inside of Yvette's wedding ring. The idea might better perhaps have been stated in reverse, for to whatever degree Yvette may have belonged to Max, it was soon evident that Max belonged to Yvette *in toto*—blindly, worshipfully.

The Yvette who emerged from what must have been at best in 1899 a highly experimental bout with surgery was a radically altered woman. Convalescence had been long, and confinement and isolation had laid her open to all that oppresses the human spirit when physical defenses are stripped away. Missing was the old brash self-confidence; hideously omnipresent, a racking uncertainty of self and future. During a year or more of invalidism she had had time to brood about destiny; about God. Living for months close to the very real possibility of death, she had seemingly for the first time experienced an active awareness of Deity. In her forced retirement it had been bitter to note how progressively she was being neglected by former admirers and friends now that her name no longer glittered daily in the press. Only an occasional reporter called at Vaux, whom she would receive languidly on her chaise longue in the shade of the chestnut trees.

There had been a little wave of happiness at the decision to embark on a new course, and then, in a backwash of reaction, she had sunk into an even deeper state of melancholy, when, during weeks and months of disability, she saw the new life, bravely planned, incapable of realization. To prepare and rehearse new programs would demand resources of physical and mental power that she simply could not offer. Such dark and constant perspectives led her to the very verge of despair.

It was during this bleak period that the devotion of Max Schiller made its first great contribution to her life. By the time her convalescence was well under way, Max had indeed come to belong to Yvette, and asked no better career than service to her needs. He cared for her physically, untiring as nurse and companion. He offered strength, and humble adoration. She took the strength and drew upon it increasingly; though never before a clinging vine, became one; recovered on his adoration.

After many months—when nature had had its beneficent way, when red corpuscles had performed their sanative miracles and had brought a gradual resurgence of the old will power and *élan*—Yvette's outlook began to improve, until eventually optimism reached the point where it could at last shape itself into plans and the plans into action.

But—

Action under what unexpected circumstances! Yvette had returned to health, altered not only emotionally and spiritually but physically as well. The "lean witch" of the famed nineteen-inch waistline was no more. The new Yvette was buxom; ample; of matronly figure. Not to put too fine a point upon the matter, fat.

Here was a situation never anticipated; a reversal of every known value in her world; a state somewhat comparable to recovering blinded or crippled. To lose the celebrated silhouette, a fundamental part of her stock in trade, had been no part of her bargain with the future. Luckily, in 1900, a degree of *embonpoint* was not fatal to a woman's rating in personal attractiveness, and Yvette seems to have accepted her added poundage as an inevitable concomitant of her recovery and to have made no efforts to recapture svelteness.

Still, and she recognized this, it was a factor to be reckoned with professionally, adding as it did years to her appearance. At that very time Paris was babbling over the scandal of D'Annunzio's *Il fuoco,* with its ruthless baring of Duse's aging body and all that the fading of beauty signified to a vain Don Juan five years his mistress's junior. Everyone knew the great actress's passion for D'Annunzio—Duse made no secret of it—and more, her dream of forming with him the poetic theater of all time; he to write, she to act his plays. How viciously his callousness must have brought home to every woman of the stage the cruelty of the crossroads: the moment when a star must cease offering the public the illusion of youth and frankly own her years, with all the lacerations to pride such a moment brings in train. But the decision Yvette had lately reached with Max—to abandon the noisy, smoky *caf'-conc'* for the sedate and gilded concert hall—was in entire harmony with the problem of her age and figure. On the concert platform, mature feminine avoirdupois was a fact of long acceptance. In Yvette's case there was even another favorable aspect: a certain suggestion of personality change. With plumpness, the gamine had begun to fade; with weight added to height, Yvette now seemed at times almost regal.

The real problem was how to return at all after so long an absence; how to resume her place in public favor, especially as she would be seeking a new public and a new kind of favor.

Obviously she must have a new repertoire, and somehow the idea came to her of using the *chansons* of old France as a principal source; of restoring to life the ballads of the medieval troubadours as well as the songs of the seventeenth, eighteenth, and nineteenth centuries; of making this practically unknown field uniquely her own. Ever since La Bodinière days the *chanson* had fascinated her. But the immensity of the undertaking! She would need much time for preparation. Research, thus far desultory and intermittent, must become constant and systematic.

As fast as physical strength permitted, then, she began haunting bookstores and libraries. In the Bibliothèque Nationale in Paris and the library of the Paris Conservatoire she unearthed many quaint airs from yellowed, crumbling sheets. In the provinces she knocked on the doors of monasteries, nunneries, and old châteaux. Many of her finds were in their original bindings, some even in original manuscript form. One leather-bound volume alone yielded a treasure of words and music for over one hundred and fifty songs, copied by some patient hand centuries dead. She began the study of Latin grammar, to enable herself to translate dim texts in Latin and old French; she read widely in the history and literature of old France; she reproduced sketches of old costumes. It seemed a natural part of her rebirth, and moreover a source of great joy, to discover hitherto unsuspected aptitudes for painstaking work of this nature.

Meantime, however, the artist in her could not wait on the scholar. Habits of a lifetime were strong; she hungered for audiences, the nightly sense of exhilaration, of conquest. She must sing, as soon as possible. Instinctively her mind turned back to little La Bodinière, former scene of her semischolastic matinee triumphs with Hugues Le Roux. In such a toy theater a minimum tax would be laid upon her only partially recovered energies. The place, she reasoned, would be ideal, as would the high cultural level of its patrons.

As to songs, since her studies in medievalism were not yet ripe, she would carry out another idea which had been germinating in her mind—to revive the work of Maurice Rollinat, whose dramatic songs *L'Idiot, Le Convoi funèbre, Dans un Champs de Colza,* and others, she had used previously with signal success, and she would also ask Rollinat to set to music certain poems of Baudelaire, including *La Mort des amants, Recueillement* and *Reversibilité.* Her acquaintance with Rollinat dated back to Montmartre days, when he used to sing his poems to his own weird accompaniments at the Chat Noir. To her those half-mad performances had been magnificent, even though he always reminded her of something out of *Tales of Hoffman.*

The composer, now in retirement in a little town in central France, flattered by Yvette's interest, consented to her proposals, and scholarly M. Arsène Alexandre, editor of *Le Rire,* agreed to serve as *conférencier.* It only remained for the singer herself to summon enough courage to enter from the wings on opening night.

On January 13, 1901, *Le Gaulois* noted with interest the reappearance of the long-lost Guilbert before a Paris audience. *"C'est une véritable résurrection,"* the columnist proclaimed, though admittedly of a new-model Yvette. The reporter had had to swallow hard, one gathers, on finding the black gloves missing and Yvette attempting *"l'art pur,"* but there was no denying the warmth of her reception or the brilliance of her performance. Rollinat's music made merciless demands, requiring a wide vocal range and virtuoso breath control. For the latter, Yvette had practiced exercises unremittingly and now, after weeks of rigid self-discipline, could toss off a passage of twenty-four measures without having to take breath.

On the morning after the concert, once more reporters were crowding into the house on Boulevard Berthier, where they found the *revenante* in high humor. She was wearing a violet peignoir, wrote Maurice Guillemet, and she chatted with the same old gay animation, using the same picturesque expressions and touches of argot.

News of the Parisian "resurrection" was not slow in traveling, and the first foreign claim to which Yvette listened was, quite understandably, that of her German admirers. In Berlin, in 1897, her relations with public and critics had been particularly harmonious; in Berlin remained also the additional lodestone of Max's family. Max's father had recently died, but the Rosenfelds were still there, living in the little suburb of Steglitz. Yet another pull might have been the cordial friendship that existed with Madame Louise Wolff, an ardent Francophile, through whose agency Yvette conducted her affairs in Germany.

Within a month, then, the Schillers were registering again in their favorite Palast-Hotel in Berlin; both Schillers, for Max had adopted the role of "manager" of the star. Yvette, they had decided, would still be known as Mademoiselle Guilbert. Best not to destroy the public's cherished image of her—unmarried and an enchantress, as in *Un Tendre,* with who knew how many affairs under the rose. As manager, Max could offer invaluable experience in personal liaison; as solicitous husband be constantly on hand to guard his wife's still precarious health.

On her opening night at the Metropol there was no trace of traditional German stolidity in the auditorium. On the contrary, the audience rose to a man when Yvette came on stage, while she, taken completely by surprise by such a demonstration, stood speechless, tears welling into her eyes. That night she sang old favorites—*La Glu, La Pocharde,* and all the others—and at the end the cheering Teutons, after encoring wildly, pressed upon her an immense wreath inscribed extravagantly "To the Queen of Song." A few days later, in a concert hall, when she ventured to offer tentatively to a select few her more esoteric program of Baudelaire and Rollinat, she created no less an impression. So great was her impact on the Berlin public that the German art cabaret, Yvette always declared, was born as a direct result of her influence. "When I think," she wrote later, "of the flock of diseuses and diseurs that sprang up after my debuts in Germany, I wonder if all those good people ever remember to thank me."

During the period of Yvette's withdrawal from the spotlight, another well-known Parisian figure had also been lost sight of. From Louis de Robert also not a word was being heard.

By the strangest of coincidences, for Louis too there had been the exchange of sunny Paris boulevards for the lowered shades of an invalid's room. In April, 1900, he had been stricken with pneumonia, a mishap more serious than at first appeared, since it may well be held that he never fully recovered, seeming to slip from the pulmonary ailment into one far more subtle and sinister. In letters written over a period of years to his close friend Paul Faure, much is unclear as to the clinical diagnosis of his malady but not as to its symptoms, which he describes vividly: sufferings of a nature to suggest those tortures that often pass under the vague term of "nerves," but which can in many instances end a man's usefulness as effectively as the bite of a rattlesnake.

In the fall of 1901, he transferred with his mother to a small estate in Sannois, not far from Paris, where he soon became that most pitiful of figures, *un homme couché*. For him, as for Yvette, life's values had been abruptly altered, but for him far more tragically. Yet, though his sensitive spirit was darkened almost to the point of giving way, he set about, from his couch, making readjustments. Life for life's sake he might be constrained to forego; life for art's sake might still be possible to a degree. Through sleepless nights and nightmarish days he clung to that tenuous hope. Though it may have been in the beginning a groping with little faith, his struggle to work persisted.

It was also in 1901, the year of her "resurrection," that a new aspect of Yvette's creative energy began to develop. Not only did Yvette begin to think in terms of scholarship; she displayed as well a bent toward authorship.

As divette, she had long been an inveterate letter writer to the press —a practice seemingly then much enjoyed in France by persons in public life—and in sundry articles had given vent to her attitudes, frequently castigatory, on a variety of subjects, mostly trivial. Her journalistic style was voluble and breezy, with a kind of sincerity and a free-swinging rhythm that made her observations easy reading, if not always convincing. Earlier, too, her preface to Bac had attracted attention, not to mention her extraordinary contribution to the American edition of *Un Tendre*. So no one seemed surprised when it now began to be rumored that Guilbert was deep in the writing of a novel.

To be sure, an observer, scanning her full calendar, might well have wondered when, in the relatively short bits of freedom between tours, she could have found time to work on such an extensive project. Possibly during March and April, after her return from Berlin and before her May and June engagements, first in Montmartre and later in London. According to a confidence she made to her friend Edmond Sée, she was certainly working on it during the sweet summer days at Vaux in July, August, and September. But probably not in October, which found her back in London, at the Olympia, and by the twenty-second of that month she had signed for an extensive tour of Europe.

In December, however, M. Sée put all rumors to rest by writing in *La Vie de Paris* that a novel would indeed be immediately forthcoming from the pen of Mademoiselle Guilbert; the title, *La Vedette*.

The book, when it appeared, was found to draw heavily on autobiographical background and hence did not go unnoticed. In fact, it was a passable success, first for its author's sake, and second for its undeniably authentic glimpses of *caf'-conc'* life.

The hero is a popular *café-concert* singer, risen from the ranks of the minor tea gardens, dance halls, and neighborhood cafés, whose name on the bills is finally printed in heavy capitals, or *en vedette*. He marries, and he and his wife star together and travel widely; here the author's American experiences provide scenes for certain of the chapters. Eventually the public tires of the pair, and they are reduced to touring in the poorest provincial companies. But through it all, the heroine is a "sentimental, devoted woman, a type very commonly met with in the *beuglants*," and despite fickle fortune the two remain faithful to each other. One night their adored child, who is ill of semi-starvation, lies on a billiard table in a café, where the wandering couple are performing. While the mother is passing the collection plate after their act, the boy cries, "*Maman,* take me home," and dies.

"There is no home," the mother sobs, while tears melt the paint on the faces of the husband and wife.

The book ends with a dismal chapter showing the crazed parents, still in the gaudy dress of their performances, alternately carrying the dead boy in their arms at night in a strange town, unwilling to go to the morgue and without a soul to give them a resting place.

The story, most of it couched in the jargon of the green room and the argot of Paris slums, is filled with scenes of squalor and misery and strange glimpses of a sinful Bohemia. Nor does it omit to satirize corrosively the current methods by which ignorant young men and girls, scraped up from the lowest ranks of waiters and dishwashers, were drilled in a space of two or three weeks to become music-hall "attractions."

Paul Bourget, after reading a pre-publication copy, said of the book to its author: "Your first effort places you among the literary artists of first rank. I have not read such significant, graphic fiction since de Maupassant's death." But M. Bourget was a friend, writing in a letter, and his generous estimate has not been borne out by the judgment of posterity. Madame Rachilde of the *Mercure de France,* also a friend, summed it up as "the work of a nervous, vibrant, passionate woman as well as that of a novelist acquainted with all the tricks of the trade." But Edmond Sée, who saw the book as merely another, longer song, temporized gracefully. He believed Yvette would succeed in literature as she had in singing, by her charm; that the book was a manifestation "hardly differing from the nature we all love . . . with the well-known face of the *artiste* discernible on each page . . . you will remember quite naturally the warm tenderness of her voice . . . the gaucherie of certain chapters will recall to you those evenings when the public pardoned her for being less than her best. For it is with women as with artists—they cannot always be infallible . . ."

With Yvette seemingly established in the new role of novelist, it must have come then as something of a nine-days' wonder when one day a certain Arthur Byl (presumably the same Byl whose name appeared as author of the text in the English edition of Toulouse-Lautrec's *Album d'Yvette*) unexpectedly revealed his part in the composition of *La Vedette* by filing suit against Yvette for services as ghostwriter.

Naturally, the press investigated thoroughly:

Who actually wrote Yvette Guilbert's "La Vedette"? . . . Yvette Guilbert published it as her own and as hers a German firm translated it into German. . . .

... The book was a success, when suddenly came the accusation, from the German publisher, of false authorship, and a Monsieur Byl obligingly stepped forward to protest himself the real writer. A mass of correspondence is put into the court—the letters written by Madame Guilbert upon the subject. ...

The affair seems to have commenced as follows. One day Madame Guilbert received a letter asking her to collaborate upon a work of "Café-Concert" life. To this she wrote back that she knew absolutely nothing about Café Concerts. At a fixed hour she drove to the building, dressed herself in a room by herself, went on the stage, sang, and drove off again. After an interview, however, she consented to the literary effort. Only Monsieur Byl, whose intentions were from the beginning frankly and exclusively pecuniary, stipulated that the publication as far as he was concerned should bring only money—the glory he left to the lady. A book published under his own name would pass unnoticed; in hers pecuniary benefit was certain, and pecuniary benefit was his one and only object.

But now comes the interesting intensification of the mystery—the climax to an extraordinary literary episode. Monsieur Byl sent his copy to Madame Guilbert in a handwriting clearly not his own. And one day in the parcel of manuscript she found a note addressed to him. "Here is the fifth installment of 'copy.' Marsolleau." So Monsieur Byl did not write his own contributions and "La Vedette" was indebted to a third contributor! The mystery is still unlifted. Certainly Monsieur Byl, who was paid generously out of the profits, cuts a sorry figure in the business. His threats when demanding still further remuneration are contemptible. Legally the case ended in a victory for Madame Guilbert. From the point of view of law she remains the authoress of "La Vedette." Assistance was rendered, but she undoubtedly not only wrote a large part of the work herself, but repeatedly urged her collaborator, or collaborators, to sign with her for publication. Also, as the judge observed, Monsieur Byl's letters alone prove him incapable of rendering anything but the very slightest literary assistance to anybody, while his acknowledgment of the money paid is given for revision, and "small services rendered" in connection with the book.

Only there is a literary moral to the story. In writing a book it is best to write it oneself, or when assistance is given, to acknowledge it, for the silence of those still capable of speaking is never in this world to be relied upon.

On January 1, 1902, in a luxury French train whose wheels were grinding out the miles across Europe, something new was being borne to the music halls of Germany, Austria, Roumania, Czechoslovakia, Italy: Yvette and a troupe. Yvette, now apparently restored in health, though always haunted by a dread of relapse, was taking a flyer as manager, with, of course, the experienced Max at her shoulder. *Montmartre en ballade*—thus she had baptized the contingent of twenty-one *artistes de la Butte* whom she had gathered up. Names of some of the singers and comedians then much in vogue float down to us—Fragerolle, Marcel Legay, Gabriel Montoya, Clement Georges, François and Dora Villé, Eugénie Nau, Jeanne Dule, Irma Perrot, Mévisto, Lagrange, Severin-Mars—names for the most part strange today in our ears. And at every engagement, in addition to their offerings, Yvette sang eight to ten of her own songs and still found time to send back from along the road travel chitchat to the Paris press.

Cologne heard the Montmartrists in its great Philharmonic Concert Hall and applauded, even though deploring the giantism of the bill, which ran four hours; Munich heard them, and Vienna. On March 17, Yvette reported in a news letter to Edmond Le Ruy:

To be truthful I have to add that in Austria and in Germany I am something of a spoiled child. This time Hungary was more hospitable than usual. This time I sang in the great theater and not the music hall of Budapest, where high society does not go. Before those Hungarians in rich array I had the sensation of a soirée at the Paris opera. In Munich my comrades and I were invited to an artists' ball; on the way there people shouted "*Vive la France!*" At the supper everyone drank to Paris and the Parisians. . . . In Vienna the public was less satisfied, but that is because in Austria French is not understood as well. . . .

Of all the cities visited, Prague was the only one new to me. *Dieu,* what a lovely town.

It was in Prague that, sight-seeing with her Jewish husband, Yvette wandered into a world she had never before experienced—the dismal world of ancient Central European ghettos—and was profoundly affected by its tragic and oppressive atmosphere:

What excursions into the old quarters. . . . And the ancient synagogue, the oldest in the world (it dates from the year 500). And the
. . . cemetery, where under the fruit trees fifteen thousand of the
sons of Israel sleep.

Rambling on, the letter describes her reception in Berlin. There,
at a banquet of well over two hundred plates, a sonnet to her had been
read; a Berlin journal carried a long article on Yvette and Wagner:
Wagner was at last at home in France, Yvette in Germany; the two
had spread balm on old national wounds. The letter closes with the
profound hope that France will show a similar hospitality to all visiting foreign artists—"Viennese, German, American, Swedish, even
Japanese"—since it is only by artists, Yvette declares, that a bridge
can be built between races of men.

This hardly sounds like the voice of the young woman who not so
long ago had declared herself willing to go to Russia, "to Berlin, no";
and certainly the sentiments indicate a cosmopolitanism not previously noted in Yvette's utterances. Could the voice actually have been
Max's, and the sentiments merely an echo of the Tolstoyan affirmation of brotherhood, a theme then beginning to challenge many
European intellectuals? In any case, the writer could hardly have
foreseen how contemptuously her words would later be remembered
against her.

Soon it was April, and Rome, another city of first appearance,
where, although seats had been quadrupled in price, houses had been
sold out well in advance. Critics soared in their reviews. Three engagements, and she was booked to return for fifteen more in May.
On her part, Yvette fell equally in love with Rome; like so many a
pilgrim there through the centuries found herself overwhelmed by
the sense of the past that breathed upon her wherever she turned:

Rome! The first time I saw you how I hated my ignorance. So
badly, and so little, did I understand my Roman history. . . . Rome is
formidable to understand without culture. . . . I began to instruct
myself, and I had to return often and read much to be able . . . to
revel in its stones . . . and still I did badly.

It must have been during this season in Italy that Yvette had opportunity to enjoy some of her most precious experiences with Duse.
During the years since their friendship began in Brussels, an affec-

tionate intimacy had developed, of a sort rarely found between two women who are public idols in the same profession. Whereas Bernhardt had consistently taken a sharp and envious rival's tone in her references to Duse, as she had earlier toward Yvette, Yvette had always felt for Duse a personal emotion close to adoration. Yet never to the blurring of judgment. With typical clearheaded unsentimentality she could observe: "No one has loved suffering like Duse."

Where shall one begin to speak of her? ... Of what was her genius made that, after having watched the actress, one was overwhelmed and captivated by her soul? Ah, her soul, how gloriously she offered it to us! How she touched us by her knowledge of the painful essences of life, how she revealed to us its many agonies, how well she knew how to measure them drop by drop as if she knew their weight, ... and how one could feel her strange enjoyment of pain; ... To suffer, for her, was to live! Without sufferings for the soul no beauty of heart; without beauty of heart there will be ugliness of mind. "*Il faut souffrir pour être belle!*" an old proverb warned the coquettes. ... And certainly her beauty shone through her martyrdom, and it was her inner loveliness that irradiated her tones as an artist. ... Not one of us was worthy of such a laying bare of a human soul. ...

Duse an actress? What actress ever had such a brain, such intellectuality, such a love of silence, or had such an obstinate desire to avoid the crowd, or such a sincere disdain for popularity? ... What actress ever refused with such ironic fatalism to beautify her face, or resisted the trammels of fashion, and all the tricks of the "footlight queens"? What actress ever lived as she did, remote from the crowd, outside the theatre, far, far from theatre folk, far from theatre habits...?

She thought that she could lead two separate lives, one of the theatre and one of her own, by doing away with the thousand and one accessories that linked them together.

For instance, she refused to have her stage dresser come to her house. She had one mirror for her work, which was allowed to reflect only her "actress" face. She used a different mirror at home. And when illness laid its hand upon her she would have no more mirrors—not even in hotel bedrooms when she was traveling.

In Vienna I saw that she had placed a screen in front of the long mirror in her bedroom at the Bristol Hotel. And to increase the shadow in which she preferred to have her being, she avoided the light on her face and turned her bed so that it faced a wall instead of a window. She never took her meals in public. She was served in her bedroom, and she used the side staircase and hardly ever the main entrance of the hotel. She insisted that she should have the elevator to herself; she hated inquisitive eyes; a keen look would make her "close up" her expression, and above the black in which she always dressed her pale face bade the enemy lower his eyes. Pretty? Oh, no, much more than that! . . .

To have known and loved Duse, to have deserved her affectionate friendship, is one of the brightest and most precious of my memories. I loved her first of all as the sublime model of an art which I reverenced, and later I loved her as a sister who had been hurt unto death and whom I wished to heal.

As to whether Yvette knew of the one-time relationship between Duse and Max Schiller, Eva Rosenfeld assumes that she did.

During those glorious spring days in Italy the two women seem to have been often together. Duse, according to an account that Yvette gave to Arthur Symons in 1926, paid Yvette the incomparable compliment of following her on her tour from town to town.

Oh, the unforgettable artist and the unforgettable friend! . . . She would appear suddenly in my dressing-room as an affectionate "surprise." She sang some of my songs. She would come, with flowers in her hands, to the hotels in which I stayed, singing—

It is May
It is May
It is the pretty month of May!

One day she gave me a great joy. She said: "Your art and mine are of the same race, you are the only artist with whom I would willingly associate 'in the work.'" Speaking of her own talent, she said: "My work." The word "work" recurred constantly in her conversation.

This is probably the last time Yvette would find her friend caroling lightly of the blossoming May. Though Duse and D'Annunzio were still together that summer in Italy, Duse must have been suffering even then from her lover's gathering ennui. Within a short two years she would have discovered in his bedroom the gold hairpin of Alessandra, Marchesa de Rudini.

Strangely enough, despite popular successes, at the end of the tour of *Montmartre en ballade* a surprising fact had to be recorded in Yvette's notebook: loss instead of profit; the amount, fifty thousand francs. A serious matter, of course, but the Schillers remained optimistic; there had been no loss in prestige.

After the disbanding of the company, Yvette, back in her role as solo performer, insisted upon continuing a packed schedule, despite the disturbing physical symptoms that had begun to harass her again —the convulsions of pain backstage between acts, the vomiting in the wings. There was Baden-Baden in July; followed by Aix-les-Bains, with the Greek king in the audience; Lucerne, Ostend, Spa, Trouville, Berk; Amsterdam, The Hague, Liège; in December a first tour of Alsace-Lorraine; London again, this time in Bechstein Hall. In January came the announcement of another equally arduous tour, to Germany, Roumania, Italy; the contract, according to *Le Gaulois,* was for one hundred performances.

The second tour was no more than begun, however, when it had to be acknowledged that the star's pace had been too forced. Suddenly from Germany came reports of wholesale cancellations of engagements; Madame Guilbert had collapsed. In Berlin hushed crowds gathered under her hotel windows, waiting patiently for news. The emperor requested special bulletins. Another operation loomed.

In this emergency the warmhearted Rosenfelds rented a house in Steglitz, at 24 Fichte Strasse, next door to their own. From here, six weeks later. Yvette, to quiet alarming rumors, wrote *Le Gaulois* that there was no occasion for concern; that she would soon return to Paris, entirely cured; that, in fact, she would sing in London the end of May.

The statement proved oversanguine. By midsummer her condition had failed to improve; had even worsened to the point where her life was in the balance again and the famous Dr. Israel had no choice but to perform a second operation. Followed still another convalescence, this even more lingering, filled with even more torturing uncertainties, and again a desperately sick woman was grateful for the rough stone walls of an old garden shutting out an inquisitive world, holding close within its quadrangle the singing silence, the seclusion, she required in order to recover. Here, too, again it was Max's love and solicitude on which she depended in those long weeks, while the deep wounds of mind and body slowly mended.

To Yvette, the most pleasurable event of 1903 was the success of her second novel, *Les Demi-vieilles,* on which she had been working for some three years. This book even Bauer, the severe critic of the *Echo de Paris,* praised. His influence was so feared that those who came under his scalpel for dissection were said to have a "good Bauer" or a "bad Bauer," as the case might be. In *caf'-conc'* days Yvette had always had an exceptionally "good Bauer." "You have chosen a magnificent subject," he wrote her now, "one of eternal tragedy. . . . 'To cease to love and be loved, this is death insupportable! To leave off living is nothing.' "

Les Demi-vieilles is the story of Esther Renot, an actress, who, though over forty, is in love with Maurice Roval, a young and successful dramatist. He, a thoroughgoing egotist, at first fancies himself in love with Esther, but when he discovers her actual age, callously sets about studying her as potential material for a play. Eventually he reveals to her that he has written a new piece about a middle-aged woman who conceals her age in order to keep her lover's affection, and brazenly asks her if she will play the role. Shocked, she refuses, but Maurice overrides her reluctance by imploring her in the name of art, and for the sake of his own dramatic reputation. Though she is sickened by his brutality, her infatuation is such that at last she agrees.

Aging actress and egotist playwright: little imagination is needed to guess the roots of this drear tale. In Duse, Yvette had seen at close range the agony inevitably in store for the woman past her youth whom destiny has marked to love a self-centered younger man. But the story, of course, is not concerned merely with Esther Renot's heartbreak. Esther is Everywoman, suffering the irreparable outrage of the years; the playwright Maurice is Everyman, in Yvette's eyes always the unforgivable source of Everywoman's martyrdom.

Chapter 2

"One cannot remain always the same," Yvette retorted to a critic who doubted the wisdom of her new objectives. "*Il faut se renouveler, se modifier.* Art is a mirror which should show many reflections, and the artist should not always show the same face, or the face becomes a mask."

It had been ten years since Yvette made her first inwardly quaking appearance before the British public, and in the meantime she had been heard again and again in London. Yet in May, 1904, in Bechstein Hall, when she stepped before an expectant and cultured audience, which included the French ambassador, with what she had nominated her "new repertoire," she experienced fully as much agony of stage fright as on that other night so long ago. For this was the moment she had selected, and this the audience, for trying out her first program composed entirely of the old French *chanson*. This would be "*l'art pur*"; the culmination of months of patient research; the risking of everything on one spin of the wheel; and there was no minimizing the crucial nature of the test.

She had not dared to offer the program in its entirety in Paris. On the contrary, she had only that January yielded to pressure from the Folies-Bergère to play almost the whole month in her old raffish vein. Even the green gown and the long gloves had been reverted to, to satisfy the hard core of oldtime Parisian *aficionados*.

But she had experimented gingerly on the road. In February she had ventured at least a part of the program in Brussels, and there had been minor samplings elsewhere. As, for example, in London in 1901, when she had successfully included among her offerings a twelfth-century piece called *La Légende de Saint Nicolas,* the grisly tale of three children slain and dismembered by a murderous butcher:

Il était trois petits enfants
Qui s'en allaient glaner aux champs.
S'en vont un soir chez un boucher;
Boucher, voudrais-tu nous loger?
Entrez, entrez, petits enfants,
Y'a d'la place assurément.

As the song progresses, the audience freezes in terror over the senseless brutality of the killing. The saint enters; the butcher knows his soul's damnation is at hand; he flees.

Quand le boucher entendit ça
Hors de sa porte il s'enfuya!

The final vowel "a," prolonged by Yvette into a long scream of deadly fear, as if uttered by the murderer—"Aaaa!"—created a searing effect; on the instant a seven-hundred-year-old legend became a contemporary event. But the gruesome tale ends on a naïve and tender note. As the good saint brings the victims back to life, each child awakens sweetly. The first rubs his eyes—"*J'ai bien dormi!*"; the second yawns, "*Et moi aussi*"; and the third in a high, baby treble announces, "*Je croyais être au paradis.*"

But despite incidental successes with the new material, it was not going to be easy, Yvette had discovered, to change the established image of herself, and she had suffered particularly from the hostility of the Parisian public. To Parisians the name of Guilbert stood for only one accomplishment—making the monkey blush. For that they would pay; for nothing else. This position they made unmistakably clear. Years later in her writings she complained bitterly of her Paris public:

... what a heartache you gave me when for years I had to say to myself: "Then after all it was my repertoire that made my reputation—my gloves and my dress, and not my talent, that made me famous. . . . I've been deceived, deceived!" . . .

When I wished to put my gifts and the fruits of my studies at the service of France, and to express my country in her many-sided picturesque aspects, her varied cadences, her satires, her jokes, her joys, and thus reveal her to millions who knew nothing of all this, all backs were turned upon me. . . . I had even to go outside Paris and even outside France to find encouragement. But I had made up my mind that either Paris should hear me in my new repertoire of the songs of old France or I would give up Paris. . . .

In my early studies what appealed to me most was the period nearest to our own, and at first I was attracted by the literature of the eighteenth century; then it was the seventeenth, then the sixteenth, and finally the fifteenth century. From that epoch my enthusiasm positively carried me away! . . .

To the fourteenth and thirteenth centuries I devoted more than ten years; then my eager curiosity, delighted with its discoveries, wished to know what was happening before that, and I went back to the twelfth century! Oh, those first difficulties, the worry of going for weeks, months, years, before I could unearth the *pièce complète* —that is to say, words and music together! . . . When, after ten years of patient endeavor, I had managed to resuscitate a few songs it seemed to me as if I had unearthed a treasure buried in a desert of sand.

When I arrived at the eleventh century I found Latin words, and these I had to have translated. When I had the translation I had the verses sung to me in Latin; then, noting the places where the stresses came, I arranged the translation myself into French verse, and gave my lines their rhythm in accordance with the Latin stresses so as to retain intact the musical style of the old theme.

The strange modernness of certain poets of the Middle Ages was so astonishing that I said to myself that some mysterious power must have impelled me toward them that I might learn the source of the satire of the Chat Noir of my early days. . . . What strength there was in our primitive tongue; what power of suggestion in the truculent speech of a Robert de Blois, a Coquillard, a Eustache Deschamp and five hundred others, . . . What do I not owe to the manuscripts of Bayeux and Montpellier, and to all those who from 1870 followed the lectures of Gaston Paris and in their turn became beacons to light the blind, such as myself? As far away as America I found disciples of the great Gaston Paris, . . .

. . . the songs of old France, collections of which had hitherto never gone further back than the sixteenth century, revealed for the first time their medieval flavor in my two volumes (forty songs) which were published by Heugel. These two volumes include the works of Bernard de Ventadour, Thibaut de Champagne, Moniot de Paris, Marcabru, Adam de la Halle, Guillaume de Machaut, the monk of Montaudon, Mahius le Jeune, Philippe de Vitry, Blondel de Nesles, Gauthier de Coincy, Guyot de Dijon, Chatelain de Coucy, Conon de Béthunes, Richard de Fournival, Godefroy de Bastard, and so forth.

. . . From the eleventh to the nineteenth century more than sixty thousand songs are before me. My dear little books, hunted for in the four corners of the world, have turned my life into a fairyland. Every possible subject for a song is there; from the most sublime to the most libertine. . . . The spirit of my country in its evolutions, its revolutions, reveals itself in its many shades, and the social classes according to their period can be seen in their heights of exaltation or in the depths of uncontrolled excitement. The Middle Ages were the forerunners of 1830, and the minstrels of the Crusaders were own cousins to Lamartine and de Musset. Politics, with its puppets, its kings, its emperors, its army leaders—the whole history of France is there written in verse! The hates of a people, which turn into loves, and loves into hates, the rise and wane of enthusiasms, heroes spurned, Napoleon insulted, dragged in blood and mire; then again Court intrigues, favorites attacked, princes flattered, and then guillotined. The songs of the people at Court, those of the mob, the satires against the Government, against those in high places, those in the fashion, actresses and musicians, and against social habits, all this written with care, with wit and elegance, by writers who did not have to consider the effect on an audience at a place of entertainment. There were no such places in those days, and these verses were sung only among people of the same world, and could circulate only in exquisite editions, little books for which the King's permission had to be obtained.

It was this literature, refined and delicate, suggesting the mystical spirit popular in the provinces as well as the romantic style and satire of the Middle Ages, that I had the temerity to offer after my repertoire of Montmartre!

In selecting her first wholly new program, Yvette had decided to concentrate on songs of two periods.

At Versailles, in the luxury-loving court of Louis XV, in the days of red heels and rapiers, when the powerful Madame de Pompadour held sway, it was the custom for singers to entertain small groups every evening, quietly and discreetly, in private boudoirs. Some of the songs were graceful, witty satires of the monarch and his favorites; others, lusty verses about pretty peasant girls and their swains. The first part of the program, drawn largely from the eighteenth century, Yvette called therefore Chansons Pompadour.

The second part, which she called Chansons Crinoline, consisted of songs that might have been found strewn on little old pianos in French drawing rooms from 1830 to 1860, during that era of romanticism when literature bloomed with color and extravagance. In those exciting, swift-moving years, rich in genius and exploited brilliantly by Balzac, Sand, Merimée, Lamartine, Hugo, De Vigny, she discovered that songs had flowered as profusely as books from the fertile soil of fancy.

To lend visual authenticity, costumes for these *chansons* were exact replicas of those worn in the two periods Yvette was bringing to life.

One, a reproduction of a dress worn by Pompadour and painted by Watteau, had cost six thousand francs. It had been made of specially selected silk threads, dyed to the precise colors of the Watteau portrait, and then woven to the precise pattern. Even the loom used was one copied from an original model and had cost more than four thousand francs. To make the gown, the couturier Paquin had lent his talent. With such sumptuousness of appearance, augmented by accessories of powdered wig and enormous hat, Yvette became a startling embodiment of an eighteenth-century *grande dame,* sometimes vivacious, sometimes gracefully languorous, again majestic and imposing, but always the epitome of elegance and the grand manner.

For the final touch of historicity, special music was provided by a group of virtuosi of the Société des Instruments anciens, in which Henri Casadesus played the viola d'amore and his wife the quinton, Marcel Casadesus the viola de gamba, Marguerite Delcourt the harpsichord, and Edouard Nanny the contrabass. The quintet would open the evening with perhaps some almost unknown work of Mozart, produced on the exact instruments for which it had been composed in Salzburg in the 1770's, or again with a gay divertissement by Mouret, or even a ballet of Monteclair, *circa* 1680. For Yvette's *chansons* the harpsichord alone served as accompaniment.

Songs in the program romped and stabbed and chilled by turn. In *Les Houssards de la garde,* a story of three hussars and their romantic adventures, the singer "hinted, insinuated, and her eyes did the rest." In *Les Rues d'Anjou et de Poitou,* her hand played an amusing part in depicting how both roads and lovers met, where

> *la rue d'Anjou*
> *Donn' dans la ru' d'Poitou.*

In *Les belles Manières,* set to a pretty melody Marie Antoinette once used to hum, a great lady instructs her daughter in the absurd social affectations of the period.

In *Le Curé de Pomponne,* a village maiden reels off her list of sins to her confessor. She has been kissed and, worse, has enjoyed it. "This is shocking," says the priest. A pilgrimage to Rome will be the only way of expiating her offense. "And take my lover with me?" "Shame!" says the curé. Then, after a pause for reflection, he orders a short cut to absolution—a kiss or two for himself.

Au confesse m'en suis allée
Au curé de Pomponne.
Le plus gros péché que j'ai fait
C'est d'embrasser un homme. . . .

Embrassez-moi cinque ou six fois
Et je vous le pardonne.
Grand merci, monsieur le curé,
Le pénitence est bonne.

Ah! il m'en souviendra,
Lairira,
Du curé de Pomponne.

The words of the song indicate no greater sin than a few kisses, but by the way Yvette toyed with the simple refrain "Lairira" she presented to her audience a maiden who looked "like the most artful of coquettes to begin with, the most ardent of kissers to go on with, and finally the most passionate of sinners."

In the poignant *La Légende Bretonne* another fair penitent confesses her love for the priest himself. "Ah! then we must see one another no more," says he sadly. "But I should die of a broken heart!" she whispers. "Then," softly, "I should bury you." "And would you weep?" the girl falters.

Non, car il faudra chanter, Simone, ma Simone,
Requiescat in pace,
Ma mignonne.

In tragic vein she sang *La Mort de Jean Renaud*, an earlier tale of a man coming home from the Crusades death-stricken on the very night his son is born to him, and his wife who will not be deceived when the old mother tries to hide Jean's death from her.

"Mother what is that knocking I hear?"
"My daughter, it is but the carpenter mending the stairs."
"Mother, I can hear singing!"
"It is the carol-singers, my dear."
"But now I hear sounds of weeping."
"It is our neighbor, poor thing, she has lost her child."

"But mother, your own eyes are wet!"

"My daughter, I can no longer hide it; your husband is dead and in his grave!"

"Tell them to dig a grave wide enough for two, my mother, and for the little one who lies in my arms."

Le Roi a fait battre tambour relates an example of royal insolence and double-dealing: a King's offer of a marshal's baton to the husband of the woman the King covets. But Majesty has not reckoned with his Queen, who knows her poisons well.

> The Queen hath plucked her flowers white,
> And made her garland ready.
> The odor of these flowers one night
> Hath slain the Marquis' lady.

Most brilliant of all, however, was the stirring seventeenth-century *Les Cloches de Nantes,* chanted to the periodic chiming of bells. Confined in a Nantes prison, on the river Loire, is a youth whom no one goes near except the jailer's daughter; she takes him food and drink, and, alas, falls in love with him. On the eve of his execution he persuades the girl, since he must die at dawn, to strike the chains from his feet. The young thing, weeping, frees him, and as the bells of Nantes start ringing, the prisoner with one bound exultantly leaps into the rushing waters of the Loire and escapes.

> *Toutes les cloch's de Nantes,*
> *Se mirent à sonner;*
> *La fillette est jeunette,*
> *Elle se prit à pleurer.*
> > *Ah! Ah! Ah!*
> > *Ah! Ah! Ah!*
> *Le prisonnier alerte*
> *Dans le fleuve a sauté.*
> *Vivent les fill's de Nantes*
> *Et tous les prisonniers.*
> > *Ah! Ah! Ah!*
> > *Ah! Ah! Ah!*

Of this song Haldane Macfall wrote in *The Mask:*

We leap into the tide that flows by the walls of Nantes, and eagerly ... we are breasting that flow of waters to the sea; and, all the while, sounds the carillon of bells, that peal forth above the towers of Nantes ... running like a litany through all the adventure of our vision and our hearing; yet, even as the youth stands fetterless and free at an inn at last, drinking to the jailer's daughter, the carillon sounds the note of pain, contracts one's heart—for in the old prison at Nantes there is another prisoner, a girl, and there are tears in the eyes of the girl who bows her head in the empty cell—alone. . . .

This is supreme acting—the indescribable, consummate, compelling thing that no mortal can teach; that it is given only to genius to do. . . . Read the simple lines in cold blood, and you are filled with wonder that from such scant fabric this graceful woman has woven so rich a tapestry.

Arthur Symons, leaning forward in his seat as the curtain rose that night at the Bechstein, was quick to catch the difference between the new Yvette and the old, and to delineate it in the *Saturday Review:*

A new Yvette ... Mme. Guilbert has long been a fine artist, in the sharp, nervous, somewhat brutal modern way, a Forain; she has suddenly become another kind of artist, with the eighteenth-century grace, precision, sensibility, and witty delicacy of a Fragonard.

As a compliment perhaps to her English hearers, Yvette had also that night resurrected from the dust of years an old English ballad, "The Keys of Heaven." To hear her sing that, said Harold Owen in the *Morning Post,* was "like seeing one's mother's wedding dress taken out of its lavender wrappings."

With such encomiums ringing in her ears, it seems a pity that Yvette could not have been tactful enough at this particular moment to forbear making invidious criticisms of her British hosts. But the tendency to public faultfinding seems never to have deserted her, and now she drew British blood by gratuitous thrusts on the lack of artistry in current London plays, attacks which moved Sir Herbert Beerbohm Tree to parry with the rejoinder that the French were always prone to confuse the obstetric with the artistic.

In spite of the success of the new repertoire in London and the fact that on her future tours, as she crisscrossed Europe again and again, carrying with her the distinguished musical quintet, she repeated it many times triumphantly, it was not until almost a year later that Yvette dared put it to the test in Paris. Finally, however, when the Chansons Pompadour and Crinoline were at last heard in a series of matinees at the chic Bouffes-Parisiens, where the memory of Offenbach still lingered, the tribute paid her by one critic was, if anything even more unrestrained than any she had received in foreign cities. "She is queen of Paris, she is queen everywhere. . . . she is the greatest French virtuoso," G. Davenay exulted.

Davenay, of course, was referring strictly to *l'art pur*. But as to the popular appeal of the new repertoire—the Guilbert box office receipts which the press of former years used to quote so breathlessly—on such matters, silence.

Chapter 3

In the early 1900's the list of English and American theatrical stars who had appeared in New York under the flag of Charles Frohman made an impressive roster: Maude Adams, John Drew, Ethel Barrymore, William Faversham, Olga Nethersole, Henry Miller, E. H. Sothern and Julia Marlowe, Mrs. Patrick Campbell, Otis Skinner, Billie Burke, Julia Sanderson, to name only a handful; and the Frohman empire of theatres, which included houses in both New York and London, was equally formidable.

In June, 1905, therefore, when the press reported that the engagements of Yvette Guilbert and London's "coster singer" Albert Chevalier at Frohman's Duke of York's Theater had been extended, it was apparent that the manager was well satisfied with his box office. Not long after this straw in the wind came the announcement that Madame Guilbert would shortly make a third trip to America, this time under the coveted Frohman management.

Much had happened on the dollar side of the Atlantic since Yvette's last sojourn there in 1897. In inventive America the turn of the century had brought, for the masses, subways, taxis, movies, long-distance phones, and the delirious prospect of universal plumbing. Even in embryo, the new marvels offered exhilarating proofs of what everyone conceded was the better world just ahead. So engrossing were they, in fact, that the truly new world being born at Kitty Hawk was hardly noticed. For the affluent, the Naughty Naughts had brought new concepts regarding wealth. Money, which to pioneer ancestors had spelled power or responsibility, had come to be regarded by many moderns of 1905 as a passport to pleasure, excess, zany behavior. At Newport, bastion of the Four Hundred, trees of exclusive estates could now be fancifully decorated with solid gold artificial fruit, and favorite horses bedded on embroidered linen sheets, while at Saratoga plaid-vested tycoons who would have felt out of place at Newport could disport themselves at the crowded race tracks and ruin their digestions with nine-course dinners at ornate hotels. By 1905 everyone of consequence was making the Continental *grand tour,* and the international marriage market had never been more active, stimulated equally by title-hunting American mammas and fortune-hunting European insolvents.

It would be, then, a somewhat more sophisticated New York that would listen to the new Guilbertian repertoire, but even so, Yvette nursed secret doubts. Not unless her American hearers were solidly at home in old-world culture, she feared, could they follow Pompadour and Crinoline subtleties. Especially she dreaded the cranky hinterland she would again have to encounter.

The *Kaiser Wilhelm II,* docking in New York on February 13, 1906, brought the Schillers back for the first time to the city where they had met. The accomplished Société des Instruments anciens did not follow them down the gangplank; for musicians, there were only the violinist Armand Forest and Yvette's accompanist, Richard Hageman. In her memoirs Yvette complains acidly that at her debarkation she was not met by her producer, as any visiting star might legitimately expect to be; that Frohman, in fact, had just sailed for Europe, completely forgetting her coming, and leaving her in the lurch in respect to advance arrangements and publicity. As to the latter charge, newspaper files do not bear out the accusation; furthermore, the date was February 1906, rather than October, 1908, as she states; apparently another instance of faulty memory after many years.

Reading the dozens of interviews, one can picture the battery of poised pencils before which Yvette chatted loquaciously as usual. Yes, she had recently appeared before Queen Alexandra at Buckingham Palace in a command performance, and the Queen had professed herself "in love" with the new songs, particularly *Le Roi a fait battre tambour*. The Queen was dressed in mauve, wearing no jewels except her customary pearl dog collar, "very slender, rather stiff, and yet very gracious." No, there had been no gift of flowers or souvenir, such as was customary from royalty. Incidentally, Yvette must have been more disturbed by this omission than she admitted to the pencils, for the next time she met King Edward she taxed him with it. But His Majesty only laughed. "When husbands are spendthrift," he joked, "wives are economical!"

To the scribbling reporters she described her mania for the talking machine and how she was carrying on correspondence with her mother by means of record cylinders instead of pen and ink. Every day she would talk three records full of gossip and anecdote and ship them by express to Paris, and exery day in her New York hotel suite she would set her phonograph in motion and listen to her mother's answering voice for half an hour at a time. On another record a pet dog, Mimette—"so little and so dear and so sweet," who could not bear to travel—yelped love. She was also making a collection of whole dramatic scenes by her favorite actresses and actors in America: Ethel Barrymore in *Alice Sit-by-the-Fire*, Margaret Anglin in *Zira*, William Faversham in *The Squaw Man*, Mrs. Leslie Carter in *Zaza*, David Warfield in *The Music Master*, Maude Adams in *Peter Pan*. Many of these cylinders had been made especially for her. And she loved also her records of the songs of Eames, Caruso, Plançon, and the de Reszkes, and the imitations of Elsie Janis.

One bit of newspaper gossip attracted attention:

> Yvette Guilbert is trying to sell her house in the outskirts of Paris. . . . now she is spending her time in the cold harsh climate of the Prussian capital. Yvette admits that she loves Berlin, and during recent years she has spent a great deal of time there. Her husband's family is there and Berlin has been very kind to her new form of entertainment—kinder even than Paris, . . .

As to the new Yvette, reporters conscientiously recorded for their respective publics the absence of the celebrated black gloves and the exorbitant costs of the singer's Pompadour-Crinoline wardrobe. Some speculated as to whether the new-old songs would catch the interest of vaudeville, where the big money then lay. Others noted the contrast of the present engagement before the select audiences of the

Lyceum with prior New York appearances before the rough-and-tumble of Koster and Bial's.

On opening night, February 19, a few of the critics studied the new Yvette with frank skepticism. Acton Davies of the *Sun* could not take the "reformation" seriously. Alan Dale, who had followed her closely during her earlier visits, was patently amused with what he found after a lapse of nine years:

> We saw a penitent Yvette with a sweet cherubic smile, and a comfortable air of plump and matronly prosperity, at the leather-upholstered Lyceum Theatre yesterday. We saw the once lank, lissome and longitudinal Yvette of the black gloves and the untranslatable songs . . . ah! so much worthier! . . . It was Yvette reformed, with a matinee entertainment for respectable people, if you please.
>
> The circus had departed from Yvette. . . . A penitent Yvette, a nice Yvette, an ask-to-dinner-to-meet-auntie Yvette! . . . no leafy glades, and no vaudeville accessories, and you couldn't smoke, and you sat still as though at a concert, and, well, so may all naughty ladies see the error of their ways, and become dear, and cute, and motherly, and tea-like, this is a wicked world. Oh pluck off me long gloves, mother dear, and let me, oh, let me be a lady! Or die!

Flippant barbs, but wickedly percipient of the singer's unacknowledged human motivations.

In other quarters, however, the new personality was received respectfully, one critic comparing Yvette's "beaming and benign charm" with that of Schumann-Heink.

Surprisingly, the new repertoire seemed to please unenlightened New Yorkers as much as it had the *cognoscenti* of Europe, and critiques as to performance were for the most part glowing: "incomparably *spirituelle*. . . . No other woman who has ever visited these shores could command so gracious and varied an art of pantomimic illustration, so minute, so finely shaded, yet so vitally dramatic."

In all the comment over the demureness of the new repertoire to which, it was said, any girl could take her parents without blushing, only one observer slyly noted that in wearing costumes copied from Pompadour and DuBarry, "king's harlots both," Yvette, under her outer innocence, was now suggesting the wickedness which she formerly disclosed freely.

Toward the end of the Lyceum engagement a surprise announcement issued from the office of Mark Luescher, representative of F. F. Proctor, vaudeville magnate. At the conclusion of the short road tour which Madame Guilbert was already committed to make for Frohman to Boston, Philadelphia, and Baltimore, the diseuse had now contracted for a series of appearances in the Proctor chain of vaudeville houses in and near New York. At least a dozen variety managers, Luescher boasted, had tried to capture Guilbert since her arrival, but she had remained elusive. But the Proctor offer (figure not stated) she had been unable to resist. It was admitted that the sum was more than Lillian Russell had received the preceding season —a broad hint, as Miss Russell's reputed salary of $100,000 for a thirty-three-week contract had been widely quoted. When it is remembered, however, that at that time where Lillian went Diamond Jim Brady went also, one can believe that Mr. Proctor's audiences got their money's worth; nightly there would be not only Beauty warbling on the stage, but the Beast, emblazoned with his diamonds, glittering from a box.

It was Proctor who had first adopted the policy of offering unprecedented salaries in order to lure into his vaudeville houses headliners of stage and opera, and perhaps one of the most striking changes in American theatrical history of the preceding quarter of a century had been the result of this policy—the mushrooming of vaudeville patronage because of the improvement in artistic quality of vaudeville offerings. By 1906, the variety show had come a long way from its small beginnings in the days of Tony Pastor, until now it rivaled musical comedy in its lavish mountings and its billings of such top names as Lily Langtry, Eva Tanguay, Harry Lauder, Nat Goodwin. Proctor, always respectful to vaudeville, claimed that it was entitled to recognition as legitimate theater. "Vaudeville is absolutely the highest paid profession in the civilized world; it is the most liberally patronized of any branch of the amusement business," he argued.

As it happened, the year 1906 marked the completion of his twenty-fifth year as theatrical manager, and for his silver jubilee Mr. F. F. had decided to indulge his fancy. His fancy having fallen on Guilbert, he was prepared to pay whatever was necessary to get her. The Proctor contract was a bonanza for Yvette, for, truth to tell, despite reviews, *l'art pur* had not been playing to capacity houses. The offer might even be interpreted, too, as a moral victory, demonstrating that Yvette reformed might hope to prosper as well as Yvette wicked.

Her Frohman tour completed, Yvette returned, therefore, to New York and Proctor. The hinterland had been unexpectedly kind, in Boston even discerning. There the *Transcript's* H. T. Parker had found the leopard's spots not really changed in spite of the new air of guilelessness: "She is steadily ironic. See this little tragedy, hear it and feel it, but, she insinuates, is it not sordid? Watch this little comedy and smile at it, but is there not malice beneath all this innocence?" Now back in New York, beginning with Easter Monday, sandwiched between acts of *The Prisoner of Zenda* or *Rupert of Hentzau,* Yvette duly began her four-week stint for Proctor before a very hoi-polloi type of audience. No one understood French, so she was obliged to substitute English songs. But worse, no one understood her subtleties, for which she had no substitute to offer. "What misery it was!" she moans.

Her dissatisfaction rose to the point where she permitted herself a few stinging remarks to the press one morning just before her departure aboard the *Kronprinz Wilhelm.* The interview took place in her suite at the Astor, in "a little boudoir full of sunshine, spring flowers, and soft colors," a room with "green silken walls, French color prints in gold ribbon frames, rose-brocaded draperies, mossy carpet, and spindle-legged chairs."

. . . But dainty as were the furnishings, it was a room where work was done. Letters and newspapers littered the tables, and everywhere on tables, mantel, and on top of the baby grand piano were vases filled with roses and daffodils, carnations and narcissus. Yvette is . . . past mistress in the art of effective touches. As one walks down the interminable hotel corridor searching for her room, one sees in the distance a tall vase of roses standing outside of a door, the door of Yvette's room, of course. She comes in rustling and smiling.

Regrettably, some of Yvette's observations lacked the delicacy of her décor. Questioned as to whether she would sell her house in Paris, she vehemently denied the rumor: "Such emptiness of brain to write such stupidities! Desert Paris for Berlin! . . . *Non, non,* one deserts other places for Paris." When the interviewer politely recalled the venerable witticism that good New Yorkers go to Paris when they die, Yvette was both amused and condescending: "Ah, that is good! Indeed they should go, poor people."

The general dearth of "culture" in America came in for more than one reference. To one reporter she proposed: ". . . why do not you New Yorkers persuade some of your enormously wealthy millionaires to found a theatre in which there shall be no such thing as financial considerations to limit artistic ambition? We have done it in France." To another she suggested that American theaters should be engaged by societies, or the government itself, on Sunday afternoons for free lectures on art and literature. In France, Sunday lectures, which had long been established, were patronized by rich and poor alike. "Believe me," she added, "this ardent worship of the Beautiful is a gratification of the senses that can be classed as the most subtle and aristocratic of voluptuous pleasures." After perhaps ten years' exposure to such civilizing influences, she predicted with her usual gracelessness, "America would have an artistic standing which is now denied it by more cultured nations."

Nor could she seem to drop the subject of English and American inferiority in matters of taste. In London, where she returned in June for another series of engagements with Chevalier at the Duke of York's Theater, she fell again into the same familiar game of baiting a host country by taunts of what was wrong with it. English drama was meretricious, she declared, with its insistence on the happy ending. Worse, it was characterized by false naïveté, whereas French drama owed its glories to its *franchise*. "Ah, *mon cher,* believe me, we French people say more than we do. And you Anglo-Saxons, you do more than you say." As an example of English hypocrisy, she took the public to task over Shaw's play Mrs. *Warren's Profession:*

. . . In America and England, Mrs. Warren was condemned immediately because the theories she pronounces appeared scandalous. In France, they would have understood the miseries, griefs, temptations and struggles of a woman who was the innocent victim of a selfish and heartless society.

And so on, in like vein. But it made good copy for readers—café singer turned Jeremiah; a famous black-gloved hand vehemently pointing sluggish and insensitive Anglo-Saxons in the general direction of Culture.

Not long after her return, George C. Tyler, indefatigable and smooth-talking, of the New York firm of Liebler and Co., came forward with the idea of a joint American tour of Guilbert and Albert Chevalier. For all his French name, Chevalier was London-born and had spent most of his life on the stages of London music halls. In the opinion of Max Beerbohm, there was a distinct kinship between the two singers, both having been innovators in method and in subject matter, but in this judgment Yvette hastened to disagree, considering Chevalier more skilful than talented and his style stereotyped and melodramatic. She did concede that he was personally a cultured man, and professionally one who knew how to choose his music and to contrive an excellent make-up; moreover, with a box-office value not to be overlooked. The plan that Tyler spread before the two was nothing less than coverage of every city of importance in the eastern half of the United States, with Texas and part of Canada thrown in.

"I thought over the proposition carefully," Yvette writes; ". . . they were ready to pay me a big price—for my name—and I needed money."

Here is an admission that undoubtedly would have surprised her contemporaries, because for years Yvette had been considered enormously wealthy. But even large fortunes can take wings. Hers had been cut into, for one thing, by those long periods of illness, with no revenue, but with living continued on the same scale of extravagance; every vase must be kept filled with fresh flowers. Also the Schillers had not been fortunate in investments. Poor Max, with all his efforts at being a hardfisted man of business, was no money-maker. And there were many personal generosities, for both Schillers were naïvely openhanded. The little foxes had been eating the grapes.

Early in October, 1906, then, two contingents gathered in New York, Yvette and Max arriving in Hoboken on the *Kaiser Wilhelm der Grosse* with maid, accompanist Richard Hageman, dachshund Soupçon, three boxes of books and manuscripts, and twelve trunks of costumes; and on the *Campania* a few days later Chevalier, with valet, accompanist Alfred West, and his own mountains of trunks. To this total was added in New York, manager Al Lehman, a baggage man, and five advance agents.

In prospect, the safari had seemed from the other side of the Atlantic by virtue of its very proportions a pleasurably exciting undertaking, but in New York elation dwindled when the task began to loom in truer perspective: a record-breaking twenty-three thousand miles by rail, more than the earth's circumference—those American distances! —in a period of six weeks, with a schedule of forty-two engagements that sometimes called for a matinee in one city and an evening in another.

Almost immediately the hardships began: missed connections, lost sleep; stalled engines, late arrivals; no time to eat—the Sandwich Tour, it came to be called. Pullman cars of the period were luxurious to a degree, gilded and tasseled, velvet-carpeted, plush-upholstered. In 1907 Lillian Russell, on a series of one-night stands, traveled through twenty-three states in her eighty-foot *Iolanthe,* which contained a drawing room with piano, a kitchen and dining room, bedrooms, bath, even servants' quarters and a small conservatory; but evidence is lacking that the Guilbert-Chevalier troupe enjoyed such accommodations. Besides, there was the jolting. Roadbeds were rough, and cars reeled and rolled, and were coupled with unexpected smashing bangs. For Yvette this constant vibration shortly became agony; almost at once it brought on a recurrence of her kidney ailment so acute that at times she could find relief only in tears. Some nights she could barely walk from the wings onto the stage. In every hall or theater the indispensable Max would hurry anxiously in advance to her dressing room. Was it warm, was it clean? Sometimes the entire building was glacial. Sometimes there was not even a dressing room, or a lavatory. For six weeks the whole company was half-cold, half-dirty, half-hungry, and Yvette's temper as well as her strength frayed under the strain. Tyler was an ignoramus, she raged, to send her into such barren and hideous towns, remote from civilization. Imagine those absurd Texas cowboys, with revolvers at their belts, trying to understand Pompadour lyrics! But the publicity was nationwide. By the time the tour was completed, though the stars might be half dead, it would have been hard to find a housewife or a bootblack or a hired hand east of the Rockies who had not heard the names of Guilbert and Chevalier.

As to financial returns for the producers, that was another story. In the records of Liebler productions, as given by Robert Grau, against these well-publicized names there appeared the cryptic initials "A.S.F.," code for "Artistic Success, Financial Failure." The stars' salaries apparently were unaffected.

Back in New York, the ever-jocular Alan Dale found the appearance of a Guilbert in hallowed Carnegie Hall hilariously funny.

> . . . the resort where the New York Symphony and the Boston Symphony prevail; where "illustrated lectures" are not unknown; where the chaste dreariness of the "piano recital" occasionally takes

place, and where we are, at any rate, always serious. Oh, Yvette, of y-verve, y-vim and y-vogue! *Que faites-vous?*

To such pleasantries Yvette for once had no reply. In a state of exhaustion she was already thankfully on the high seas en route to Europe, where a surgeon's delicate fingers would once more set to work, trying to repair the effects of thirty-three nights of martyrdom aboard a savagely jouncing, bouncing, rattling, hurtling, swaying American train.

Chapter 4

Yvette's reasons for making a couple of forays into the legitimate theater the following season can be easily surmised. The years immediately following the turn of the century constituted one of the most brilliant eras in the history of the Parisian stage. Theatrical personalities enjoyed unprecedented prestige, and both plays and players were ever-lively topics of conversation. "The theatre was the new cult," says Bertaud, "and the whole of Paris a vast, gossiping green-room." Moreover, the dramatic stage, being like the concert stage many degrees removed from the detested music-hall milieu from which Yvette was determined to disassociate herself, had been long in her thoughts.

The previous June, at the end of her London engagement, Yvette had told an interviewer that this would be the last season she would devote exclusively to songs; the following year would see her in a play already selected, *L'Eau Trouble;* the place, Brussels. The announcement created no great stir. Hints were continually being dropped that Guilbert was about to be starred in such-and-such a play; or that such-and-such a dramatist was engaged in preparing a vehicle especially for her.

In February, 1907, however, the present statement was found not rootless. Somewhat to the public's surprise, Guilbert did appear in the piece named, and in Brussels. The play, which had been written by a friend of many years' standing, a society woman, Madame Paule de Gardilanne (pseudonym, Jean de Hinx), and doctored by the experienced playwright Edmond Guiraud, had probably attracted Yvette's interest because of the distinct echoes it contained of *La Demi-vieille.*

The story concerns a young Italian woman who, weary of a boring marriage, deserts her husband and small son to go on the stage. The son, when grown to manhood, becomes a successful dramatist. Years later, he chances to meet his mother and, unaware of their relationship, offers her a part in a play he has just completed. Though she knows their relationship, she accepts. The play is a hit, and the young man, fired with success, falls in love with her. The mother fears to reveal the truth, and to save him shock tells him that she loves him but not in the way he desires. Uncomprehending, but recognizing the finality of her decision, the son commits suicide.

Perhaps because of its resemblance to her book, perhaps because the unpopular role of *demi-vieille* was one she nevertheless had lately been strongly espousing, Yvette had accepted the part:

> I want to supply the stage with a character, a type which it does not possess—the *demi-vieille*. The type is representative of the woman of "40," with her ardent joy of living, because she knows how to live. I shall not imitate those actresses who refuse those parts which make them mothers of girls of "21," under pretense that it ages them. . . . I shall make my debut in the part of a woman, a true woman.

Brussels rather than Paris had been chosen for the run of the play because Yvette feared to face the Paris public in her first return to drama, and even in Brussels the opening was an unnerving experience. Though she had been six weeks in rehearsal, on that first night at the Théâtre Royal du Parc she was in as abject a state of panic as any amateur. In the end, of course, she triumphed over the condition, to emerge with a degree of praise, and the play ran some thirty performances.

After the usual extensive spring concert tour, followed by a London engagement in July, the Schillers vacationed for the month of August in Marienbad, one of those luxurious German spas where the international set could "take the cure" for fashionable ailments and at the same time keep up a sophisticated social life. For many seasons past, with health her major problem and Germany now a dear favorite country, Yvette had sought the restorative power of various waters, at Baden Baden, Wiesbaden, and others. These pilgrimages Max and Yvette were in the habit of taking alone, leaving Albine at "La Rive," where the Broutin relatives kept her company.

224

Of all the spas they frequented, Max and Yvette were particularly fond of Marienbad. Here for seven summers the English king habitually repaired with staunch British regularity, and here, according to his biographer Virginia Cowles, his presence notably enlivened the local scene:

The little resort with its cluster of hotels, its forests, its cafés, and its famous cure attracted some of the richest men in Europe; consequently it also attracted dozens of beautiful adventuresses of every nationality. . . . Since the King always visited the resort *en garçon,* accompanied only by two equerries, it was not difficult for him to arrange a good many assignations. Despite his years, he was still extremely virile. His amours were never dramatic or even serious, but he continued to crave the stimulation of female company, and he preferred it to be varied and plentiful. Sometimes the King invited these ladies to his hotel to take supper with him; sometimes he took them for drives in his carriage; sometimes he asked them to stroll with him through the forests.

Sometimes also he invited the more respectable ones to luncheon parties, as for example the day, presumably this summer, when Yvette and Beerbohm Tree lunched with him. On that day Tree proposed to Yvette that she play Lady Macbeth. But the King disagreed: "No, no, she has no rival in her own field; let her remain Yvette Guilbert. No tragedy!"

In spite of the royal advice to "remain in her own field," autumn, however, found Yvette opening in another play, this one in Paris. Here she co-starred with the darling of the matinee crowd, comedian Max Dearly, in Louis Artus' frothy *L'Amour en banque,* in which "I Want You, Mah Honey" had somehow contrived to be included. Ironically, the theater was the famous Variétés, where long ago a young Yvette had played out a grimmer kind of comedy. The redoubtable Brasseur, formerly of the Nouveautés, was of the company, and the perennially straw-hatted Samuel, most magnetic of stage managers was still there. But though these two now treated her like an old friend, and though critics were not unkind, there must have been other tensions, if one reads correctly between the lines of certain interviews and articles which shortly began to appear. When Yvette professes wholesale disenchantment with playwrights, as she did in London in July of that year, in a press scrimmage with England's dramatist Clyde Fitch, and again later in a letter to *Figaro,* one can only surmise that in this respect her renewal of theatrical life had proved uncongenial:

> The author . . . will not admit that despite all his efforts he never produced anything but a half-dead child. The talented actor animates, nurses, consolidates, fortifies and clothes it, suggests the proper gestures and attitudes, infuses his own health and strength into this weakling, gives it blood and, so to speak, makes it live. The playwright contributes the soul, it is true, but the soul being intangible, it is only a pitiable gift as far as the dramatic art is concerned. . . . Under the pretext that they know their metier the professional playwrights substitute their own mannerisms to the instinctive art of the interpreter. The author in such a case is quite satisfied, whereas the actor has only achieved an art made up of constraint, and has become a servile parrot in his hands.

It is a truism that performing artists often deliver themselves of much nonsense concerning their medium. Seldom are they wise talkers or writers, and Yvette, warming to her thesis of actors' wrongs, in one interview even went to the extremity of suggesting that the only true theater is one in which the author is eliminated altogether—a theater of improvisers, a *commedia dell'arte:*

> There have always been from time immemorial certain "grimaciers" of genius who could act without the text of others. The day the comedian refuses to interpret his work the dramatist will simply starve.

Again it is the managers who come under Yvette's censure:

> . . . this continual rod of iron which is held over most young players by many managers is apt to kill their originality of method, and thus one who has ideas of her own—one who can think out for herself the real heart and soul of a part—may frequently . . . have her natural histrionic and artistic talent crushed by a too severe discipline.

When the last curtain had fallen on her season of 1907, professional results must have seemed inconclusive. The great Guilbert had not failed in plays, nor particularly succeeded either. Nevertheless, acting was an experiment that had had to be tried. Over the years there had been too many discussions pro and con regarding the desirability of her invading the ranks of the theater. These abortive attempts should have demonstrated, however, that, for all her genius, the legitimate drama was not her true métier; she was too pre-eminently the solo artist. Though she would continue from time to time to coquette with producers, it should have been clear by now that a woman with her extreme individualism of temperament and singular ability of being a whole theater in herself could hardly submit happily to the yoke of corporate effort.

The renewal of her contract with the theater did result, however, in one incidental and quite unexpected by-product—the foundation of a charity destined to be of far-reaching benefit to struggling young women of the profession. Yvette had known of old how harsh the theatrical world could be to the penniless; now, almost twenty years later she saw that conditions had not changed. One day a pretty young thing came to her in distress; she had been offered a role that required a bridal gown but could not afford to buy one; could Yvette lend her something? Yvette had nothing suitable in her own wardrobe, but with typical generosity she managed to secure for the girl the proper outfit.

The incident made its mark on Yvette's tender heart, and from it was born the idea of creating an organization that would collect and store a wide variety of handsome dresses for the benefit of young players who could not afford to costume themselves properly. *La Vestiaire du Théâtre,* Yvette called it—The Theatrical Cloakroom. At her solicitation Baron Rothschild headed the subscription list; the couturiers Worth, Armand, Martial, Drescoll, Beshoff contributed gowns; Queen Nathalie of Serbia, Princess George of Greece, the Duchess de Rohan, the Duchess d'Uzès, the Princess de Ligne, and scores of other women sent trunkfuls of discarded dresses and accessories. Yvette herself organized a benefit at the Théâtre Sarah-Bernhardt, and within a few months the Vestiaire had become an established center, eventually offering not only raiment but advice and assistance. In its first year its founder helped thirty troubled girls to find engagements.

The next season marked another professional experiment: the inauguration of "Yvette's Thursdays," a series of concert-lectures at the aristocratic Gymnase Théâtre, which proved so popular that from

1908 to 1910 similar series were offered between foreign tours. On these "Thursdays," Yvette not only sang but also doubled in Hugues Le Roux's old role of scholarly commentator.

One of the new lectures, entitled *La Femme dans la chanson,* took Woman as its theme, using as illustrations such ballads as *L'Enfance, La jeune Fille, La Mère, Le Jaloux et la menteuse, L'Hypocrite, L'Enigmatique, La Tendre, La Buveuse d'absinthe, L'Ouvrière, L'Heroique,* in which were depicted feminine types from the Middle ages down—women wise, audacious, cunning; faithful, coquettish; hypocritical, fatal, forsaken.

Other lectures dealt with Francis Jammes and Jules Laforgue, both of whom Yvette had lately added to her list of favorites. Jammes was a bucolic poet, brother to Theocritus and Virgil; a devout Catholic, whom she considered "like a being from another world . . . akin to Saint Francis of Assisi—tender, exquisite, his heart going out to all living things," and his poems struck a strange, unexpectedly sweet note in her repertoire, rising above the discordance of those poems of pessimism and bitterness that she had so long preferred.

Jammes looked on womanhood with compassionate eyes; Laforgue, on the contrary, complex and cruel, treated scaldingly the theme of the never-ending duel of sex. Every woman hides behind a mask, he assumed, changing it constantly to suit the role she feels obliged to play. "Clothe her in rags and she will play the part—in riches and she will be the splendid demoiselle." A compulsion to discover woman's essential self behind her artifices, to solve the mystery of the eternal feminine, was a popular sentimental fad of the time which flattered women and intrigued men, and Yvette took as a Laforgue *étude* the poet's *Notre petite compagne.* In this song, against the background of a tawdry night scene, the symbol of feminine enigma is a woman of the Paris cafés who has savored every sordid experience, plumbed every vicious depth. She, the woman who is all women—THE WOMAN —is nonchalant, cynical, indifferent:

> *Si mon air vous dit quelque chose*
> *Vous auriez tort de vous gener*
> *Je ne le fais pas à la pose;*
> *Je suis la Femme, on me connait.*

These lines Yvette and her composer Gustave Ferrari adopted as a leitmotif, repeating them as a refrain after each stanza, and set the

228

whole composition to a bromidic air by De Waldteufel that was then being heard on every street corner in Paris:

If I please you, take me as I am. (Spoken, cigarette in hand.) Handle me as you like, roughly or smoothly. I am woman. Don't you know me? If you would have me a saint, I pull my hair down smoothly over my forehead like a madonna; if you would have a chorus girl, I put up my hair and look reckless; I play a part for every taste. Choose your style, each to his liking; and I am it and I will make you mad. But whatever outward part I play, I am always One—I am Woman. . . . Drink of my lips, not of my soul. Do not look for more. You cannot understand. Nobody understands me— not even myself. . . . My aim is lost in the stars. I am the great Isis. . . . Dream only of me for what I can give you; don't pretend, don't try to understand Me. . . . I am the Incomprehensible. . . . So—if my ways attract you, take me as I am. I am a woman. Everyone knows me. But, duchess or girl of the gutter, I am the same—always the One—WOMAN!

Somewhere in the song Yvette would begin to dance, weaving about "to the refrain of the worn-out waltz tune, with paint on cheek and fineries and fripperies, the smoke of cigarette curling into the air . . . ," contriving to suggest a whole gamut of self-pitying and neurotic melancholy. Mawkish as the idea may appear today, by artistry the performance became another Guilbert chef d'oeuvre.

In 1909 came another solicitation from America; a seven-weeks' contract, beginning in October, to play a chain of vaudeville houses under the management of Percy Williams. Yvette quailed at the idea of facing moronic vaudeville audiences again, but again fees were high, $2500 weekly, and il faut manger. Since her last American visit, the months as they flew by had consistently shown no balance of profit. Even though earnings from Continental tours had been supplemented regularly in London, by variety shows at the Coliseum or the Palace or by concerts at Bechstein Hall, debits seemed always to swallow up credits. There was nothing to do but accept.

Not only were the summers spent at German watering places delightful to the Schillers because of their health-giving effects; Germany was home to Max, and he valued every opportunity to renew family ties. Theodor Rosenfeld had died in 1907, leaving Max's sister

Rose to fill her husband's shoes as best she could as co-manager of the Passage Theater. These were the years when little Eva, to whom both Max and Yvette had always been deeply attached, was growing up. One summer Yvette presented Eva with a dachshund puppy that had been given her by the Kaiser's brother, Prince Heinrich, a fellow guest at the Palast Hotel, and from that moment the child's affection for her celebrated aunt soared into sheer adoration.

Yvette loved Germany for her own reasons. In that country her popularity was always flatteringly evident. More and more she was becoming discouraged over the coldness of the Parisian public to the new face she was showing in her art, and more and more feeling drawn spiritually to the *gemütlichkeit* of German culture. She recognized the debt she owed to German critics:

> The German critic was always, always most attentive to my offerings, noting precisely all the essential points of my progress. . . . Germany alone never ceased to analyze seriously, . . . what I brought interpretatively to the works . . . which composed my numerous and varied programs, ten centuries of songs, humanity across the ages. Paris was interested only in the humanity of its own Boulevard.
>
> It is to German reviews, superbly generous, that I owe the fact that for thirty years I have found audiences educated by them, always eager to listen to me, thanks to the importance that never ceased to be given to each of my visits. . . . What audiences! What understanding! What sympathy! What constant encouragement!

Also, there was the charming Madame Wolff, and through her the large circle of friends the Schillers had made in Berlin. Madame Wolff was more than an efficient manager of Guilbert bookings in Germany; she was also a hostess of charm and intelligence who delighted in bringing together cosmopolitan groups of celebrities at her intimate after-concert parties. At these stimulating gatherings Yvette met such European personalities of the day as Arthur Levysohn and Theodor Wolff, successively directors of the *Berliner Tageblatt;* Ludwig Fulda, translator of Molière and Rostand; Gerhardt Hauptmann; singer Lilli Lehmann; Joachim the violinist; the orchestra leaders Muck and Richard Strauss and Weingartner; the great Moissi and Ysaye and Casals. Hardly an artist of standing could be named whom the Schillers had not at one time or another met in Berlin.

That summer of 1909, again Yvette was far from well, and after only a brief stay at Marienbad, Max rented a house in the ancient university town of Heidelberg where he hoped she could recoup her physical forces more quickly, freed of all social demands. Instead, it was not long before new complications arose; hospitalization followed, and another severe operation, with all its attendant suffering and phantasmagoria of fears. Operations indeed were to become for Yvette a way of life. Years later she wrote, concerning her "sixteen years of martyrdom":

> . . . six times the steely kiss of the surgeon's knife. Six times the table on which the body lay awaiting the unknown, six times the nightmare, the ghastly anguish of saying good-bye to those one leaves behind, sixteen years . . . of the question, "Shall I live or die?" . . . My life struggled for, death kept at bay by twenty-eight of the most famous surgeons of the world, for I used to fall ill in the midst of my journeys—and four times it has been impossible to move me.

Weeks passed in Heidelberg; it was autumn, nearing October and the date of the Percy Williams contract. Though Max had lovingly nursed her through the blackest of the shadows, Yvette was still far from completely recovered. But she insisted on fulfilling the vaudeville contract. She must gamble on her strength; stoop to one more picking of the golden American apples.

To report on her opening at the Colonial Theater in New York on the night of October 11, 1909, is to invite comparison with a certain woeful night in 1889 when a raw, awkward amateur of a songstress was booed off the stage of the Lyons Casino. For incredibly, unexpectedly, heartbreakingly, history repeated itself in New York, and a woman who for years had ranked in the best critical opinion of two continents as an artist of first rank was subjected to such jeering and catcalls that she could barely proceed. Furthermore, that the *Times* and the *Sun* next day cried vigorous shame on her tormentors produced little effect on future audiences. For the entire two weeks of the Colonial engagement public reaction ranged from hostility to boredom. Her novelty had worn off, *Vogue* thought. In Brooklyn, hooligans would not let her open her mouth. Though she fared slightly better in other houses on the circuit, it soon became clear that she would be foolish to expect to match in popularity the swimmer Sam Mahoney for whom the management had provided an Arctic Sea, complete with aurora borealis, in which that hardy gentleman swam nonchalantly about—among cakes of *real* ice!—or that she could offer anything but anticlimax when it was her bad luck to follow immediately the singer of such a howling success as "Just a Splinter from Me Father's Wooden Leg." Seeing herself so clearly unwelcome to the public, demanded the New York *Telegraph,* why did not Guilbert have dignity enough to abridge her contract and go home?

Finally, to relieve the shameful situation, Belasco reached out a helping hand by offering her a theater where, with Elmer B. Harris, dramatic critic of the *Globe,* as *conférencier,* Yvette was able to give concert matinees before audiences of her peers. Caviar to the general, here she was once more in her proper sphere.

In spite of critical declarations in her behalf that it was American vaudeville audiences that were deteriorating, not the star, relations between Yvette and her vaudeville public eventually reached the point of no return. In Pittsburgh so "icy was her manner and so ungenerous" that not a single encore did she offer. Clearly this was not the Yvette of old, singing, singing, without stint, until the curtains closed on her breathless *"Je n'en puis plus!"* No, this was The Dilemma showing its taunting face again. The *Chicago Tribune* put it into blunt language:

> Swinburne was denounced for the erotic poetry that he used to write, but who cared for his verses when he became respectable. Yvette made a furore that prospered her in New York when she sang indecent ballads ... but now that she has improved the morals of her songs ... she is disregarded. She is as ever an artist, but dull instead of spirited, ...

Under such circumstances it is perhaps understandable that the Guilbertian talent for invective was not slow in coming into play. When a Philadelphia headline sneered, "Oh, Such a Grouch Has Mme. Guilbert," Madame retaliated with sweeping indictments of everything American: the boorishness of customs officers, the stridency of female voices, the vulgarity of lady press agents—rashly naming in particular one Nellie Revell—the trickiness and greed of managers, and everywhere the lack of gentility. Only one topic came in for approval: woman suffrage, then just showing over the political horizon. On this subject Madame took a resolute stand, fierce as always in her recollection of the long history of women's wrongs.

In December, when the trial by fire was over and the Schillers, with accompanist Ferrari, embarked for Europe, Yvette, her pride in ribbons, was smarting under the inescapable belief that another of the world's most important cities was no longer hers: she had been popularly rejected in Paris; now openly insulted in New York. Well, there still remained London (the English provinces would have none of her or she of them), and all of Europe except Paris. She would continue to defy The Dilemma.

Fortunately, the following year, 1910, brought an event that did much to sweeten self-esteem, for this was the year of the publication, in London, of *Struggles and Victories,* a volume from the joint authorship of Yvette and a British writer, Harold Simpson. 'Tis pleasant sure, runs the old saw, to see one's name in print; a book's a book although there's nothing in't; and while it would be exaggeration to apply the couplet literally here, it must be confessed that, as to content, *Struggles and Victories* is a strange, mongrel mixture, consisting of a short and superficial autobiography by Yvette, presented both in French and in translation, followed by an equally sketchy biographical addendum by Mr. Simpson which features culled critiques, uniformly laudatory. In partial extenuation, however, it should be remembered that Yvette had worked on her part of this book under extremely difficult circumstances—in bed following one of her several operations. Yet disappointing as her document is in general, it is not without interest. Intimate in tone, written in emotional leaps and bounds, it is filled with the force and drive, and yet *tendresse,* characteristic of her temperament. True, the long dedication, "To God First of All," "a prayerful rhapsody," was viewed with disfavor by the more careful English critics, who found it not entirely "free from histrionic taint." The whole work might have been charged also to abound in vagueness, lack of candor, and inexplicable inaccuracies; to have been written for self-advertisement, like so many other popular autobiographies of theatrical personalities of the day. It tells little of the writer's years that had not already been repeated ad infinitum in the press. But it does suggest a life of monumental self-will and towering ambition. Nor can the significance be ignored of an unexpected emphasis on spiritual attitudes, as found in the preface. From a former professed freethinker, here are statements indicative of deep changes. "I have always been a mystic," Yvette defended herself to an interviewer. "An artist without religion—ah, I cannot fancy that. . . . I am not speaking of belief in forms, in dogmas, in words, but of faith in the large, spacious sense."

The year 1910 was also one of sorrow. It was the year when the hearty, affable presence of Edward VII passed from the world scene, and in many quarters, including, one may be sure, the house on Boulevard Berthier, his death was felt as a personal loss. More poignant by far, however, was Yvette's grief over the beloved cousin. In 1910 Lina Gaillard died, she who had wept when Yvette decided to go on the stage because the two girls' dream of a hat shop would have to be abandoned; Lina, who seems to have held such a unique place in Yvette's universe that her body was placed in Yvette's own tomb in Père Lachaise Cemetery.

As to relatives in general, it is puzzling to note that in speech as well as in writing Yvette made it a lifelong practice to avoid details regarding anyone except her parents. Once only in print are the grandparents Lubrez mentioned, and then with no comment. From Yvette the public would never have known of Aunt and Uncle Broutin in Asnières, and their three children, a son Albert and two daughters Jeanne and Marcelle. Of Hippolyte's family, too, never a word, until fairly late in life when, as if momentarily off guard, she refers, but only casually, to her father's and her mother's sisters; not from Yvette would one know that Hippolyte had also a brother Martial who had two daughters. While a lack of social intercourse with members of the father's family is understandable and would account for a lack of references to them, it is not so easy to account for what seems a deliberate veiling of relationships with the mother's family.

Lina Gaillard, the cousin from Sedan, was the notable exception; concerning her there was a slight lessening of censorship. The hat shop dream had come true for Lina, in a sense, for Yvette, after becoming wealthy, had set her cousin up in business for herself in a smart little *boutique* called New House, Rue de Clichy. When, for the Salon of 1896, Henri Alberti painted Yvette in her dressing room surrounded by a group of five intimates, "la petite cousine"—no name —was one of the five, along with Louis de Robert, Redelsperger, A. Ricard, and Ferdinand Bac. At Yvette's marriage Lina, who had herself been disappointed in love and was overcome with emotion that day, was one of the six guests at the very select and secret wedding party.

Yet, knowing all this, one still knows really very little about Lina.

She remains a shadowy figure, joining those others whose outlines Yvette delights to blur by vague references—Zidler, Hugues Le Roux, Louis de Robert—though concerning the latter better guesses can perhaps be made as to reasons for Yvette's reticence.

Struggles and Victories appeared in April, 1910, and by odd coincidence before the year was over a novel entitled *Le Roman du malade* had appeared from the hand of the invalid of Sannois.

Louis de Robert, for a decade now immured with his nightmares, his insomnia, his weakness and panic fears, through it all had been painfully hammering out page after page of this novel, as his strength permitted, doggedly maintaining at the same time some contact, though faint, with the world of letters. Paul Faure remained his constant correspondent, and there were others who wrote, though less often—Colette, for example. But when *Le Roman* finally appeared, and first as a prize-winning serial in *Figaro,* its author found himself again in the center of that long-lost world.

Of the congratulatory messages that poured into his quiet retreat one of course was from Yvette, who wrote warmly and lovingly. Through the years Yvette, Albine, and Max had remained on terms of family intimacy with Louis and his mother. Now Yvette speaks of the new tie that exists between her and her one-time suitor—the shared experience of surmounting physical suffering; illness is the greatest teacher of philosophy:

> *Moi aussi, j'ai toujours dit que la maladie était le plus grand professeur de Philosophie—on apprend avec elle, la valeur des individus et des choses! ... par elle on arrive à savoir, les possibilités, les probabilités des multiples bonheurs, securités et autres assurances de la vie—et la clairvoyance est si aiguë alors, que des certitudes naissent en vous, et qu'un guide surnaturel vous conduit là óu vous hesitiez d'aller.*
>
> *Comme je t'embrasse tendrement, "petit Robert." ... Et travaille! travaille, tu as un beau talent!*

"Work! Work!" It was the old refrain.

Like Yvette's return to public life, Louis' book was another veritable resurrection, in this case bringing, surprisingly, even love in its train. Louis was now close to forty, but a certain buoyant young lady named Thérèse thought only of his honors and not his graying hair. The affair was prolonged some two or three years; "a compensation life owes me," Louis wrote Paul defensively. He was still the semi-invalid, but until Thérèse was won by a younger man, we see him feeding once more on lovers' meetings and letters in violet ink, suffering at love's death over the discovery that the beloved's heart was "little" and "mediocre," and having in the end no choice but to consign youth and beauty to the devil: "*Qu'elle aille au diable.*"

It was now the very height of *la belle époque,* and Paris had never been so good a place to live in. Even by 1910 the face of the city had not changed greatly since the turn of the century. There were taxis now, to be sure, and motorbuses, and in the brilliantly lighted underground the exciting Métro; the American bar had made its appearance, following in the wake of culture-hungry overseas tourists and that ever-increasing colony of expatriates centering on the Left Bank. But there were still the thronged boulevard cafés, beloved as ever, even if a hint more garish under electric bulbs than formerly under the flattering flicker of gas mantles. For the frivolous there was the world epitomized by Maxim's; there was also that other world of leisured women whom Poiret draped in furs and laces and velvets. In artistic circles naturalism had become passé; intellectuals spoke of Wilde and Burne-Jones instead of Zola; for earnest souls it was an era of conscious aestheticism, and an ecstatic capitalizing of such words as Art, and Being, and Light, and Joy.

As to entertainment, the city was flooded with foreign artists of every stripe—magnificent, revolutionary, precious. One among them, variously claimed by some contemporaries to fill all these categories, was a young American dancer who was creating a vigorous stir by virtue of certain *bizarreries,* both personal and professional. Even to blasé Parisians, the young woman's record as *amoureuse* was admittedly staggering, and professionally she attracted even wider attention by an approach to dance that challenged every accepted concept. At a time when the vast, bureaucratic Imperial Russian Ballet, ossified by its rigid tradition of acrobatics, personified the public ideal of dance as an art, the appearance on an almost empty, blue-curtained stage of the solitary figure of Isadora Duncan, uncorseted, seminude, must have been at first rather puzzling. Also, the strange creature had displayed the further originality—impertinence, some called it—of appropriating to her purposes music designed for opera or concert hall, even claiming that she *danced* the music, not *to* the music. To cap all, she was articulate as to certain iconoclastic theories; she proclaimed herself a dancer with a mission: to win converts. Self-appointed apostle, she proposed nothing less than to overthrow the whole sterile ballet system, which she considered as stupid as any act of dancing bears; she would set free bodies deformed by ballet, awaken spirits dulled by it. She would teach. She would revive old pagan graces by founding a school of dance based on classical Greek models. Her addiction to dressing in flowing white tunics and barefoot sandals and flaunting a gold fillet in her hair seemed only to add further piquancy to her repeated assertions that she was herself a Hellenic reincarnation. As early as 1901, she had been quoted as stating that she would "rebuild the Temple of Paestum and open a college of priestesses."

The notion of artist as priest was not original with Isadora. Flaubert, enunciating the same doctrine, had stood before his novelist's altar with equal consecration. Art to him was avowedly a sacramental experience and required of its servants priestly dedication. In fact, the concept of art as something practiced in a temple seems not at that time to have been confined to a limited few; in this context the subject may be found in assorted references during the period. But the doctrine deserves more than passing note in view of the fact that Yvette too was of the same persuasion. For her, Flaubert may indeed have been the immediate source of the cult, since there is evidence that she knew his works, and certainly she matched his infinite labor and pains in her worship of perfectionism.

During the entire first decade of the twentieth century, rebuilding the Temple of Paestum was the burden of Duncan's song. Over and over, the length and breadth of Europe, the idea was reiterated, until at last pertinacity earned its reward. Eventually, since soule is forme and doth the bodie make, Duncan did become the founder of a school of dance; in fact, a succession of schools.

Bernhardt had dallied with the dream of a school, and now, in 1910, Yvette paralleled both Bernhardt and Duncan by actually founding one of her own. Other parallels were already in existence between Yvette and Duncan. Like Yvette, Duncan had studied in museums works of sculpture and figures on Greek vases; like Yvette she constantly emphasized the virtue of work. "*Travaille, travaille!*" cried Yvette; "Practice, practice!" urged Duncan. Duncan too, brought a *conférencier* into her matinees to add scholarly luster; she too made use of ancient musical instruments; where Yvette brought to life songs of the Middle Ages, by 1900 Duncan had "interpreted" Italian Renaissance paintings to the accompaniment of fourteenth-century Italian music. It is certain that Yvette regarded Duncan with an admiration second perhaps only to that which she felt for Duse, terming her "the artist who resuscitated the art of dancing; ... a genius, ... an Athenian goddess, divinely pagan." And it is probable that by now Yvette and Duncan had met. They moved in similar circles, played the same cities, had friends in common; Isadora had already made the acquaintance of Duse in Berlin.

The little school that Yvette opened in October, 1910, for children of working-class parents, *L'École de la chanson,* was in itself inconsequential enough. It did not continue long and it left no mark, its only significance being perhaps the place it occupies as precursor of a later educational project of larger scope. An idea had been born with Yvette that would remain alive, even if not the miniature *École de la chanson.*

One day at Vaux, in the summer of 1911, Death, that hath ten thousand doors, quietly opened one of them before Albine Guilbert and courteously bowed that tired old lady through, by his gentleness making what amends were possible to a woman who, by and large, had known little gallantry from Life.

The cardiac seizure Albine suffered had been quick and comparatively painless, yet on Yvette the shock fell heavily. It has been said that there is an eloquence in the death of the aged that nothing can match; links with the past snap forever asunder. So now it proved. "La Rive," which more and more in recent years had been left in Albine's care while Yvette and Max vacationed in Germany, now seemed meaningless. The estate must go, it was decided, as part of a bygone era; life was hurrying the Schillers too fast now in other directions. Yvette must dispossess herself of the once-precious spot—sunlight, moonlight, peace of its murmuring river and all.

Yvette mourned her mother sincerely, but it must have been a mourning alleviated by the knowledge that henceforth the affection she had always felt for Albine could be wholly and with clear conscience transferred to Max. Had she not long ago described her ideal mate as one who could "love her like a mother"?

Chapter 5

It was from Roumania, where she was touring in 1912, that Yvette set off on her first journey to the Near East. Though she looked forward keenly to a change of scene—Europe was by now a very old story—the trip had not been planned primarily for pleasure. She would still be on tour as a singer, with engagements to fill in Constantinople, Smyrna, Athens, Alexandria, and Cairo. As events proved, however, the sight-seeing and the concerts were to remain unimportant in retrospect in comparison with the singular psychic experiences that overtook her there.

Yvette had long wondered over her thousand talents; even half believed, as Duncan fully did, in a thousand pasts; and on the day when she first found herself walking the streets of Constantinople she was startled by a sense of unexpected familiarity. Surrounded by so many images of antiquity, she felt her brain begin to swirl; was seized by an unnerving conviction that she had walked these streets before. These were scenes that she was returning to, not discovering. She already knew these mosques and minarets and tombs; these arcades and vaults, and the porticoes succeeding and enmeshed in one another. She recognized the hundreds of sidewalk merchants, turbaned and robed, squatting beside their narghiles. The bazaars— that bewilder-ing sea of treasure extending in every direction—she had already bargained here, among objects such as perhaps Salammbô once fin-gered: embossed gold and silver daggers, enamel spurs of desert riders, carved copper braziers, chests made of fragrant woods; slippers, tur-quoise-encrusted and fit for a princess from *A Thousand and One Nights;* Persian damasks shot with sparkling threads; coffers of jewels —necklaces, bracelets, diadems. Down whatever alley she turned, she felt herself, in a kind of mounting ecstasy, on remembered terrain. The very air she breathed was familiar, with its mingled aromas of musk, rose water, incense, spices, dried fruits.

"What is happening to me?" she cried to herself, almost in fear. "This is my first trip to Constantinople! Why do I feel that it is not? When have I ever seen Byzantium?"

The sense of participation in the past had already suggested itself to her in Rome; now a certainty seized her that she was possessed of multiple souls and that in the Levant she had returned to the land of her beginnings. At the phenomenon of discovering herself, as she rapidly became persuaded, spiritually Byzantine in origin, her whole being was shaken by a perception of the immense distance her personal humanity had traveled through the centuries. Imagination began to riot, and romantic fantasies to form, mixtures of pagan suppositions with deistic and even Christian overtones. Did all the Oriental sumptuousness with which she was here surrounded, she asked herself—the bronze doors, ivory beds, marble floors, golden tables, silver chairs, flagons set with pearls—explain the insatiable desire for splendor she had always felt in her own depths, deadened but not dead? If so, as she theorized, the desire must have existed only to be transmuted, during the course of many incarnations, by passing through "filters of misery" such as, in her present existence, the poverty of her youth. Perhaps it was God's way of purifying her ostentatious and—who knows?—her cruel ways during that century when she was a Byzantine and lions dragged her chariot.

You, Byzantium, you knew me when I was beautiful, abusive, tyrannical, and proud of my beauty. Today ... the plainness of my face is perhaps a punishment for my former pride; but beneath your skies, as I breathe in your ruins, I recognize the air of your country. Was I once born in your land? Was I a celebrated Greek brought you from Athens? A servant, a slave, a queen of Egypt? I do not know. Was my father one of those learned Jews, spreading Oriental literature to the Occident, to inculcate in me a thousand years later this love for books, arts, human curiosities?

Have I already sung those sobbing Hebraic laments, captive in Babylon, or on my return to Judea in Cyrus' time? Was I among the Afaph, Heman, or Idithun singers during David's reign? Was I a member of the Mosaic choirs, and was I the soloist chosen at the bank of the Red Sea to win the people across with my chant and the rhythm of my tambour? Was I a chorister that day when King Solomon married the Pharaoh's daughter, and who knows whether I was not an interpreter of the *Song of Songs* which was "played" in the fabulous temple and which Origen reconstituted in all its chanted scenes? The Hebrews had in their prophets their first trained and rigorously disciplined singers; am I descended from their race?

My emotion over the ancient legends, my taste for Noëls reviving sacred history—do these rise in me because I assisted on the Mount of Olives at the Great Death? Or ran screaming through Jerusalem behind the mob? Could I have been Pilate's wife, or Mary Magdalen, or Veronica of the sacred napkin?

Did I sing in Greece the hymn to Nemesis . . . ? Perhaps I led the choir in the song of the Katabasis. Did I sob to the Stavrothéotokion, together with the first Christians? That song of the Cross . . . transposed sixteen hundred years later into a lament that I now sing under the title *La Passion*—did I once sing it in Greece?

What was I before I became the little working girl of Paris turned artist? . . . Why at the age of twelve was I so taken by the statue of the discus thrower? Had my subconscious returned it to me, and was I rejoicing over it like an old friend I believed lost and now found again? Yes! Yes! I am a daughter of these ancient races, and I have been singing Life for many thousands of years.

Convinced that in none of her myriad lives could she ever have been anything other than a singer, Yvette began to search for the songs she could believe she might have sung, and found many. In an emotional transport she almost wept when she heard issuing from her lips—re-issuing, she was ready to swear—words translated from the Greek which she herself had rhymed in French. In the simple alignment of the notes she found, she says, an exquisite beauty, and in singing them the voluptuous joy a woman knows when she holds her beloved and is intoxicated by the odor of his flesh.

In Smyrna even greater tumult of spirit assailed her the day she was taken to a small temple to witness an astonishing religious ceremony performed by fifteen whirling dervishes. It was a singular privilege to be present at this particular celebration, which was a sacrifice to Allah. Only four other spectators besides herself were admitted.

The ceremony consisted of a dance in which the men, dressed in full white skirts with corded edges and accompanied only by a small flute, whirled in an exhibition of dexterity and endurance that dumbfounded the onlookers. Around and around they spun on the same spot with incredible lightness, revolving on feet that moved so fast they seemed not to be moving at all, the great white skirts spreading like open umbrellas. As they spun, their faces took on an expression of ecstasy; some with eyes rolled completely back, others with sealed lids; the mouths open, one palm outstretched toward Allah to receive, the other lowered in thanks. It was a terrible dance that lasted two hours without break; perspiration bathed the votaries, foam spread over their lips, the pallor of death was on every face. Only four of the fifteen were able to finish without fainting. Afterward all were obliged to sit for long hours in complete silence before they could either breathe normally or resume awareness of the world. Not a word, not a gesture; only a sense of soul ascending, and mystery.

During the performance one of the dancers particularly held Yvette's agonized attention, a man with a long thin face, a black beard, eyelids blued with suffering, violaceous lips stretched tautly back to the gums, arms that dangled, flabby, livid, lined with black veins. Suddenly she recognized the figure. It was the crucified Christ! Indubitably the Christ in descent from the Cross that she had seen in innumerable Italian primitive *Pietàs!* The Christ in person before her! Yvette was so shocked, so profoundly moved, that for days she lived as in a trance, unable to return to the daily round of existence. For days she could think of nothing but the exaltation of that terrible moment; her brain ached with it. "... I saw, I saw, agony dance!"

Athens agitated her less; whispered in fainter tones than had Pompeii, where she had felt years before that life still pulsed in the chariot-rutted streets. Though she had long ago learned to reverence Greek art in European museums, to her surprise she felt little rapport with Greece itself. Athens to her was a sarcophagus; a silence; the Parthenon haughty and subtly cold. Only two spots moved her: one where Plato daily met his disciples, the other the theater of Bacchus, which set her to dreaming of its great expectant audiences and the odes she may once have sung there, "alongside the couplets of Aristophanes," to the suburban Athenians.

The theater where she actually played in Athens had been offered her by the courtesy of King George, who after the concert sought her out in her dressing room, accompanied by his son the prince and two of the princess daughters, to compliment her. Later that night, as she left the theater, she was approached by a gentleman who remarked that her work evinced a great knowledge of life; she might be another Hypatia.

"I don't know Hypatia. Tell me about her," demanded Yvette.

"She was very intelligent and clairvoyant. She was martyred in Alexandria."

"*Flûte alors!*" cried Yvette. "Tomorrow I'm due there!"

The incident, too frivolous to be taken seriously, nevertheless seemed to add one more whiff of persuasion to the fast-growing feeling of consanguinity with Mediterranean peoples of antiquity. It reminded Yvette, too, of an explorer whom she had once met in Berlin and who had exclaimed on meeting her that her features were those of *une Atlantide*.

In Alexandria the sense of being haunted continued to intensify. As she debarked, her eyes were ravished by the physiques of the men she saw working on the quays—plastic statues of bronze, glimpsed through floating robes of blue, rose, green, saffron. Those who rode horses held their reins very high in one hand, with the other arm glued along the body; when they disappeared, it was in a flash, seeming to be carried away like gods, straight and rigid. She was breathless at their elegance. The ancient athletes, she thought, or the chariot drivers in the circus, could not have displayed more superb style. Later she noted the people as a "race," the fineness of wrists and ankles, the faces that seemed a blend of Mediterranean and Asiatic. At sight of the robes, the turbans, the curled beards of the silent men who dwelt in tents, Biblical patriarchs sprang to life in her mind; she watched the graceful, barefooted women, black-veiled; was awed by the pride of the Bedouins who honored her by demanding alms: "Bless me, passer-by, for having proved to God your charity"; and with every class felt a kinship. Suddenly she was of Alexandria, too. She felt wedded to the beginning of the world—and, equally, to its end; a link in a long chain.

In Cairo, during her concerts there, a beggar crouched every night in the street outside her dressing room in the theater, singing strange chants with modulations unknown to her. As she sat before her mirror putting on her make-up, she would listen carefully, and every evening would go away with many of the tunes memorized for her own use. Later, to her intense surprise, she discovered melodic echoes of her beggar of Cairo in certain manuscripts of the Middle Ages, and by investigation learned that these European versions had been brought back by the Crusaders and that the Greeks, the Byzantines, and the Egyptians, from whom the melodies had been picked up, learned them centuries earlier from traveling Hebraic singers, reputed to be scholars. The chain was a very long one indeed.

"My planet is my country! I am of The Earth!" she exulted, in a new vision of the eternity and universality of art. The artist's duty was to imitate the whole Earth.

More dramatically, however, than any of the cities she had thus far visited, it remained for Cairo to offer what seemed to her the final and incontrovertible proof of her former existence.

She was well conditioned for Egypt. Nineteenth-century imagination had long been aquiver over ancient worlds. Wherever archaeology had led the way, disinterring old civilizations, romance had followed on its heels, reanimating the disinterred. The Pharaohs especially, in their mummified majesty, had captured public fancy, and the spell of the Near East was deep in the hearts and minds of many who knew no more of Egypt than what they had read in such tales as Gautier's *Roman de la momie*.

Loti had told her of the famous mummy of Sesostris in the Cairo Museum, that great conquering Sesostris of the Twelfth Dynasty whose army, according to a fascinating little book she picked up in Cairo, numbered six hundred thousand foot soldiers and twenty-seven thousand chariots; who subjugated Ethiopia, forcing it to pay a yearly tribute of ivory, gold, and ebony; who at the head of four hundred ships sailed through the Red Sea, seizing all the coasts. His supremacy was recognized in Syria, Armenia, Cappadocia. Even as late as Herodotus' time, monuments had been seen to him, great obelisks bearing the inscription "Sesostris, King of Kings, Sesostris, Lord of Lords, has conquered this country by force of arms."

Now, still unbelievably well preserved, the shrunken body of this lord of lords lay in the Cairo Museum, available for the humble to gaze upon, and around it clung a strange story. One morning, it was said, an attendant had found one of the arms that for uncounted centuries had been resting rigid beside the king's body pointing straight upwards as if electrified. First on Yvette's sight-seeing list in Cairo was Sesostris.

Quite unprepared for the shock that awaited her, she went immediately on arrival at the museum to Sesostris' bier, leaned over the glass case that enclosed it, and gazed down upon the varnished, shining face of the man who had been a legend even thousands of years ago. As she gazed, she all but swooned. The face she was looking at so intently was the face of her father! There he lay—the hated and adored, the captivating, talented, glibly persuasive, irresponsible ne'er-do-well and deceiver—whom she had reviled bitterly for years for his faithlessness but whom she could never forget. She saw "The same curve from the forehead to the tip of the slightly arched nose, the same protruding cheek bones, the same arched and prominent eyebrows, the same short chin . . ." At home she had a portrait of Hippolyte Guilbert that might have been a portrait of Sesostris.

Her emotion was so extreme that she fell into a state of uncontrollable trembling. Even fifteen years later she remembered the moment so vividly that she could write:

I was in a state of ecstacy! My living eyes were absorbing this dead man . . . he was penetrating me, encrusting himself into the the cells of my brain. . . . I carried Sesostris away with me, and when I shall be placed in the earth, then he will find his tomb again . . .

In Constantinople Yvette had already speculated on her ancient paternity; all through these lands had carried a father-awareness with her; and here at last she had found the awareness objectified. Here, in the safety of the Middle Kingdom, under the impact of total surprise, the enemy-lover-daughter at last acknowledged herself "penetrated" by Hippolyte Guilbert.

After Yvette had left Egypt and returned to Paris, she received a newspaper critique of her last concert at the Théâtre du Printania in Cairo, significant in its suggestion of the enlargement and elevation of spirit that must have been manifest in her personality at this time and in its implication that these psychic changes were affecting her as an artist and foreshadowing a new freedom from limitations of literalness:

Yvette is becoming more and more stamped with mysticism and a unanimistic religion. I see her as a Vestal Virgin, . . . priestess of a fanaticism of art . . . letting fall her lamp in order to stretch herself out naked and joyful on an altar.

Stamped with the supernatural, she abandons herself to it with fervor, a divine abandon. This is because Yvette is a poet, more of a poet than anyone has thus far recognized, and of times less worn and degenerate than our own—the times of the Greeks, or Milton, or Dante, when art moved in ordered tumultuousness . . . In our day art as idioms, as languages, becomes analytic . . . we search more for sensation than for sentiment. This is false Realism, erring more precisely because of its system of induction. And that is why the apostles who digress from it and renew the high traditions of the past . . . walk toward the Future.

Chapter 6

March of 1913 found Yvette again on tour in Italy. Events of the months intervening between her trip to the Levant and this one had been of hardly more than routine interest. An operatic version of the legend of Sister Beatrice which she had written and attempted to produce failed to materialize. There had been the usual round of engagements—Berlin, Dresden, London—with an occasional change of pace attempted by the introduction of some slight novelty in repertoire. In 1912 she had resurrected *Le Sabot Perdu,* a divertissement first presented in Paris in 1781, but even with rewritten choruses and dances and reorchestration, it proved of no more than historical importance. At another time she had appeared in *La Vie du Christ,* a program of *chansons* devoted to episodes from the life of Christ, reconstructed from poems and music of the fourteenth to seventeenth centuries, but even her devoted Berliners found against this offering. She had been slightly more successful in a series of concerts at the elegant Salle Gaveau in Paris that autumn with material that had come to her hand almost by accident. Rummaging one day in a clutter of dusty, faded sheets of music that had accumulated in her house on Boulevard Berthier, she had discovered under an old hatbox a collection of gay ariettes, pastorals, and drinking songs. The find intrigued her, such a wealth of fun and humor suggesting that Frenchmen of a few hundred years ago might have been more spontaneously lighthearted than those of the twentieth century. As entertainment, these songs had made only mildly amusing evenings, but as curiosities they had attracted scholars from the Sorbonne, the Collège de France, Oxford; philologists to study early provincial dialects; historians; musicologists.

The critic Henri Brisson applauded such revivals. It was often deplored by the French, he said, that three-fourths of the treasures of their past had been lost; that acquaintance with literature went hardly back of the sixteenth century, with four preceding centuries as unknown to the average Frenchman as Chinese. If Guilbert could save no more than a dozen songs of that period—even granting the inevitable mutations which they would have suffered—she would be doing in his eyes a great service to France.

Now it was spring again in Rome, and inevitably her thoughts turned to the woman she loved as a sister, who had followed her from city to city on that other Italian tour in 1902 and whose heart had since been "hurt unto death."

D'Annunzio's break with Duse had not seemed to affect the playwright, who remained as busy with his amours as with his muse. In 1910 he had arrived in Paris at the height of his fame, and there continued to flatter and charm one mistress after another. The lives this man crossed! Even that of a semi-invalid in Sannois. By 1913, according to confidences penned by Louis de Robert to his alter ego Paul, an unidentified Marguerite M., of famous beauty, was maintaining simultaneous friendships with both novelist and playwright. Under the circumstances, then, it is perhaps not strange that Louis of the Drawn Shades betrays a certain modest sense of triumph in recording to Paul the fact that one night Invincible waited in vain for Beautiful. We note the lovely Marguerite with more than passing interest, for if we understand Louis correctly, the dance pattern of a strange sort of *ronde* was thereby completed, one in which since 1892 six figurants had woven in and out in a constant change of partners— Marguerite and Louis and Yvette and Max and Duse and D'Annunzio—forming and reforming their series of love triangles through the years.

About all such dalliance, however, probably neither Yvette nor Duse now knew or cared. In 1910 Duse had abruptly withdrawn from the theater, offering no explanation. According to Isadora Duncan, she had not acted from reasons sentimental, but for lack of capital to carry out her ideas of art. But Yvette, who had been close to Duse for longer than Duncan, had some time ago recognized health as the fundamental problem:

Her health worried me so much that my husband and I decided to arrange for her to come and consult a specialist in Paris. She came, and was ordered to go to the Black Forest . . . to take an open-air cure. But alas! her poor lungs were already attacked. She returned to Italy, lived a halting life, and left off acting. Having spent two years resting in the sunshine, dreaming away her days in her own thoughts, without the incentive of work in the theater, . . . she seemed gradually to have lost the idea of returning to it, and her physical strength seemed to be ebbing away little by little. But when I came to see her I felt that if she were not given the illusion that she lived by her art she would die all the sooner in the body. This magnificent beacon was burning low.

I then set to work to rekindle it with the only fuel that could set it aflame again—work!

She let herself be taken in by my friendly snare, and my visits to Rome made her leave her bed. . . . I was not a little surprised to see my Duse in the audience, in Rome, in Florence, in Milan, where she followed me. She used to come with her eyes bright and her face betraying how moved she was by the great success I was having: through me she was getting in touch again with the life of the theatre. . . . I felt myself to be a wholesome example for her, and I played on her. "Come, come! Courage, begin again, my Duse!" and her eyes would shine with hope. And then, the day after my concerts, she would be coughing from having been out late, and black despair would come back, and discouragement would fall upon her, and there followed letters, pathetic little notes written in bed, always in pencil, and sometimes long telegrams in which her whole heart disclosed itself.

Now in 1913, when Yvette saw Duse again in Rome, she thought her wondrously improved:

Her cough seemed to have passed off, and her breathing to be more regular, so I shook her up: "Here you are, splendidly fit, and yet you're doing nothing! Look here, would you like to do a tour with me? . . . You . . . could play three nights a week, and I could sing for three. . . . that would not tire you so much. . . . Is that agreed?" She looked at me overcome with delight. That night I received the following letter at the Manzoni Theatre (I leave it in her Italian style):

Hotel Eden, Rome
March 1913

Take care, my kind Yvette.
Perhaps what I say will never come to pass.
Perhaps it is the agony of illness, of the isolation of heart and mind; perhaps it is mere vanity, triviality of the artist or woman of the theatre (as the *canailles* call it) that makes me write . . . still—still, if you put aside all this stupid surface of things . . .
perhaps "your soul"
can see
better and further

than what I speak.

Listen! If I look at the sky I think I have a possibility of activity,

If I watch the stars I seem to get nearer to myself, I can feel myself live.

I have a life within myself, and it is not yet dead,

I whisper this to you: If I watch the night, peaceful and quiet . . .

I seem to understand everything, even art. . . .

I am dying, I am dying here, but not quickly enough, that is the trouble.

I have gone over things so often, I know, that everything is my fault, and yet nobody's fault. . . .

But here I am dying. I am dying. I feel what it must be like after death.

It takes too long. . . .

Yesterday, you did me good, so much painful good to my heart, and even this morning my heart is welling up.

Alas! . . . I don't know how to write, I am shy of words.

Listen.

Don't say a word to anyone else, for perhaps I shall never be well again, and never again shall I be strong enough for work.

But with you perhaps I should get back my faith.

But for me to start off, very far away, and alone, still bound to the footlights, *No!* I couldn't.

But with you, as a sister in soul and in work, perhaps your strength would awaken mine.

The same journey, the same aim, and two art mediums.

Three evenings a week: you.

Three evenings a week: me.

and far!

In North America there are university towns where thought and things of the mind have their value.

You, your treasure is already prepared.

But mine is not, but as I am the more sheltered of the two I could hasten my preparation.

I have a work of poetry in my heart, which I venture to say, no one has ever loved as much as I.

It is the work of one of the great, which has been badly played. But when I am suffering, and I have hardly the breath to live, I close my eyes and I call up *My Vision* and I know it to be beautiful.

I give you in confidence the name of my consoling vision, but (and a dying woman speaks) don't mention it (yet) to anyone.

My beautiful comforter in the hours of my soul's agony is *The Lady from the Sea,* by Ibsen.

She is comforting and lovely, as changing as the sea itself, and her name reveals her completely to whosoever is fit to understand.

The work is an old saga (old Norwegian legend).

I have "composed" it in my heart, it is made of the colours of the sea, the gentle breeze, and the wave that breaks and disappears.

I, I know.

Everything is formless when I speak of it, but it takes shape in my being in the silence....

Alas, it fades away when I speak of it.

But
you
you
are art,
and to you one can tell it
without its magic disappearing in thin air.
If I could carry it
with you
beyond the sea,
eh?
There!
Do you understand?

But, be careful, don't make any contract with those *canailles* of the theatre.

To-day perhaps my fever is higher, and I dream perhaps of the impossible.

But you,
you are art
and I have told you of my sorrow and my joy.
Keep the heart of

Leonora

After Yvette left Rome to fill engagements in other cities of Italy, here and there Duse would take her by surprise by coming to see her en route. On one of these occasions Duse seemed hopelessly dispirited; she would never act again, she said; she hated the theater.

Yvette, deeply troubled, decided to try to rouse her friend by a little ruse:

I wrote to her, in an offended tone, saying no doubt she did not think my talent worthy to be associated with hers, and asking her, if this were so, why she had for years covered me with flowers and praise, etc., etc.

The ruse worked. In Genoa Yvette received a telegram.

Received your letter, you have judged hastily, and misunderstood, will talk over everything, am gathering my strength to come to Nice to speak to you ... will discuss heart to heart, for whether or no I am capable of work, I keep of you an ideal, as an artist and a woman, that I must make you understand. *Au revoir* from my heart....

Eleonora

Another message followed in Milan:

My thoughts are working. ... if hope is realized, then we must see each other and plan an artistic scheme, the best time for work would be January to April. Must avoid all theatre milieus, and turn to university towns quite outside usual theatrical tours. Must talk it over, for the moment heart cheered by hope. Tender greetings. Be beautiful tonight. Devotedly

Eleonora

In Nice, where the tour was ending, Yvette received a note from Duse, who wrote from her hotel. She had actually come.

Yvette, who arrived at two o'clock to-day, is to sing to-night. She will be beautiful! She will be Yvette! and she must be given time to rest, to be herself, so I shall stay by the sea all day, and to-night I shall go

and see
Yvette.

So ... during the day
Silence
for both of us.

Leonora

Yvette dashed off a reply that she would expect Eleonora to lunch the following day.

> Dear, [wrote Duse in reply] to see you tonight takes the place of everything else. But lunch to-morrow? I fear not.
> I slept like a log during the journey, but to talk and get about is much harder. Although I am rid of my fever which I left in my hotel bedroom in Italy! But I am stupidly tired. . . . I am looking forward to night with affectionate and anxious eagerness. Then luncheon to-morrow. No, I can't . . . but at three o'clock, if you are free, I could either come and fetch you or wait for you here, you can answer me to-morrow, to-night, you must think only of your work. (Oh, Life, Life!)
>
> Leonora

That evening Duse went to the concert, but at witnessing the torrent of physical energy that Yvette poured forth in her performance the invalid was struck with dismay over her own weakness. Next day she wrote in a panic:

> . . . Yesterday evening, seeing you again with my eyes, and in the night in my soul, I could no longer find the one I used to be, I could not find myself. . . . How can I begin again? What can I do? . . . I have nothing to offer you! Yes? Then how? When? What is to be done? Everything founders in an indescribably little anguish of the heart which does not understand itself, neither can it find its way, and I am terrified of the crowd and of the glare of the footlights! If I close my eyes, if I hush my heart, I understand so *clearly* your effort, and each thread that consolidates that enormous power which guides and inspires you. I, I haven't got "work" that I love sufficiently to make me change my mind, and perhaps to be silent has its nobility too. . . . Yvette, I don't know! Nothing is any use without strength and power. . . .

By the time the two women met at three that afternoon, the only thing Duse could contemplate doing, she said, might be a program of recitations, great Italian poems, or scenes from plays, which she could interpret sitting in a chair and which therefore might not be

252

beyond her physical powers. Could Yvette find material that would be in harmony with the different periods of her own *chansons?*

Thus the idea of a collaboration was born, and there for some time it rested. From Paris Yvette shipped frequent parcels of books to Rome, but later learned that Duse had gone back to her own house in Florence, ill again:

> Yvette, thanks for your letter. For the last fortnight have been again in bed with a heavy chill. Have fallen back into the same bodily and mental depression as last winter. On Thursday consultation on where to spend summer. Keeping your books in hope of seeing you somewhere during summer. Best and faithful love. No forgettings.
>
> Eleonora

Though her heart bled over her friend's condition, Yvette continued to pretend optimism in regard to the projected collaboration. Duse apparently found enough strength later to take herself to Paris and still later to Basle, where she stayed ill for weeks in a friend's house on Lake Maggiore, Yvette constantly writing, trying to sustain the sick woman's courage.

Months afterward came a reward for all these efforts. When Max and Yvette called on Duse one day in the spring of 1914 at the Eden Hotel in Rome, they found her looking entirely changed:

> The long rest and assiduous care had transfigured her! How beautiful she was! She received us, my husband and me . . . in her little room. . . . She had hung the room with white muslin, for hygienic reasons, and from her balcony she could see the whole of the magnificent city of the Campagna Romana. The delicious air allowed her to breathe freely. No sound could be heard from her chest, and I thought her cured.
>
> She came to lunch with us, . . . She then offered to take up once more the plans for work . . . And it was settled that in October 1914 we should go somewhere and "work" together!

When this decision was made, who had ever heard of Sarajevo? By October, 1914, who had not?

It was during this visit to Rome that Yvette made an unexpected announcement to an interviewer from *Theatre:* arrangements were even then in progress for her return to America in the fall of 1915. During the *fiasco glorioso* of 1909, when she and the American public had feuded so fiercely, spitting at each other daily in the press like enraged cats, Yvette had sworn never again to set her foot among such vulgarians, and the vulgarians themselves had seemed not ill pleased to have it so. But that had been five years ago, and in five years tempers can cool and conditions change.

The prime condition that had changed was the type of booking newly available in the States. Instead of playing in cheap vaudeville houses, with their cigar-chewing trickster-managers, she now had an opportunity to appear under the dignified concert management of Catharine A. Bamman. Under such auspices cultured audiences would be assured, and tasteful settings in which she could be seen to best advantage. Financial returns would be more meager than in vaudeville, but *l'art pur* would have its day. Yvette was pleased at the prospect.

Chapter 7

In the early summer of 1914, just before the world first caught fire at Sarajevo and *la belle époque* was reduced to ashes overnight, Yvette and Max had gone to Berlin. Suddenly the word "War!" was flashed the length and breadth of Germany, and within a few hours the Schillers, stunned with surprise, had found themselves jammed into a sweltering express train with hundreds of other French nationalists, racing through the night for the Belgian border; racing the guns for home.

The somber reversals they encountered on their return to Paris were not concerned solely with citizen anxiety over the military situation, precarious as that situation was. Profound changes in emotional climate had swept over the city. Paris was no longer smiling; Paris was on the rack. Those who saw the heartbreaking lack of nursing and medical facilities for the thousands of wounded soon pouring back from the front could think only of finding ways to alleviate suffering. Personal concerns were quickly dwarfed.

To offer freely the resources of her art was for Yvette a natural first instinct, and she now began singing for soldiers as generously as she had formerly sung for needy stage performers; singing in hospitals to amuse patients, in theaters to raise funds.

She contributed in other ways, too. One day Les Dames de France appealed to her for six hundred yards of linen; special shirts were needed at once for men with arm wounds to be dressed. Here was an emergency in which an ex-seamstress could function with efficiency. How well Yvette remembered from her girlhood those gloomy tenements of the needle-trades district! How well she knew what doors to open, up what corkscrew stairs to toil! She climbed, she solicited, she charmed, and wherever she went, she got what she asked for. Not only was the material donated; shirtcutters sat up nights to cut it, satisfied for their services with nothing more than her autographed photograph. Then she borrowed sewing machines and hunted up women to do the stitching. Later, for the same charity, she wheedled pillows for the wounded from Le Printemps by reminding that great store that she had once been one of its humblest saleswomen. Under the auspices of Pierre Loti she organized a gala benefit at the Gaîté. At Christmas she collected bonbons and toys and clothing for fatherless children.

Of her own saddened personal life very few then knew, but letters written by Yvette in late 1914 and early 1915 to a young American student, Margaret Farnam, reveal some of the inner stresses. In Berlin, Carl Rosenfeld died in 1915, bringing the Passage Theater to an end and leaving Max's sister Rose in financial uncertainty; Max himself had become thin almost to emaciation from anxiety. Yvette's relatives, the Broutins, who still lived in Asnières, were in equally bad case, the old parents grieving themselves so literally to death over the loss of their beloved son "missing in action" that the young girl cousins, Marcelle and Jeanne, Yvette well knew, would soon be orphaned. "And one lives among the dead, the wounded, the mutilated," Yvette wrote Margaret Farnam, "and one sings, my dear, one sings! ... France is wrapped in a gorgeous flame of energy, of courage, and of faith in victory."

Though physical mutilations were soon to become commonplace, there was one unexpected shock in store for the people of France that would sicken every heart. The beloved Bernhardt had been ill for a long time. She was old, and in the general holocaust her death would have been accepted as only one more; but who was prepared for the amputation of a leg? A wave of agonized pity swept the country.

Yvette, to her infinite credit, had a few years earlier graciously offered an olive branch to her erstwhile enemy, which had been as

255

graciously accepted. It happened in London, during an engagement at the Coliseum, where the two women were appearing by chance on the 'same bill. The clouds were already closing in on the Divine One, but even here, on music-hall level, she had kept one shred of panoply fluttering. Every night, when her act was called, she required her secretary to offer his arm and escort her with due ceremony to the wings. Yvette, to spare Bernhardt the embarrassment of an accidental backstage encounter under such circumstances, acted promptly and correctly by calling at her dressing room and sending in a card. Bernhardt, who also had mellowed with the years was sweetly cordial, seeming to think it quite natural than an old rival should have dropped in to give her a kiss, and from that day on, the two met on higher ground than jealousy. Now, at the time of this most cruel blow, Sarah again kept her public on leash when she took her unforgettably gallant stand against misfortune. Madame Bernhardt, it was promptly announced, would not leave the stage; she would henceforth play her roles seated. *Quand même!*

Even in letters to her *chère petite Marguerite* in America, Yvette made no mention, however, of the really serious situation that was beginning to build up around herself. Paris did indeed overflow, as she had said, with faith and heroism. Unfortunately, it manifested also an uglier quality—a war hysteria in which fears of espionage and rumors about possible spies proliferated. Like all war capitals, the city was undoubtedly infiltrated, and among the names of French nationals suspected of disloyalty that of Madame Guilbert soon came to be whispered. La Guilbert was married to a German, *n'est-ce pas?* And didn't she and her husband spend as much time in Germany as in France? Furthermore, of late years had she not openly expressed her love of that country, even making uncomplimentary comparisons between French and German ways of life? The very location of her house on Boulevard Berthier bred suspicion—near the fortifications and hence easy of access by enemy agents. There is little doubt that in previous years, with her extraordinarily wide professional acquaintance in Berlin, many Germans must have come and gone freely through her door. Now sinister interpretations arose. Threatening letters began to show up in her mail; newspapers dealt in dark hints. In vain Yvette tried to set up a defense by telling an Associated Press reporter: "I have reason to be proud, first of my French birth, second of my American nationality acquired by marriage." But even the man in the street could recognize this claim as mere stratagem. To him Madame Guilbert would remain Frau Schiller, and in strong probability an ally of the hated *Boches*.

As unsavory incidents multiplied, Yvette and Max began to live in fear, as if caught in a poisonous vapor seeping up from the very stones of the streets. The final insult came when accusations were scrawled on the walls of Paris street urinals: "*Yvette Guilbert, femme d'un espion allemand*."

"She is queen of Paris, she is queen everywhere. . . ." To think it was less than ten years ago that these words had been written!

Ironically—so goes the whirl of the wheel—the Schillers found themselves adopting a new attitude toward the forthcoming American sojourn. They began to count the weeks before the sailing date; to plan, moreover, for a stay of indefinite duration. The tour that had been accepted for profit only took on the aspect of a providential deliverance, and references to Americans became of a sudden ingratiating. Writing to Miss Bamman, her manager, Yvette made obvious overtures:

And should I not avow that it is my desire to escape for a time from the agonizing vision of universal mourning, . . . from the sight of these thousands of men so awfully mutilated, from all the horrible recollections which will never be effaced from my memory? After all these visions of hell, my trip to America to me is like unto the divine grace of entrance into the Promised Land . . . into a Paradise of Peace. I have an ardent desire for the charity of silence on all that is and has been of horror and disaster, to the end that in your generous country I may again find my equilibrium. I am sure of the hearty, helpful good-will of the American people.

Apparently unnoticed, the Schillers slipped quietly out of Paris in November, and after a tense crossing of the submarine-infested North Atlantic, finally found themselves back in Manhattan. And Paradise indeed it was to sleep soundly once again, blessedly far from the menacing growls of the Big Berthas and the even more imminent danger of arrest.

In the event that awkward questions should be raised in America as to her patriotism, Yvette had apparently determined her answers before leaving France. True, she could always claim reasons of health for an extended stay in America, but she must have recognized that health alone would be a shoddy excuse at a time when the whole French nation was suffering untold physical hardships. Instead, on the excellent principle that the best defense is an offense, she planned to announce at the outset that her trip carried national overtones; that her professional engagements were actually a cultural mission from France, her immense repertoire of the old songs of France being the most vivid and comprehensible history possible of the people of France and the soul of the nation. Her case would have been invulnerable if she could only have persuaded the French government to endow her with some official title indicative of semidiplomatic status. In this respect she was disappointed. But she had interviewed M. Georges Leygues, a member of the government, more successfully on another idea:

> "I should like you to . . . allow me to photograph the tapestries that have been saved from the cathedral at Rheims. I will show them on the screen in America, while I give some of the old songs belonging to the period of Jeanne d'Arc. In this way I can hope to attract the sympathy of the United States toward our invaded homeland, . . ."

This request had been granted, and she had been able to sail with at least official photographs to display. These should serve as governmental endorsement of her loyalty.

The Knickerbocker, the Schillers' economical choice of hostelry this time, though far from being the Savoy of earlier visits, was nevertheless favored by the theatrical profession. Those who had interviewed Guilbert previously noted personality changes in the woman freshly come from a nation in combat—"eyes . . . clouded with a certain sadness"; a new kind of dignity—changes not to be wondered at in one whose teachers of philosophy now included perhaps the sternest of all. To *la maladie* and the six steely kisses of the surgeon's knife had now been added *la guerre*. No one seemed aware of the cloud under which she had left Paris.

Unashamedly enjoying once more the succulent fleshpots of the vulgarians and reveling in the coziness of a deliciously warm hotel such as the vulgarians knew so well how to build, the Schillers were nevertheless not long in noting changes even in New York. Immediately they became aware of new tensions. America was war-conscious. How long could the United States escape involvement? everyone was asking. In the streets newsboys shouted war extras; armchair strategists pored over maps and moved battle lines of colored pins back and forth as the fortunes of the Western Front rose or sagged. People spoke in horror-stricken clichés of "the rape of Belgium" and "the unspeakable Hun." It was fashionable to be Francophile. French visitors, many of them fund-raisers for relief, were made much of; the tricolor was flown freely; at the Metropolitan, Duncan had electrified crowds by her maenad miming of the *Marseillaise*. Even while Woodrow Wilson was patiently explaining to the world that his nation was too proud to fight, impetuous young men were flocking to join the Lafayette Escadrille. Never in the history of the country could a better time have been hit upon for an unpopular Frenchwoman to return to New York.

As Yvette came on stage for her first concert at the Lyceum Theater, the sumptuous Paquin costumes brought rounds of applause.

. . . she might have stepped down from one of the great canvases with which Titian or Veronese were wont to hang their glowing Venice. In them they wrought figures of women in the physical opulence of middle years, in ripened and rich beauty, in dignity and nobility of pose and glance, in the panoply of multi-colored and embroidered stuffs, with the full radiance of full living on mind and body and spirit, like a deep halo around them. . . .

The program opened with two of the most telling songs of the *La Vie du Christ* cycle. These, which she titled *Les Légendes dorés*, "The Golden Legends," set forth the birth and death of Christ. In the first, variously called *Le Voyage de Joseph et Marie à Bethléem* and *La Naissance du Christ*, Joseph tries to encourage the fainting Mary onward:

> *Nous voici dans la ville où naquit autrefois*
> *Le roi le plus habile—David, le Roi des Rois.*
> *Allons, chère Marie—près de cet horloger*
> *Est une hotellerie—Nous y pourrons loger.*

In gentle cadence the characters move under the Judean stars: Joseph timorously asking shelter from inn to inn; the hosts all refusing, each after his fashion; Mary, with hands crossed fearfully over her travailing womb, conveying an expression of anguish such as is sometimes seen depicted in carved figures in thirteenth-century churches. To make use of time as a vehicle in the drama—time moving ineluctably forward—Yvette added to the story a watchman who called the hours at the end of each fate-laden verse, his tones coming always from a distance and long drawn out; sometimes high, drifting, mournful; again shrill, like a note of warning; at last, soft, with assurance of repose. In Constantinople, in the voice of a muezzin calling the hour for sunset prayer from the top of a minaret, she had heard the exact timbre of this voice. The total effect was of something unearthly, beyond mortal knowledge, at once sorrowful and triumphant. Six hours was the turning point; in six more, Mary would "yield her eternal fruit." Since the original text ended with Mary finding shelter in the stable, Yvette resourcefully added a verse of another legend from the same cycle to round out the conclusion—a jubilant coda, a climactic cry of rejoicing, a "chant as of a host of angels, trumpet-tongued":

> *Noël! Noël! Noël!*
> *Il est né le Divin Enfant!*
> *Sonnez, hauts-bois! résonnez, musettes!*

Many of the audience present that opening night must have remembered *La Soûlarde* from another opening and reflected that the distance from that pitiful drunken wretch to the Virgin Mary represented an impressive span in the singer's development.

The second Golden Legend, *La Passion du doux Jésus,* was a ballad that in the sixteenth century used to be chanted at Eastertide before the portals of every cathedral in France:

> *Avant qu'il soit vendredi nuit*
> *Vous verrez mon corps pendre*
> *Vous verrez mes bras étendus*
> *Sur une croix si grande.*
>
> *Vous verrez mon chef couronné*
> *D'une aubépine blanche*
> *Vous verrez mes deux mains clouées*
> *Et mes deux pieds ensemble.*

Vous verrez mon côté percé
Par un grand coup de lance
Vous verrez mon sang découler
Tout le long de mes membres.

Vous verrez mon sang ramassé
Par quatre petits anges
Vous verrez ma mère à mes pieds
Bien triste et bien dolente.

Because the scene of the Crucifixion is here only a foretelling, the singer is spared the crudity of any attempt at realistic treatment, and Yvette's interpretation seems to have abounded instead in suggestion subtle and powerful. "By what magic of evocation," one viewer asked, "by what conscious relaxing of muscles and drooping of the head, did Yvette make us see in her the crucified Christ?" Boston's Philip Hale must have been made to see Him too, for he wrote of "the image of Jesus upon the cross . . . a spiritual mystery of personation that is beyond all analysis of tones and mimique . . ." She sang the entire legend with a mounting crescendo, while the audience, enraptured and terrified, scarcely drew breath; the mere act of listening was a participation in the Passion; a shattering experience.

Now Nature responds with tumult to the agony:

Vous verrez la terre trembler
Et les pierres se fendre
Vous verrez la mer flamboyer
Comme un tison qui flambe.

Les étoiles qui sont au ciel
Vous les verrez descendre
Vous verrez la lune et le soleil
Qui combattront ensemble.

Over such songs as these, angels might indeed swoon.

And critics rave. Not since those early days at the Concert Parisien had any press so fluted and trilled as did the New York press in the following weeks. "Mystic," Yvette was called; a "great soul, which is manifesting itself to us with irresistible force because it has been through Gehenna!" Those early indecencies for which she had been scored on previous visits were hardly more than legend to younger hearers, and as weeks went by, almost an aura began to surround her name.

Of the New York critics who wrote rapturously of the Guilbert of 1915, none was more adulatory than Clayton Hamilton. To him—and he stated his opinion unequivocally on more than one occasion— Guilbert was one of the greatest artists of the world and indeed of all time. In her work he saw a unique synthesis of all arts through a perfect mastery of rhythm:

> You come away from her performance, swimming in a phosphorescent sea. For two hours you have worshipped in a temple where beauty is truth, truth, beauty; and now you know that nothing else on earth is worth the knowing. You have been seeking, all your life, for Art; and at last you have met it face to face. . . .
>
> There is no word in English for that medium of Art of which Yvette Guilbert is the supreme and perfect master. It is not acting, it is not singing, it is not recitation; yet it combines the finest beauties of all three. It offers simultaneously an interpretation of literature and an interpretation of music; and it continually reminds you of what is loveliest in painting, in sculpture, and in dancing. . . .
>
> . . . All the arts are merely so many different languages to give expression to the same essential entity; and this essential entity— which constitutes the soul of art—is rhythm. . . . By her bodily movements, her gestures, her facial expression, she makes patterns in space to charm the eye; and by her enunciation of words and music, she makes patterns in time, to charm the ear. . . .
>
> But Yvette Guilbert is not only a great artist, she is also a great woman; . . . She is a great woman because—in Whitman's phrase —she "contains multitudes."

Mr. Hamilton's known ardency as a Francophile need not wholly cancel professional acumen in this critique, for the topic of "rhythm" was marked also by the *Musical Courier*:

> Several of her songs were "*sans musique*" and her unsurpassable delivery of them a mere triumph of rhythms: a rhythm of meters, a rhythm of the pitched voice, a rhythm of gestures . . . a rhythm of facial expressions and last, though by no means least, a rhythm of

costumes. . . . Even in the songs with music . . . Always and ever the rhythmic element predominated.

The emphasis on the unique ability to suggest a synthesis of the arts echoed what José Granier had only recently declared on the other side of the Atlantic. It was no news that as a singer Yvette had always possessed the voice that was no voice musically; actually more a speaking than a singing medium; that as an actress she was always miming without playscript. Now, in her ripened work, M. Granier too had seen techniques of the dance and the visual arts:

Madame Yvette Guilbert is more than an actress, more than a singer . . . no nation has, nor will have, another Yvette Guilbert, for the simple reason that the art of Yvette Guilbert is her own creation. And that is her foremost title to genius. Greek Dance, at the time of Pericles, would have crowned her Queen of Greece, this astonishing Yvette Guilbert, in whose rhythmic movements, instinct with the science of harmony, sculptors and painters find eternal inspiration. The Greek tragedies were "danced." In the classical sense of antiquity, Yvette Guilbert is the greatest dancer in the world. . . .
She inherits the grace of the "Primitive" painters, she sings as Van Eyck and Memling painted, with the careful and experienced preoccupation for drawing and construction that every great work and every great artist must possess. . . .

The new repertoire was by no means entirely religious. Most of the old *chansons* were earthy enough. There were songs of every class: the gentry, the commoners, the king's soldiers, the vinegrowers and scissors-grinders. Yvette repeated two old song cycles which she had presented the season before at the Salle Gaveau in Paris. One, centered on Jeanne d'Arc, had been gleaned from manuscripts written during the lifetime of the Maid and shortly thereafter and later gathered up and presented to Charles VII by a chevalier of France. The other she called "Songs of David," translations from the Hebrew made in 1646 by Antoine Godeau, Bishop of Grasse, with music by Auxcousteaux, *cappelmeister* to Louis XIII. Still another program was the series *La Femme dans la chanson,* also already given in Paris, which ended always with the old favorite, Laforgue's enigmatic Woman herself, "ultra-modern, ultra-realistic, tragic, and allegorical."
Of the Moyen Age group there were also teacup-fragile little pieces

like *Les Conditions impossibles* and *Le petit Bois d'amour; Le Lien serré,* a cynical warning to women too eager for marriage; advice to parents in *La Defense inutile. Ma Cousinette,* belonging to a type known in French literature as *Chansons à danser,* tells merely of a girl who goes to the garden to pick flowers for her lover; Yvette chose to pick the flowers with a low bending of the body from the waist, slow-dancing a series of seductive poses. There was broad humor in *Une Dame mariée à un puant,* the droll tale of a woman whose husband is as offensive to her spirit as to her nostrils, and *Pourquoi me bat mon Mari?,* the plaint of a simple wife who, though she has *un ami,* wonders why her husband beats her. At the other extreme was brutal tragedy in *Les Anneaux de Marianson,* the ballad of a wife falsely accused by a rejected suitor. The lord, believing the charges against his lady, goes berserk with rage and drags both wife and child to death at the heels of a galloping horse. The dying wife forgives him her own death, but not that of their child.

Though Yvette had begged of her impresario, Miss Bamman, "the charity of silence" regarding the war, it was not in the Guilbertian nature to contribute to the silence. Among all the Allied propagandists who came and went in the United States in those days, Yvette, who had taken her place from the first on a permanent basis, by poetic license always referred to herself as an "ambassador" of good will from the French people; as interpreter of the French *chanson,* she wished to be considered an authentic representative of French life and culture. Yet if the quasi-ambassadorial status she implied was questionable, her patriotism was not, and her French-accented, glowing English served ideally at financial or recruiting rallies. Before each of her own performances, too, she lectured on France's need of United States help in men as well as money. As flaming pacifist, Yvette was often heard to inveigh against wicked old men in seats of power who were responsible for the wanton waste of young lives in war. But consistency never having been a hobgoblin of her mind, she apparently saw no reason why, as French patriot, she should not in the next breath turn recruiter and urge more young Americans into the French armed services. After listening to her dramatic pleas, even mothers usually felt it their duty not to discourage their sons from volunteering, so that eventually, by virtue of her constant, spirit-stirring appeals, in the eyes of American audiences Madame Guilbert did come to stand, even without diplomatic brevet, in a general, vague sense for France.

It is pleasant to remember Yvette during this period, when she is again for a time the public idol, praised on all sides as a great mystic-genius-artist-patriot. Seldom, however, has idol been so determined to parade its feet of clay. Unfortunately the journalist-captious critic-reformer in Yvette could not long be silent, and in certain of the articles and interviews that soon appeared with predictable regularity under her name the American public came to glimpse its deity in aspects less than imposing. What Clyde Fitch once called her "faculty for *réclame*" probably accounts for some of the trashy effusions— "Love of Home-making Brings New Civilization," "It's Wicked to Let Your Gowns Outshine Yourself," "What My Art Means to Me," and so on. On matters of love, too, saccharine nothings were dispensed:

The young girl is a bud—charming, yes, but hard and without much perfume. . . . The man who loves the woman of forty finds the perfect companion, the mother heart, the sister soul.

"But do women always want to keep love?" a sulphitic lady reporter once surprisingly countered. "Do you really believe in our ghastly fidelity? Isn't it one of our unnatural vices—one of the traits man has imposed upon us? Do you think the natural woman is any more constant than the natural man?"

Not much more [Yvette admitted], but where can you find me a natural woman? The love of woman is supernatural. Man feels nothing like it. A woman will cling to a man who crucifies her— worse yet to a man who bores her . . . did you ever know of a man who kept vigil beside his dead love . . . ?

Yet though many utterances were trivial or publicity-tainted, a few were of a more thoughtful nature. In relation to popular American music, Yvette joined moralists in charging that lack of ideals in art would inevitably be reflected in lack of ideals in other phases of national life:

Ragtime is degrading you. It is profaning your ideas of love; it is filling your divorce courts; it is making your young women vulgar and your young men purposeless. . . .

The danger in ragtime is evident to . . . all those who consider music's intense power over the emotions and passions. . . . The rhythm of the music itself, irrespective of the lewd words which so often accompany it, is barbaric and yet without the vigor of purely savage music. . . . Your cabarets owe their moral destructiveness more to the music that is played by their orchestras than to the liquor which is consumed at their tables, for the orchestral performers know for what they are hired and they do their duty as they see it. They emphasize the blood-firing strains in their selections. They set the wailing violins and throaty saxophones to chafing emotions that need soothing and to whetting appetites that should be dulled. The syncopated time which marks the dance music has nothing of the languor which saved the waltz from utter sensuality. It is a rapid, ceaseless throbbing of exciting measures and it mounts higher and higher . . . and faster and faster . . . until it comes to an end with a shrieking, exhilarating climax.

If I had a son who danced in your cabaret halls every afternoon I would shut him up in a monastery. . . .

Speaking on the American theater, she criticized the prevailing emphasis on merely commercial values, accusing the great monopolies of stifling individuality in favor of "attractions" and "shows." She deplored the passing of the stock company, that invaluable training ground for actors. If the stock system could have survived Augustin Daly and Albert M. Palmer, the American stage, she believed, might have become the leading stage of the world; but these great managers left no tradition. Charles Frohman she blamed for wholesale importation of foreign plays to the point where a national drama had been stifled from coming into being. Belasco she called the American Sardou, commending especially his *Girl of the Golden West*. She looked into the future when she called for acting in the round, physically three- instead of two-dimensional, on a stage surrounded by audience.

But it was in her roles as feminist and suffragette that Yvette was most the extremist. Even in her repertoire, echoes of feminism were plentiful in the innumerable characterizations of wronged women, especially McLeod's *La Prière des femmes,* a "poignant appeal of all womanhood for Woman (victim and culprit at once, by some strange fatality in the eternal conflict of sex.)" In the press again and again she openly indicted man for his fiendishness in creating the horrors of war. In an impassioned "battlecry for women," the daughter of Hippolyte Guilbert melodramatically charged the whole race of men with fouling and dishonoring human existence:

O the rottenness of the customs with which ye have covered the earth! O your manifold of wickedness, your low cunning and your vices. . . . On your knees, O ye women, to ask of God for strength for the labor that is nigh. For men have sowed death, ye women must sow life. . . . For men have made of earth a wilderness, ye women must cause it to bloom again. . . .

In article after article the theme of war-as-murder was repeated; women, suffering victims of men's evil hearts, were the true heroines of the present conflict. Mothers of the future would have to take full responsibility for the keeping of world peace; it was they only who could teach sons from infancy to love their neighbor as themselves.

As a suffragette, she was openly militant. In 1914, in an article in the British press, she had reproved English suffragettes for acts of violence. Now, in 1916, as speaker before the Congressional Union for Woman Suffrage, she revealed a striking change in attitude. "Be brutal!" she urged the sisterhood seeking women's political emancipation. "You have never accomplished anything by your sweetness and smiles. Your Statue of Liberty is a joke."

Woman must have suffrage to save civilization from Man, always the destroyer; even to save Woman herself from her fatally weak inclination to love:

Man cannot be helped—by woman less than any one! No one can help man—neither God, nor science, nor art, nor family, nor love, nor even life nor death. Nothing will prevent man from being what he is, what he ever has been—the eternal fighter, the eternal killer and destroyer!

All that we women build up man will demolish. . . . We will make children and they will make cannon. In truth, I tell you, the time has come to reflect. . . .

But alas! Woman can never be independent. . . . No matter what . . . [a man may] be—drunkard, gambler, thief; whether he be indelicate, a liar, a hypocrite, or cruel or evil or sick, unclean, malodorous—there will always, always be found one woman, nay ten women, who will lavish upon him their smiles, their kisses, all their gifts. . . .

Let us aid the woman of to-day that she may not die of hunger, but, above all, let us aid her that she may not live by love! Herein lies her rescue.

In the light of such persistent and immoderate denigration of man, individually and collectively, an anomaly seems to exist in Yvette's obviously happy relationship with her husband. The mutual devotion between herself and Max apparently had never lessened by one jot from the day the two first met. The Schiller-Guilbert marriage was everywhere looked upon as ideal.

Max's contribution to this marriage has been carefully described by his niece, the psychiatrist Dr. Eva Rosenfeld, as a vocation for service:

> I remember the death of my grandfather [Schiller] in the suburb of Steglitz near Berlin, where the families of Schiller and Rosenfeld had congregated. . . . The evening after my grandfather's death, . . . I was sent across the road to his apartment, to sit with my grandmother and look after her. I remember her taking my hands and saying: "Listen, my child, tonight will be the first night in more than 60 years that your grandfather will not kneel in front of me and untie my bootlaces."

How could the picture of a fond man kneeling before a woman, which from his earliest years the sensitive, sentimental Max must have witnessed times without number, have failed to leave its stamp on his child mind? But Max in his own marriage went further than to untie the boots of his beloved. Though he had already demonstrated himself a competent biochemist, on the day he married Yvette Guilbert his career as scientist knelt to hers as artist.

> He became Yvette's most devoted servant, [writes Dr. Rosenfeld] . . . and the moments were rare indeed in which he regretted having thrown away his own career and his chances to be someone himself. Yvette not only understood this from the beginning, it was really she who insisted on marriage at a time when he would have never thought of it. He traveled with her, he took her to every concert and waited for her behind the scenes, he was her manager, her secretary;

she never as much as carried a purse from the time he came into her life. In later years he dyed her hair, he chose her dresses, carried her music, he fought with every concert agent in the world for her rights, and of course he did the housekeeping, the engaging and dismissing of staff.

Yvette, whose instincts in respect to her own career were remarkably sure, must have known how increasingly demanding would be her personal needs, and she must have recognized from the beginning the potentialities for self-renunciation in this man. It was really she who insisted on marriage, says Dr. Rosenfeld. But of course. With Max, marriage, bourgeois as it might be, had to be insisted on; Max was popular with women. Free love, beginning then to be much talked about, might be well enough in the ideology of modernism, but where Max was concerned, Yvette's Norman caution would dictate taking sanctuary in legalism. This man represented invaluable and unfailing supply; in his devotion would be found the emotional shelter she had never known; on his clever abilities she could lean like a child for fulfilment of every practical necessity. His reward would be an extension of the passionate adoration she had always professed for her mother and an exemption from the hostility toward her father.

On Max's part, the danger of course would be extinction. There is a certain type of cannibal-artist that feeds, albeit frequently with all tenderness, on human flesh. Sometimes, in the same person, the cannibal-artist is also an artist-cannibal to such a degree that the human victim, after he has loved and embraced, accepts his fate of being devoured as unprotestingly as his insect counterpart, the mate of the female praying mantis. Besides career, Max's name too would be largely lost sight of—a lot not uncommon for men who marry celebrities. Except to a few intimates Yvette would be eternally Guilbert. By a strange compulsion, after her death he would even take on her great name: sign himself "Maxyvette."

Yet even with name and career absorbed and self-effacement a rule of life, it is cheering to reflect that with regard to women Max retained his identity, even carrying himself in that respect with a certain intact self-confidence. Not that he flirted; he merely remained attractive to women, and knew it. He was never jealous of men who admired Yvette, says Dr. Rosenfeld, though flickers of hatred were sometimes seen in Yvette's expressive eyes when women paid too much attention to Max.

269

The characteristic image of Max most vivid in the minds of all who knew him is probably the one described by Eva Rosenfeld as she recalls her uncle in those brief half-hours when he would sometimes break away to visit his family:

> I used to note that for at least forty years he lived with his watch in his hand—Yvette is waiting, Yvette needed him.

Indeed Yvette intensely needed him, even if not in the role of mate. Though she might never have gone to the length of subscribing to the ideal of parthenogenesis, yet any emotional dependence on the male principle as a fertilizing influence either in her art or in her life seems to have been as negative as if she had. Her genius would continue to self-fertilize. Again to quote Dr. Rosenfeld:

> In him she loved and possessed "the eternal maternal principle" (*das ewig Weibliche,* Goethe calls it in Faust) which fails one if it is not perfect.

Very fortunately for Yvette, in Max the maternal principle *was* perfect.

Chapter 8

Just before the outbreak of the war, in a gathering of "royalty, diplomats, artists, intellectuals" who had been invited to a Berlin greenroom to meet Madame Guilbert after one of her matinees, there had been present a young Brooklyn girl, starry-eyed with a sense of drama—Emily Gresser, a student of violin. She had been brought to the reception by her American teacher Sam Franko, a friend of Dr. Schiller's. That day, she says, ". . . Mr. Franko tried to introduce me. The crowd in the artists' room was suffocating, but I managed to look at her and she smiled at me as if she were a Queen." For an impressionable young girl, the smile was enough. Yvette had the power to capture hearts with that smile, and words became unncessary.

After her return to the States from Germany, Emily received one day in January, 1916, a most unexpected call from Mr. Franko. Dr. Max Schiller, now in New York, was looking for a violinist to go on a long American tour with Madame Guilbert. Would Emily care to try out? She was an excellent musician, this favorite pupil of Mr. Franko's, and at the audition Max was sufficiently impressed by her warm tone and temperament and her excellent schooling to take her to the Knickerbocker to appear before Yvette, who was equally pleased. "They asked me to be Yvette Guilbert's assisting artist," writes Emily Gresser, "and so four years of concertizing in the United States started for me."

That season of 1915–16 twenty concerts were given in New York alone, most of them at the Lyceum or the small, intimate Maxine Elliott Theater. Between January and May the company took to the road: Detroit, under the Alliance Française and the entwined flags of France, Belgium, and the United States, where Yvette could not fail; Washington, where she was fondly received; Boston, where she was by now a darling of Back Bay and basked in the favor of the Olympian H. T. P. of the *Transcript;* Quebec, where Canadian-French audiences rose and cheered; to name only a few of the bookings. There was little open time.

Among the New York concerts of that season was Yvette's first appearance at the Neighborhood Playhouse, at Grand and Pitt streets, a so-called "little theater." As early as 1912 the little-theater movement had begun to make itself felt on the hither side of the Atlantic; an outer ripple of those widening cricles that for several decades had been reaching out from the avant-garde dramatic centers of Europe. Soon all over the United States groups of insurgent and imaginative amateurs were springing up, and by the time of Yvette's arrival in 1915 several such experimental companies were in existence in New York, devoted to productions with which the commercial theater did not care to concern itself. Of these, the Neighborhood Playhouse was a little theater with a large difference, first because it flourished in the heart of an East Side slum and, second, because, far from operating on the proverbial shoestring, it was liberally subsidized.

Moreover, Neighborhood productions had been singled out for praise by critics Joseph Wood Krutch and Clayton Hamilton. The latter considered that, except for the Washington Square Players—a company that later developed into the Theater Guild—this center "provided by far the finest theatre that New York has known since the death of Augustin Daly in 1899." The success of the enterprise was all the more remarkable because the two dedicated and genteel sisters who tripled as donors, sponsors, and directors were generally thought of more as philanthropists than as working members of the theatrical profession. Alice and Irene Lewisohn were daughters of a wealthy family already famed for public generosity, and the playhouse which they had recently built and presented to the Henry Street Settlement had originally been intended as a focal point of cultural activities for newly arrived immigrants. Naturally, as Mr. Hamilton said, no dramatic critic expected anything of it on a professional level:

But we soon discovered that our pessimism was mistaken. The theatre itself was a little gem of architecture. Its lighting equipment was at that time, the most modern that had been installed in any playhouse in the country. The scenery and costumes, designed and executed by the workers of the Henry Street Settlement, gave evidences of the joyous labor and loving care of a group of people who were working not for money but for art; and the subtle lighting of the stage sets was almost miraculously revolutionary. . . .
Great actresses and actors frequently appeared at the Neighborhood Playhouse for the sheer joy of working in a theatre that was permeated with an atmosphere of ideality. . . .
But the superlative achievement of this institution rested in its choice of plays. . . The Misses Lewisohn ransacked the ages, spoiled the climes. . . . They were never bothered by any inhibitions originating from the jitters of the box office. . . .

Almost at once Yvette and these exceptional women became fast friends, and during her stay in New York she made repeated appearances on their stage.

By the end of the 1915–16 season, Emily Gresser had become a favorite of the Schillers, and that summer they took her with them to a retreat they had discovered in the resort town of Interlaken, New Jersey—a simple little cottage not far from the ocean but apart from the crowded beaches and the expensive hotels. The summer was supposed to be a vacation, but, as the young girl discovered, vacations actually offer little rest in the routine of a serious artist. Yvette wasted neither time nor thought on housekeeping, such details being left as usual to Max and the cook. Instead she worked constantly. Research never ceased; more songs must be examined; new song material must be prepared; manuscripts written. The Schillers and Emily liked Interlaken well enough to return there in following seasons, and it was in that obscure spot, surprisingly, that Yvette's path again crossed Bernhardt's.

Fulfilling her promise that despite her disability she would continue to be seen in all her old roles, Bernhardt arrived in New York in the fall of 1916 for a tour of the United States. She had brought with her however, only a small repertory company and had accepted bookings indiscriminately, even in improbable and graceless places. Since she returned to France early in 1918, it must have been during the summer of 1917 that chance led her to Interlaken, where Yvette saw her, and wept over what she witnessed:

She had already had her leg amputated, and was giving a performance of *La Dame aux Camélias* in the summer at a seaside place where I had a little cottage. My heart quaked. A cinema-hall, an audience of nursemaids, a wretched orchestra between the acts; she played without conviction, seeming to improvise her words and surrounded by a very modest cast. On the curtain which she took with her on her tours was displayed her terrible yet magnificent motto: *Quand même.*

There was to be one more meeting in America between Yvette and the death-doomed Sarah. A few months later, when the poor woman lay ill in the Mount Sinai Hospital in New York, Yvette visited her:

I found her terribly made up and powdered, her eyes thick with black, her lips scarlet, her red hair crimped and fluffed up—a lion in bed! She terrified me. Heavens! think of not being oneself in the midst of fever and agony, and to be ever wearing a mask and stage-trappings, to deceive—whom? . . . At one moment she took my hand, held it in hers on the eiderdown, and said: "You are really kind, Yvette . . . I thank you for having come. . . ." I had to go, for . . . I felt that I was going to cry; it wrung my heart to see her. I should have liked to wash the paint from her poor face and give it its last beauty. I kissed her and left her.

The enticing idea of someday founding a school of her own began about this time to show signs of resurgence in Yvette's mind. Almost as soon as she arrived in New York, Yvette had concerned herself with the talents of a few selected private pupils. But these were not enough to satisfy her. As with Duncan, the dream of lengthening her shadow

273

into an institution became obsessive; particularly so, no doubt, because of what must have seemed the favorable circumstances prevailing in New York at that time.

The increasing number of little theaters and the rise of interest in drama generally in the United States had been accompanied in several of the larger cities by a rash of new studio schools of acting and theater techniques, and Yvette was probably correct in assuming that a genuine demand existed, which she was qualified to supply, for practical instruction in singing and acting.

But she went further in her assumptions: namely, that beyond the recognized need for this instruction lay the basic American need for Culture, which she could also supply. Americans were Uncouth.

This charge was, alas, no news to Americans. From the days of Henry James down, visitors from foreign shores had seemed to feel privileged to speak their minds freely; to criticize their hosts for every sin in the calendar, from nasal twang to faulty table manners. As a result, by 1916 it might almost be said that something approaching a national inferiority complex had been created in many a native breast; that with the possible exception of a few stiff-necked individualists the average man had been browbeaten to the point of conceding that culturally there was no health in him. An America that was then both drama-hungry and deficiency-conscious Yvette might well have reasoned would respond gratefully to the kind of school she had in mind.

With all the naïveté and nebulosity of the amateur educator, she poured her plan into the ear of the press one day in the spring of 1916:

My object is the creation of what will be at once a center of instruction and what I might define as a *salon* for the exercise of various forms of high artistic activity. That is to say that while the day will be devoted to teaching the evenings will find the school transformed into a club, so to speak, a gathering place for literary, musical, dramatic and artistic personalities of the highest rank for the interchange of aesthetic ideas and for the practice of artistic pursuits in an atmosphere ideally congenial. It is my aim to produce at these soirées something like the famous French *salons* of the eighteenth century, but of a fundamentally democratic nature. There shall be every incentive toward brilliancy of conversation— and Americans have much need to acquire this faculty—and occasion to perform unfamiliar music, such as the old French songs of

274

Jeanne d'Arc's time, artistic dances and plays. Think of the great cultural possibilities latent in this periodic association with brilliant minds! In the classes proper I shall teach a variety of matters—French diction (which, heaven knows, is not one of the strong points in Americans!) conversation, literature. I shall seek to inculcate abstract qualities of beauty—beauty of thought, grace of expression, distinction of manner. I find that Americans, for all their innate brightness, are not taught how to think, how to study.

Almost as if to foster the new ambition, shortly there came from Bryn Mawr College a request to appear in May of that year before the student body as lecturer-singer on the French *chanson*. Yvette of the black gloves would hardly have been bidden to the groves of Academe; such an invitation, therefore, seemed the well-earned mortarboard of scholastic recognition for fifteen years of unremitting labor in a highly specialized field. It lent her name a new luster, that of erudition, which she had long craved.

Out of the invitation developed a new and valuable personal association. As soon as the lecture was announced in the press, Yvette received a letter from Jean Baptiste Beck, of the Bryn Mawr faculty, expressing delight at the opportunity the writer would soon have to make her acquaintance. The delight was mutual, for Professor Beck was one of France's most distinguished authorities on the history of music; Yvette had already studied his scholarly *La Musique des Troubadours*.

"Now at last I do those things I have so long planned for. I have my classes in New York, and my lectures, and my songs—and my dear pupils!" It was the fall of 1916, one year after escape from her calumniators in Paris, one year of sweet acclaim, and Yvette was again in full stride. Except for occasional bouts with rheumatism, her health was apparently much improved, and the stamp of suffering that some reporters had noted on her face when she arrived seems to have faded. To an interviewer that fall she now presented her old vital self:

Crackling with personality, electric with ideas and opinions. Courteous and responsive, busy and business-like. Cordial and capable. Brisk and humorous. Sincere, unaffected, frank. Utterly without pose. Sensible. Charming. Could one ask more of a woman?

The acquaintance with Dr. Beck had ripened during the summer, and some of the lectures of which Yvette spoke were including him as *conférencier*. In Beck she had recognized another ideal Hugues Le Roux, and the autumn found the two appearing together at the Maxine Elliott Theater.

The overpowering urge to teach also prompted Yvette to experiment here and there with lectures of her own on the arts of the diseuse and the singer, luring audiences to play the role of students. Seated at a table with manuscript and reading lamp, she would read from notes, interrupting herself occasionally to improvise; now and then rising to demonstrate her precepts. In the intimate atmosphere she created, audiences happily placed themselves *in statu pupillaris* and settled back comfortably in their seats to enjoy the graphic quality of her commentary and the animation of her whole enkindled being. Carl Van Vechten thought she had never been more incandescent or more authoritative than during these lectures, even though it must have been obvious that, with all her candor, every word she spoke only underscored the impossibility, try as she might, of explaining her genius:

> She told how she studied the words of her songs, how she planned them, what a large part the plasticity of her body played in their interpretation, and when she was done all she had said only went to prove that there is but one Yvette Guilbert.

At about this time Yvette must have had already in mind turning her lectures into a book. *How to Sing a Song,* in fact, was published in English by Macmillan in New York in 1918, and, like the lectures, also purported to reveal a diseuse's every technique. But if the text too failed to communicate uniqueness, to create other Guilberts, it should be no real matter of wonder.

It is a kind of Alice-in-Wonderland manual, in which the first rule laid down seems to be that there are no rules to be laid down; that the way to learn is to ignore the teachers, especially of opera. Yvette once described her own art as that of the "comedian at the service of a singer without a singing voice, who demands an orchestra or a piano to do her singing for her," but this little book indicates no barrenness of musicianship. The technical devices she considers most important for a diseuse-chanteuse are the knack of coloring phrases, perfect breath control, and, most important, the ability to substitute for mere musical rhythm the rhythm of speech, not however, forsaking it so completely that the singer cannot slip back into musical form when the moment demands. Also important are facial expression, tempo, plastic, selection of texts, observation of life, and—charm. The way to the latter lies through Soul. Art is Love. "Know your fellow-creature as you know yourself and you will be an artist," she advised the tyro; "love . . . as yourself and you will be a genius; worship God and his creation, sing its praise and you will be immortal!" Yet with all its inaccessible truths, its *obiter dicta* that could not possibly apply generally, the book was praised for its sincerity, passion for perfection, and instinct for beauty.

For other lectures she turned to individual poets. In one she described the life of François Villon, analyzed his poetry, sang his songs. In another she included an analysis of the works of several members of the Pléiade group of Renaissance poets, with illustrations from Belleau, Baif, Ronsard. In still another she discussed a contemporary. The aging Parisian *poète-chansonnier* Jehan-Rictus had always fascinated her by his subject matter—the sufferings of the poor. In reading him, Yvette said, she never failed to experience the same shiver as in reading Villon. Molière, though he demanded admiration for his style, failed to move her. But with Villon or Rictus, forgetting diction, she was conscious only of the poet's beating heart; François Villon and Jehan-Rictus bled! In New York one day she had reduced some of her moneyed but tender-hearted students to tears by reading to them Rictus' *Les Soliloques du pauvre.*

Yearly also the country-wide tours continued. In 1917 the itinerary carried her far: Toronto, Ottawa, Windsor; Chicago, Toledo, Cleveland, Milwaukee, Grand Rapids, St. Louis, Denver, Colorado Springs; even to Los Angeles, Santa Barbara, San Francisco. But she was not always a drawing card. There were plenty of disappointments. In the Middle West audiences were often distressingly small, and the farther west the company moved, the smaller in general the audiences became. Then it would be back East again, to Boston, Providence, Plattsburgh, Newark.

In 1918 the Western tour touched such principal cities as Louisville, Indianapolis, Milwaukee, Omaha, Chicago, St. Louis, Grand Rapids, Salt Lake City, San José, Sacramento, Los Angeles. In 1919, still another tour, again as far-flung as San Francisco, Fresno, and Los Angeles. In San Francisco, where the company remained this time for five weeks, Yvette conducted a formal series of courses in voice, drama, and pantomime.

By now the famed Madame Guilbert had become, even without benefit of school catalogue, almost an institution in American cultural life. Unfortunately, however, that first fine careless rapture with which the thrushes of the press had greeted her return in 1915 had tended with the passing of time to tone down as familiarity bred its inevitable contempt and the marvel of her genius became somewhat taken for granted. Too, the type of audience became slightly more fixed, limited in general to a faithful coterie of earnest intellectuals, mostly women, a few French folk, a seasoning of curious youth. A minority critical opinion speculated occasionally, like Burns Mantle, on whether the *chanson per se* was worthy of a Guilbert's gifts, and popularly the consensus came to be that Yvette was a connoisseur's item; a phenomenon rather above the head of the man in the street.

To Emily Gresser, the only young girl in the sober, dedicated little troupe that made the long cross-country tours, the routine of travel with a celebrity was a challenging experience. Every day there was for her the invariable violin practice; midday hotel dinner with the Schillers; sometimes a sedate afternoon drive of sight-seeing with them; then rest, a light supper, the concert, and always afterward in the Schillers' suite a refreshing spread of cold cuts, bread and butter, and hot milk. Yvette as usual spent her every spare moment in reading and studying, reviewing her current program and planning others, never wasting ten minutes whether in train or hotel. She suffered from the fear of forgetting her words. "Before concerts, in her dressing room, she would repeat and repeat the words of her songs (although she must have sung the songs hundreds, if not thousands, of times)." And constantly she fought the rheumatic pain that often crumpled her in the wings, but never on stage. Every performance left her exhausted.

As manager, Max too would be occupied every moment: transportation, hotel accommodations, public relations, correspondence, lighting, programs, platform arrangements. Especially he and Yvette's maid must see that the star's dressing room was immaculate. The Schillers had a phobia for cleanliness; registering only in the best hotels, wiping forks in restaurants, never shaking hands with strangers ungloved. And though Max shied away from social groups after performances, scrupulously avoiding ever stepping into his wife's limelight, he was omnipresent as protector, appearing when necessary, as he was fond of saying, to play the part of Cerberus, pretending that Madame Guilbert must catch a train if he saw that she was becoming bored or overfatigued. No one could reach her by telephone except by his permission; he was censor of all mail.

Emily Gresser never lost her unbounded admiration for Guilbert during these tours, though she was conscious, even at close range, of a fundamental aloofness; ". . . her warmth was genuine but cerebral, expressed more in her art than in personal relations." Sometimes, when things went wrong and defenses were down, the girl witnessed moments of unredeemed bitterness and gloom.

Following the appearance on the Bryn Mawr campus came other academic invitations, from Columbia and Smith. In October, 1917, the series of Columbia Arts and Science concerts included "The Great Songs of France Reconstructed by Madame Yvette Guilbert from the Literary Monuments of the Poets: Trouvères, Jongleurs and Clerks." In this program were two groups which Yvette called *Chansons courtoises* and *Chansons à toiles,* dating for the most part from the twelfth and thirteenth centuries, the latter presented as supposedly chanted by noblewomen while spinning or doing needlework to lighten the heavy hours of their husbands' absence at the wars.

At Smith, donning costume of corduroy trousers and felt cap, Yvette dramatized ballads of brigands and outlaws—sensational tales of the Middle Ages. There were also stirring soldier songs: songs from the fifteenth century; from the armies of Charles le Téméraire; seventeenth-century marching songs, once roared out by the troops of Maurice de Sax; songs popular with the armies of Louis XVI, among them the famous *Malbrough s'en va-t'en guerre.* The sophisticated audience at Smith also found delightful Verlaine's *L'Heure exquise,* Francis Jammes' *La jeune Fille,* and Baudelaire's *La Causerie.* Comparatively little attention had thus far been given in the States to Baudelaire, and Yvette's passionate admiration of this poet unquestionably stimulated respect for his work.

In New York, other program novelties followed. When Jacques Copeau invited Yvette to give a group of recitals at the Garrick, where he and his troupe from Le Théâtre Vieux Colombier were playing, she included in the series her Pierrot creations.

Yvette was a unique Pierrot. More than two hundred years had elapsed since this stock character had come to France from Italy. Beginning in Italian farce as a comic embodiment of such childish vices as greediness or fibbing, who lived in constant fear of a cuff or a boot-thrust, he had passed through many modifications. Yvette introduced one more, a radical one. Her Pierrot was no grimacing mountebank; with her, he became a thinker, an idealist; dreaming of universal love and spiritual regeneration. To Emily Gresser, Yvette's Pierrot seemed a Christ, symbol of pity as well as of aspiration, with outstretched arms.

In January and February of 1919 Yvette made her first and only appearance as actress on the English-speaking stage. The play was *Guibour,* a medieval French miracle in translation. Though under the handicap of speaking in a foreign language and thus far from being in her top form, she nevertheless turned in a satisfactory performance, playing against superb mountings by Robert Edmond Jones and well supported by Rollo Peters. Incidental choruses and chants had been selected of course from her immense medieval collection.

The play, typical of its genre, is an artless story. A devout woman murders her beloved son-in-law to prove that the malicious village gossip that links her name with his is unfounded—a motive that even for the fourteenth century seems a little far-fetched—and for the crime is condemned to be burned at the stake. But the pitying and understanding Virgin intervenes. When the crowd watching the execution sees the flames recede, they recognize that a miracle is taking place, and emotions change from hatred to religious fervor.

The production, impeccable as it was in every detail, was clearly not one to capture popular fancy, and *Theatre Arts,* though politely admiring, had to confess that the play held "more of an antiquarian interest than of illusion and enthralment."

Chapter 9

During all these months the beloved school project had been kept vigorously alive in the hope of raising funds. Surely, in the land of easy money, an entrepreneur of culture might logically suppose that an endowment for such an excellent purpose should not be difficult to come by. As far as teaching itself was concerned, Yvette had no need to institutionalize. She had had pupils for some time at the David Mannes Music School on East Seventieth Street, in addition to private pupils of her own. But she was in the grip of an *idée fixe:* she wanted to establish the principle of what she called "interpenetration of the arts" as the *sine qua non* of dramatic education, there being no distinction in her mind between the interpretative and the creative arts, so-called. She would prove that art itself is single in impulse, though multiple in expression.

The interpretive artist of tomorrow will be able easily—and very easily—to be, at the same time not only an actor, but a singer, a dancer, a mime, a painter, a decorator, a musician—in a single word, an artist.

Ars una, to be sure, was not a new idea, and Clayton Hamilton was quick to note that her central theory was "historically sound." Da Vinci, for example had espoused the principle that "a master of one art must be a graduate student of them all."

In an article entitled "The Actress of Tomorrow," originally published in 1906, in the New York *American-Journal,* now reissued in *Theatre,* Yvette laid down her formula of preparation. The well-rounded actress should be fond of travel; have a command of several languages. Before undertaking a professional career, she should devote six years, from the age of eighteen to twenty-four, to a study of liberal arts as well as of acting techniques. She should be at home in history, in order to understand plays which deal with tales of yesterday. Further, the well-rounded actress should make the visual arts her special province, since it is only through these that she will learn how to reduce truth to its simplest expression:

. . . for where is the professor who can teach plastic art with the *maestria* of Michael Angelo? Titian and Rubens are excellent masters in attitudes, poses. . . . There are Phèdres and Medeas to be seen in the faces of several of the martyrs in the pictures of Guido Reni, and I have seen the misery of Marguerite Gauthier in the faces of his women who follow our Lord. . . . What marquises, soubrettes, or ingenues of the seventeenth and eighteenth centuries can be better used as models than those who inspired Watteau, Lancret, Greuse and Fragonard? Those actresses who play "les grandes coquettes" will have Gainsborough to dress them, and to teach them, too, the haughty and disdainful pose which fits their part.

281

There are mouths which an actress must see before she can give expression with genius and with success to terror, grief, joy, prayer and love. There are hands which an actress must see to realize what fingers can and must be able to express. Art has all arts for its servants. . . .

In another context, she testified to the contribution that visual arts had made in her own study:

. . . Taste, plastic art, line, science of colors, styles, schools of art —it is my eyes that taught me these. My visual culture is great, my culture through books has been less, enchained as I was every hour of my life with work that absorbed too much of my energy and exhausted me. The poet Arthur Symons wrote that I was one of the best-read women he had ever known. It is true that I have read much, but still not enough . . . it is easier to see the works of all the museums than to read all the books published. . . . I was a workman in art, a passionate gourmand in art, that is all. My insatiable curiosity . . . was my only teacher. . . .

All my original revelations came to me from myself; later when I came to books, I discovered nothing new, for I had mysteriously understood "the art of the arts" by the simple instinct God had given me.

Now, ten years later, she went even further in her prophecies respecting the actress of tomorrow:

In her the woman will disappear, yielding her throne, a throne which this time will be respected, to the High Priestess of Expression. . . .

Strange as it may seem—was it because of the ascendancy of feminism?— no one seems to have so much as blinked, even in 1916, over the challenging concept of a future stage peopled with priestesses.

The reasons for Yvette's failure to obtain funds for her projected school, for which she campaigned with such messianic fervor, may have stemmed from two sources: one, an unfortunate timing; the other, herself. In 1916 the little theater movement had not yet generally taken root on American campuses, and the study of drama as performance was far from being accepted as a proper segment of formal education. Harvard College was notably cool to Professor George Pierce Baker's dramatic laboratory, the pilot project that later came to be known so far and so favorably as 47 Workshop; and in the same tradition most of the other older institutions confined the study of plays to the printed page. Public performances, if any, were extracurricular, and instruction in the techniques of interpretation was most often relegated to private teachers of "elocution." Most of the highly developed and academically accredited departments of drama, now taken for granted in the American college scene, were then nonexistent. To try, therefore, to find a tycoon willing to divest himself of any of his millions on a project claimed by the fund-raiser to be educational but which educators themselves classified as frivolous would have been from the first to court heartaches.

It may well be, too, that there was something in Yvette's personal attitudes—her instinctive assumption of cultural superiority on the basis of her nationality, together with her lack of restraint in speech —that defeated her ends, even with the most tolerant. Yvette had never practiced diplomacy. Americans were "gasbags"; America was the land of "bluff" and the "dollar" and the worship of success; how many times she had reiterated these charges!

At the same time she defended the foreigner who coveted American dollars:

. . . Americans who travel do see their country as it really is, and they escape from it every year to Europe where the air seems to civilize them and to smooth off their rough corners. . . . But the strange thing is that, once back in their own country, they are bitterly offended when they hear an artist confess that he comes to the United States for the sake of making money. Honestly, for what other reason can you Americans suppose that an artist would come? What inspiration do you think the country can offer him? . . . What delights for his soul could he find in that country? . . . An artist needs spiritual food. What ice-cream do you offer instead!

That the experiences of a fund-raiser are likely to contain more disappointments than donations, to lead to more resistance than assistance, is one of the sterner facts of life, but one for which Yvette seems to have been unprepared. She could not understand why any rich American, man or woman, should not promptly, even gratefully, underwrite the school which had become such a fetish to her, and as she received one rebuff after another, a deep resentment developed within her, which even years later she took pains to record, with acrimony, in her memoirs.

In some of her unpleasant encounters, however, one can but sympathize with her; for example, those occasions when cheeky dinner hostesses would dangle the bait of an opportunity to meet "influential people" to whom she might appeal; of course, she would sing a few songs after dinner? This happened more than once.

Probably her most sizzling scorn was reserved for a gentleman whom she refers to under the flimsiest possible disguise—he who runs may read this identity—Mr. E., Lord of the Dark Rooms, whose home was in Rochester, New York. She had once sung in this gentleman's lordly mansion; Emily Gresser, who accompanied her that night, says that this was the only occasion when she ever saw Yvette in a rage. Emily did not know what had happened; only that Yvette left the house in a fury, storming incoherently about American vulgarity and ignorance.

A year later Yvette met Mr. E. in New York at a friend's dinner party. "I specially noticed the sharp light in his pupils as he looked at me. He knew that I wished to found a school in New York." At table Mr. E. expatiated on a project of his own, a school of music staffed with the best teachers procurable, which he was planning to establish in Rochester and make self-supporting by profits from a movie theatre in the institution. Yvette was "horror struck," presumably at the idea of a school paying its own way.

Later in the drawing room Mr. E. said to her:

"You want me to help you to create a School for the Art of the Theatre?"

"Yes."

"Well, if I were to help you what would you do to ensure that it would be a success, for you know it has to be a success?"

So, looking him in the eye, I replied: "First of all I should open the doors wide and free. You understand, free of charge and for nothing, to all who were really gifted, and yet had not the money for their studies and their artistic careers, and then——" O God! what a laugh he gave as he interrupted me: "For nothing! For nothing!"

"To help make artists, monsieur. A school is not a business house;

284

it is a temple, a holy place. For a country to create art it must be ready to give it."

If this is an example of her approach to prospective donors, perhaps it is not wholly to be wondered at that Yvette met with small success in wooing fortunes into her hands. Perhaps the hardheaded men whom she interviewed wondered whether the Frenchwoman's feet were really squarely on the ground. Perhaps they became a bit confused by all this talk about temples and priestesses and holy places, when what they thought they were discussing was merely the establishment of a school where a talented young man or woman might study acting.

The war dragged on to its bargaining close, and after the Armistice had been signed in November, 1918, and American doughboys began coming home from Over There, there remained no political reason why Yvette should not return to France. But now she did not want to return permanently. She was not prepared to give up her dear Idea in New York. However, an excellent reason did exist for her to go back temporarily: for four years her house on Boulevard Berthier had been standing closed and she wished to find a tenant for it. Plans were accordingly made early in 1919 for a brief business trip.

Just before her departure, an incident occurred which sent her heart rocketing. A wealthy New York furrier, identified only as A.N., unexpectedly declared himself a prospective benefactor ready to provide a house on Fortieth Street in which a school of theater and its workshops could be installed. In the highest of spirits the participants met—Max and Yvette, accompanied by the Lewisohn sisters, and Mr. N. and his wife—to draw up a plan of action. At this conference it was agreed that while Yvette was abroad Mr. N would sign a three-year lease for the house; she would ship from Paris enough of her furnishings to equip it; the school would open under its own roof that fall. Yvette was ready to the kiss the furrier's fat cheeks.

In the few short weeks which the Schillers had allowed themselves in Paris, Yvette accomplished under forced draft the grueling task of packing and shipping fifteen cases full of carpets, curtains, draperies, bedding, linen, silver, pictures, ornaments; in a whirlwind finish and a run of luck found ideal tenants to whom she rented her house; and then, with business all concluded, had nothing to do but wait as patiently as possible for the return sailing date a few days distant and dream of the happiness ahead.

The fifteen cases could hardly have been more than midocean when one morning, just before the Schillers were to embark, a cable arrived from New York. It was signed "A.N." and the message was stiletto-short: "I have changed my mind."

Yvette collapsed.

That fall, nevertheless, the long-heralded school did open, though in miniature, and lacking both buildings and endowment, under the name of "Yvette Guilbert's School of the Theatre." The first brochure lists the Hotel Majestic, where Max and Yvette were living, as the school's headquarters: "Owing to unforeseen difficulties regarding the school building, the classes will be held until further notice in the Red Room (1st floor) . . ." In the brochure Miss Mabel Poillon appears as executive secretary, her name followed by a short roster of faculty, mostly part-time, but all specialists in their respective fields.

Scholastically, the two stalwarts of this group are Professor Jean Beck ("University of Strasbourg, Ancien Élève de l'École des Hautes Études, Paris") and Charles Sears Baldwin, both doctors of philosophy. Dr. Beck is listed as offering, together with Madame Guilbert, a course entitled "The Development of Music from Its Beginnings to the Present Day." Though the impressively detailed description of this course would lead the avid student to expect a most painstaking consideration of centuries of evolution of musical theory and composition, actually the instruction seems to have been offered in a series of twelve Friday evenings; presumably more of those combinations of learned comment by a *conférencier* and illustrations by Madame Guilbert which Yvette had been fond of since the days of La Bodinière. Dr. Baldwin's course, "Medieval English Literature in Its Dramatic Bearings," was handled in five Friday evening lectures.

Six other Friday evenings were devoted to "Lectures on the Modern Drama," by Mr. Clayton Hamilton, who, as critic and author, was another qualified man in his field, and was appearing also about this time as lecturer at Columbia University. On six Thursday evenings was offered a course entitled "Highest Lights of French Literature of the 19th Century," in which Mr. William Van Wyck lectured; to quote the catalogue: "Excerpts and poems in French from these noble works will be read and recited by Madame Guilbert and her pupils. Artists and literary people will be invited to these lectures which will be followed by a reception and informal program; music, singing and dancing. These reunions are planned to create intellectual and artistic relations for the students and to prepare them for their artistic life."

In professional courses the schedule followed more or less the usual order of the day in schools of this kind: "Culture of the Speaking Voice," offered by Miss Dagmar Perkins, who was billed as "Former Special Lecturer at Harvard and Bryn Mawr"; "Eurhythmics," by M. Placido de Monteliu, former assistant to Jacques Dalcroze, Geneva, "Bryn Mawr College and New York University"; courses in crafts of the theater, held in the Neighborhood Playhouse, which included "Designing and Execution of Scenery and Properties," with Mr. Warren Dahler; "Dyeing," with Miss Amy Mohler Hicks; and "History of Costume Designing and Execution." Mr. Edmond Rickett, listed as "Chorus Director," and Miss Rosetta O'Neill assisted Madame Guilbert in "Folk Songs and Period Dancing." Also a course entitled "French Language" was offered by Mademoiselle Alice Blum.

The main body of instruction, and that which, one assumes, must have most whetted the neophyte's appetite, comprised the courses conducted by Yvette herself: "Dramatic Interpretation," "Lyric Interpretation," "Improvisation—Pantomime," and "Plastique." Other features valued by students naturally would have been the opportunities to participate in public programs at the school, act as "super" in Neighborhood Playhouse productions, and even, for those of special proficiency, appear with Yvette herself in her professional engagements. Granted the bill of fare may have been more inspirational than perspirational, all in all it probably looked very tempting to the young aspirant to dramatic fame who could afford the tariff. Tuition was far from cheap—five hundred dollars a year—but it was eased by the proviso that a student who could not afford the full course might enroll for any part thereof. In fact, a few scholarships were offered.

Writing in *Vogue,* Mr. Hamilton lavished endorsement on the project:

If Raphael could return to earth to reopen his academy of painting, if Donatello might resume his interrupted school of sculpture, if Mozart should migrate to our shores to conduct a conservatory of music, or if Keats could come to us with an open offer to teach apprentices the art of poetry, the high occasion would be chronicled as epoch making in the march of history. Yet Yvette Guilbert—

although her life has been devoted to an art that is not, alas, like theirs immortal, an art that flowers to fruition in ecstatic moments than can never be recorded for posterity . . . —deserves a ranking with these giants of the high and far-off days by virtue of her perfect mastery of a finally perfected medium. This verdict is not uttered by the present commentator in an unconsidered moment of enthusiasm. It has been, for twenty years, the verdict of all the leading critics of all the leading nations; and it has been supported by the tributes of nearly all the leading artists that are living in the world. . . .

Furthermore, her appeal as instructor should not be limited merely to the tyro, Mr. Hamilton believed:

Her classes might profitably be attended by every actor and actress who enjoys a current prominence upon our native stage. Though America now leads the world in painting, any of our native painters would leap forth to enjoy the privilege of serving an apprenticeship to Leonardo; and none of our native sculptors would hesitate to go to work, without remuneration, in the busy studio of Michelangelo. . . . Speaking merely for myself, as an apprentice to the craft of setting words together, I wish to God that some great artist in the realm of literature would come to New York and offer a curriculum of personal instruction to any ambitious aspirant to his craft! How eager I should be to go to school again if Tennyson or Stevenson should come to the Hotel Majestic. . . ! And if I were Mrs. Fiske—who is perhaps the greatest artist who recurrently appears upon the American stage of today—I should lose no time in seeking the personal tutelage of Yvette Guilbert in the little matter of enunciation.

From the first a note of high idealism seems to have been struck in the little group at the Hotel Majestic. It should come as no surprise that Yvette, besides teaching, should take upon herself also the mantle of prophet; that one who spoke of a school as a "holy place," who saw the ideal actress of the future as a "priestess," should exhort her followers in passionate, even if slightly confused, vein to some sort of nobility; or that, being Yvette, she should include the work ethic in her credo. A fuzzily fervent composition entitled "Work," inscribed on a plaque, hung constantly before her students' eyes:

Rise, youth of the world, seize the riches of the universe and make them yours. The true riches, forethought, wisdom, honor, truth. Grasp what is noble, what is enduring, the eternal and essential forces that lead to real riches and real success. Take them, make them yours, and then, "up and doing," yes, up and doing, to-day, and with might and main. Trample upon all that is slackfibred and base. Look afar towards the visioned future; see it clearly; see it beautifully. Stand apart from the universal unrest. Place your pride and strength in surpassing your own ideals. You can be rich. Be so, to full and overflowing, rich in heart, in soul, in will of upward fire.

O work, fair and wholesome, work noble and joyous, song of heart and hand and brains, in you is strength, in you salvation, free-dom, purification, pardon, reward.

Barrier against evil, temple, altar, chalice, O great and beautiful spirit of work, take pity upon us, enter into, possess our wayward hearts. Hear our prayer and make us all your own, for you are the strong, imperishable foundation of mankind, you are the true king of the world.

That work can bring scholarly as well as spiritual rewards was a fact thrillingly dramatized one day in December, 1921, when the directress received the following letter from M. Henri Lemaître, secretary of the learned French Société des anciens textes:

Madam,

I have the honor of informing you that at a board meeting yester-day the council of the Société des anciens textes ratified your ad-mission into the society and that your name was then announced to the general assembly in the list of its new members.

We hope, since you have familiarized the Americans with our old French songs, that you will also inspire them to read our na-tional epics and our poetry of the Middle Ages. . . .

Later she received a letter congratulating her on her American achievements from M. Joseph Bédier, probably France's greatest living authority on medieval literature. In Yvette's mind, these were honors to surpass any she had thus far received.

To understand the satisfaction it afforded Yvette to become head of what she considered an educational institution, even though all its classes were conducted in one salon, one must remember her early educational deprivations, the intense hunger for learning her magnificent mind had suffered, the constant awareness she must have felt of the gap in formal schooling between herself and her husband, and the instinctive deference the self-educated always pay to organizational trappings. She yearned for status in the world of scholars and educators, not realizing—how could she?—the exclusiveness of that world or its set patterns. She could not know that in its rigidly caste-ridden system academic Coquelins and Melbas were to be found, and that in the final analysis her highest rating would always derive from quite another field, the one in which she was unsurpassed.

In all New York no one could have better understood Yvette's objectives or been more sympathetic to the cause of theater education than wealthy, philanthropic Alice and Irene Lewisohn, who had become during these past seven years, next perhaps to Duse, Yvette's most cherished friends. Why did these two women not supply the building and endowment that Yvette sought? Yvette never discussed this point except to say:

> Alice and Irene Lewisohn were the first to appreciate the special value of the art that I was bringing to America, and it was they who helped me to found my school at the Majestic Hotel, my school to which I gave all my strength, all my zeal, all my life, and they were for me what they were to so many others—sisters.

Just what form the help took is not clear. That Yvette's students were allowed to make use of the excellent facilities in theater crafts afforded by the Neighborhood Playhouse and to appear there in public productions were privileges of real financial worth. No doubt the Misses Lewisohn also exerted what influence they could socially; gave good practical advice; possibly even primed the pump. Yet the fact that students paid tuition, and a fairly high one, would indicate that self-support was expected.

Early in 1922, however, it became evident that the venture was drawing to a sorry end. The darling enterprise into which Yvette had poured, as she said, "all my strength, all my zeal, all my life," could struggle on no longer merely on tuition receipts. Even the house on Boulevard Berthier had been sold in desperation and the proceeds tossed in, and now, after three consistently losing years, Yvette perforce bowed to the logic of arithmetic. In the face of a dwindling box office for her concert performances, stamped as too recherché for the mob, and an insolvent school treasury, nothing remained but an inglorious retreat. She must try to start anew in her own country, now that peace had been restored; pick up where she had left off.

In the seven years Yvette had spent in the United States her life had been a kaleidoscope of tours and teaching, concerts and classes; she had been praised far more than dispraised; honored in academic circles; surrounded by a coterie of warm friends and loyal student-admirers. Yet as she sailed away from American shores for the last time, a woman nearing sixty, facing an uncertain future, she knew there would be no brass blaring in Paris to signalize this home-coming. Her sense of failure was acute, and all because, as she would always believe, those loutish American millionaires, ignoramuses every one, had spurned what they should have knelt to and the Idea that would have regenerated dramatic art in this century had been still-born.

II

1922–1940

Ah! ... Si je pouvais arracher de mes bras
ces gants noirs qui firent mon succès
mais qui maintenant font
mon désespoir....

—Ah! If only I could tear
off these black gloves
that once made my success
but now are my despair.

Chapter 10

If Yvette had been phenomenally lucky in chancing to return to
America in 1915, at a time when the heroism of the French nation was
lending a shimmer of glory to everything French, she was no less
unlucky in the time she hit upon for her resettlement in France. For
these were the Roaring Twenties, with the jazz age in full swing,
when even Paris had begun to reverberate to the slide trombone and
the song of the Dodsworths was being heard in the land. It was again
an era of giant dislocations, a present at odds with the past, and the

293

demand for change was shrill. To create a new world had become the categorical imperative—and who cared how raw, if only different? Let music lose its old harmonies, art its old meanings; where there is no novelty, the people perish.

Could Yvette have realized, one wonders, the full implications of what she was attempting when, against this background of frenetic futurism, she chose to arrive from New York with her cargo of medievalism? Even before the war, Paris, that had once been her lover, had quarreled with her on this freight; what would it say now?

In a more intimate sense, too, life in Paris had changed. With the Boulevard Berthier house lost, home was now a suite of rooms in a hotel. A very pleasant suite, to be sure, in the quiet, exclusive Hotel Regina, on the Rue de Rivoli, its windows overlooking the Tuileries gardens. But hotel living carried a sense of transiency, and it was only in the murmur of French all around her, as sweet in her ears as the humming of bees around a flower, that Yvette could feel that she had come home.

Of the personal threads she would have liked to pick up, many were broken. In 1920, while she was still in New York, the expected deaths of her aged Aunt and Uncle Broutin had occurred. Her young cousin Marcelle had written her at the time, and the letter Yvette sent in return overflowed with sympathy, generosity, and ripe wisdom:

... Do not forget that you will be lacking in affection if you hesitate in case of necessity to come to us. .... Above all, don't get married stupidly, just to avoid celibacy! ! ! ... That is shame of body and bitterness of soul. .... Have faith in what God has in store for you. Patience in all things. Hurry nothing. Life, stronger than you, works for you. To wait is the supreme wisdom. The age of happiness is not absolutely the age of youth—understand that well. Wait for happiness; it will come in its own time, not in yours. If at thirty you were not married, that would mean only that you were not chosen by unhappiness and that happiness is making you wait in order to better choose the gift that it owes you.

One night, soon after her return, Yvette and her old friend Léon Xanrof, in a nostalgic mood, risked a return, as auditors, to one of the old *caf'-conc's*. What would it be like, they wondered, the version of 1922? Yvette went heavily veiled, fearing the rush of memories would be too much for her and she would "weep like a dog." To her surprise, as she watched the acts, she was conscious of nothing but a vast dreariness of spirit. Ugliness, coarseness, and vulgarity paraded before the footlights. Several times she and her companion exchanged despairing glances. Finally she whispered, "Was it really like this— *then?*"

"No!" Xanrof exploded. "Things were different in our day!"

"In our day!" What a milestone that phrase reared!

In spite of poisoning uncertainties, however, regarding her future, to interviewers who shortly began calling at the Hotel Regina she showed a bold front, speaking with consummate assurance and authority, bluffing where necessary. In her years abroad, she said, as unofficial ambassadress of French culture she had been able to convey to the American people through her songs the true soul of the French nation. Furthermore, her New York school of the theater was known all over the United States.

Now she had larger plans. She wished to found a similar school in Paris, with the same motto, *Tous les arts dans un art.* As to students, she would begin with a nucleus of beautiful and talented American girls brought over from New York. Only the year before on a brief visit she had introduced to Paris a small group of her *belles Américaines,* who had everywhere created the most favorable impressions. They had enjoyed the honor of being entertained at the Élysée by the President of the Republic and his wife, Monsieur and Madame Millerand; Bernhardt had granted them an audience and had been most gracious; and when Yvette, presenting a series of three concerts in Salle Gaveau, had included them as extras on the program, critics had exclaimed over their fresh charm and crisp enunciation.

But the school was only part of her present project. She was about to found also two new theaters. One, "*le théâtre religieux du Moyen Âge,*" would be devoted to the religious drama of the Middle Ages; "exclusively and burningly Catholic." In the other, "*le théâtre de la vieille France,*" austerity would be banned and gaiety abound. The laughter of an olden time would be given back to France.

The scholars Joseph Bédier and Gustave Cohen had already volunteered to help by rediscovering mysteries and miracle plays, old farces and *soties,* chivalric romances, monologues and fables, songs of troubadours and trouvères. She herself would sing and mime ballads spanning the seventeenth, eighteenth, and nineteenth centuries, down to and including songs of *fin de siècle* days. The couplets that the "gallant" priests were wont to sing; Béranger's refrains; the songs on men's lips when Murger's *La Bohème* was a living reality—all these would provide continuity from the Crusades to the heroic times of the Chat Noir.

Nor would the present be neglected:

"I desire also to reserve my stage, several times a week, for modern plays, of a new form. . . . I want to create a theatre liturgical, medieval, lyric, dramatic, pictorial, choreographic . . . and ultramodern. Medieval and utramodern. Exactly. . . . Bruant, Rictus, Verlaine, Laforgue, Donnay, Salis are all descendants of Aristophanes. But I find them too in the poets and writers of the older time. Only there the spoofing is more farcical, cruel, lively. Medieval art is the complement of my audacious 'modernity,' and these poets the nearest to the ones I knew in my youth. . . ."

"What exactly do you mean by the ultramodern theater, Madame?"

". . . I would like to find young writers, expressing their dramatic ideas in absolutely different form . . . more direct, less prepared. The cinema, where interior action and thought are exteriorized and materialized, could influence this new literature."

At this point, a reporter who must have felt some stirring of skepticism over the practical aspects of such extensive undertakings wondered openly whether Madame Guilbert actually believed that she would be able to realize all these several and costly ambitions.

With cool confidence, Yvette assured the inquirer that she believed she would. Only recently, in the magnificent Byzantine hall in the home of the Comtesse de Béhague she had presented an evening of religious drama to an invited group of a hundred and fifty Paris clergy. Cardinal Dubois, Archbishop of Paris, had been deeply impressed. As to the secular type of entertainment, on another evening in the Comtesse's home some three hundred guests had listened approvingly to risqué specimens of the past. She foresaw no lack of patrons.

The idea of a religious theater sponsored by Yvette of the Divan Japonais and the Moulin Rouge elicited, as might be expected, some delighted japes in the press: So our Yvette has returned a veritable Abbess Hroswitha, eh? Well, well—and with a conservatory of wise virgins!—An apostle, *parbleu!*—"Saint" Yvette! *Ohé! Ohé!*

As one cynic summed up the matter: "Yvette may psalmodize us all she wishes, she will always be Yvette. . . ."

Nevertheless, in the Salle Gaveau, the Théâtre Edouard VII, and the Théâtre Albert I, Yvette, as producer, for some weeks thereafter spread before Paris generous samplings of her so-called *théâtre religieux* and *théâtre de la vieille France*. In candor it must be admitted, however, that this unfamiliar and high-sounding packaging turns out on examination to be no more than a new dress for an old friend. One of the programs, for example, is found to consist, in the first part, of two scenes from *Guibour;* in the second part, of Moyen Âge ditties which Yvette had been presenting for some years.

Visually, the *Guibour* scenes were conceded to be heart-stopping. At least three critics felt as if they were seeing illuminations of some precious old missal come to life. Such scenes of hieratic beauty, they agreed, such atmosphere of mysticism, they had never before experienced in the theater, and through these scenes the American students, acting as extras, were near-perfection in diction and grace. Dutifully the press recorded names: Mademoiselles Buyko, Meade, Meyers, Kelley, Maud, Moffat, Mandell, Hessler, Barry, Folwell and Mesdames Churchward and Walker. Pulchritude, too, was noted. When action dulled dramatically, as apparently it frequently did, one jaded reviewer confessed frankly that at such moments he was able to lose himself in contemplation of the pretty faces and poetic attitudes of *les belles Américaines*—whether functioning as golden-robed angels immobilized in a stained-glass window, or dancing peasants, fustian-clad, or allegorical creatures floating in pastel gauzes.

As to the second part of the program, all agreed that Madame Guilbert's power of suggestion was more astonishing than ever. With her, an old song came to life like a forest in April when birds return. A few notes and strophes, and this incomparable woman could evoke a country and an epoch. And as for wit! One should see her as a coquette of the time of Eustache Deschamps in *Dites-moi si je suis belle!*

Yet despite the program's transcendent beauty and perfection, stubbornly some voices were heard to mumble in protest. *Mon Dieu,* what tedium! How sad to see such painstaking effort wasted! Why resurrect childish *chansons* anyway? Even the great medievalist Gaston Paris had admitted that miracle plays have only feeble worth as literature; that being elementary in construction and lacking in artifice, they quickly became monotonous and often almost grotesque. Besides, fretted other voices, it was disconcerting to feel that one was at Mass instead of the theater. Too boring; too severely liturgical—thus ran the negative report, as opposed to that which declared that here was a real spectacle, something all Paris should hasten to see.

Unfortunately for the box office, all of Paris did not hasten.

Among those who came to the star's dressing room, one evening in July of 1922, to kiss and applaud Yvette in her new guise, was Eleonora Duse. The friendship between the two women was as deep as ever. On Yvette's part, according to Emily Gresser, there was always a special tenderness; Yvette yearned over Duse "as a goddess might over a fainting nymph." Only intermittent correspondence had been possible during the war years, and it was not until after the Armistice that Yvette, while still in New York, had learned that Duse was in serious financial straits. Duse too had given months of patriotic services—entertaining in camp shows for Allied troops in Italy, working in canteens—and now her slender strength was exhausted, and her money. Though she had tried to sell her memoirs, she had failed to find a publisher; she was at rope's end.

Promptly Yvette had written: "Why not come to America? If you can pay your journey I will pay your hotel, your life here. I am at the head of a School of the Art of the Theatre. You will always find something to do with me. Come!"

It is intriguing to speculate on what might have been the future of a school in which a neophyte would have studied under two such geniuses as Guilbert and Duse. But Duse did not accept the invitation, though she replied gratefully: "The "come" in your first letter remains in my hours of discouragement like a light before the eyes of my soul."

An exchange of letters and cables followed; several times Duse seemed on the point of departure. Finally, shortly before the Schillers left New York, Yvette again held out inducements. Why not allow Max to find an American manager who would bring her over in a play? Duse responded tardily to the idea, cabling just as Yvette and Max were about to sail to ask whether Max, or some other impresario, would book her immediately for twenty or twenty-five evenings in April and May. But Max thought it would be a pity to spoil her very excellent chances in America by coming in the spring; in October and November audiences would be larger, he replied, and if she could wait until then, he would personally manage her. And so it was arranged, though management by Schiller was another plan that was fated never to materialize.

Now in Paris, seeing Duse after so long an absence, Yvette was secretly horrified at her friend's condition:

And I saw her again! And, God! what did I see? I saw her ill! Ill! Disfigured, and coughing, spitting, breathless, but as though she were burning up her last embers. . . .

Oh, that spring of 1922 to which my last memories of her are linked, when my hopes, blinding my judgment, counted too much on her delight in work for overcoming her illness! I trusted that mind would conquer body; her beautiful eyes would be so bright as she told me of the ovations that had crowned her successful return to the stage that I said to myself: "Such eyes cannot be those of a dying woman!" It is true that her fear of the spring wind and her nervous shivers alarmed me a little. But at a luncheon given at Foyot's . . . she chatted gaily and seemed to defy the possibilities of a sinister future. . . .

The night Duse came backstage in the Théâtre Edouard VII and found Yvette surrounded by her American pupils, she surprised Yvette by expressing unqualified disapproval:

"How good you are, Yvette, to let these schoolgirls appear with you! . . . But do these little creatures appreciate it? And do you imagine that you can teach your gift? No, no, Yvette! Did some one teach you what you know—you? No, no! And I, did anyone teach me my talent? No, no! Can you give them souls? No. Can they even comprehend yours? No. Well, then, keep yourself to yourself— give yourself only to your art, and not to them!"

"But it encourages them, Duse!"

"A proof that they are fools! For you are the most discouraging example in the world, Yvette! No, my dear; our talents cannot be taught; if one has not 'God under one's skin,' as the poet said, there's nothing to be done."

Prophetic words, for truth to tell, among all the students, first and last, upon whom Yvette lavished herself, gifted as the best of them might have been, there arose no second Yvette. No "God under the skin" was ever discerned.

Shortly thereafter a tour was announced for Yvette and a company made up of a core of her best Americans, aided by a few professionals, through Holland, Switzerland, and Belgium. In Brussels, where the troupe gave twenty performances, Yvette enjoyed the personal friendship and patronage of saintly Cardinal Mercier, idolized by the Belgians for his valor during the war. In France, mystery plays and song programs were given at scores of church institutions as well as theaters.

From such preoccupation with what she had termed "intensely and burningly Catholic" drama, it might be conjectured that Yvette in her own spiritual life was beginning to turn back to the faith in which she had been born. But this did not happen. Though by now a profound believer in God, she never returned to the formal practice of the Roman Catholic religion. To the end of her life she continued in the position she had earlier expressed: "I am not speaking of belief in form, in dogmas, in words, but of faith in the large, spacious sense."

As to the hoped-for school in Paris, disappointment again lay in store. Yvette still seems to have dreamed of eventual endowment from private fortunes; but France, bled white by the war, was concerned only with rehabilitation. For the comparatively few students who enrolled, classes were held in rented quarters, the banquet hall of the newspaper *La Fronde* serving as atelier. Since expenses had to be severely limited, emphasis was placed on techniques of acting only, in order that properties and stage sets might be dispensed with as far as possible. There was little publicity; the whole enterprise was a disheartening, uphill fight. Yvette, who was past mistress of keeping up her guard with the press, must have been sore oppressed in spirit that day when she cried out despairingly to a reporter:

I asked a place in France where I could found a school of art . . . people smiled and talked of something else. They would sing, almost in my face: "*Un fiacre allait trottinant. . . .*"

So things dragged along another twelvemonth. There was another tour with *les girls* to Austria, Hungary, and Czechoslovakia; and Yvette went on without her troupe to Warsaw. Changes took place; some of the American disciples were marrying, others returning home; it became impossible to continue, and finally, in 1924, the school was formally liquidated. One more fiasco.

Her "theatre" too, that grandiose, pitifully unrealistic scheme, had never really come to fruition; and small wonder. There was simply no commercial market for the idea. Both the religiosity of it and the exclusive concern with medievalism put it hopelessly out of step with the times. So far as Paris was concerned, the implacable edict remained: "Yvette may psalmodize us all she wishes; she will always be Yvette." Plenty of voices suggested that the old Montmartre repertoire of aphrodisiacs would still command a hearing, but to these she would not listen.

These were dismal days too of personal shocks and losses. In March, 1923, Bernhardt died. Yvette had seen her, apparently not long before, under rather unhappy circumstances. Gordon Craig, relating the incident, places the date as 1920, but as Yvette was then still in New York, an old man's memory must have faulted.

Lunching one day with the Schillers, Craig had been lamenting his inability to carry out his aims in the theater in England because of lack of funds, while Yvette, ever sympathetic, listened attentively. Finally, "What can we do to help poor Craig?" she propounded to Max, seeming to have it in mind that, somehow, someone ought to be appealed to in his behalf. Then, after a little reflection: "We'll go to Bernhardt!"

What Yvette thought Bernhardt could do for Craig was not clear; nevertheless, the three hastily called a cab and shortly presented themselves at the house-of-the-coffin on Boulevard Péreire. Here they were shown into a small room where they sat for three-quarters of an hour. Finally they were ushered into the presence; Bernhardt, seated in a high-backed chair behind a table, greeted them in a kind of rapid, low, murmuring monotone, which she kept up without pause but which seemed lacking in either animation or pleasure; the voice of gold was no more. Several times she asked Craig, "And how is that dear Mr. Irving?"—to Craig's severe embarrassment, for Mr. Irving had been dead at least fifteen years. The murmur continued for some minutes, then ceased; the audition was at an end, and the visitors rose and soberly withdrew.

On the day of Bernhardt's funeral, dramatically and literally Yvette's and Sarah's paths crossed for the last time when Yvette, standing on a street corner in Paris, saw the cortège approaching, the hearse heaped with flowers. As it passed, Yvette was glad that she had long ago been able to forgive the sorely afflicted woman and could now "salute her with pitiful tears on her last journey."

In June of that same year the exotic Pierre Loti died; another wrench. Yvette's mind went back to their many happy meetings, especially to that extraordinary one in 1897, when soon after her marriage, while she was on tour in the south of France, she and Max had stopped at Rochefort at Loti's invitation. She remembered the wretched exterior of the house, and its breathtaking interiors—room after room of treasures gathered from Loti's global travels. It was "the house of a poet of the Thousand and One Nights," from the enthroned Hindu god before which all had to burn incense on entering, lest the divinity play tricks on them, to the pink marble fountain taken from a mosque, whose murmur lulled Loti to sleep each night as he lay on his ivory satin mattress, "wrapped in a splendid golden robe embroidered with birds and flowers. . . ."

She remembered the day during the war, before she left Paris, after Loti had been assigned on a naval mission, when he called at Boulevard Berthier to say good-by—heavily rouged as usual, magnificently uniformed in pale blue, his chest crossed by the red moiré ribbon of the Legion of Honor and glittering with a profusion of jeweled medals.

But the deaths of Bernhardt and Loti were as nothing compared with the fearful loss to come. A few months later, Eleanora Duse, during the American tour to which she had finally committed herself under other management, was seized by a severe chill. The end came suddenly, a confused nightmare of finale, in a hotel bedroom in smoky, icy Pittsburgh. Long ago Duse had given Yvette a flower-embroidered, deeply fringed green silk shawl; now Yvette buried her face in it and wept.

In hardly more than a year, Bernhardt, Loti, Duse—all swept away.

In the end the quarrel between Yvette and the Parisian public was resolved by Yvette's capitulation. One evening in March, 1924, at the luxuriously appointed new Empire in Paris of which Dufrenne was manager, a red-haired woman once more stepped on stage, wearing a legendary green gown and long black gloves and prepared to sing once more *Le Fiacre, L'Hotel du Numéro 3,* even *Le Petit Cochon,* and all the others.

Yvette, to be sure, had freely reverted to the rabelaisian all during her years as concert artist, when funds were low or for special reasons. During one of her flying visits to Paris from New York, for example, she had been seen at Paul Poiret's Oasis, the great couturier's brief experiment in bringing back the past by a simulation of old *caf'-conc'* days. In this attempt at revival of a bygone era, Kam-Hill, Paulus, Judic —all favorites of the golden age—were impersonated by contemporary music-hall players, and Yvette, who happened to be on the scene, brought herself back in person. But these appearances had been sporadic, incidental, potboiling, or tongue in cheek. Here at the Empire was a different situation. Here, survive or perish, she was a bona fide performer taking her place in all seriousness on a bill that included musical elephants, acrobats, Negro jazz players, and cowboy stunt men. Here, if she survived, it would have to be on proved contemporaneity. Would she be "modern" to a new generation? Or dismissed as merely an archaic oddity? She had worried a good deal over the young people she would have to face, their tastes in entertainment ruined, she feared, by the jazz rhythms she so heartily detested.

When she came down to the footlights that night, she was trembling violently from stage fright, as her audience could not but perceive. They must have recognized the emotion sympathetically and known that it came from respect to them, because almost immediately she became conscious of the old, familiar wave of love, the old overwhelming tenderness, sweeping up over the footlights. When this happened, she realized she had nothing to fear. The *caf'-conc'* crowd had always understood her. It understood her now; especially this one so thickly studded with white heads.

Inevitably her return to the music hall was made much of in the press. "Triumphal!" trumpeted Pierre Varenne, and Henri Jeanson caroled: "Her sacred fire, I swear to you, is no fire of straw. . . . She has not betrayed our memories." When she left the stage and did not come back, in spite of the continued cheers and the stamping of feet, she was hiding, Jeanson thought, "no doubt to weep over our having been so moved."

Had Yvette been in any doubt about the verity of that wave of love she believed she felt, her mail the next day should have confirmed it. "Ah, Madame, last night at the Empire it was our youth you brought to life, and you—you are still the Yvette of our thirty years. Oh, thanks, Yvette, thanks! No one will ever be what you are. My sons heard you for the first time and they are mad about you, yes, yes, astonished and delighted as their old father once was. Ah, those evenings at the Divan Japonais. . . . Do you remember one night when a whole cortège of us walked beside your carriage to Rue Saint-Lazare—do you remember?" "Madame, you were perhaps twenty-five, and I was madly infatuated with you. Every night I went to the Ambassadeurs, timid and happy, to listen to you and to look at you. . . . I do not know any actress . . . who has given me the emotions that I owe to you. Besides, who has your talent? No one! I have sent you roses, Madame, because in my youth I had the audacity to shower you with the same flowers, and now I am home, overcome with joy at having seen you again, feted by a new generation." "What emotion yesterday at the Empire! . . . if I dared I would say that we took you in our arms and embraced you. . . . Excuse the lyricism of an old man, happy at seeing you still beautiful and young—yes, Madame, young! Such an emotion does not come twice in a lifetime. I kiss your hands."

In July, 1924, a certain Alphonse Franck, director of the Théâtre de l'Étoile, engaged Yvette for one hundred performances of an operetta, *Les Amants légitimes*, by Marcel Ballot. The piece opened successfully enough, but shortly thereafter Yvette had the misfortune to suffer an attack of laryngitis. As no understudy had been provided, she continued to appear in her role, speaking the lines perforce, however, instead of singing them. The solution proved unwise, for the play collapsed, and M. Franck sued for thirty thousand francs on the grounds that the contract had been broken when the star failed to sing.

It was many months before the case came to trial, and when it did, in 1926, it must have afforded spectators almost as much entertainment as the operetta which gave it birth. Lionel Nestory, a specialist in theatrical law, representing Yvette, contended that the illness of a player constituted no fault; that the management, on the other hand, had been at fault in providing Madame Guilbert no understudy and that by not keeping her dressing room heated it had been directly responsible for the laryngitis. In view of those circumstances, Madame Guilbert, in playing at all when she was ill, should have been commended for courage and devotion to her manager's interests.

Moreover, N. Nestory submitted the ingenious argument that Yvette had been engaged not for her voice but for her diction and her powers of mimicry; as a diseuse, not a chanteuse; and by continuing to offer these gifts she had thus not violated the terms of the contract. Could any director as sophisticated as M. Franck have seriously engaged Madame Guilbert for her singing voice? In opera, for example? Ridiculous. Besides, in a musical comedy the degrees of difference between lines spoken and sung are variable, vague, and open to interpretation. Messieurs André Messager, Reynaldo Hahn, Léon

Xanrof, and Tristan Bernard, who took the stand as witnesses for the defendant, agreed that it would be unreasonable to require of a diseuse like Madame Guilbert nothing but song, her art being so uniquely personal. No, the ugly truth was, averred counsel, that M. Franck, who had sold his theater meantime, was seeking a pretext for getting rid of obligations to his star. The defendant, moreover, was placing a counterclaim against the plaintiff for seventy-five thousand francs damage for breach of contract on his part, on the grounds that M. Franck had not provided the hundred performances agreed upon.

When tight-lipped justice finally spoke, it was to absolve Yvette from all charges against her and also, in respect to her own suit, to award a neat little windfall of thirty-five thousand francs.

It may have been, in part at least, the proceeds from the despised *caf'-conc'* public that enabled Max and Yvette in 1924 to set up a home of their own once more. Yvette's fifteen packing cases of furnishings and bric-a-brac, which in the summer of 1919—in that period of wild optimism over the promises of her faithless furrier-Mycenas—had been shipped to America, had ever since then been gathering dust expensively in a New York warehouse. Now, at last, when she was able to raise the king's ransom necessary to redeem them, the Schillers joyfully removed from the Hotel Regina to a fifth-floor apartment at 120 Rue de Courcelles. And a charming and luxurious home it became, when the dear possessions of a lifetime had been retrieved and placed therein. At least, so it appeared to her affectionate young friend Emily Gresser, now Mrs. David Liebowitz, who often visited her there, and to the various reporters whom Yvette received from time to time in her "petit salon rose."

"Her very own personality completely dominated her apartment ...," gushed one of these callers. "Flowers and birds are there too, and in the far off workroom the distant click of a typewriter tells of future plans for the versatile woman who has been, and is, the joy of two generations." One entire room, as usual, had to be given over to sculptures, photographs and paintings of Yvette. An interviewer who wanted to know the names of some of the artists represented was rather bowled over by the number of celebrities rattled off: Toulouse-Lautrec, Puvis de Chavannes, Degas, Forain, Seurat, Jacques-Émile Blanche, José Granier; Yvette may well have mentioned also Anton Van Welie, Métivet, de Losques, Bennewitz von Loefen, Maurice Neumont, Bernstamm. Burne-Jones by good rights should have been

305

in that gallery, too. He had once asked her to sit, but as she always told the story, with a little *moue* of regret, in her youth and ignorance of the honor that was being offered her she had declined!

As Yvette reminisced that day with the reporter, her voice often trembled and her eyes swam. She seems to have become increasingly emotional during this period of her life, and she often recounts incidents never told before. That day she spoke of the profound pity she had always felt for prostitutes; of one girl in particular whom she had noticed long, long ago when she was playing at the Nouveautés. It was a cold winter night, and the girl was obviously ill, coughing harshly. "How much do you earn?" Yvette had asked her. "In good weather, fifty francs, Madame," was the answer, "Here," said Yvette, opening her purse, "I will pay you fifty francs every night while you are ill. Go home until you are well."

After the Empire engagement Yvette went to the once-loved Ambassadeurs again, for now the new fad started by Poiret was spreading with Parisians, a revival of affection for the old *caf'-conc'*. The year following, it was to the Odéon, and then another return to the Empire. Again and again the posters bearing the great name went up. And again and again, to whatever the black-gloved figure sang, a critic choir, in antiphonal chant, lifted their voices in monotheistic affirmation: *"Il n'y a qu'une Yvette; il n'y a qu'une Yvette."*

Yet almost concurrently, during both 1924 and 1925, the same figure, but without gloves, was appearing in concerts of an entirely different character. At the Salle Gaveau, with Madame Béatrix Dusanne, a brilliant and learned member of the Comédie Française, serving as lecturer on the multiple *rapprochements* between theatre and song, Yvette continued to present *chansons* and more *chansons,* in seemingly endless number, and small, élite audiences continued to listen with undiminished admiration. As indeed did certain critics. "She alone," affirmed Edmond Sée, ". . . now preserves *la chanson* in the domain of art."

Soir once called upon its readers to recognize how easy it would have been for Madame Guilbert to have kept on jogging along in *le fiacre qui allait trottinant*. Instead, she had not been satisfied to be merely a model of a certain kind of song; she had aspired to be Song itself. From the first, she had not been understood in her new endeavors. How ridiculous, some had scoffed, to give herself so much trouble; to submit herself to the fierce discipline of study; to seal herself away in the city of books; to labor to reanimate the rhythms of another age when it would have been so simple and profitable merely to take her stand among all the babble and madness of the contemporary. But Yvette Guilbert had not listened to the counsels of sloth; she had continued to climb; to dare.

Quasi-reverentially, the *Soir* writer ends in a near Hail Mary:

Respectfully Hail, Yvette, full of graces; the genius of France is with thee; persevering art thou amongst women, and blessed is thy adoptive offspring, *La Chanson*.

Chapter 11

In February, 1926, Max Schiller wrote to Emily Gresser Liebowitz: "We are in Berlin where my wife—for the first time after the war—appeared again with a tremendous success at the Bechstein Saal." Though this seems a purely routine announcement, happenings leading up to that Bechstein concert had been far from routine.

As soon as they returned to Europe in 1922, both Yvette and Max had longed to resume professional contacts in Germany, but it was some time before they dared seriously to consider crossing the so-lately-flaming frontier. Official peace had been made in 1918, but hatred had not died by treaty and the Schillers dreaded a possible contretemps. It was the greatest of pities that Yvette's appearances there had been interrupted, because nowhere in Europe had her genius been more extrolled than in Germany and Austria. During *la belle époque* Paris had stood to most educated Germans as the symbol of freedom, inspiration, wit, *joie de vivre,* and because to her Germanic devotees Yvette was Paris, she had been able to intoxicate their minds, transport even phlegmatic temperaments. With the war, however, the rapport that had existed between artists of France and audiences of enemy nations had been so shattered that there was still question as to how soon, if ever, it could be mended.

In the years of the Schillers' absence in America, Max's favorite niece Eva had grown up, chosen psychology as a profession, married, and removed from Berlin to Vienna. Nevertheless, though personal ties were not as strong in Berlin as formerly, though stray nationalistic land mines might yet explode, Yvette and Max continued to yearn for Unter den Linden, and in October, 1925, they finally decided to risk a cautious experiment. They would slip in quietly as tourists and feel out for themselves the attitude of the Berliners.

Nothing could have been more naïve than to believe that a woman as widely known as Yvette Guilbert could pass incognito anywhere in Europe, especially in Berlin. Within forty-eight hours she was recognized, and what inevitably followed was that, as word spread, flocks of old friends began crowding in on her and Max in their hotel suite. It was equally inevitable that in the warmhearted, excited reunion talks that followed, regretful references should occasionally be made to the unhappy memories that still lingered as an aftermath of hostilities, and several times the idea was voiced that some kind of Pont de la Concorde ought to be established between the two still sensitive nations; that especially among artists and scholars differences should be mended as soon as possible. Yvette, always the impassioned pacifist, intensely wished she might be the engineer of such a bridge.

As she searched her mind for a method, opportunely one presented itself. The producer-manager Max Reinhardt, who had placed a box at her disposal in each of his theaters for the duration of her stay in Berlin, often brought talented newcomers of the theatrical world to present to her during intermissions in performances. Her acquaintance being thus rapidly enlarged, one day the thought occurred that it would be a pleasant gesture to offer, as a return courtesy, a matinee of her own songs, for the profession only. In theatrical circles this might be considered as a small olive branch. When she told Reinhardt her idea, his expressive eyes showed that he recognized her motive. *"Bien,"* was all he said, but he put his theater Die Komoedie at her immediate disposal.

He did not, however, limit invitations to the Guilbert matinee to members of his companies. He invited also all persons of prominence in the city, including personnel of every foreign embassy. The house was crowded to the roof.

That afternoon, as she stepped on stage, Yvette was greeted by an ovation the ardor of which exceeded anything she had ever before experienced. The applause and shouting lasted many minutes, and then before she quite knew what was happening, one of Reinhardt's players had appeared at her side and was delivering an elaborate speech of homage to her in German.

Yvette was so moved that at the end of the concert she felt impelled to make an address herself. Speaking extempore, but with eloquence and unmistakable sincerity, she told her audience of the hope she cherished that a new "bridge" between France and Germany could be established; that French and German hands would soon be joined as before in amity:

At that minute emotion was indescribable! Handkerchiefs came out of every pocket, people cried, applauded, stood for half an hour, ... others left their seats to come on stage to seize my hands, to kiss them, women wiped their eyes distractedly, saying, "Thank you! Thank you! God bless you! Ah, how good you are, Madame!"

Suddenly ... I saw standing in a box close to the proscenium a very old woman in mourning, her hair quite white, looking at me, questioning me with desolate eyes. Without saying a word she was calling me, I felt it and I went to her. She wanted to speak to me and she could not. She choked to control herself and to put an end to our tortures I said: "Tell me, Madame, as a sad sister in France, what you want to say to me." Shaken with emotion, she murmured ... : "I am in mourning for my four sons. Tell me why I have such a sweet, happy feeling at seeing you here, Madame, and at honoring you for what you have done."

Breathless with emotion, I pressed my lips to her hand. Ah! that old mother in black, recalling to me our own mothers—my God! how overcome I was! All my life I shall not forget her. . . .

The press was wonderful, and at a reception given by Madame Louise Wolff, director of *La Vie Musicale* in Germany, who for thirty years had handled my affairs there, I met again Francesco de Mendelssohn, who organized in honor of my return a dinner following the reception. . . .

The ice thus broken, it was only a question of time until other French performers began venturing across the border, timidly and singly, until in 1928, with the engagement of the Comédie Française in Cologne, the cultural separation of the two countries seemed to come formally to an end.

As for Yvette, after the Berlin triumph she was soon including in her itineraries all the major German cities as of old. Of the incident in Die Komoedie she said: "I felt the joy of Christ stilling the tempest by walking smiling on the waters. My soul was uplifted."

Only the year before in Vienna, Yvette had also played the role of dove. She recalls the date as February, 1924, and if her memory serves, this may have been during one of her tours with *les girls*.

Yvette had always loved Vienna. To the Carltheatre she had brought her Société des Instruments anciens; to the theater An der Wien, her troupe of *Montmartre en ballade;* she had appeared alone in the classic Grosser Musikverein Saal; had given two concerts with the celebrated orchestra Tonkustler-Verein under the direction of Alex Birnbaum. Not even at the Paris opera could greater opulence have been displayed than at her Vienna programs; tiaras sparkled throughout her audiences, and streets were jammed with varnished equipages driven by elaborately liveried lackeys. What tributes she had invariably received from Vienna's journalists! Dr. Singer, director of the *Wiener-Tageblatt,* had always referred to his journal as "hers," and when he went to Paris, he visited her.

But now—what changes!

One day when Yvette was lunching at the French Embassy, table conversation turned to the uppermost topic of the day, *"rapprochement,"* a matter of grave concern to Ambassador Pierre Lefèvre-Portalis because, as everyone admitted, the healing of the nations was not proceeding well. Viennese could not easily forget the famine they had suffered during the late war, nor forgive the wholesale deaths of their children from malnutrition.

During the conversation Yvette kept thinking of Vienna as she had last known it, sweet, joyous, laughing, prosperous; now it was ragged, sad, lamentable. She thought of the friends she had revisited whom she had found living in the dead of winter without fuel; of the stories of professors picked up on benches in the Ring, unconscious from privation; of the many suicides. The new generation especially was far from tender toward the French. Most hostile of all, she now heard, were the students of the University.

"We ought to win back the youth," the ambassador said anxiously, "conquer the University itself—professors, students, the whole lot of them. That's where the serious resistance lies. But the University double-locks its doors and there's nothing that can be done."

After the guests, in a mood of deep depression, had adjourned to the drawing room for coffee and liqueurs, an idea began to take shape in Yvette's mind:

"Suppose I try?"

"Try what?"

"Why, to open the doors of the University. . . . I have been a pacifist all my life, and nothing in the world pleases me like bring-

310

ing together those who are separated. It is such a joy to my heart
... that I would throw myself into this, body, heart, and soul."

"Of course, Madame, but—have you a plan?"

"Yes, and here it is: to offer a concert at the University, presided
over by the French ambassador."

A great silence, then from all: "Impossible."

"Why, gentlemen?"

"First, because the opportunity has never been given to any artist
to be heard there; next, because the Embassy cannot appear where
it has not been invited."

"But if they invite you?"

Everybody laughed. "Ah, you are an optimist, Madame, to believe
that everything can be arranged because one wishes it."

Pursuing my idea: "Can you, M. Lefèvre-Portalis, tell me the
name of the philologist who holds the chair of French literature at
the University?"

"Yes. Professor Kuchler."

"Have you confidence in my tact, and do you wish loyally, and for
the good of the cause, to honor with your presence a fête where you
have been invited, according to protocol?"

"Absolutely, Madame."

"Very well, gentlemen, I swear to you that I shall have you all as
auditors at the University of Vienna."

Yvette lost no time. The very next day Professor Kuchler, to his
astonishment, it may be imagined, found in his mail a graceful note
from Madame Guilbert, setting forth the writer's long interest in
French medieval literature and her desire while in Vienna to present
an evening of ancient French songs. For this she would need the
assistance of a competent medievalist who could lecture on troubadours in general, with specific commentary on the ballads she would
offer. The French Embassy had recommended Professor Kuchler as
the most distinguished authority in this field in Vienna; would he
care to call at her hotel and discuss the matter?

The flattered scholar, of course, rose straight to the glittering lure,
like a trout in spring to a Royal Coachman. He called, and fell under
the spell of the Guilbert charm. Such a program, he could not but
agree, would indeed be a cultural contribution; he would be honored
to collaborate; but in what language would Madame propose the lecture to be given? The response was prompt.

"In German, Monsieur, in German! . . . I will sing the French texts about which you lecture."

As to choice of hall, Madame was a trifle vague. Some place of distinction, of course, appropriate for an élite gathering. The professor thought two weeks at least would be required to bring together a proper audience. Very well; at that time she would be in Budapest, but she would return. On parting, the two shook hands warmly.

The opening maneuver had been an exhilarating success, but with inspired finesse Yvette let the matter rest where it was for the moment.

The second meeting took place a few days later when the professor and his wife invited Yvette to their home to discuss the content of the program. Madame Kuchler was French born, the atmosphere was cordial, and in the easy and genial teatable conversation that glanced about from one subject to another the professor at one point found himself confiding that he wished he were rich, in order to be able to provide some sorely needed books for his Department of Romance Languages. "We are in such a state of distress . . . it is heartbreaking!" he sighed.

Here was the opening Yvette had been looking for.

"Really?" with quick sympathy. "Well, then, why not give all our receipts to your University?"

Oh, no, the Professor protested, much embarrassed. He had not meant—! One simply could not accept—! Oh, no—! Oh, no, indeed—! But Yvette sweetly overrode every objection. Why, they ought even to donate the gross receipts; she herself would meet expenses. Naturally, if the Professor could find her a hall at a reduced price, that would be helpful. And then the crowning subtlety: "Perhaps in the University?"

The Professor sadly shook his head. Impossible. Stage shows were never given there—never!

"Stage shows! A lesson in the history of literature, with examples, a stage show?"

"But you would sing, Madame!"

"Professor, how can one speak of trouvères and troubadours without illustrating their works in totality—that is, with their music which cannot be separated from the texts?" . . .

"Besides," suggested Madame Kuchler, "if you hold to a severely academic program, where the idea of 'learning' takes precedence over 'entertainment'—"

"Your wife is right!" I cried. "I will provide you with some Gregorian themes to which words were added later in the vernacular. I will sing the texts first in Latin and later the others—"

". . . you will sing in Latin!"

"But of course, Professor. So come now, do get me a room in the University—it will be such an economy for me."

"But would they give it to us? You cannot realize, Madame, how the war has changed hearts here . . . a Frenchwoman, singing in French . . . in the University itself? For myself, *parbleu*, all I want is peace, but—"

"Professor, are you sincere . . . ?" And I looked at him straight.

". . . Well, then, . . . you will go to see your rector, tell him the offer I make to his library, ask his understanding and exception in regard to me . . . and you will invite the French ambassador."

At this Kuchler jumped! "But he will never come, Madame!" he exploded violently. "He will never come, unfortunately. . . . It's always the same—neither side will take the first step. Oh, if only he would come—but he will not!" The little man paced the room nervously, his arms behind his back.

"But one can try—one must not doubt miracles but invite them. . . . See your rector, and when I have his answer, with his promise to make an *entente cordiale* of the occasion presided over by my ambassador, I will see M. Lefèvre-Portalis. . . . *Ça va?*"

"*Ça va*," said Kuchler. And I kissed both him and his wife.

The affair of course went off brilliantly. On the appointed date the staff of the French Embassy was received at the University with full-dress pomp by the entire Faculty, and Yvette sank the *Kyrie* in six different arrangements, the while her heart sang *Alleluias*.

Her compensation came a few days later when M. Lefèvre-Portalis extended to her, in the name of France, official thanks for a significant service to her country.

It was Eva Rosenfeld who was instrumental in bringing about Yvette's friendship with Sigmund Freud. Eva, while studying psychology in Vienna, had become acquainted first with Freud's devoted daughter Anna and eventually with the whole household.

Freud had long been an ardent Guilbertian, his interest dating back to 1889. That year, while he had been attending a Congress on Hypnotism in Paris, he had yielded one evening to a friend's urgings to go to hear a new *caf'-conc'* singer—"for relaxation." Instead of relaxation, however, he had experienced that night a deep excitement that he never forgot.

After the Schillers' return from America, Yvette learned through Eva of Freud's regard for her, and feeling highly honored—for the name of Freud even in the '20s was one to conjure with; it came up on every hand—she sent him through Eva a photograph flowingly inscribed: *"À un savant d'une artiste."* To this compliment Freud courteously responded in kind with a photograph of himself, and thus was laid the basis for the eventual meeting of the two in Vienna.

The friendship that sprang up between them was instant, tender, and enduring. In Freud Yvette seemed able to confide more than in any other person except her husband. Perhaps his patriarchal appearance and qualities of benevolence, his reputation for knowing the springs of being and conduct, created for her the perfect father image. After she had resumed her annual concerts in Vienna, which again, as in pre-war days, were considered among the choicest intellectual and artistic events of Viennese society, she never failed to send Freud seats in the middle of the front row. Though by then he had already entered into his long martyrdom to cancer and had given up all social life, he nonetheless never omitted, ill as he might be, to be present, gallantly sending Yvette flowers after each performance, and often he and his wife would come for tea to the Bristol Hotel, where the Schillers always stayed. *"Cher grand homme,"* Yvette would address him in her letters, and *"Mes mains bien affectueusement dans les votres"* warmly subscribe herself. Dr. Ernest L. Jones, in his biography of Freud, recalls that in May, 1926, in the deluge of congratulations that showered down upon the old man at the time of his seventieth birthday, Yvette's tribute was placed with that of Georg Brandes, Einstein, Romain Rolland, and the Hebrew University of Jerusalem as those which pleased Freud most.

By the mid-twenties then Yvette seems to have come full stream once more in a schedule of strenuous tours, both provincial and foreign —the south of France, England, Belgium, Hungary, Czechoslovakia, Germany, Austria. At sixty she was finding it necessary to conserve strength a little more than at forty; resting all day before a concert and drinking only a cup of chocolate before she went on stage. But aside from such minor retrenchments she spent herself almost as prodigally as ever. Max, as always, kept her insulated from every practical problem.

314

Yet with all the tours, all the concerts, all the activities, the Schillers were not actually prosperous, not in the sense of *fin-de-siècle* days, and, typically, neither could quite understand why. With all the hard work, they kept asking themselves, why was there always a nagging deficit? Perhaps some of the reasons lay in their high overhead. Travel was expensive, and both still demanded uncompromising standards of comfort. Appearances must be kept up. Personal generosities, too, continued on much the same scale. For the Schillers, economy was a hard word to learn to spell.

From the time of her return from America, Yvette had never been long out of the Parisian spotlight. There had been journalistic head-waggings and I-told-you-so's over the failure of her visionary theater ventures; the epic outburst of adulation on the occasion of her return to the music hall; the chuckles of amusement over the bizarre lawsuit; certain acid strictures on her willingness to be the first French performer to appear before the Boches. But in none of these connections had she provided anything comparable to the seismic shock she created one bright day in May, 1926.

On this day, at a restaurant in the Champs Élysées, a select group had gathered, the occasion being a luncheon tendered by the association of foreign correspondents in Paris to their confrères of the French press. At the head table, in the place of honor, sat the veteran statesman M. Aristide Briand. The guest list included, besides journalists, most of the leading editors of France, many theater directors and better-known personalities of the stage, social leaders—in short, *Tout Paris.*

The meal ended, speakers rose over the liqueurs, one after another as called upon by M. Briand, for the customary postprandial observations, and in the convivial atmosphere that prevailed wit and compliments mingled gracefully. Suddenly Madame Guilbert, who had been seated near the head table but who had not been invited to speak, nevertheless, to M. Briand's obvious surprise, arose and entered into an extended address. Almost immediately a slight chill fell on the assembly when it was recognized that the tone of her remarks was uncomfortably personal and emotional, out of keeping for so light an occasion, and as she proceeded, the head table began to show signs of nervousness. After all, there were present representatives from practically every newspaper of importance in the world, and Yvette was not noted for public discretion. Wakened now from digestive torpor, correspondents leaned forward attentively. When Yvette turned to M. Briand, and said, "I am happy to find myself near the president of the *Conseil* and minister of foreign affairs because I have something to say to him," that gentleman turned a vivid pink and was heard to whisper warningly: "Madame, you are in danger of creating a diplomatic incident!"

But Yvette when well launched in words was as easily diverted as an Alpine avalanche. Continuing implacably, she reviewed for the gathering her long career and its staunch values. Then:

"But there is one thing that has never been offered me, that has never been asked for me, so I ask it for myself: I ask THE LEGION OF HONOR!"

Though the lack of that inconspicuous mark of distinction, the little red ribbon of the Legion, was indubitably a worm i' the bud in the heart of every undecorated man and woman of accomplishment in France, Yvette's unabashed public admission to that effect was probably the first of its kind on record. The silence that fell was resounding.

It was a long silence, while people avoided each other's eyes and Yvette stood through what must have seemed an interminable interval, waiting out the embarrassment, the shock, even the distress that her words had produced. Finally came a scattering of perfunctory Hear, hears!, as a few guests recovered enough poise to try to bring the situation to a decent end.

"One is never so well served as by himself," Briand was heard to mutter *sotto voce*.

At this point Yvette might well have seated herself, a half-success. Instead she chose to continue, to elaborate her cause, while the chill deepened and spread. When at last she sat down, and while eyes were still glued on plates, there was fortunately present in the gathering one person possessed of the tact and imagination to know how to break the horrid spell. This was the talented Madame Rachilde of the *Mercure de France,* a friend of Yvette's and herself a holder of the ribbon. Quickly Rachilde rose from her seat and removing her own decoration, gracefully pinned it on Yvette, following the pinning with a pretty word and a kiss. It was a charming action that permitted the thoroughly uneasy company to start chattering again and eventually to escape from the room in grateful relief.

"Do you know what you have just done?" Briand afterward commented sourly to Yvette. "It is called direct diplomacy." Had the

316

minister only known, he would have recognized it as the diplomacy a starving girl had once used to wangle a roast chicken.

The incident naturally afforded Parisians a new and piquant topic of conversation that night about their unpredictable Yvette. First-class humor, laughed some; nothing but bad humor, retorted others. Some argued that the challenge was entirely justified; as long ago as 1914 Bernhardt had been made Chevalier of the Legion. Still others wondered why all the pother over that particular bit of ribbon anyway, considering how indiscriminately it had been bestowed of late.

But Michel Georges-Michel of *L'Art* brushed the whole episode aside as only another endearing example of Guilbertian *niaiserie:*

"*Ma chère Yvette, ma chère Yvette,*" he chided gently, "*tu as été joliment et sympathiquement maladroite ... !*"

Chapter 12

Probably most sexagenarians consider themselves moderns, and Yvette, it is to be presumed, was no exception. She had already endorsed the new mechanisms of film and phonograph as mediums charged with incalculable potential in the service of song and drama. She had been, in fact, willing to entrust her own art to them and must have assumed that such participation stamped her as of the decade. Yet in her choice of repertoire in the 20's, despite oft-repeated assertions that she hoped to "discover" new poets, as she had done in the 90's, poets who would express twentieth-century ideas in twentieth-century forms, almost none of the postwar *chansonniers* had made their way to her heart. The generations of Baudelaire, Verlaine, Richepin, Laforgue, Rollinat, Jammes, were the last to which she was willing to be fundamentally committed.

Of her present preoccupation with the *chanson,* Gustave Fréjaville, writing in *Comoedia,* had noted disapprovingly that Guilbert was actually pulling against the current: "On the great flood of art ... the prow of her bark is turned toward the sources; but human sensibility does not know how to turn back the course of the centuries." Without to any degree minimizing Madame Guilbert's accomplishments, he believed that her present success was based on personal prestige and incomparable art. Yvette, he said, had retreated from life universal when she consecrated her talent to the glory of France as symbolized in the *chanson*. Instead of remaining one of the most vital and vibrant voices of contemporary France, she had for two decades plunged into the dust of libraries to pursue phantoms of past centuries. Yvette had entered erudition, he feared, as another woman might enter a convent. Erudition is a respectable enough passion but can easily become a mania, and this particular artist was now as much a slave to it as if it were opium. Its pleasures were purely those of intellectual curiosity; its effects in art merely laborious reconstitutions; sometimes no more than conjectural even in authenticity. Logically, too, it could hardly be supposed that works of the past would move a modern crowd, which lacked taste and culture even to comprehend them. Twentieth-century attitudes were vastly different from those held by the good people of the Middle Ages for whom these archaic ballads were composed. And oh, the pity of it! If only this artist, instead of having been borne by her spirit out of her generation, had willed with equal force and perseverance to create a series of beautiful living songs, springing out of her own time! Ah! When one thinks what has been lost to the archives!—Thus, and much more, in critical reproof.

Yet even Fréjaville and other moderns could hardly have foreseen that their postwar world, reeling as it was from its late buffetings, was soon due for still others. The marching boots of the Hun had not been able to trample out time and space; a reasonable residue yet remained for mankind's sedation. The next step toward the annihilation of these blessings was a feat reserved for a modest, gangling American youth named Lindbergh, of whom comparatively little had been heard up to 1927.

One morning in May of that year, this young unknown, with a letter of introduction tucked in one pocket and a sandwich in another, climbed into the cockpit of a single-engined plane at Roosevelt Field, Long Island, expertly lifted the nose of his fragile ship into the blue ethereal, and set a course in the general direction of Paris. The young man's confidence in arrival at his destination was not generally shared. All through that day and night, innumerable vigils of prayer accompanied the tiny speck of daring across the Atlantic immensity, and when, thirty-odd hours later, the little craft was learned to have spiraled down safely to Le Bourget—even taking time out first to wreath the Eiffel Tower with a couple of deft circlings—America went mad. Not only did the exploit seem the most heroic in the nation's air history, but all the more admirable because of having been such a masterpiece of advance understatement. It had also set concepts of time spinning wildly. Overnight the past had received its rudest shove toward oblivion, and the future seemed suddenly present, with sirens already wailing warnings of unimaginable changes.

If Fréjaville had been right that Yvette's medievalism was hopelessly inapropos to a large section of the pre-Lindbergh public, he might well have asked now how that repertoire would be received in a world that must inevitably and immediately take on prodigious new dimensions; how much longer Yvette could continue to address any segment of the public in terms of those two preposterously limited worlds of hers—Paris of the 1890's and France of the Middle Ages. Surely with the opening of the global phase of the air age, a new breed of men was about to be born—men shortly to become birds; ride shooting stars. True, at the Empire in 1924 she had charmed a brash postwar generation by sheer *élan,* magnanimity, aristocracy of the entire personality; had been hailed as ageless. But the new challenge might be more formidable.

The fear of her material becoming "dated" seems never to have troubled Yvette. "From the time of her first successes," wrote A. Legrand-Chabrier in 1928, "the epithet 'modern' has been attached to her manner of singing." Had the question of "keeping up with the times" ever been posed, there seems little doubt that she would have continued to take her stand on *l'art pur* and its cosmic pre-eminence. Against the new technology that would tend to shrink planetary space and de-emphasize the past, she would have pitted that immemorial absolute as capable of illuminating all time and space. As she stated in 1930: "One is not only of one's own time; one belongs to all time. It is the ignorant and the spiritually limited who sing only their own epoch...."

The manuscript which the typewriter at 120 Rue de Courcelles had been busily tapping out during the past months appeared this year on the Paris bookstalls—a new volume of Guilbertian memoirs, *La Chanson de ma vie.* Lives of music-hall singers had always delighted Parisians. Years ago the Great Thérèsa had recounted her career under the Empire; in more recent days Josephine Baker and Maurice Chevalier had become subjects of deep interest.

The present work was more extended than *Struggles and Victories,* that first joint effort in 1910 with Harold Simpson, and was, moreover, entirely Yvette's own. Full of her subject—herself—and possessed of a lively sense of self-dramatization, the writer needed no assistance in setting down volubly, often picturesquely, and always sentimentally, the account of a little working girl's spectacular rise to fame, in a tale frequently interrupted by emotional outbursts and philosophical reflections.

Contemporary reviewers who took note of the volume were, in general, kind. "Alert and gay," they termed it; "pathetic and poignant"; "impressive in the verity of its accents"; "soaring into a chant of victory, a hymn, a march triumphal."

> With moving simplicity, a sincerity that holds the reader captive, she recounts her unhappy childhood, her difficult beginnings in the heroic age of the *café-concert,* her struggles for success, then her sudden ascension to glory. Paris adopts and worships her, Europe acclaims her, and the entire world celebrates her. She is the spirit, the goddess of song.
>
> Then this unique artiste, arrived at the apogee of her career, withdraws from the plaudits of the crowds; sacrifices herself to the realization of a dream which she has long pursued—the resurrection of the old French *chanson,* the rediscovery of all the masterpieces which have cradled the French soul in the course of its long history. At the cost of difficult research she reassembles the marvels of our folklore; she gives them life again.... But the memoirs of Madame Yvette Guilbert not only bring us a shining sheaf of memories; they also contain a moving lesson of energy and valor.

Today's critics, if perhaps not as fervid, might nevertheless see the book as the work of a brilliant literary amateur and find in it much of interest. They would surely rate it as lacking in craftsmanship; the story jumbled; full of suspected concealments and equivocations; historically untrustworthy; marred in places by animus, especially against America and Americans, and by flashes of coarseness; a highly personal and defensive document, such as often appeared in that period under the category of autobiography, especially from members of the theatrical profession.

"An artist," Yvette once said, "is an exaggerated human being," and in the pages of *La Chanson* she presents herself, in her unquenchable vitality and inflexible will, a shining exemplar of her own definition.

On July 8 of that year, Isadora Duncan, recently back from Russia and a shattered dream of living under Communism, danced again in Paris at the Mogador Theatre. She was in good form that night, and in the audience Yvette, always one of Duncan's most devoted admirers, helped lead the applause.

This casual encounter may well have been Yvette's last sight of the unfortunate Isadora. The next month the dancer left for Nice, never to return, for it was at Nice that she met her death through an accident which in its strangeness is hard to match. On a mellow September evening, Isadora stepped gaily into an open car, a sporting new model that she was about to try out, and, waving farewell to friends, called back happily: *"Je vais à la gloire!"* She was wearing a long, fringed scarf, one end of which was wound twice about her neck; in the fast departure and her mood of excitement she did not notice that the other end was trailing over the front wheel. As the car shot off, the friends screamed warnings, but too late; before brakes could be applied, the trailing fringe had spun tightly around the hub of a wheel of Death.

The artist in Duncan had always spoken to the artist in Yvette, and in her new book Yvette paid extravagant tribute to Duncan's genius:

> Isadora Duncan . . . was the Living Revelation of the Greek Dance. . . . What a miracle that such a tender blade should have grown on such a stony soil as America; like a voluptuous blossom in a garden of snow, heat born of ice, harmony born of chaos! . . . A creature of extremes, you could not but be American! . . . Genius of flesh and blood, human and yet superhuman, may Olympus welcome you!

In October of 1927 Yvette returned to the Scandinavian countries. Her first appearance in Copenhagen had been in 1898, when she had been almost mobbed by student admirers. Her second, in 1903, with her Société des Instruments anciens, had also been triumphal. Now in 1927, after twenty-four years' absence, she suffered pangs of apprehension over her reception, the weight of her age heavy on her soul. Stockholm, even worse, would be seeing her after a lapse of twenty-nine years.

In both cities, however, reporters crowded to meet her, and in Stockholm her evening at the luxuriously appointed Academy of Music was an occasion of almost royal dignity. To her surprise, the audience, which might have compared favorably to one at the Paris Opéra, or Comédie Française, or the austere Salle Gaveau, understood French so thoroughly that not a nuance was lost. On her part, Yvette fell thoroughly in love with Sweden and Norway. She marveled at the grandeur of the scenery, the well-scrubbed look of the cities, the wholesome sanity and *joie de vivre* of the people. At Oslo, which she now visited for the first time, she was met by her impresario "the amiable Rasmussen," and the distinguished comedian Knudsen of the National Theater, accompanied by a corps of photographers. A soirée of welcome had been prepared for her by a club of some two hundred painters, sculptors, musicians, actors, poets, and writers. At the Great Royal Theater where she played, her inscribed photograph was added to those of the beloved performers who had preceded her on those boards—Bernhardt, Croizette, Reichenberg, the Coquelins, Mounet Sully, Christine Nilson, Duse; ovation followed ovation, until at the end of the tour Rasmussen flung both arms about his star, in his enthusiasm over her conquest of his countrymen.

The following year Yvette's literary career was furthered by the publication of *L'Art de chanter une chanson,* a French translation of *How to Sing a Song,* first seen in New York in English in 1918. While some French reviewers thought this work a fitting supplement to *La Chanson,* the distinction of the author lending it a compelling interest, the discriminating Fréjaville found in it "paradoxical counsels, which are truths for Yvette only and dangerous snares for others," and ventured a minority opinion:

> None more than I admires the finesse, skill, *verve spirituelle,* or dramatic power . . . which the great artist Yvette Guilbert displays before us in each of her songs. But I believe that what she does is so unique and personal that any artist who risks following her example deceives himself irremediably.

Earlier, in 1926, in an article entitled "The Hundred Faces of a Comedienne," Yvette had tried, or pretended to try, to explain her use of her mask, the face. The limitless number of facial transformations, without benefit of make-up, which audiences witnessed as she changed from character to character, night after night, song after song, invariably gave rise to the gasp of astonishment: "How *does* she do it?" It was a question Yvette always professed to be more than willing to answer, perhaps because it gave her opportunity to ridicule the typical actress who in a lifetime, as Yvette loved to gibe, would be quite satisfied to appear in hundreds of roles with only one face. She found it distressing that even such an artist as Bernhardt would play

Joan of Arc or Saint Thérèse with the face of the Lady of the Camellias. The answer to the question, "What then does one do about the face?" she declared was very simple. "My little glory," she wrote demurely in this article, "will be to have opened and shown the road to follow . . . creative thought is the only thing that matters."

Very simple indeed.

For the Schillers the decade of the 20's had brought a variety of activity but a monotony of reward. The financial pinch never let up. To make both ends meet, there had had to be the continual swallowing of pride: the return to the variety show, or the occasional role in some inconsequential revue. One day in January, 1928, in front of the Bobino Music Hall in the Rue de la Gaîté—an old hall of a less-than-chic district lately rejuvenated and aspiring to elevation in tone—posters might have been seen announcing: "*La grande divette Yvette Guilbert dans ses chansons.*"

"Yvette Guilbert—it can't be true," remarked one couple as they sauntered in.

But it was true. There she was, past her sixtieth year, elaborately featured in a garish Loie-Fulleresque, sunset-vivid effect of crimson and yellow lights played against a gold curtain. The atmosphere of the hall was chokingly thick with tobacco smoke, and before she began to sing, she stopped the orchestra and held up her hand to the audience. At once a stilly silence fell. "*Mes enfants,*" she chided gently, "if you thought about the women who come to sing to you, you would throw away your cigarettes." Away went the cigarettes.

As the war had interrupted her appearances in Germany, so it had also in England, and it was not until 1928 that her visits there were resumed. That June, in a series of recitals at the Arts Theatre Club, Londoners had the opportunity of seeing their old favorite for the first time in thirteen years, and again, as on the Scandinavian trip, Yvette worried acutely over her loss of youth. Again she need not have.

I fancied I was forgotten, but in June 1928 I found again the success of thirty years before! My sixty-three years took nothing away from the first impression, and journalists, critics, and audiences of the new generation verified the approbation of thirty years ago. . . . I was enormously touched . . . to find the younger generation coming and coming again to my sixteen recitals, and, just as in the old days, writing to me in enthusiastic strains such as a woman whose youth has gone had ceased to expect. For so many of us, success turns away from faded faces, and talent bleeds to find itself buried alive before the body's death.

Yvette does not exaggerate in respect to her critical reception. Said the *Times:*

> She is at once music and the musician; an instrument that plays with exquisite skill upon itself. There comes on to the small stage ... a woman no longer young. . . . She is draped in voluminous shimmering robes; a figure of seemingly no particular presence or vital glow. But then she smiles and instantly life flows into the picture; she speaks and there radiates forth a personality of infinite variety ... in *Dites moi si je suis belle* she exploits the eternal feminine of the coquette with such ageless success that you do not merely forget the crude fact of her actual tale of years—they simply have no existence.

While she was in London on this visit, Yvette was invited to lunch with the George Bernard Shaws, whom she had not seen since she last lunched at their house in 1914. Yvette's acquaintance with Shaw dated back, of course, even further than 1914, for it was in 1894, when she made her maiden voyage across the Channel, that Shaw, then a music critic, had first seen her and recognized her genius.

> If I had known his disposition better then, how I should have feared that there was irony concealed behind so much cordiality! Nowadays we always look for leg-pulling at the back of Bernard Shaw's seriousness. At a later date I twice had the honour of lunching at his house. . . . He made a delightful host, distinguished and simple. . . .
>
> Shaw's eye is quite different when he is listening from what it is when he himself is speaking. His whole face also changes. His faun-like aspect disappears when he is attentive to the speaker, his mobility of expression is strangely held in check; it is like a mask he quickly takes off and puts on again at will, for when we were having coffee in the little drawing-room he planted himself with his back to the fireplace and, face visibly ready to amuse us and lips quivering with fun, threw at us quips of which he made himself the willing target. . . .
>
> His bellicose intelligence, which misses no contemporary happen-

ing and attacks every stupidity, fills me with delight! I adore people who find everything wrong—they are the only people capable of helping to do everything better. . . .

What is amusing in Bernard Shaw is that you can feel that he is amusing himself, enjoying himself over himself. I do like that. The rebel turn of his disposition predisposes him to farce; he is a comedian, a very great comedian who gets a lot of fun out of his part. . . .

Bernard Shaw, of you I preserve a gay memory—and a proud memory too—of having come in contact with your superb intelligence, and having divined beneath your high-handed effronteries your jarred sensitiveness, all your human heartburning at seeing humanity still so stupid and pitiful!

In the late 20's, with smart theaters moving west, the old Eldorado, scene of Yvette's earliest *caf'-conc'* adventures, wore a neglected air and was attracting only working-class audiences. Though in the same vicinity La Scala had continued to lure the top-hat crowd, Eldorado patrons were the simplest of souls, laborers in blouses, puffing on dirty pipes, their caps glued to their heads, with here and there in the auditorium a baker's dozen of grubby housewives, or pairs of young lovers, arms entwined.

But one night late in 1928 a number of top hats and fur evening wraps might have been seen mingling with the greasy caps. The bill at the Eldorado was nothing more than the opening of another routine operetta, *La Hostellerie de vertu,* by Jean Guitton and Henri Verdun, and it was not until late in the evening that the regular patrons came to realize why the top hats were there. In the revue, in a minor role, had been announced a player who was supposed to resemble Madame Yvette Guilbert. Somewhere in the second act, however, when the exigencies of the plot had left this character alone on stage, the lady, dropping her disguise, revealed herself as the authentic Yvette.

The surprise this appearance caused touched off such wild rounds of hand clapping and foot stamping that the show was literally stopped. For moments Yvette stood in the center of the stage, waiting for quiet, while the storm of applause went on and on, her eyes as usual beginning to overflow with gratitude at such a demonstration of affection. Finally she stepped forward.

"*Quelle émotion!*" she began hesitatingly. "*Quelle émotion, mes enfants——*"

Her voice broke; she could say no more. But it was enough for the simple hearts and hard palms before her. Until nearly midnight, when the Paris subways closed, top hats and greasy caps alike were kept tossing in the smoke-filled old Eldorado. "With almost all her old verve, her amazing ability to create a whole scene with a crook of her thumb, with a phrase half sung, half spoken from the corner of her mouth, the famous diseuse went through her famous repertory. . . . It was the same Yvette, . . . the same irresistible way of giving the final fillip . . . by jerking the culminating word forcibly from the corner of her carmine mouth, her expression remaining ridiculously serious as her listeners nearly split their sides with laughter."

The operetta was never finished, but nobody seemed to notice.

By now it began to be clear that Yvette Guilbert had achieved simultaneously two existences—one in her living self and the other in her legend. Louis Léon-Martin, in his book *Le Music Hall et ses figures,* published in 1928, could say nostalgically of the legend: "She is the old La Scala, the *caf'-conc',* the Lautrec poster, the delicious, careless and lighthearted era of the end of The Boulevard, the vogue of Montmartre . . . of dying Bohemia, the era when, to be an artist or a poet, one had to drink his half dozen pernods every night, the era of the Prince of Wales, of the Chat Noir and Maurice Donnay."

By 1929 still another autobiographical document by Madame Guilbert had been offered to the Paris public—*La Passante émerveillée. The Astonished Passer-by,* however, is a book subtly different in tone from its predecessors, one which leaves the reader with the impression that in spite of all the piquant observations it contains and the warm-hearted expressions of love of life and humanity, the voice that speaks is that of an embittered woman. It is a book in which for the first time may be fully measured the depth of the author's resentment and scorn of practically every aspect of America. In it Yvette remembers with malice her American experiences, particularly those with financiers, every one of whom she found worthless in promises, full of "sublime bluff," and reeking in vulgarity. Almost half of the book is given over to these stinging reflections. The other half offers impressionistic recollections of her tours, country by country—England, Belgium, Holland, Denmark, Sweden, Norway, Switzerland, Germany, Austria, Hungary, Czechoslovakia, Poland, Russia, Roumania, Italy, Greece, Egypt, the Near East, Spain, Portugal, Algiers. It is a dizzying record, even more in what it suggests than in what it states; in geographical scope alone outlining a breadth of professional travel such as few singers have ever equaled. In it, says Legrand-Chabrier, Yvette stands revealed as more than French. She had long been, he says, "the *grande dame* of the French *chanson* of all ages"; now she stands pre-eminently also as "European."

All in all, ever since that first controversial preface to Bac in 1896, Yvette had kept her name so actively before the reading public, as well as the theater-going public, than no one could have been much surprised when on October 14, 1929, the Société des Gens de lettres rather tardily got around to electing her to membership. As this membership was ordinarily the first title to which a literary beginner might aspire, and as Madame Guilbert, besides her many magazine articles and book prefaces, had already a very sizable list of book titles to her credit (in French, *La Vedette*, 1902; *Les Demi-vieilles*, 1903; *La Chanson de ma vie*, 1927; *L'Art de chanter une chanson*, 1928; *La Passante émerveillée*, 1929; English versions in *Struggles and Victories*, London, 1910, and *How to Sing a Song*, New York, 1918; a German translation of *La Vedette* and both English and German translations of *La Chanson* and numerous edited works of song collections, such as Heugel had published)—in view of all these accomplishments, to many observers the Society's election must have seemed long overdue.

Only recently she had had occasion to congratulate Louis de Robert, and from the heart, it goes without saying, when he received his red ribbon. Louis, still writing from his invalid's room in Sannois, had been through the years the pattern of industry that Yvette had always urged upon him in those days of their "affair"; since the war, producing a book almost yearly. His personal life, too, had not been without incident. Only a few years before, he had met Jeanne Humbert, when he was fifty-three and she was twenty-one, and from that moment his letters to Paul Faure had been embellished with romantic confidences. He was frantically in love; he knew it was crazy; he lived in dread of his beloved mother's death and the thought of being left alone. There was opposition to the match; the marriage would have to be in secret. Unexpectedly, however, the opposition was withdrawn.

As Louis had anticipated, it was an emotional catastrophe for him when in August, 1929, his mother died. Fortunately the marriage with Jeanne had taken place by that time; fortunately, too, there had been compensation in the form of other honors added to that of the red ribbon: being photographed by the New York *Times,* for example, on the occasion of receiving the Lasserre Prize in literature.

More pride-swallowing followed for Yvette in January of 1929, when it was necessary to play a return engagement in the Bobino, the program another one of those attempts then so popular in Paris to revive the spirit of the old *caf'-conc'*. Between the clowns and the card tricks, Yvette made her appearence, and whenever she stepped on stage there would fall throughout the house that absolute, breathless silence of anticipation that is for the performing artist the most precious and delicate homage.

In May, at the Theatre Marigny, a revue entitled *À la Mode de chez nous* was reported in English and United States papers as well as Parisian. Of Yvette's two scenes in this trifle, one was thought to have been "lugged in," merely to afford the star a chance to sing old favorites. But in the other she scored. Here she played a fatuous eighteenth-century marquise, "rich, elderly, raddled, painted, but in her glass, blinded by vanity, she still sees herself as twenty. The Marquise believes that her vulgar fiancé loves her for herself; chance reveals him after the lady's money-bags. . . . Hiding her face, the Marquise staggers from [behind] the screen, where she has overheard the truth, and collapses into a chair, while through the mirror, still elderly but beautiful in the simplicity of her face, steps the woman's true image. . . . At this moment Madame Guilbert looks startlingly like Ellen Terry twenty years ago."

About this time photographs began to appear in American newspapers with captions heralding a projected return of Madame Guilbert to the Land of the Dollar. The announcement, following as closely as it did on the publication of the scorching *La Passante,* lends itself to only one explanation: that, despite her open detestation of Americans, Yvette would bow again to financial inducements.

But the project did not materialize. Perhaps because of something very unexpected—an economic phenomenon commonly referred to subsequently in the Land of the Dollar as The Great Depression.

Chapter 13

It must not be supposed, however, that by the dawn of the decade of the 30's Madame Guilbert's professional life had been reduced merely to music halls and *boui-bouis*. Such engagements Yvette considered only potboiling interludes between her larger concert commitments, the tours that since the renewal of her contacts in Germany in 1926, had been taking her again yearly throughout Europe. The woman who had come back from the United States in 1922, defeated, almost empty-handed, to begin life anew at fifty-seven, was once more an international prestige attraction.

In 1928 Max had written to Emily Gresser: "The life of an artist is a frightful struggle and requires an immense physical effort. And perhaps my wife masters them both because I am helping her with all my courage and all my efforts." An examination of a typical year of this period will bear out the truth of Max's statement.

In 1930, for example, after the usual series at the Salle Gaveau in January and February, Yvette was off on a circuit that whirled her from Barcelona to Budapest, to Vienna and Berlin. In May she was again at the Gaveau; in June in London. A month's cure in August at Bad Kissengen, Germany, was followed by a series of thirty concerts between October 13 and December 13 in Brussels, Copenhagen, Stockholm, Berlin, Dresden, Leipzig, Munich, Vienna, Budapest, Prague, Geneva, Lausanne. And still, to critics' never-ending astonishment, she was artistically what she had always been, "queen of French song," despite time, despite changes in public tastes. ". . . like Rachel, Sarah, and the Duse and like the saints whom we honour with only one name—Yvette is a whole epoch. . . . Her performance of 'Je m'embrouille' is, like Duse in 'Ghosts,' Mary Garden as Melisande, and Massine in 'The Three-Cornered Hat,' one of the things I shall never forget," said a reporter of her London engagement that year.

In Paris, too, the appearances in the Salle Gaveau in one new song series after another, under varying rubrics, drawn from her treasure store of the Moyen Âge, were prestige occasions. *"Notre grande Yvette,"* she was beginning to be called; "probably the most powerful actress we have," one critic affirmed.

Even her song collection itself had attained fame—more than eighty thousand original texts, some dating from the sixth century. From every corner of France they had been garnered and more were constantly being added, including discoveries as they came to light in the Vatican library. Only the scholarly M. Bédier could boast a larger trove. J. Delini, writing of the collection in *Quotidien,* begs his readers, however, not to speak of it as archives, but as a monument to Yvette's authority. On her writing table M. Delini was shown a letter in which some unknown inquirer was being given priceless information concerning songs of the Court of 1686—off-color quatrains written by courtesans, courtiers, abbés, for intimate royal suppers. Not half a dozen persons in France could have answered that inquirer. Unhappily, however, there is evidence that, whenever she contemplated the truly magnificent proportions of her library of *chansons,* Yvette suffered from a sense of futility. "The only sorrow of my life is that, when I am dead, nothing will be left of all this. I have spent my life collecting all these works and saving them from oblivion. I have consecrated my talent to interpreting them lovingly. I have tried hard to interest artists in this difficult art. But our century lacks sensibility —the sacred fire."

As to monuments, Yvette had already been memorialized in marble, in a statue of Song in the Paris Hôtel de Ville, concerning which Raymond Escholier noted in *Le Petit Journal:*

> If tomorrow anyone should want to rear a monument to the French chanson, I know well what face that statue should have; the face of Yvette Guilbert. Moreover, the statue already exists, and it is a masterpiece, but unfortunately inaccessible to the greatest number. To the admirable figure of Song executed for the state dining room of the Hôtel de Ville, the old master Dalou has given the exact features of Guilbert. . . . I ask only that this be removed from its shadowy niche and installed in broad daylight in some garden in Montmartre, or Belleville, full of the songs of birds, of midinettes, and children.

She had aspired to be Song itself, *Soir* had said. A pity that M. Escholier's plea was disregarded.

Another activity of this crowded year today seems slightly moonstruck. The cult of the *chanson,* and her proselytizing zeal for it, prompted Yvette that spring to don her black gloves as a Crusader might his armor and to found what she hoped would become a Movement, enlisting to her ends the aid of Jules Levy, president of the literary Club des Hydropathes of *fin-de-siècle* fame. The project, which she called *La Boîte aux gants noirs,* would function through monthly luncheon meetings designed to revive and popularize the antique Norman custom of singing old *chansons* at table on festal occasions. At the fraternal *agapes* of *La Boîte,* members were to be encouraged to burst forth, solo or chorus at will, somewhere between the pear and the cheese—*la chanson au dessert,* as it was termed. The practice, Yvette claimed, would relax twentieth-century tensions and recapture the lost lightheartedness of a gayer and more innocent past.

330

If one wonders at the May madness that inspired such a scheme, one must also remember Yvette's overpowering sense of commitment, her almost monomaniac urgency to propagandize. The very justification of her life work was at stake in the winning of converts to her specialty. She may also have hoped it would prove a counteroffensive against jazz. As pathetically as Dame Partington, she had taken broom against this wave of the future, and her bitter scorn of "the American music," as she called it, was to become more and more evident through the years. It is no surprise surely to learn that the scheme failed to catch on. As the past has always sensibly declined recapture, the Movement never really moved.

In 1930 there were also new literary efforts. In that year the Paris *Soir* began publishing a signed column entitled *Guilbertinages,* which was to run intermittently for several years. In this, Yvette commented on the contemporary scene, reminisced, or prophesied, as the spirit dictated; by turns chatty, biting, opinionated, learned, mocking, indignant, but always pungent. Articles and anecdotes range from how Paris mobs may be manipulated to how Paris streets were named, century by century; gibes on the new art of renting anything, that permitted four-flushing hostesses to flaunt changes of jewels, silver, *point de Venise,* tapestries, servants, for each dinner or reception; reflections on the coquetry of men's beards; the ways of bargain sales; France's neglect in wooing American tourists; the obsequies of Maréchal Joffre as contrasted with those of Molière and the all-but-forgotten composer Grétry; the new sport of gliders; a current craze to secure the autograph of a certain Prague executioner "hot from murder" (there was a superstition that to be parent or friend of a hangman was assurance against hell-flames; in Paris, in 1894, Jean Lorrain had seen lace handkerchiefs dipped in blood from the guillotine at La Roquette); eugenics by castration (what a monotonous world, Yvette conjectured, if one were surrounded exclusively by intelligent and normal beings—surely God creates contrasts for His amusement); vignettes on abortions; modern scientists as engineers of death—creator-destroyers; the inherent lubricity of the French as revealed in their centuries of scandalous songs. Whatever caught her imagination her quick pen flung on paper.

Meantime, in his quiet home, 19 Berggasse, Vienna, Dr. Sigmund Freud was pursuing the uneven tenor of his suffering days and ways, carrying on activities to the limited extent permitted by his health.

Eva Rosenfeld was still studying with him; was, in fact, undergoing analysis. In 1930 he had spent fruitless weeks in Berlin for treatment, and it was during this period that he had had his first exposure to the nascent philosophy of Nazism, a political doctrine which his sanity had not been able to take seriously; which he had eventually dismissed as out of character for Germans and Germany. "A nation that produced Goethe could not possibly go to the bad," was his final judgment.

Then one day in February, 1931, there arrived from 120 Rue de Courcelles an effusive and excited letter; the good Queen herself never underlined with more abandon. In a forthcoming book Yvette wished to define herself.

From the beginning of her career the inexplicable quality of her genius had tantalized observers, one after another attempting in vain to account for her effects. Only recently J. Kessel, writing in *Gringoire*, had been another to throw up his hands over the impossibility of analyzing her art: of explaining, for example, how, from a little *chansonnette* of the eighteenth century, this woman could create such a tragic, desperate, unforgettable chant as he had just listened to; except indeed to explain by paradox—by referral to the unexplainable —to that *"indicible démon"* which, ever since the Dionysiacs, had seemed to take possession of all who make true theater.

Now Yvette, who had decided to try to solve the mystery herself, wished to test her theories in the light of the new science of psychology:

February 28

My dear Professor

I am going to prepare a new book to follow "my memoirs," which will be titled

Mes lettres d'amour

—what I myself call *my* letters of love, and which come from those who help in my concert work. I shall put together these numerous letters from the public telling me "their impressions." I would combine my correspondences with some very important *poets interpreted* by me—some Parisian celebrities of my youth. In the preface that I am preparing for my book, I am trying

to *"explain myself myself"*

I am attempting to reveal my system: *effacement of my own per-*

sonality in order to take on all those others whom I personify among the characters of my songs—now I ask you, my dear professor, *to tell me,* whether what I say of myself has been experienced by you? What impression have you experienced in listening to me? In the prologue I am sending you do you find that I am *fair with myself?* Or am I *fooled by myself?*

Four lines in German (my husband will translate them) will make me wild with joy.

My hands in yours, faithfully

Yvette Guilbert

To this plea for professional opinion Dr. Freud replied promptly and generously, not limiting himself to four lines:

Vienna IX, Berggasse 19
8. 3. 1931

Dear Friend

I wish I might be near when your dear husband translates this letter for you, for because of my bad health I was able to profit so little from your last visit to Vienna.

It is very fine to learn that you want to write once more something about yourself, and if I understand correctly, to reveal the secret of your work and your success and you imagine that your technique consists of setting aside your own personality in order to replace it by the character you wish to present, and you ask that I give my opinion as to whether this process is improbable and whether it is the case with you.

I wish I knew more about the process and I would certainly then tell you all I know, but not knowing much about all that, I beg you to be content with the following observations: I believe that what seems to you to be the psychological mechanism of your art has been often, even generally accepted. But this theory of the displacement of the proper personality and its replacement by the personality to be presented has never entirely satisfied me. It says so little, it does not teach how one can do it, and above all it does not explain why this [end] to which all artists apparently aspire is more successfully reached by one performer than another.

I theorize rather the additional influence of a mechanism quite opposite, which the proper personality has in no way dismissed but which springs from it; for example, from faculties unde-

333

veloped, suppressed desires are made use of for the presentation of the imagined character. It is thus that they manifest themselves and give to the character the appearance of real life.

This is less simple than the transparency of your own ego which you put forth.

I would be very curious to know whether you experience anything of this other situation.

In any case it is only one contribution to the solution of the great secret as to why we shiver before *La Soûlarde* and answer "yes" with all our hearts to the question "Dites-moi si je suis belle?"— But one knows so little!

In affectionate remembrance. . . .

Yours

Freud

In reply, Yvette vehemently, almost incoherently, resisted the opinion she had solicited:

March 14

My dear great friend

Thanks for your letter! *No,* I do not believe that what *comes out of me* on stage is "the surplus" suppressed and made use of, for if life has made me understand many things I am still ignorant of so much! However, I would know how to imagine without having *"experienced."* I could be the Tsarina, the Tsar, Saint Francis of Assisi if a *text were given me* in order to express them,—I would feel the *physical* side because of my habit of carrying over from my *brain* to my *flesh* everything that I want my public to see.

It is by my eyes that I learn most about the *lives of others*—to me my eye is the great revealer—I see—I think—I decide—all this *very quickly*—My personal knowledge includes all human beings who have known *poverty, love, illness,* and all the struggles to overcome these three dangers—I do not possess all the virtues, but neither do I have all the human vices, but my sensitiveness, my painter's eye, help me *to divine everything* about what I do not know and *to reveal* everything I do know. I believe, myself, on the contrary, that it is what we have not yet been that makes it possible *in art* for us *to become that* for *the public.* Artists are full of electricity. . . . For example, the atmosphere indicates to me *physically* the coming of snow, or rain. A face tells me sympathy for me, or the opposite—

I *sense* very readily at the *approach* of a person (whether he is *sincerely* my *friend*—or simply amiable. My soul (what I believe to be my soul) prompts me always to want *to be beautiful,* it is a form of pride? perhaps! But I *have cultivated it in myself* and I try *always* to tear out the human and habitual nastinesses from *that soul*—I have never had vices—I have had some meannesses and weaknesses from which I have suffered which when I have to *interpret* them in others, the heroes of my songs, I have felt a sense of pity mixed with a little scorn and *it is of myself that I am thinking* when I express a sadness, for both cause and effect—I am often quite bare on stage, and I offer myself unclothed of all lies—my heart is bare—my soul—my spirit—my temperament—my character— stamped with the sins of the universe, I add those of others to my own, *I adapt myself to them.* But they are not "suppressed"? No! No! they were never mine? I become on stage what I want to become *by a force of the artist's cerebral will,* and if I succeed in being *Beautiful* (as you say) when I sing: Dites-moi si je suis belle—it is because my *brain* knows what I lack

                    to be that

and I create "the illusion."

Ah, well . . . all this at bottom is such a mystery, is it not, my dear and wise friend . . . ? We are animals, very complicated and at the same time very simple. . . . *The great battle* is the search for *Happiness*—in *Truth,* and our follies are only our rages over finding only *Lies!!* For *myself* it was the torment *of my life*—Truth, Truth, and again Truth, I wanted only Truth and I have found only Truth —here and there—and which lasts so short a time.—I was born for the "*Eternities*"—the absolutes—*exaggerations in everything!*

And human beings are so poorly endowed. . . . I have known how to make my happiness with what they have given me however—To you, my friend Freud, all my friendship, loyal and firm

                                        Yvette Guilbert

Protestations as jumbled as these shed little light; seem to intensify rather than dissipate the mystery of the uniquely Guilbertian creative impulse. One point seems evident, however: that Yvette prefers to to the psychological theory of "suppressed desires" something akin to parapsychological; she "divines" through "sensitiveness"—at least, in part—what she does not know.

On receipt of her impassioned scrawl, Dr. Freud found himself, as he humorously expressed it in his reply of March 26, enjoying the "very interesting experience" of defending his theories to "Madame Yvette and Uncle Max":

Actually, I don't intend to yield much beyond the confession that we know so little. Just recently, for instance, Charlie Chaplin was in Vienna; I almost caught sight of him, but it was too cold for him and he left in a hurry. He is undoubtedly a great artist—although he always plays one and the same part, the weak, poor, helpless clumsy boy for whom life turns out all right in the end. Now do you think he has to forget his own self in order to play this part? On the contrary, he invariably plays only himself as he was in his grim youth. He cannot get away from these impressions and even today he tries to compensate himself for the humiliation and deprivation of that time. He is of course an especially simple, transparent case.

The theory that the achievements of artists are conditioned internally by their childhood impressions, vicissitudes, repressions and disappointments, has already clarified many things for us, and we therefore think highly of it. I once dared to tackle one of the very greatest of all, Leonardo da Vinci, of whom unfortunately too little is known. I was able at least to point out that "The Virgin and Saint Anne," which you can see any day in the Louvre, couldn't be understood without some knowledge of Leonardo's peculiar childhood....

Now you may point out that Madame Yvette doesn't play just one part, that she plays with equal mastery all kinds of characters: saints, sinners, prostitutes, the righteous, criminals and *ingénues*. This is true and testifies to an unusually rich and adaptable psychic life. But I wouldn't hesitate to trace back this whole repertoire to experiences and conflicts of her early youth. It is tempting to continue on this subject, but something holds me back. I know that unwarranted analyses call forth antagonism, and I don't want to do anything that could disturb the warm sympathy that dominates our relationship.

There is no evidence that Yvette, with all her veneration for her "*grand savant*," ever subscribed to the Freudian explanation of her unique abilities, though from time to time she continued to puzzle over them. "When I sing the vices of my life," she once said, "I have

336

the feeling that I am whipping them, that I am freeing the national reputation of the transgressions of a minority."

Besides a moral therapy, she also theorized for a while that a mental therapy, potent but dangerous, might possibly be found in her art. One day not long after the Freud exchange, an alienist invited Yvette to sing at his mental hospital and afterward to lunch with him and six friends. The other guests were introduced as a naval lieutenant, an engineer, an obstetrician, a well-known horsewoman, a violinist, and the cashier of the hospital. Conversation was urbane and lively. The lieutenant wanted Yvette to be taken on a tour of the hospital after lunch to meet the inmates. He especially wanted her to see the sixty-year-old woman who thought she was a fish and swam on the pebbles in the courtyard. "She is so funny, Madame Yvette, you would die laughing." The violinist, a very intense young woman, talked incessantly of Sarasate, her teacher, and her planned tour of Spain. "I am never separated from my Stradivarius. I keep it with me always. The doctor will show it to you later; it is in his closet." When lunch was over, an intern appeared. "It is two o'clock, sir," he said to the naval lieutenant, "and your ship will soon be leaving." The lieutenant rose immediately, courteously kissed Yvette's hand in farewell, and departed smiling. A moment later another messenger entered. The engineer was urgently needed; a ceiling had just fallen down. After the engineer had made his excuses and withdrawn, a nurse came in and said to the horsewoman: "Your horses, Madame, are getting very restless," and the lady left. Then the doctor opened his closet and took out a large red-leather case which he handed to the violinist: "Here is your Stradivarius, Mademoiselle." The young lady opened the case and looked at the instrument almost piously. "How beautiful it is! What color, what tone! Touch it, Madame—Sarasate will be jealous."

By now the realization that she had been lunching with inmates of the hospital had dawned on Yvette, and she was dumbfounded. What serenity in these poor creatures' demeanor! All had been playing the roles they would have wished to play in real life, and, their goals achieved in fancy, they were satisfied and modest.

The incident was disturbing and lingered in her memory. The insane, she seemed to see, impersonated one life, assumed one mask, lived one delusion. But she lived a hundred lives in her songs, putting on one mask after another. Was this playing dangerously close to insanity? Or did it save her from insanity? Was art the savior of man?

337

Without it would the world go mad? Sanity is a fragile thing, she saw. As for art, if she had respect for it as a healer, an ameliorator, conversely might she also see possible danger in it as a promoter of delusions, a distorter of reality?

It was an enigma that she could not at the moment resolve.

The year 1932 brought into Yvette's life a new friend in the person of a new accompanist, the talented Mademoiselle Irene Aïtoff. As Mademoiselle Aïtoff remained for the next seven years Yvette's only accompanist, rehearsing at 120 Rue do Courcelles regularly at least three times a week, she had opportunity to observe closely Yvette's habits of study. For Yvette was still the sedulous student. With her the gospel of work had never been idle mouthing; work was unalloyed joy. With a repertoire by then so large that she could easily have continued her concerts to the end of her life without the addition of another song, it was nevertheless psychically impossible for her to halt in the unresting search for new light.

> When she started to learn a song [writes Mlle. Aïtoff], she would memorize it by singing it with the words in front of her. Then, when memory was sure, she would search for different effects and colorings. Once, after two weeks of work on a song, she said to me: "I am beginning to be moved, so that means it's coming along." When there was a change of thought in a song, she would pause, so that inwardly she would have time to feel what was coming next. . . . When she sang *Malbrough,* she saw a crowd at the windows, in the streets, who accompanied Malbrough as he left, and she would wave her handkerchief as if to signify: "Come—look! He is leaving!" It was extraordinary how she made one actually see the crowd.

Years earlier, speaking of Yvette's consecration to work, Marcel Prévost had said: "This conscience to be always doing better, this rage for artistic effort, has been shown by many great writers, but in the theatre it is rare. Mademoiselle Yvette Guilbert is a great moral example."

Though Yvette was by this time no stranger to honors, the one decoration she had most deeply desired and even publicly demanded had still been withheld from her. Now that citadel of resistance was to crumble when, on October 29, 1932, M. de Monzie, Minister of

National Education, officially pinned on her breast the emblem of the Legion of Honor.

Around her for the presentation had gathered close friends and admirers, many of years' standing, grown gray in devotion. The charming Rachilde was there, to witness her symbolic and surpassingly graceful gesture of a few years ago now realized; dear old Léon Xanrof, of course, and the faithful colleague Madame Dussane; André Antoine and Pierre Brisson; Francis de Croisset, Pierre Lalo, and a host of other celebrities.

The press burbled pleasantly over the event, recounting to newer generations the great Guilbert's legendary hours of hunger as a young girl, as well as those magical *fin-de-siècle* days when astonished Parisians first began to recognize that what they were witnessing at the Concert Parisien was not only the birth of a new star but that of a new art as well. Character, too, was noted. Madame Guilbert had always been *une honnête fille,* "a decent girl." Her personal life had been *toute unie, toute simple, toute pure,* one lived in the broad light of day, in which scandalmongers had found nothing to cluck over. Significantly, the word "grandeur" occurred, and "generosity."

"Maman aurait été bien contente," Yvette was heard to murmur.

The entire year of 1932, in fact, was one in which the press showed even more than average interest in *notre grande Yvette.* In the many interviews that appeared, her history was rehearsed again and again and her art analyzed and reanalyzed. Her views, too, were often respectfully solicited.

Yvette, who held positive opinions on practically every subject and enjoyed nothing better than an opportunity to express them, minced no words in her replies. On the subject of France she was particularly blunt. She had had to listen, she said, in the course of her foreign travels, to many animadversions on her country with which she had been reluctantly forced to agree. France, it was charged, was letting itself turn to ugliness; pride in beauty was being lost. As to Paris, why was the city so ill-lighted at night? Nothing more sinister than the Trocadéro quarter, and as to the Tuileries, who would dare venture there? Was the study of mythology really going to be struck out of French school curricula? Why, mythology was the alphabet of the antique world! Without it how could future generations even discuss antique works of art? France was one of the richest nations in the world, but look, she cried, at its ruined laboratories and discouraged scholars! And where was the cultural life of the provincial cities—Chartres, Rouen, Albi, Lyon? Here, in musty cafés, young men already old were finding today nothing better to do than push dominoes by the hour, or shuffle dirty cards. The provinces stank with ennui.

There was undeniable bitterness in her cry from the heart that the art of the *chanson* could never be renewed in France without material support, both popular and governmental. A kind of temple was needed, where the *chanson* could be properly studied and presented, with orchestras of true musicians, not dance-hall performers. Further, period songs demanded period dress; and to be most profoundly, fully performed, choruses should be added. The *chanson* should not be considered an inferior art, but should rank with opera.

As to music-hall singers aspiring to this realm, most of these— sarcastically—would have to begin by learning to speak French. Hence a conservatory of the *chanson* would be useful. Why double —or triple—a single "l"? Why sound silent letters? As she talked, her voice vibrated with scorn.

For the comedienne as well as the diseuse [she said in defining her own art], the technique is the same. The science of speaking well demands the same care and study. To articulation and es- pecially to pure pronunciation . . . must be added the art of lighting up or blowing out the words, of plunging them into the shadow or the light, according to their sense, of lessening or enlarging them, caressing or biting them, sending them out or bringing them back, clothing them or stripping them bare, . . . in a word all that makes a text come alive, or die, or vibrate with force, color, style, elegance, or vulgarity . . . this is Diction!

In 1932, when Yvette and Max made their customary Central European safari—forty recitals this season—their itinerary included as always the many well-remembered trails leading through Germany, where again as always, in city after city, hearty *Auf Wiedersehens* echoed in their ears as they departed. Through German friends they gleaned that disturbing political changes were more and more evident in the name of National Socialism, but since to most Europeans poli- tics was a chronic malaise—and to the Schillers particularly a pro- found mystery—the situation did not actually alarm them. Certainly no one expected then that in hardly more than a year, on March 23, 1933, the course of history would be changed by the new Nazi party.

340

On that date, as events were to prove, a pliant and deluded Reichstag would vote dictatorial powers to a hitherto almost unknown leader, a house painter from Austria, an undersized little man with an absurd mustache and hot, fanatic eyes, behind which smoldered psychopathic hates.

Chapter 14

The black year of Hitler's accession to power saw no slackening in the pace at 120 Rue de Courcelles. In that year *Mes Lettres d'amour* appeared, its preface containing the disputed theories that had been the subject of Yvette's heated letters to Freud. Still stoutly sticking to her guns that the source of the mysterious powers animating her art was "effacement of my own personality in order to take on all those others whom I personify among the characters of my songs," Yvette gropingly attempted in this document to define her artistic technique:

To be no longer more than a heart that laughs and weeps, a soul that reveals to souls all their pains, joys, virtues, shams, and vices, and in order to do that, to juggle myself away, disappear, become the living mists of others of whom I sing, with here and there a return to myself when necessary. A quick sketch, a dash of the pen . . . but at my pleasure to force my hearers to forget me, to lose sight of me . . . I become the painter, the sculptor remaining behind his screen. . . .

It may have been disappointing to a few that the book, in spite of its teasing title, contained not one titillating reference to erotic adventure; that it was merely a collection of admiring letters from and reminiscences regarding a few critics and writers of varying degrees of prominence whom she had counted as friends at some time during her life—Jean Lorrain, Rollinat, Donnay, Laurent Tailhade, Henri Bauer, Francis Jammes, Paul Déroulède, Fagus, Pierre Louÿs, Jehan-Rictus, Loti, Xanrof. Those who rememebered and looked for Louis de Robert found only a casual allusion to him as "a friend of the family." Some might say that the emphasis of the book on personal tribute marks the work as that of an aging woman, whose mind was beginning to dwell on the glories of her youth.

In April Yvette presented what was variously titled a "musical comedy" and an "operetta," in which she ranked as librettist as well as star, with a miniature supporting cast of four, the music composed by Fernand Raphael. Either of the terms applied to the composition seems ambitious; probably the author herself was nearer right when she referred to *Madame Chiffon* as really no operetta at all, only an eighteenth-century chanson a little more developed than some. The negligible plot deals with an aging but still amorous modiste who is besieged by two suitors, one young, one not so young. But Madame is capricious; she loves to coquette. Finally she discusses the choice with her young niece Suzon. Shall it be Colin? Suzon sulks. Mathurin? Suzon's face lights up. Kindhearted Madame, therefore, maneuvers pretty Suzon into the arms of Colin and, with no more than a little shrug of resignation, accepts for herself the soberer Mathurin. The piece was only a trifle—one act in three tableaus—played before screens in the Salle Chopin, but the press made much of it.

"And she had already given nineteen concerts that season!" a reporter exclaimed, almost in unbelief that a woman in her sixties could compass even the repertoire such a schedule would presuppose, much less meet its physical demands.

She had also given a lecture of more than routine interest. In 1931 the fiftieth anniversary of the Chat Noir had been passed. "God created the world, Napoleon founded the Foreign Legion, but I made Montmartre," Rodolphe Salis once modestly put it, and Paris, in its nostalgic mood of the 30's, remembered this fact. Among the various programs celebrating the *cinquantenaire* of the fabled Chat Noir— although the cabaret itself had long since disappeared—was one offered by Yvette in March, 1933, an evening of her own reminiscences, punctuated by songs written by some of the distinguished members. To a generation of Pharaohs that knew not Joseph she related the history of the club's founding: how Rodolphe, originally an artist of sorts, one day suggested to Emile Goudeau and other members of the Club des Hydropathes, who used to meet informally for *soirées littéraires* in a little Latin Quarter café on Rue Cajas, that they join their membership with his own comrades of Montmartre, who were artists and musicians, and how when he opened his cabaret in its first quarters on Boulevard Rochechouart he found in a dusty corner a cast-iron black cat for which he named his enterprise. A marriage of the Latin Quarter and the Butte, Yvette called it, this merger of artistic and literary talent that was to dazzle Parisians with its novelty and

342

glitter. Often in the early days of the cabaret, when the evening was well advanced, the men would leave off their animated discussions and fall to singing old French *chansons*. Charles de Sivry, brother-in-law of Verlaine, would sit down to the piano, and Claude Debussy, in shirtsleeves, would conduct choruses with a tin fork. Such a roar of melody invariably attracted crowds outside in the street, who enjoyed lifting their voices to join in, to the stern disapproval of the gendarmerie.

Laughter at the Chat Noir, said Yvette, was a sort of cult. One held to it religiously; *l'esprit* was the God one wished accessible to all. The laughter was of all tones and colors; *l'esprit* had its greater and lesser priests, and if Donnay was pope, the clerics of his entourage were nonetheless highly talented. In the second and more commodious quarters of the Chat Noir, on Rue Laval, someone painted on the wall a great black cat putting his paw on a startled and bristling goose, a composition which Jules Lemaître regarded as symbolic; the mischievous cat was *l'esprit,* the goose was the bourgeoisie. But the goose, Lemaître declared, was benefited by the cat, for "if the laughter of the Chat Noir has, as it is claimed, influenced the literature of its time, it has also created a humanity less sottish . . . in the choice of its pleasures."

Especially Yvette recalled the cabaret's entertainments and entertainers. A *première* at the Chat Noir ranked with one at the Théâtre Français, and on the nights when Donnay recited his poems illustrated on a screen, the silence was as deep as at Bayreuth on a Wagnerian evening. Like a litany, she recited the names of its famous habitués.

Astonishing, brilliant, beloved, long-vanished Bohemia!

Although her film career was brief and intermittent, Yvette nevertheless appeared in three roles of undoubted interest. In 1926 she had experimented in the silent movies by playing Marthe to Emil Jannings' Mephisto in the German Ufa production of *Faust,* which was widely shown in many countries. Less well known had been her first role as Biddy Mullens in *Les deux Gosses* (*Two Little Vagabonds*), directed by Louis Mercanton, in a story that had first been read in a book written by Pierre Decourcille and later seen in a dramatization by George Sims and Arthur Shirley. Also she had made a number of song shorts in France in the early years of sound.

Almost from the first, the film medium had been committed to youth and pulchritude as main requirements for starring roles. But Yvette had a missionary zeal for it as a means of bringing art to the masses and for herself was willing to accept unattractive character parts, to forego trappings, and even to submit to the most unflattering make-up for the sake of realism. The result was that in the film *Les deux Orphelines,* in the early 30's, her appearance dismayed both audiences and critics. In this story, already known in France, Germany, and the United States under various titles and in various versions, she played the role of Mother Frochard, a hideous and terrifying old creature. Dressed in loathsome rags, with stringy white hair, thick eyebrows, and piercingly evil eyes, Yvette presented the character as an out-and-out hag, a type she may well have encountered not infrequently during those bitter childhood days in the Rue du Temple.

The other sound film, *Les Pêcheurs d'Islande,* made at about the same time, had happier overtones. This was an adaptation of a novel by Pierre Loti, and hence for Yvette a labor of love. The filming itself, done on location in a Breton fishing village, was an exhilarating novelty, and in this picture the sympathetic starring role of the grandmother did not jar her admirers' nerves.

To a reporter who interviewed her during rehearsals of her first movie she admitted a lively curiosity about seeing herself in the finished product. And she also, a little wistfully, admitted more—the yearning every woman feels over that poignant irrecoverable, the girlish self:

> It's going to give me a shock to see myself walking, talking, playing, living on the screen. But ah—I would give a hundred—a thousand—a hundred thousand—I don't know what I wouldn't give—to see again, today, in a movie, the little debutante of the Divan Japonais.

In 1935 Londoners heard Yvette again, this time at Wigmore Hall. At least, a few of them did; public response was at first disappointing. Reviews were mixed. As to songs: "The voice may be as the singer confessed, hoarse, but how expressive.... It is a reflection upon the public taste that there should have been so many seats unoccupied at this rich feast." Comments on her Baudelaire lecture-recital, however, were less affirmative: "Baudelaire's complicated nature tempts all manner of explanations, ... Madame Guilbert's attempt to establish him ... as '*le poète théâtral,*' as a '*metteur-en-scène*' of genius had, however, been sensibly thought out; and though at the end we did not all share her view, we had heard not a few illuminating comments. . . . She read certain of the poems well, if not superlatively well; and she interpreted others, half in speech, half in song, over somewhat banal piano accompaniments in the manner of the 'melodrama.' In this manner 'Une Martyre' was made horrifyingly realistic, . . ."

Thus tepidly opened what was to prove an annual series of visits to London for the next several years. For London in the late 30's offered to the Schillers some of the family attraction formerly felt in Berlin and Vienna.

In 1936 Eva Rosenfeld and her husband, more politically aware than Yvette and Max, had wisely removed from Vienna to London. In Germany, in June, 1934, the first of Hitler's "blood baths," though conducted within the Nazi party, had given chilling augury of the future under Nazism. While the world, in fascination of disbelief, watched the Goebbels propaganda machine creating its new concept of a "master race," the Saar had been suavely recovered by plebiscite in 1935. By 1936 Germany, now arming to the teeth, had remilitarized the Rhineland. By then, too, anti-Semitism had become flagrant. Yet even so, many Jews, hoping against hope, held by lifelong ties, refusing to believe that the monstrous new doctrine of germanization could literally be as evil as it seemed, tended to linger on. Though Germany in European eyes had long been considered a dichotomous nation—on one side kindly, earnest, devoted to learning and the arts; on the other bullying, treacherous, and sadistic—the militarists, it was argued, had surely learned their lesson in 1918. At the beginning of the 30's, it had seemed to most observers that old hostilities were fading and that an atmosphere of internationalism, at least in cultural and educational areas, was becoming evident. Certainly no one was prepared for the sudden rearing into power in 1933 of the spirit of hypernationalism. Surely nothing so preposterous could be taken seriously. But by 1936 it could be, and by that time thousands of Jewish Germans, like Eva and her husband, had begun quietly to relocate outside the frontiers of madness.

For the next few brief years then, Eva and Yvette were able to meet regularly again, but under what changed conditions. As the newspaper-reading public saw Yvette in her many interviews, through the eyes of respectful and often bedazzled reporters, she was a legend, an international figure, a fixed proud star in France's firmament of artists. Magazine articles repeatedly depicted the scholarship, the

345

prodigies of physical energy expended in a multiplicity of forms: at home, the concerts ranging from music hall to Baudelaire, benefits, film roles, recordings, appearances before audiences of children in the new and much-touted children's theater movement; the constant addition of new repertoire; the flood of energy spilling over even into literary works and journalism; abroad, the continuing extensive itineraries.

But seen from back stage, as a woman, as Eva saw her now in London, that star of France, once so high in the fine old days, was showing alarming signs of sinking. Not only were audiences sometimes scanty, and thus finances; Yvette herself, writes Eva, was fighting her old enemy, rheumatism:

Her body was so tortured by arthritis by then that I had to push her upstairs and help her down. She had no longer the means to keep a dresser, so I flew behind the stage in the intervals to help her change her dresses. She was bathed in perspiration and exhausted beyond recognition. She crawled onto the stage, one might say. But as soon as she was out there, she sat in a swing and she was 15 years old. She sang, she was gay and she convinced us all.

The grim sight of empty seats began to plague her in Paris occasionally, too. In November of 1936, when the three knocks sounded backstage on opening night at the Théâtre Michel where Yvette was offering a series of *causeries,* there was only an embarrassing handful of an audience. Wearing the drop of blood of the Legion of Honor on her breast had not filled the house, nor even singing those incomparable verses of Murger for which Dumas once said he would exchange everything he had ever written:

> *Non, ma jeunesse n'est pas morte,*
> *Il n'est pas mort, ton souvenir,*
> *Et si tu frappais à ma porte,*
> *Mon coeur, Musette, irait t'ouvrir.*

Despite every discouragement, however, Yvette continued with the formidable itineraries. In 1937 she again covered Germany, Austria, the south of France, Belgium, Holland, the Scandinavian countries, and England. Apparently the days of the full house were not entirely over; attendance may be said rather to have become variable. As *Variety* laconically reported from The Hague on January 8, 1937: "Yvette Guilbert, French star, was a bad flop at Diligantia Hall. She had been here this summer and drew quite an audience, but this time got very few attendants."

But this season Londoners flocked when she appeared in Grotrian Hall, in spite of the fact that for the Verlaine recitals Yvette now had to seek vocal assistance. Since some of Verlaine's poems had inspired Fauré, Debussy, and Reynaldo Hahn to musical settings requiring a range that she could no longer command, she had had to introduce a younger voice, that of Mademoiselle Germaine Cernay.

The Baudelaire lecture, which Londoners had sniffed at the year before, was appraised in quite different vein by *L'Ere Nouvelle* when it was heard in Paris in 1937 in the Salle Chopin and later at the Sorbonne:

One went to the Salle Chopin a little out of curiosity. How would a music hall singer speak of a writer whom some people compare to a father of the church? Now Madame Yvette is as learned as penetrating. She made in her lecture three points:

The idea that many poems of Baudelaire suggest a stage set, so that one could say that this artist was a dramatic poet; the declaration that Baudelairian hysteria is not an indication of sexuality but hypersensitivity; and a corrosive and moving evocation of the life of Baudelaire.

So went the seesaw of opinion regarding Baudelaire. But no one denied the saltiness of her performance of Mrs. Peachum in a revival of *L'Opéra de Quat'Sous* at the Théâtre de l'Étoile that season.

Looking back to those crowded days of the '30s, a young lady named Sidonie Baba set down in the early 40's her earliest recollections of Yvette Guilbert. A late October sun was shining through the yellow taffeta draperies of the little salon in the Rue de Courcelles apartment when Sidonie, as a very frightened child, had first been brought into Yvette's presence. "Ah!" murmured Yvette sympathetically when she learned that the child was newly orphaned and saw tears trembling in her eyes. "Then I adopt her! She shall choose me for godmother. Kiss me, my godchild. I bring good luck. Let me present you to my husband."

The man who took the child's hand in his was smaller than Yvette, "as if to live better in her shadow." He had black eyes and white hair, and he smiled and looked at her closely; the child thought that he was wondering: "Will you love her enough to deserve her?"

On another afternoon, years later, when the grown-up Sidonie was calling to take tea with her "godmother," Yvette chatted confidentially about Max.

"He is a mother to me, that husband of mine. Look, he has been out of the house over half an hour. He said he had to buy something. He could have sent the maid, but no.—He's gone to buy *me* something!"

In a few moments the maternal Max returned, wearing a mysterious smile and keeping his hands behind his back. He did not know that the bunch of violets he was trying to hide was being clearly revealed by a mirror. Yvette and the girl exchanged smiling glances. "Oh, dear," Yvette sighed, "how I wish you had brought me a little bouquet of flowers!"

"*Le voilà!*" cried Max, delightedly producing his offering. "*Le voilà!*"

The somber implications of the recently conceived Berlin-Rome Axis became manifest to the world in March, 1938, when Mussolini allowed Hitler, in a surprise coup, to occupy Vienna. It was this coup that created a crisis in the life of Sigmund Freud.

Even as early as 1933 Freud had been advised to leave Vienna for France or Switzerland but had not been able to persuade himself that Nazism would ever present a serious threat to Austria. Besides, he was old and ill; he needed the medical attention he believed he could get nowhere else, and he feared finding himself penniless in a foreign country. Some of his family had transferred to London, and in 1937 Yvette had written of having been with them there. In fact, she and Max must have indicated at that time some passing thought of living in England themselves, for to her letter Freud had replied under date of December 19, 1937:

> ... What you wrote about your meeting with my children in London, I already knew, but it was indeed a pleasure to hear about it again from you, as well as to hear the news of your magnificent success and the hint of the possibility of your settling there. London society will most certainly receive you with open arms. ...

348

Another woman, with whom, as with Yvette, Freud had for some years enjoyed close, friendly association, was the Princess George of Greece. The Princess had been originally a patient of his and had later made psychoanalysis one of the main concerns of her life. Now, after the Vienna coup it was she who undertook to save her old friend from Nazi extinction.

Within a few days after the shouts of *Heil Hitler* had begun to resound in the cobbled streets of Vienna, the Princess set about the task of getting the Freuds out of Austria. Weeks of negotiation were required, however, even for a woman in her high position, assisted also as she was by American diplomatic intercession. The price demanded for release she promptly advanced. But there were continuing inquisitions, the threat of the concentration camp was never absent, and it was not until early in June that the feeble old man, his wife, and daughter Anna were finally able to board the Orient Express for Outside.

That night in Paris the Princess gave a reception in honor of the Freuds, at which the Schillers were present, and Dr. Ernest Jones, who had come over from England to escort the refugees to their destination, London. It was an occasion of exaggerated gaiety, with everyone reacting almost hysterically to the miraculous escape. In unexpurgated mood Yvette kept the dinner guests in gales of laughter by ribald stories one after another. It must have been an evening like the one Hesketh Pearson recalled at George Alexander's house in London: "I remember thinking afterwards that if her stories had been told by anyone else they would have been received in dead silence." When later in the evening Dr. Jones asked her to sing *Il était seul,* a particularly "ambiguous" song, as he terms it, she readily obliged, following it with the equally "ambiguous" *Elle avait le nombril en forme de cinq.*

How safe they all felt that evening, and how they must have thanked God for the security that would soon be theirs behind the impregnable Maginot line then under construction. There, everyone was saying, was a magnificent system of defense. When that buffer of fortification was completed, it would certainly guarantee every Frenchman against the knock in the night.

Notre grande Yvette! hundreds of times this affectionate term had been spoken or published in France during the decade of the 30's by a public that seemed to have entirely forgotten the innuendoes and accusations it had hurled at the same woman in 1914. What had once been the wasp waistline was now too, too solid flesh; the stark silhouette in green had given way to elderly shapelessness masked by fluttering mauve-and-silver draperies; the homely face was chiseled with cruelly deep lines; but what matter? At seventy-three *notre grande Yvette* had become an institution; she was now the grand old lady of song.

It is not clear to whom the revelation first came that in 1937 Yvette had been behind the footlights a round half century and that quite as much as the Chat Noir she merited public tribute. In the Chat Noir mood of Paris throughout the 20's and 30's the remembrance of a gayer past had been strongly evidenced, and a yearning to experience again the lost *fin-de-siècle* spirit. Now, in the late 30's, as bloody instances multiplied across the Rhine, how even more blessed seemed those sweet years, not beyond man's memory, when hearts were not loaded with foreboding.

The idea of honoring the chief symbol of those years soon caught on, and plans were set in motion for a gigantic Guilbert love feast to take place the following year, June 21, at the Salle Pleyel. The "Jubilee," as it was popularly referred to—a term Yvette detested—would be under the patronage of the Minister of Education, Jean Zay, with a committee presided over by Georges Huisman, Director-General of Fine Arts, and including such personal Guilbert devotees as George Bernard Shaw, Maurice Maeterlinck, André Antoine, Edouard Bourdet, Maurice Donnay, Marcel Prévost, Jacques Rouché, Reynaldo Hahn, Jean Giraudoux. On the program there would be the inevitable oratory; singing by Fanny Heldy from the Opéra; declamation by Madame Marquet from the Comédie Française; contributions of one sort or another from a score of other performers.

The Jubilee proved indeed circus-sized; "more like a national function," wrote one New York correspondent, "than like anything that comes under the ordinary terms of entertainment," beginning at ten at night and ending some time around dawn. On the program were statesmen, men of letters, singers, dancers, pianists, humorists, vaudevillians, radio announcers (Yvette had lately begun to be heard over the air in talks on Molière), actors, and actresses. Yvette herself, statuesque in white lace, of course dissolved in tears over the tributes and only barely managed to bring off her *Fiacre* and *Soûlarde*.

Even across the Atlantic there were participants *in absentia*. Next day New York critic John Anderson, recalling those many occasions when he had watched Guilbert from his seat on the aisle at the Neighborhood Playhouse, recorded in his column the fact that among the greetings that reached Salle Pleyel the night of the Jubilee had been a gift from American friends.

Notre grande Yvette! "As French as the profile of Marianne on a five franc note," was the way Anderson summed her up.

As the shadow of the swastika lengthened in Europe, the innocent Schillers found even their lives affected. After Vienna and the Freud incident, it could hardly be considered safe for Max to travel again in Germany and Austria, and the extensive loss in this concert territory immediately cut earnings to the bone. They did go to England, however, in 1938, where Yvette not only gave lectures in London on Verlaine, Montherlant, Jammes, Laforgue, Baudelaire, and Rimbaud, but appeared in the Malvern Play Festival held annually in honor of Shaw. Optimistically, she also secured French rights to Hugh Walpole's *Old Ladies,* perhaps with a view to producing the play in Paris, or even acting one of the roles. She talked to a reporter of a hoped-for trip to Italy, Egypt, and Palestine. Particularly she wanted to sing her songs of Nativity and Crucifixion in the Holy Land itself.

In 1939 death began to press heavily again on the Schillers; in this year Max's sister Rose died, and Freud. More particularly, on a certain sunny day of June Yvette herself may perhaps have felt that she too had died a little, for it was on that day, in the Municipal Theater of Sannois, that the Société des Amis de Louis de Robert gathered to conduct a Jubilee of sorts for their friend; one quite different from Yvette's, however; one with sable trappings and arms reversed. The occasion was a program of commemorative exercises for Louis, who had died in September, 1937, and whom now the municipality of Sannois, where he had lived so long and to which he had brought a measure of fame, wished to honor by naming a thoroughfare "L'Avenue Louis de Robert."

The ceremonies were lengthy: an address by Edmond Sée, president both of the Société des Amis and the Association de la Critique Dramatique et Musicale; another by M. Ignace Legrand; reminiscences by Mme. Marcelle Tinayre and M. Maurice Rostand; readings from Paul Faure's pages by Mme. Simone Damaury of the Comédie Française, followed by excerpts from one of the author's latest works, *Paroles d'un solitaire;* a *conférence* on the general works of the novelist by M. Lucien Dumas; readings from letters addressed to him by Colette, Loti, Proust; a passage from the prize-winning *Roman de Malade* by M. Jean Hervé of the Comédie Française.

And not least in interest, surely, songs by Yvette Guilbert.

During the program, as Yvette listened to the tributes, what images of half a century past must have crowded through her mind, of a slim youth with eager eyes waiting for her in the tiny dressing room of the Concert Parisien; sitting beside her in the carriage going home; escorting her to the "five o'clocks"; everywhere wooing her—in the pretty little Rue Saint- Lazare apartment, on the breezy lawn at Vaux or the shining river. How impatient she had always been: "*Travaille! travaille!*" she had belabored him. Well, he had worked, and though his voice would not perhaps become a major influence in French literature, he had not gone unrewarded.

"*Hélas! ma jeunesse!*" Louis had once sighed in a letter to Paul Faure as the toll of years began to oppress his spirit, and "Alas, my youth!" must have echoed in another heart that June afternoon in Sannois before the program was over and an old woman had turned again home to Paris: home to her seventy-four years, to the gathering war clouds, the hoarsening voice, the constant struggle against disability and poverty, but—thank God!—still the motherlike Max.

III

1940-1944

*Mon livre de chevet? La Bible! Parce qu'elle
seule totalise en ses pages la médication de mon
âme. . . . Comment cèderais-je aux découragements
si je* LIS, *et* RELIS *dans la Bible que:*

> *La course n'est pas toujours facilitée aux plus agiles,*
> *Ni le combat aux plus vaillants,*
> *Ni le pain aux plus sages*
> *Ni les richesses aux plus savants . . .*

—My bedside book? The Bible! Because
it alone contains in its pages all the
medication for my soul. . . . How could I
give way to discouragement if I *read* and
reread in the Bible that:

> The race is not always to the swift,
> Nor the battle to the strong,
> Neither yet bread to the wise
> Nor yet riches of men of understanding . . .

for all are subject to time and circumstance.

353

Chapter 15

In spite of Hitler's violation of the Munich Pact and spreading German conquests in Europe, most Frenchmen, even as late as March, 1939, were stubborn in their conviction that nothing disastrous was likely to happen to France. Those war clouds were filled with more wind than rain and one of these days would all blow away. France was mobilizing, yes, as a result of Mussolini's seizure of Albania and Hitler's entrance into Bohemia and Moravia. But mobilization was a precautionary, "antiaggression" measure shared with Britain. Even in the late summer of 1939, when the Polish situation reached the seething point, the French as a people declined to become emotional. It was not until September, when Hitler actually invaded Poland, to which France and Britain were committed as allies, that the governments of these two countries were finally constrained to utter their intentions of war on Germany.

The declaration aroused no patriotic response in France; no spirit of Verdun blazed up. Of the general public, too many remembered too searingly the million and a half killed only a generation ago; hardly a French home but had its vacant chair. The French had always looked down their noses at the Poles, and after Poland fell under Hitler's *Blitzkrieg,* popular opinion held that that nation had been shamefully lukewarm even in its own defense. "Die for Danzig?" scoffed the man in the street. There was, to be sure, some gossip about the threat from within known as the Fifth Column, but on the whole this phenomenon was not taken seriously in spite of the fact that in a surprising number of salons more and more highly placed persons were being heard to express pro-Nazi sentiments. A good thing that Germany was expanding in Eastern Europe, they argued. Bolshevism would be far worse. At least, one could do business with Hitler.

Besides, what was there for France to worry about? Hitler would not be mad enough to attack a country in defensive posture, and it was agreed that the French Army was invincible and the Maginot Line impregnable. Nothing worse was likely to happen than that the Maginot and Siegfried Lines would continue trying to outstare each other for a few more months, and then someday there would be clever maneuvering by the gentlemen in the pin-striped trousers at the Quai d'Orsay and the unpleasantness would be painlessly over.

Complacently, therefore, Parisians accepted the new total war footing, persuaded that the minor inconveniences they now had to put up with would prove only temporary. There were blackouts, of course, and alerts. Identity papers became more important; police examined these carefully. Trains were congested and slow; military news scarce and unreliable. But all in all it was not a thoroughly uncomfortable war. Life had not been seriously disrupted. Financial uncertainties might skulk in the Bourse, but the Café de la Paix was as packed as ever and readers browsed as usual at the bookstalls on the Seine. About the only real change to be noticed was the increasing scarcity of men of military age. Indubitably, and most comfortingly, it was a "phony" war.

For 1939 Max had attempted to carry out a "farewell tour" of the States, but arrangements had had to be canceled, because of the outbreak of hostilities. The Schillers were bitterly disappointed. Remembering the haven America had offered during the First World War, they must have been counting heavily on the expedient of another American sojourn during the present crisis. Naturally, Yvette need not literally say farewell to public life.

But since the gods ruled otherwise, and since their only course was to continue in the few European countries still open to them, Max booked for the spring of 1940 an itinerary through Belgium, Holland, Denmark, Norway, and Sweden, to be followed by three recitals in London and radio engagements with the British Broadcasting Company. Their visit to London would be darkened by the loss of Freud, but Eva would still be there.

Meantime in Paris difficulties began to confront them. A fuel pinch was being felt that winter, and in December, as a result of singing in an unheated auditorium, Yvette fell victim to bronchitis. The condition lingered and worsened, perhaps because she was suffering also from lack of heat at home. Sometimes, too, lame as she was from rheumatism, she was obliged to climb the five flights to her apartment when elevator service failed. A further complication was that funds dwindled sharply, to a point where emergency measures had to be taken. To sell one's clothes was an old Rue du Temple expedient, and Yvette's costly wardrobe, almost in its entirety, found its way to the Flea Market. It may have been at this time, too, that certain collections of letters that had been quoted in *Mes Lettres d'amour* were sold—the Francis Jammes correspondence, for example, which was eventually to be found listed in a catalogue for 85,000 francs, though it is doubtful that Yvette received half that amount. At any rate, the Schillers converted what they could into cash and hopefully awaited their projected European tour.

But this tour, too, proved a mirage. Early in April of 1940 Hitler overran Norway, and the débâcle was on. On May 10 he was in the Low Countries, sweeping through to the French border, down through Sedan, following the historic route of invasion. Events began to race: bombs over Brussels, parachutists over Holland, traitors everywhere; French towns blitzed, as the German columns pushed on; constant crises in the French Cabinet; gloom; conflicting rumors; the Dutch government in exile; streams of Belgian refugees pouring south, choking the road. Abruptly the "phony" war had come to an end, and Paris began to take on an altered aspect; cafés were half empty now, bookstalls shut, there were no buses in the streets and only a few taxis, there was no Métro. Everywhere people were buying shoes and suitcases and mattresses.

In the midst of these alarming developments, a letter from Max to Emily Gresser, dated June 16, brought reassuring news to anxious American friends. The Schillers were no longer in Paris; they were in the south of France. "The very day you wrote your letter (May 20th)," Max said, "we decided to leave [Paris]. . . ." To another corespondent he clearly implied that it was Yvette's bronchitis that had prompted the sudden departure to a milder climate. But surely Max was writing for the possible eye of an enemy, and the recipients of these letters would have guessed that greater issues were involved. Surely when a Jew fled from a city as Hitler approached it, some connection between the two actions might reasonably be assumed. It had not taken the Schillers long to make ready to depart, only long enough to pack trunks and valises. The Freud incident was fresh in their minds. It would not do to get caught.

Rhododendrons were in bloom the day they left. Paris was having a spell of hot, bright May weather; the sun beat down and there was smell of new-cut grass in the Tuileries gardens. To Yvette it must have been monstrously inconceivable that for the third time in her life she should find herself at the mercy of the Germans—ironically, the Germans whose culture she had come to love.

It was lucky they left as they did. By June 10 the banks were evacuating and the Government was in flight for Tours, its new provisional capital. By then the great exodus from Paris had reached its height, and hundreds of thousands of French refugees were being added to the millions of Belgians already on the roads of France. Max and Yvette were lucky, too, in knowing a door that was open to them, for many were fleeing with no destination. In the tiny village of Eguilles, near Marseilles, they would be guests for three weeks of a friend, Madame Gasquet, widow of a minor French poet, in her pretty little Villa Fontlaure.

On June 16 the Germans were advancing in France as far as Burgundy. Yet—another irony—this was the very day on which Max, the dust of Maginot Line censorship still in his eyes, was writing: ". . . we do what all french people do wait for victory."

Actually, had Max only known it, France was far from being in heroic mood. By this time, Dunkirk was a matter of history and Italy was formally in the war. The Germans had entered Paris, and the Champs-Élysées had quivered once again, as in 1870, under the heel of the marching horde. Paris had not been bombed. Toward France the Fuehrer was using the velvet-glove treatment, apparently convinced, and correctly, that a separate peace was all but in his hands. The French Army had practically collapsed.

As to the impregnability of the Maginot Line, that myth had exploded. Within days the Line had capitulated, astounding even tongue-in-cheek journalists who had visited it and talked with its men and who knew the sagging patriotism of the rank and file, demoralized by long hours of idleness, worry over neglected affairs at home, and the insidious propaganda daily pouring forth from the German radio. Their own radio news these men distrusted because of its unreliability. They distrusted their allies, the British. Every Englishman, the Germans assured them, was prepared to fight to the last drop of French blood. After Dunkirk, French troops in Flanders threw away their arms and deteriorated into a heartsick rabble. In Paris, soldiers on leave shouted in their cups: "*À bas la guerre!*" The rottenness of pacifism and defeatism was widespread.

In only six days more, on June 22, France's final humiliation would come with the birth of the infamous Vichy regime, when Pétain, the aged and once-loved marshal of 1914, now the head of government, would sue for and be granted an armistice. That day the whole French nation would listen to their radios in shame and heartbreak as the old man tried to justify to them the act.

Yet although Max and Yvette were now in unoccupied territory that would for some time to come be designated as Free France, they were not free from fear. In the letter to Emily, written that Sunday in June from Eguilles, Max had concluded by asking that future replies be addressed to Madame Yvette Guilbert, *without* my name," and the word "without" was double-underlined. Neither here nor in other letters does Max ever openly refer to his danger, but from such emphasis there can be no doubt that he knew it existed. This one poignant detail tells all.

The pressing problem of escape temporarily solved, there yet remained for Max and Yvette the equally pressing one of subsistence. With their small revenue from investments cut off by reason of the Occupation and all hope of concert tours abandoned, net income plummeted to zero. In the days of good fortune Yvette's purse had always been open; times without number she had played the role of *dea ex machina* to mortals in distress, and now that it was her turn to be in need, it is pleasing to record that friends immediately stepped into the breach with substantial checks. She accepted the aid philosophically. With an almost Oriental disdain she had once written: "Money achieves dignity only when it serves love."

There did remain, however, one new professional avenue to be explored, even within the narrow limits of the war situation. For some time Yvette had been dabbling in broadcasting. The medium appealed to her because of the vastly increased audience it provided, both for the beloved *chanson* and the literary chats she enjoyed giving, and in Marseilles there was an important radio station. If a regular program could be scheduled here, it would provide in part at least for her needs.

With the fall of France in June, 1940, radical and immediate changes took place in respect to the government-owned Radio-Télégraphie in Occupied France. Through Article XIV of the Armistice terms, the Germans, who had long ago learned the importance of radio propaganda as a weapon of conquest, became masters of the French air. When every French voice had been silenced in occupied territory and every transmitter surrendered, it was German propaganda experts who henceforth controlled all programming, their objective to condition captive listeners, "to shout down thought in Europe." But Marseilles had remained free to operate under only a judicious self-censorship, and now, when the station was presented with an opportunity to add an artist of Guilbert's stature to its list of performers—with entertainment, moreover, that would rank as politically innocuous—an arrangement was speedily effected.

After concluding their visit to Madame Gasquet, Max and Yvette decided to settle in Aix-en-Provence, a few miles inland. The choice seems both natural and sensible. Aix, known since Roman days for its hot mineral springs, appealed to Yvette in her search for health, and both she and Max must have enjoyed its beauty. It was a slow-tempoed city, of ease and dignity, many of its streets reminiscent of a vanished aristocracy; a city of fountains, where the sound of splashing water was refreshing in the heat of summer. Moreover, its location was strategic. Transportation was available to Marseilles, making it possible for Yvette to carry on her radio appearances there, but more vital were the obvious advantages in being close to one of the few remaining ports of exit. If the worst came, there might be at least an even chance of getting out of the country by sea or by air, perhaps to French North Africa.

The Negre Coste Hotel, which they selected, was a faded pastel of early-nineteenth-century elegance. At the time it was built, it was considered the choicest hotel in Aix, but by 1940 its importance had shrunk chiefly to its location on the Cours Mirabeau, Aix's stately main boulevard. Nevertheless, even in semisenescence it preserved a pleasant air of graciousness and hospitality. In front, a small sidewalk café, bright with flowers and snowy-white tablecloths, was modestly inviting, and upstairs back of the tall, shuttered windows that looked out onto tree-lined Cours Mirabeau, the rooms were high-ceilinged and spacious. In one of these rooms Max and Yvette now unpacked their trunks.

"The tragedy," wrote Max to Mrs. Vladimir Gurewich, a family friend, "began in 1941, just on my birthday . . . on the 17th of July. I opened the morning paper and I read a note, wired from Paris: 'The apartment of Madame Guilbert entered during the night by burglars.'"

But this misfortune was slight compared to what followed. A few weeks later, reported Max cryptically, the apartment was seized by the Germans—"in consequence of a denunciation." The nature of the anonymous "denunciation" is not hard to guess. The ethnic background of Madame Guilbert's husband had been brought to official attention by some fanatic, and somewhere in France Max's dossier was now lying on a Gestapo desk.

For the Gestapo was already at work in France. On June 2, 1941, anti-Jewish laws had been drafted, and a Department of Jewish Affairs had been created soon thereafter. Arrests became common; there were deportations, even firing squads. The situation of non-French Jews was particularly grave, because for them, it was openly declared, no attempt at protection could or would be offered by the French government.

After the "denunciation," it was only to be expected that mills should begin to grind, and with Teutonic thoroughness. Suppose it should be discovered that Madame Guilbert was Jewish, too?

Madame Guilbert was not hard to locate; her broadcasts could not well have been disguised. Until now there would have been no reason to try to ban her from the air, for not only was she favorably known in the Fatherland, but as recently as 1929 there had appeared in *La Passante émerveillée* those frank statements of the gratitude she had always felt for her appreciative German audiences and critics, sentiments that should have been eminently satisfactory to the Nazi overlords. But, it must have been argued, if this woman, married to a Jew, proved to be Jewish herself, might there not have to be a reassessment?

So it was that correspondence had to begin and questionings; and from that moment on, Max and Yvette could not know at night whether in the morning they would still be free. Those steps in the quiet Cours Mirabeau during the small hours—would they turn in at the Negre Coste? The pleasant hotel room became a torture cell. There was only one hope to cling to, and that a small one. By late 1941 the V signal was beginning to be flashed: the underground Resistance movement was gathering strength.

Yet the anti-Jewish hysteria continued to mount through 1942. In September the London *National Review* asserted that "the same shameful and terrible conditions as prevail all over Germany are now enforced in France. The story of this new horror was told in a letter published by the Swiss paper *Berner Tagwort*." Curfew for Jews was at eight o'clock; Jews were being arrested in the streets. In November, after the Allies had invaded North Africa, Hitler annulled the Armistice of 1940 and the Germans occupied Vichy, from which henceforth operated a special *Police des Questions Juives*. During this dark period, while the investigation of her parentage dragged on, month after month, Yvette clearly showed the effects of severe nervous strain, and one day in December of 1942 she was close to death from a heart seizure.

The winter of 1942 was cold; there was snow at Aix, and the poor suffered. That inveterate Parisian gossip, André de Fouquières, though he was not himself in Aix that winter, nevertheless has his bit of tattle to relate:

One of my friends, who was sojourning in Aix-en-Provence in 1942, was taking a walk one night on the Cours Mirabeau. The night was clear, thanks to a dazzling, thick woolen carpet that the snow had woven, with only a black rent around the warm fountain. My friend had seen that afternoon a *chauffoir,* a "warming-room" for old and wretched men, and he could not get this sad picture out of his mind.

Suddenly there appeared before him a spectral figure claiming his attention, a figure almost mummylike, but at the same time with something majestic about it, that immediately drove from his thoughts the gloomy remembrance of the *chauffoir.*

"Did you recognize her?" he asked the friend who accompanied him.

How could he not recognize her, even though this Parisienne had become a very old woman, floundering in the snow of Provence? Yvette Guilbert had passed by without seeing them.

Was it not Bismarck who said of a conquered people: "We will leave them their eyes to weep with"?

For almost two years the investigation continued. It was not until March, 1943, that the Commissariat Général des Questions Juives were able to establish to their satisfaction that Yvette was not of Jewish birth, and while the receipt of the Commissariat's official document to this effect unquestionably halved the strain under which both Yvette and Max were living, the strain was halved only. Max's future still remained in doubt.

During this entire period of exile, living as she was under persecution and suffering ills of the flesh, Yvette had nevertheless been working, in a fever of pathetic courage, on yet another volume of memoirs, *Autres Temps, Autres Chants.* She was now seventy-eight, and in this book, as in *Mes Lettres d'amour,* she again looked back over her shoulder to a happier past and again as she set down hitherto unpublished reminiscences of the Chat Noir and texts of old songs of the period, tried to recreate those lovely lost days of the *fin de siècle.* Occasional flashes hint the color of the writer's spirit. "To give, always to give one's soul, one's heart, one's smiles and joy, is to furnish others with forgetfulness of their afflictions and their transgressions. It is to pray."

A journalist who interviewed Yvette in the Negre Coste about this time noted that the Toulouse-Lautrec hair, kept henna-red through so many years, had been allowed to turn entirely white.

On the morning of Thursday, February 3, 1944, Yvette felt too ill to get up. Coming back from her broadcast the previous Friday, she had caught a heavy cold that had turned into bronchial pneumonia, and for the entire week Dr. Riou, a local physician, had treated her, and Max had tenderly nursed her. But she had found it hard to recover, perhaps because her heart was already weakened; perhaps too because of the oppressive knowledge that all too soon it would be Friday again and somehow she must rally to make that weekly trip in to the radio station.

This morning the feeling was strong upon her that she could delay no longer in putting forth an effort to rouse herself. She must at least sit up in bed and begin to collect her thoughts. The room was chilly, but at her insistence Max wrapped her in blankets and propped her up against the pillows. Later she asked for pencil and paper. Some ideas had come to her for her broadcast the following day, and she wanted to jot them down.

"Mon livre de chevet" she entitled Page One, in a handwriting that was still surprisingly bold and vigorous.

> My bedside book?
> The Bible!
> Because it alone contains in its pages all the medication
>   for my soul.
> All human dementias have their causes and remedies, which
>   the Bible reveals to me—
> From it I draw daily strength, wise counsel, helping me
>   to escape base contagions.

As she continued to write, her face took on an expression of happy absorption in her work, and soon she seemed even to be gaining in strength. A little later, while she was still sitting up, Max, reassured over her apparent improvement, left her briefly with her thoughts.

He was out of the room for only a few minutes, but when he returned, the white head had fallen back gently on the pillow and the busy pencil had slipped from fingers now lying limp on the coverlet. On the paper the words Yvette had newly written stood out firm and clear.

"How could I give way to discouragement," she had just been chiding herself, "if I *read* and *reread* in the Bible that

> The race is not always to the swift,
> Nor the battle to the strong,
> Neither yet bread to the wise
> Nor yet riches to men of understanding . . .
> for all
> are subject to time and circumstance"?

Epilogue

... And I was left [wrote Max, in his quaint English] for an aimless, senseless and solitary life. And there I am in the same room she died [in], I am sleeping in the bed she died [in,] my head on the same pillows where she had rested. I am surrounded by her trunks which she had packed, by her books, her music, all is there only she is not there. ... I am writing this letter with her stylo. She held it in her hand the Tuesday before her death on Thursday morning and wrote down in her diary "Plume, plume qui continue la pensée de l'homme." ... I am alone, really alone. I have no friends here (outside the doctor who has remained faithful to me) and if I bear this solitude it is only that I am in fact always, constantly in touch with Yvette, she lives with me, in me, around me. ...

After the war, Max had the dear body brought back to Paris, to Père Lachaise Cemetery, and the city knew a day of mourning for a beloved daughter. In the flood of necrology that followed Yvette's death, the scholarly accomplishments of her later life had been scantly remembered. Instead—a final irony—much had been made of the Rabelaisian black gloves, those attributes that in the end had become her horror. On her grave Max erected a memorial stone on which two angels, with folded wings, brooded contemplatively over the precious clay that lay beneath.

He lived in a small room at the Grand Hotel in Paris, alone, corresponding with a few friends and relatives, kept alive by old memories. Every night he kissed her photograph before he went to sleep. Eva saw him frequently and George Bernard Shaw wrote occasionally—one old man consoling another: "Dear Fellow-Widower,

This is to assure you that you are not forgotten." He was quiet, resigned, patient.

One thing troubled him a little. He could not help believing that somewhere Yvette must be needing him. He had never kept her waiting before.

Selected Bibliography

Books

Albert Chevalier, Brian Daly, ed., London, Macqueen, 1895.

Aubry, Octave, *Le Second Empire,* Paris, Arthème Fayard, 1938.

Bac, Ferdinand, *Femmes de théâtre,* preface by Yvette Guilbert, Paris, H. Simonis Empis, 1896.

Barton, Lucy, *Historic Costume for the Stage,* Boston, Walter Baker Co., 1935.

Beerbohm, Max, *Around Theatres,* New York, Alfred Knopf, 1930.

Benson, E. F., *King Edward VII,* New York, Longmans Green and Company, 1933.

Bentley, Eric, *A Selection from the Music Criticism of George Bernard Shaw,* New York, Doubleday, 1955

Bertaut, Jules, *Paris 1870-1935,* London, Eyre and Spottiswoode, 1936.

Bessière, Emile, *Autour de la butte,* Paris, C. Joubert, 1899.

Bordeux, Jeanne, *Eleanora Duse,* London, Hutchinson, 1924.

Boutet de Monvel, Roger, *Les Variétés, 1850-1870,* Paris, Plon-Nourrit et Cie., 1905.

Carco, Francis, *La belle Époque,* Paris, Gallimard, 1954.

Chevalier, Albert, *Before I Forget,* London, T. Fisher Unwin, 1902.

Constantin, Marc, *Histoire des Cafés-Concerts et des cafés de Paris,* Paris, Renauld, 1872.

Coquiot, Gustave, *Les cafés-concerts,* Paris, Librairie de l'art, 1896.

——, *Toulouse-Lautrec,* Paris, Librairie Ollendorff, 1921.

Cowles, Virginia, *Gay Monarch,* New York, Harper Brothers, 1956.

Daudet, Alphonse, *Trente ans de Paris,* Paris, Marpon et Flammarion, 1888.

D'Auvergne, Edmund B., *Pierre Loti*, New York, Frederick A. Stokes Co., 1926.

Delteil, Loys, *Le Peintre graveur illustré*, Vols. 10, 11, Paris, 1920.

Donnay, Maurice, *Autour du Chat Noir*, Paris, Bernard Grasset, 1926.

——, *Des Souvenirs*, Paris, Arthème Fayard, 1933.

Duncan, Isadora, *My Life*, New York, Boni and Liveright, 1927.

Encyclopédie du théâtre contemporain, Paris, Collection théâtre de France, Vol. 1, 1957.

Febvre, Frédéric, *Au bord de la scène*, Paris, Paul Ollendorff, 1889.

——, *Journal d'un comédien*, Paris, Paul Ollendorff, 1896.

Ferrari, Gustave, *Selection from Collection Yvette Guilbert;* English translations by Ezra Pound, London, Augener, Ltd., 1912.

Fouquières, André de, *Mon Paris et ses Parisiens*, Vols. 1–4, Paris, Éditions Pierre Horay et Cie., 1956.

Freud, Ernst, *Letters of Sigmund Freud*, London, Hogarth Press, 1961.

Freud, Martin, *Sigmund Freud: Man and Father*, New York, Vanguard, 1958.

Geffroy, Gustave, *Yvette Guilbert*, Paris, André Marty, 1894.

Grau, Robert, *Forty Years Observation of Music and Drama*, New York, Broadway Publishing Co., 1909.

Guitry, Sacha, *If Memory Serves*, New York, Doubleday, Doran and Co., 1936.

Hanson, Lawrence and Elisabeth, *The Tragic Life of Toulouse-Lautrec*, New York, Random House, 1956.

Harding, Bertita, *Age Cannot Wither*, Philadelphia, J. P. Lippincott Company, 1947.

Henderson, Sir Nevile, *Failure of a Mission*, New York, G. Putnam's Sons, 1940.

Hornblow, Arthur, *A History of the Theatre in America*, Vols. 1, 2, Philadelphia, J. B. Lippincott Company, 1919.

Ibels H. G., "Le Café-concert et la chanson," *Les Spectacles à travers les âges*, preface by Denys Amiel, Paris, Éditions du Cygne, [193-?].

Jasper, Gertrude R., *Adventures in the Theatre*, New Jersey, Rutgers University Press, 1947.

Jones, Ernest, *The Life and Work of Sigmund Freud*, Vol. 3, New York, Basic Books, Inc., 1953.

Leavitt, M. B., *Fifty Years in Theatrical Management*, New York, Broadway Publishing Co. 1912.

Leon-Martin, Louis, *Le Music Hall et ses figures*, Paris, Editions de France, 1928.

Les Demis-Cabots, Paris, Charpentier et Fasquelle, 1896.

Le Senne, Camille, *Le Théâtre à Paris*, Vols. 1–5, Paris, Le Soudier, 1888–90.

Lord, Walter, *The Good Years: From 1900 to the First World War,* New York, Harper and Brothers, 1960.

Macdougall, Allan Ross, *Isadora: A Revolutionary in Art and Love,* New York, Thomas Nelson and Sons, 1960.

Mack, Gerstle, *Toulouse Lautrec,* New York, Alfred A. Knopf, 1953.

Mapes, Victor, *Duse and the French,* New York, Dunlap Society Publications, New Series, No. 6, 1898.

Marcosson, Isaac F. and Frohman, Daniel, *Charles Frohman: Manager and Man,* New York, Harper and Brothers, 1916.

Marston, William M. and Feller, John Henry, *F. F. Proctor, Vaudeville Pioneer,* New York, Richard R. Smith, 1943.

Matthews, J. Brander, *The Theaters of Paris,* New York, Charles Scribners Sons, 1880.

Maugham, W. Somerset, *Strictly Personal,* New York, Doubleday, Doran and Co., 1941.

Menetière, Albéric, *Les Binettes du Café-Concert,* Paris, Librairie Centrale, 1869.

Morell, Parker, *Lillian Russell: The Era of Plush,* New York, Random House, 1940.

Odell, G. C. D., *Annals of the New York Stage,* Vols. 14, 15, New York, Columbia University Press, 1927–49.

Otéro, Caroline, *Les Souvenirs et la vie intime de la belle Otéro,* Paris, Éditions Le Calame, 1916.

Parker, H. T., *Eighth Notes; Voices and Figures of Music and the Dance,* New York, Dodd, Mead & Co., 1922.

Pearson, Hesketh, *Beerbohm Tree,* New York, Harpers, 1956.

Perruchot, Henri, *La Vie de Toulouse-Lautrec,* Paris, Hachette, 1958.

Renard, Jules, *Journal inédit,* Vols. 1, 2, Paris, François Bernouard, 1926.

Rheinhardt, E. A., *Life of Eleanora Duse,* London, Martin Secker, 1930.

Rich, Daniel C., *Toulouse Lautrec "Au Moulin Rouge,"* London, Percy Lund Humphries and Co. [1949].

Robert, Louis de, *Lettres à Paul Faure, 1898–1937,* Paris, Les Editions Denoël, 1943.

———, *Un Tendre,* Paris, Charpentier et Fasquelle, 1893.

———, *The Eternal Enigma,* New York, The Judge Publishing Co.,

Richardson, Joanne, *Sarah Bernhardt,* London, Max Reinhardt, 1959.
1897.

Robida, Michel, *Le Salon Charpentier et les impressionistes,* Paris, Bibliothèque des Arts, 1958.

Roger-Marx, Claude, in *Yvette Guilbert vue par Toulouse-Lautrec,* Paris, Au Pont des Arts, 1950.

Sarcey, Francisque, *Quarante ans de théâtre,* Paris, Bibliothèque des Annales, 1900.

Sheean, Vincent, *Oscar Hammerstein I*, New York, Simon & Schuster, 1956.

Shercliff, Jose, *Jane Avril of the Moulin Rouge*, Philadelphia, Macrae Smith, 1934.

Stoullig, Edmond, ed., *Les Annales du théâtre et de la musique*, Paris, Charpentier et Cie., 1876–1912.

Symons, Arthur, *Colour Studies in Paris*, New York, E. P. Dutton Co., 1918.

———, *Eleanora Duse*, London, Elkin Mathews, Ltd., 1926.

Thétard Henry *La merveilleuse histoire du cirque*, [Paris], Prisma, 1947.

Van Vechten, Carl, *Interpreters and Interpretations*, New York, Alfred A. Knopf, 1927.

Waxman, S. M., *Antoine and the Théâtre-Libre*, Cambridge, Harvard University Press, 1926.

Werth, Alexander, *Last Days of Paris*, London, Hamish Hamilton, 1940.

Winwar, Frances, *Wingless Victory*, New York, Harper and Brothers, 1956.

Guilbert, Yvette, *L'Art de chanter une chanson*, Paris, Bernard Grasset, 1928.

———, *Autres temps, autres chants*, Paris, Robert Laffont, 1946.

———, *La Chanson de ma vie*, Paris, Bernard Grasset, 1927.

———, *Les Demi-Vieilles*, Paris, Félix Juven, 1902.

———, *How to Sing a Song*, New York, Macmillan Company, 1918.

———, *Mes Lettres d'amour*, Paris, Editions Denoël et Steele, 1933.

———, *The Song of My Life*, trans. by Beatrice de Holthoir, London, George Harrap and Co., 1929.

———, *La Passante émerveillée*, Paris, Bernard Grasset, 1929.

———, *La Vedette*, Paris, H. Simonis Empis, 1902.

Guilbert, Yvette, and Simpson, Harold, *Yvette Guilbert: Struggles and Victories*, London, Mills and Boon, 1910.

Newspapers and Magazines

As the newspapers and magazines consulted in reference to this work are too numerous to be listed in full, the authors will mention only those which have been most productive of information.

Among foreign publications: Les Annales Politiques et Littéraires, Berliner Lokal Anzeiger, Bloc-Notes Parisien, Comoedia, Courrier de l'Étudiant, Courrier de Paris, Courrier Français, Current Literature,

(Manchester) Daily Dispatch, Dramatic Mirror, Dramatic News, L'Étincelle, Le Figaro, Le Figaro Illustré, Le Gaulois, Graphic, Gringoire, Illustration, Illustrated London News, Intransigeant, Journal des Débats, Justice, The Mask, Mercure de France, Le Monde, Monde Illustré, Le Monde Moderne, Musical Standard, Les Nouvelles Littéraires, Oeuvre, Pall Mall Budget, Paris Concert, Paris Midi, Paris Soir, Le Petit Journal, La Revue Blanche, Revue d'Art dramatique, Revue des Deux Mondes, Le Rire, Spectacles et Concerts, The Sketch, Le Temps, London Times, La Vie de Paris, La Vie Heureuse, Volonté, Zeit.

Publications in the United States include relevant numbers of practically all leading metropolitan dailies, and among magazines Excelsior, The Literary Digest, Musical America, The New Republic, Saturday Review of Literature, Theatre Arts, Vanity Fair, Variety, Vogue, Yellow Book, and many others.

Index

378